THE UNIVERS OLL
WIN CHEST

Sport Psychology for Coaches

Damon Burton, PhD
University of Idaho

Thomas D. Raedeke, PhD
East Carolina University

Library of Congress Cataloging-in-Publication Data

Burton, Damon, 1949-
  Sport psychology for coaches / Damon Burton, Thomas D. Raedeke.
    p. cm.
  Includes bibliographical references and index.
  ISBN-13: 978-0-7360-3986-4 (soft cover)
  ISBN-10: 0-7360-3986-4 (soft cover)
  1. Sports--Psychological aspects. 2. Coaching (Athletics) I.
Raedeke, Thomas D., 1963- II. Title.
  GV706.4.B85 2008
  796.01--dc22
                                    2007040652

ISBN-10: 0-7360-3986-4
ISBN-13: 978-0-7360-3986-4

The Web addresses cited in this text were current as of October 2007, unless otherwise noted.

Acquisitions Editor: Amy Tocco; **Developmental Editor:** Christine M. Drews; **Managing Editor:** Carla Zych; **Copyeditor:** Tom Tiller; **Proofreader:** Anne Rogers; **Indexer:** Nan N. Badgett; **Permission Manager:** Carly Breeding; **Graphic Designer:** Bob Reuther; **Graphic Artist:** Francine Hamerski; **Cover Designer and Photographer:** Keith Blomberg; **Photographer (interior):** © Human Kinetics unless otherwise noted; **Photo Asset Manager:** Laura Fitch; **Photo Office Assistant:** Jason Allen; **Art Manager:** Kelly Hendren; **Associate Art Manager:** Alan L. Wilborn; **Illustrator:** Lineworks, Inc. unless otherwise noted; **Printer:** Sheridan Books

Copies of this book are available at special discounts for bulk purchase for sales promotions, premiums, fund-raising, or educational use. Special editions or book excerpts can also be created to specifications. For details, contact the Special Sales Manager at Human Kinetics.

Printed in the United States of America   10 9 8 7 6 5 4 3 2 1

Human Kinetics
Web site: www.HumanKinetics.com

United States: Human Kinetics
P.O. Box 5076
Champaign, IL 61825-5076
800-747-4457
e-mail: humank@hkusa.com

Canada: Human Kinetics
475 Devonshire Road Unit 100
Windsor, ON N8Y 2L5
800-465-7301 (in Canada only)
e-mail: info@hkcanada.com

Europe: Human Kinetics
107 Bradford Road
Stanningley
Leeds LS28 6AT, United Kingdom
+44 (0) 113 255 5665
e-mail: hk@hkeurope.com

Australia: Human Kinetics
57A Price Avenue
Lower Mitcham, South Australia 5062
08 8372 0999
e-mail: info@hkaustralia.com

New Zealand: Human Kinetics
Division of Sports Distributors NZ Ltd.
P.O. Box 300 226 Albany
North Shore City
Auckland
0064 9 448 1207
e-mail: info@humankinetics.co.nz

To my parents, Nada and Don, who planted the seed and nurtured my love of sport, my thirst for knowledge, and my desire to help others;

to my mentor, Rainer Martens, who helped me develop a passion for sport psychology, refine my teaching, helping, and writing skills, and understand the "big picture" in sport and life;

to my students and colleagues who have taught me so much and enriched my life with their friendship;

and to my three sons—Drew, Frazer, and Price—who are my greatest joy and who provide my inspiration to make sport a more positive experience for all.

Damon Burton

In memory of my brother Gary, who left this Earth way too soon.

Tom Raedeke

CONTENTS

PART IV   Integrating Mental Training Tools and Skills   203

ASEP SILVER LEVEL SERIES PREFACE

The American Sport Education Program (ASEP) Silver Level curriculum is a series of practical texts that provide coaches and students with an applied approach to sport performance. The curriculum is designed for coaches and for college undergraduates pursuing professions as coaches, physical education teachers, and sport fitness practitioners.

For instructors of undergraduate courses, the ASEP Silver Level curriculum provides an excellent alternative to other formal texts. In most undergraduate programs today, students complete basic courses in exercise physiology, mechanics, motor learning, and sport psychology—courses that are focused on research and theory. Many undergraduate students are looking for ways to directly apply what they learn in the classroom to what they can teach or coach on the court or playing field. ASEP's Silver Level series addresses this need by making the fundamentals of sport science easy to understand and apply to enhance sport performance. The Silver Level series is specifically designed to introduce these sport science topics to students in an applied manner. Students will find the information and examples user friendly and easy to apply in the sport setting.

The ASEP Silver Level sport science curriculum includes the following:

Sport Mechanics for Coaches—an explanation of the mechanical concepts underlying performance techniques; designed to enable coaches and students to observe, analyze, develop, and correct the mechanics of sport technique for better athletic performance.

Sport Physiology for Coaches—an applied approach to exercise physiology; designed to enable coaches and students to assess, initiate, enhance, and refine human performance in sport participation and to improve sport performance.

Sport Psychology for Coaches—a practical discussion of motivation, communication, stress management, mental imagery, and other cutting-edge topics; this text is designed to enhance the coach–athlete relationship and to stimulate improved sport performance.

Sport Skill Instruction for Coaches—a practical approach for learning to teach sport skills, guided by a practical understanding of the stages of learning and performance, individual differences and their impact on skill acquisition, and the critical elements required to create a learning environment that enhances optimal sport skill development and performance.

A variety of educational elements make these texts student- and instructor-friendly:

- Learning objectives introduce each chapter.
- Sidebars illustrate sport-specific applications of key concepts and principles.
- Chapter summaries review the key points covered in the chapter and are linked to the chapter objectives by content and sequence.
- Key terms at the end of most chapters list the terms introduced in that chapter and remind coaches and students, "These are words you should know." The first occurrence of the word in the chapter is boldfaced, and the words also appear in the glossary.
- Chapter review questions at the end of each chapter allow coaches and students to check their comprehension of the chapter's contents.

Answers to questions appear in the back of the book.

- Real-world application scenarios called practical activities follow the review questions. These scenarios provide problem situations for readers to solve. The solutions require readers to describe how the concepts discussed in the chapter can be applied in real-world scenarios. Sample solutions appear in the back of the book.
- A glossary defines all of the key terms covered in the book.

- A bibliography section at the end of the book serves as a resource for additional reading and research.
- A general index lists subjects covered in the book.

These texts are also the basis for a series of Silver Level online courses to be developed by Human Kinetics. These courses will be offered through ASEP's Online Education Center for coaches and students who wish to increase their knowledge through practical and applied study of the sport sciences.

PREFACE

Coaches increasingly recognize the importance of sport psychology and their role in helping athletes learn how to master the mental game. This book is aimed at helping coaches understand the mental side of sport and how athletes act, think, and feel when they practice and compete. More important, it also provides critical information coaches can use to help athletes develop the mental training tools and skills necessary to enhance their mental toughness and achieve excellence in sport and life. *Sport Psychology for Coaches* is one in a series of texts comprising the American Sport Education Program's (ASEP) Silver Level curriculum for aspiring and experienced coaches who want to develop a more in-depth understanding of sport science to enhance their coaching success.

This book helps you, as a coach, gain a better grasp of sport psychology by presenting a clear, understandable roadmap for teaching and implementing mental training. *Sport Psychology for Coaches* is organized into four parts. Part I contains three chapters designed to provide you with a solid foundation for conducting mental training. Chapter 1 highlights the importance of developing a coaching philosophy and presents information on how to construct and fine-tune your own philosophy. Strong communication skills are essential to coaching success, and Chapter 2 helps you understand the communication process and how to become a more effective communicator. The third chapter provides an introduction to mental skills training and is designed to teach you the importance of mental training and provide a systematic process for using mental training techniques to develop mental skills.

The four chapters in Part II teach you how to help athletes master four important mental training tools and use them to build their mental training program.

Chapter 4 illustrates the importance of goals, identifies how they work, outlines the most effective types of goals, and specifies the keys steps for implementing an effective goal-setting program. Chapter 5 provides you with an understanding of basic imagery concepts, information on how to help athletes develop their imagery skills, and a blueprint for using imagery effectively. Chapter 6 on relaxation and energization focuses on helping you develop an understanding of these two companion mental training tools and teaches you how to help your athletes learn to relax or energize when needed. The final chapter in this section, chapter 7, explains what self-talk is and how it works, identifies the dangers of negative thoughts, and shows how to reprogram thinking patterns and counter negative thoughts.

Part III is made up of five chapters designed to guide you through the process of developing the mental skills necessary to increase enjoyment, improve life skills, and enhance performance. Chapter 8 teaches you the critical aspects of motivation and how to build and sustain intrinsic motivation during times of success and adversity. The ninth chapter of the book, on energy management, provides you with an understanding of arousal and its impact on performance and shows you how to teach athletes to control their arousal. Chapter 10 helps you understand the attentional challenges athletes face and how to help athletes learn to focus on the task at hand, block out distractors, and sustain their focus using a systematic program for developing athletes' attentional skills. The eleventh chapter explains what causes your athletes to become stressed and how to help them develop stress management skills. Chapter 12 on self-confidence provides you with a basic understanding of the nature of this important mental skill, how it impacts performance, and how to systematically enhance your athletes' confidence.

Integrating Mental Training Tools and Skills, the final part of the book, contains two chapters that demonstrate how to combine mental training tools and skills into mental plans and training programs that maximize mental toughness and help ensure top performance. Chapter 13 shows you how to integrate mental training tools and skills into mental plans that will help athletes attain and maintain an ideal mind-set that enables them perform their best. Finally, Chapter 14 presents a master plan and systematic strategies to help you construct and implement mental skills training programs successfully.

Sport Psychology for Coaches is designed to be easy to read, understand, and use. Each of the chapters in the first three parts of the book includes foundational information about a critical part of the mental game and describes how coaches can develop an essential mental training tool or skill. Chapters preview each topic by providing a list of learning objectives and conclude with a summary of key points and a list of key terms. Review questions are provided to check your comprehension of chapter content and your ability to apply the information effectively. The book concludes with a complete glossary of terms, a list of references and resources, an index, and other useful resources to help you successfully implement mental training programs for your athletes.

ACKNOWLEDGMENTS

Sport Psychology for Coaches is a revision of Rainer Marten's classic text, *Coaches Guide to Sport Psychology*, arguably the best sport psychology text ever written. Thus, we'd like to acknowledge Rainer's numerous contributions to this book through his development of the mental skills approach, his pioneering conceptualization of a number of mental training tools and skills, and his ability to distill these concepts into a format coaches can readily understand and use. We hope that this book is a worthy follow-up to its predecessor and that it will prove to be a valuable resource that will help coaches develop mental training knowledge and skills to guide their use of MST programs with their athletes and teams.

PART I

Creating a Solid Foundation

This first section comprises three chapters designed to help you develop a solid foundation for conducting mental training. Chapter 1, Coaching Philosophy, helps you understand the importance of having and regularly utilizing a coaching philosophy to guide your coaching. The chapter also takes you through the process of developing and fine-tuning your personal coaching philosophy. Chapter 2, Communication, is based on the premise that effective communication is essential to successful coaching. This chapter helps you understand the basics of communication and provides guidance on developing good communication skills and determining when and how to use these skills to be a more effective coach. Chapter 3, Introduction to Mental Skills Training, teaches the importance of mental training; provides a systematic format for developing mental training tools, skills, and plans; and provides guidelines for implementing mental skills training programs.

Coaching Philosophy

After reading this chapter you should be able to

- explain the importance of developing a sound coaching philosophy;
- understand the process for developing a coaching philosophy;
- understand competition and how it helps shape effective coaching philosophies; and
- describe how to use competition to motivate athletes, improve the quality of performance, develop positive character traits, and teach athletes to cooperate.

Like most coaches, I (Damon Burton) have several regrets about my coaching experience, including a few big games that we let get away and a handful of athletes I didn't reach who could have developed into good players. However, my biggest regrets are the few times that I overreacted and did or said things that damaged my relationship with a player. I found these situations particularly frustrating because my relationships with my athletes were the most rewarding aspect of coaching. One of my biggest regrets involves Randy, a bright, talented player who had the potential to be an excellent point guard. Randy was a rebel, with a desire to display his independence by being different in whatever he did, from how he dressed to how he practiced and played. Randy was often a distraction because he insisted on doing things his way—an attitude that is problematic in a sport like basketball, where teamwork is critical. Nevertheless, he was well liked by his teammates, and his talent was a great asset to the team.

One day at practice, I completely lost my patience with Randy. It had been a horrible day, and I had not done a good job of setting aside my personal problems before coming to practice. After sparring with Randy several times early on, I finally lost my cool when he did a bad job of getting us into the right play to exploit the defense, then compounded that mistake by making a bad pass. I went off on Randy for perhaps 30 seconds. I can't remember most of what I said, but I ended with this: "Everything has to be about you and on your terms. Teams can't function when key players put themselves above the team and play only for themselves. When are you going to quit being so selfish and self-centered? It's about time that you put the team first."

I had gone too far, and I knew it immediately from Randy's reaction. I pulled him aside after practice and apologized, and I worked conscientiously to mend our relationship. But it was never the same. Coaching is about creating and utilizing relationships to foster an athlete's development, but those relationships are fragile, and when they are damaged they are often virtually impossible to put back together. It doesn't matter why we do those things we later regret, or how many extenuating circumstances were involved. We all have bad days, or other things on our minds. Once the damage has been done, it often cannot be undone, and, more important, our ability to make a difference in that athlete's life is irrevocably damaged.

What can coaches do to reduce the chance that they'll lose their composure and do or say something that damages their credibility? We believe the answer is to develop and implement a well-designed coaching philosophy. This chapter will help you develop a coaching philosophy to meet the needs of your athletes and the demands of competitive situations.

Developing a Positive Coaching Philosophy

The word *philosophy* turns many people off, and we certainly used to be in that category. What could be more impractical than philosophy, especially for eminently practical people like coaches? But the more we've learned about philosophy, the more we understand that nothing is as practical as a well-developed philosophy, both for competition and for life. Our philosophy guides us every day. It helps us interpret the events in our lives, and it gives direction to how we live each day.

To us, developing a **coaching philosophy** means pursuing personal wisdom. Philosophy helps us answer fundamental questions about what, why, and how things work. Our philosophy is a set of beliefs that dictate the way we view experiences in our lives; it's the way we perceive people and our relationships with them. Most of all, our philosophy reflects the values we hold in life. The key to developing a philosophy of coaching and life is learning to know yourself and prioritizing your competitive objectives. In the next two sections, you are asked to seriously consider why you should develop a coaching philosophy, and we explain how to start the process of doing so.

Why Develop a Coaching Philosophy?

How can a coaching philosophy help you be a better coach? Your coaching philosophy is a set of beliefs and principles that guide your behavior. It helps you remain true to your values while handling the hundreds of choices you must make as a coach. Each time you are confronted with a difficult choice, your philosophy should make your decision quicker and easier, because your decision must be consistent with your principles.

To develop a coaching philosophy, you will need to prioritize what's most important to you. Life and competition are full of choices. Some are easy, such as what play to call or what defense to run, but others can be extremely difficult, such as whether to discipline players who are breaking training rules—or whether to cheat and win, or follow the rules and lose. Most of us handle the easy choices in life with little problem, but the difficult decisions can test our character. When you develop a coaching philosophy, you decide what is important so that you can make the right decisions.

Most of us find that we make better decisions when we take time to think through problems in a thorough, relaxed, and thoughtful fashion rather than reacting in the heat of the moment. Thus we can make systematic decisions that are based on facts and sound reasoning rather than knee-jerk reactions driven more by emotions than logic. The fast-paced action during practice and competition often doesn't lend itself to thoughtful decision making. That's why you need to take time away from your sport to develop your philosophy. Then it will be ready when you need it—ready to help you make split-second decisions that you can live with and feel good about later on.

A good coaching philosophy doesn't provide specific answers to each problem you may encounter. Rather, it provides a set of principles to guide your decision making. It reduces uncertainty in handling problems related to training rules, team discipline, conflicts with your athletes or team, codes of conduct, off-season conditioning programs, athletes' outlooks on competition, short- and long-term objectives, success and failure, and many other facets of competition. If you invest time in developing and maintaining a coaching philosophy, it will help you focus more keenly, reduce stress, purposefully push your limits further, find greater enjoyment, and, above all, coach better.

How to Develop a Coaching Philosophy

This is not a one-time process but an ongoing journey that requires frequent reflection and systematic updating. A coaching philosophy should always be a work in progress. Your philosophy has to be personalized to fit your experience, attitudes, values, and beliefs, but it must also fit with the norms of the society in which you live. If your coaching philosophy conflicts with society's values, you are sure to invite problems. At the same time, you cannot simply acquire a philosophy by reading this book or adopting one from a coach you admire—or from any single source. It is something you develop out of varied experiences in your life, and it is useless unless you embrace and nurture it. It is continually cultivated and refined to enable positive competitive experiences for your athletes. Developing a coaching philosophy requires you to develop clear awareness of what you value and to prioritize your competitive objectives based on those values.

Developing Self-Awareness

To understand what your coaching philosophy should be, you need to know yourself. **Self-awareness** will heighten the speed and success at which you and your athletes learn and perform the skills discussed in this book. In addition, the philosophy you develop will give you direction as you implement these mental skills. You already have a philosophy about life and probably about coaching. Your philosophy may or may not be well developed. You may be conscious of your perspective on life, or it may reside more at an unconscious level. Even if you have a well-developed philosophy, remember that it is a work in progress and that it should be continually modified throughout your career.

We recommend that you enhance self-awareness related to your philosophy in two ways. First, think about your values and monitor your thoughts and actions regularly. How true do you remain to your beliefs and values when you coach? What factors keep your actions consistent with your beliefs or push you off course? Careful scrutiny of your thoughts and actions will help you identify key patterns. Maybe you have trouble remaining true to your beliefs and values when you're playing an archrival, have a lot riding on the outcome of a contest, are playing in front of a large crowd, or have a number of people you want to impress. Once you are aware of these tendencies, you can develop effective strategies to overcome them.

Second, get feedback from people you trust to help you better understand whether your perceptions of your behaviors during competition are consistent with others' observations. Occasionally, our judgment gets clouded by the heat of the moment or by our personal blind spots. Friends can provide us with emotional mirrors: They can give us accurate feedback that breaks down our defenses and encourages us to address personal deficiencies constructively. These two approaches will help you determine what is truly important to you and develop strategies for remaining true to those values when you coach.

Prioritizing Coaching Objectives

As a second step toward developing your personal coaching philosophy, prioritize your competitive objectives and develop clear strategies for achieving them. In *Coaches Guide to Sport Psychology* (1987), Rainer Martens identifies two broad coaching objectives: to win, and to help athletes develop physically, psychologically, and socially. No other decision you make about your coaching philosophy will be as important as the one you make about the emphasis you give to each of these objectives. It will form the foundation of your coaching philosophy.

Striving to win is an important objective to pursue in sport; it is, in fact, a founding premise of sport. But at what costs are you willing to pursue the goal of winning? Are you willing to risk your athletes' health or the health of their opponents? Do you put winning ahead of personal development, ahead of friends and family? What is a proper perspective on winning? These are important and difficult questions, but you will have to answer them every day that you coach. Phil Niekro, the famed knuckleball pitcher, had an interesting perspective on how to prioritize winning and development. Niekro came into his own as a pitcher in his early 30s. Why did success take so long? Niekro reports that he spent much of the early part of his career letting his ego get in the way. He worried about how much he pitched, what spot he occupied in the rotation, and, most of all, whether he got the win. Then, when he was 32, a funny thing happened: Niekro stopped worrying about winning and started just pitching the best he could. Success followed his insightful change in priorities (Martens 1987).

The challenge of reprioritizing winning—Why do coaches and athletes become win centered? Perhaps they succumb to pressure exerted by the media, parents, booster clubs, administrators, or even themselves. Some coaches live vicariously through their athletes, while others model their coaching after professional, win-oriented coaches. For still others, it's simply easier to evaluate success based on wins and losses and focus on the short-term goal of winning rather than the long-term goal of athletes' development. More than likely, however, coaches and athletes become win centered because they associate their self-worth with wins and losses. Winning becomes all-important, and losing becomes a threat to their self-worth, one to be avoided at any cost. When competitors link their self-worth to winning and losing, their goals are self-centered: They no longer care about what they can do for others—only what others can do for them. Do you coach to win for any of these reasons? Has coaching become a personal ego trip? Do you link your worth as a person to wins and losses? Or do you understand what Phil Niekro learned after years of professional baseball?

Rainer Martens coined the motto "Athletes first, winning second!" to help guide coaches to a more appropriate coaching philosophy. This athlete-centered philosophy places the highest priority on the people being coached, whereas a win-centered philosophy places greatest importance on the outcome of competition. We propose a slightly broader motto that can be applied to competition and to life. Our motto is "Personal excellence—the foundation for success!" This philosophy emphasizes that striving to learn and improve should be coaches' and athletes' highest priority, with winning a natural by-product of this enhanced personal development. As you strive to improve, you recognize that progress will be inconsis-

tent and that you will have ups and downs. Evaluate your current coaching philosophy in terms of these philosophical guidelines. Then decide whether you want to make any changes in your philosophy.

The philosophy encapsulated in the motto "Personal excellence—the foundation for success!" means that your first priority in every decision you make is to develop your athletes' skills and enable their personal growth as fully as possible. This pursuit of **personal excellence** should also increase their chances of winning, but it approaches winning as secondary to maximizing athletes' physical, psychological, and social development. These two objectives—winning and development—actually fall on a continuum. The extreme excellence-centered competitor always considers what is best for personal development with no concern for winning. On the other extreme, the win-centered competitor worries about development only to the extent that it affects winning. Excellence-centered coaches see sport as existing to help athletes learn and develop their skills, whereas win-centered coaches see development as a prerequisite to winning.

Look at the continuum shown in figure 1.1. Where do you place Bobby Knight on the continuum? Put a *BK* where you think Knight belongs. Where do you place John Wooden? Put his initials in an appropriate place. How about Michael Jordan or Jürgen Klinsmann? Add their initials. Do the same for other coaches or athletes you are familiar with. Now, where do you place yourself on this continuum? Insert your initials. Then put a *C* where you think your assistant coaches or supervisor would put you and an *A* where your athletes would likely put you. Think about your position for a few moments. Would you like to see it change?

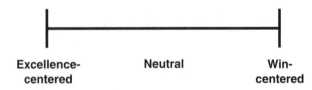

FIGURE 1.1   Continuum of excellence-centered and win-centered philosophies.

As you think about what coaching philosophy to adopt, you might consider that of John Wooden, the legendary UCLA basketball coach who emphasized learning and development over winning. Coach Wooden's philosophy represents his cumulative wisdom over a lifetime of playing and coaching. He did not begin coaching with the philosophy he espoused at the end of his career, nor should you expect to have all the answers immediately. Keep an open mind, examine your beliefs and values from time to time, and benefit from the experience of wise coaches such as John Wooden.

John Wooden's Competitive Philosophy

Few will dispute that John Wooden was a master coach. The Wizard of Westwood guided the UCLA Bruins to 10 NCAA Men's Basketball Championships in 12 years and won 88 consecutive games, including 38 straight NCAA tournament games, all while turning out numerous college All-Americans and NBA All-Stars. Wooden has become a coaching icon not only for his amazing success but also for how he achieved it. His competitive philosophy is illustrated by his famous Pyramid of Success, which defines success in terms of striving for excellence (see figure 1.2).

Without question, Wooden valued development ahead of winning. He believed in preparation and viewed success as a journey. His former players report that he never talked about winning, only about playing to the best of their ability. Wooden's pyramid has 14 building blocks of competitive greatness that reflect his belief in developing talent through hard work and perseverance: industriousness, friendship, loyalty, cooperation, enthusiasm, self-control, alertness, initiative, intentness, condition, skill, team spirit, poise, and confidence. Wooden considered himself an optimist and thought optimism was based on proper preparation and attention to detail. At the same time, he enjoyed competition and found it brought out the best in people. Wooden felt there was great joy and satisfaction in competing against

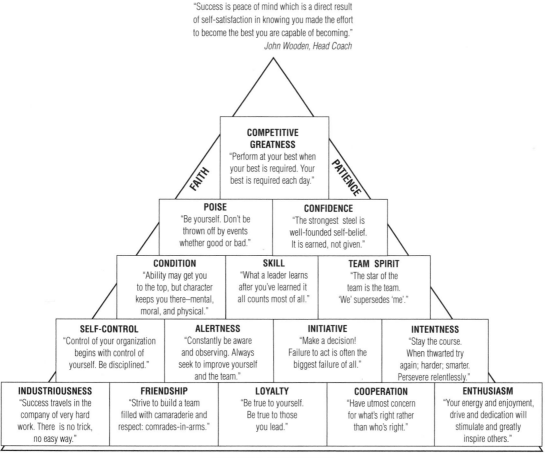

PYRAMID OF SUCCESS

FIGURE 1.2 John Wooden's Pyramid of Success.

From *Wooden on Leadership* (McGraw-Hill) and www.CoachWooden.com.

(continued)

(continued)

an opponent who forces you to dig deep and produce your best effort. The worthy opponent is the only one who can bring out the very best in each of us.

Wooden acknowledged making many mistakes but never failing. He believed that no one failed if they played to the best of their ability. He also believed that mistakes were prerequisites for success, and he often repeated a slogan from his college coach at Purdue, Piggy Lambert: "The team that makes the most mistakes will probably win." The truth is that the doer makes mistakes, and mistakes come from doing—but so does success. The player who is mistake free is also probably the one who is doing nothing to guarantee success, which may the biggest mistake of all.

Finally, John Wooden's competitive philosophy focused on team play. He wanted each player to make the effort to contribute to the best of his ability based on his individual talents. Wooden wanted players who would lose themselves in the team for the good of the team.

The True Competitor—We believe that excellent coaches are **true competitors** who have prioritized their competitive objectives appropriately. True competitors recognize that striving to win is much more important than actually winning, and they understand that when they achieve their goals they will increase their opportunities for victory. They also realize that the pursuit of excellence is never linear but has a series of peaks and valleys that will test their tenacity and resolve. True competitors view success as a journey rather than a destination. Coach Bill Snyder, who transformed Kansas State from one of college football's worst teams to one of its best, emphasized that success is not about winning but about improving as athletes, students, and people. Snyder evaluated success based on athletes' enthusiasm for the game, life-skill development, graduation rates, future career success, and character development (Shoop & Scott, 1999). This is a model that other coaches might do well to emulate.

True competitors also understand that competition is best when both sides compete on a level playing field. Thus they play within the spirit, as well as the letter, of the rules. When ideal competition occurs, both competitors flourish. For example, world-record holder Jesse Owens was on the verge of elimination from the long jump competition at the 1936 Berlin Olympics after fouling on his first two attempts. Owens got a tip from his most talented rival, the German Lutz Long, to move his mark back 6 inches (15 cm) to avoid fouling on his third attempt. The suggestion worked, and Owens won the gold medal. Pushed by Owens' outstanding performance, Long jumped a personal best. Both competitors were overjoyed and they left the stadium arm in arm, much to the dismay of Adolf Hitler. True competitors understand the cooperative nature of competition and the

need for competitors to push each other maximally if excellence is to be pursued fully. We hope your coaching philosophy will remain congruent with the principles of being a true competitor.

From Principle to Practice

"Personal excellence—the foundation for success!" is a simple, straightforward philosophy, and we have met few coaches who disagree with it. We have also met few who consistently put this philosophy into practice because many of us overemphasize winning. Remember, a philosophy is not the principles you preach; it's the values you live by. When confronted with the question of prioritizing winning and development, many coaches contend that they coach to achieve both, rightfully pointing out that winning can help athletes develop by giving them self-confidence and earning them many attractive rewards. But at times you will have to choose one over the other. Consider the following two real-life examples. What would you do?

A favored team's star player received an unwarranted technical foul early in a semifinal game of the state basketball tournament. Team rules dictated that any player receiving a technical foul must sit out the remainder of the game. Did the coach follow his philosophy and bench his star? He did. Even though he knew the player had not deserved the technical, he sat him for the remaining 28 minutes, sharply reducing his team's chance of winning. Fortunately, several other players stepped up to compensate for the loss, and the team won. The benched player later wrote a letter to the editor about the valuable lesson he learned from the experience and the admiration he felt for his coach's integrity. He concluded that the experience would make him a better person—the kind of person, it turned out, who later received an appointment to the U.S. Air Force Academy.

In another situation, the coach of a fifth-grade team in the championship game of the largest three-on-three basketball tournament in the country found his team overmatched. He chose to resort to the legal, though questionable, tactic of having his players intentionally foul an opposing player on every attempted shot within 15 feet (4.6 m) of the basket. Because tournament rules neither fouled players out nor gave bonus free throws for excessive fouls—and because the other team shot free throws poorly—the strategy worked. The fouling team squeaked out a 1-point win when its opposition missed 5 of 6 free throws in the final 30 seconds. Thus the opportunity to win this prestigious tournament prompted the coach to use a strategy that taught his players that winning is clearly more important than competing with integrity, a decision that may well have negatively affected these young athletes' long-term character development.

How you would respond to these situations likely depends on your coaching philosophy, particularly your values concerning winning and development. These are difficult decisions, but **competition** is a process that challenges your character and skills in many ways. Most competitors genuinely subscribe to the "Personal excellence—the foundation for success!" philosophy, and our personal experience in over 150 coaching education clinics attended by more than 4,000 coaches confirms that a majority of coaches rank development ahead of winning. The problem is implementing this philosophy—keeping your actions consistent with your beliefs. Winning is immediate and clearly defined. Success or failure is quickly discerned when the contest ends, and the rewards of winning are attractive and abundant. In contrast, achieving the goal of helping athletes develop into better human beings physically, psychologically, and socially is neither immediate nor clear-cut. Success may be difficult to discern, and only rarely are the rewards public.

With a well-established coaching philosophy of putting athletes' development first, you will have an easier time maintaining your values in the heat of battle when you get an unjust call, suffer an agonizing defeat, or feel frustrated with an athlete. A well-developed philosophy of life and competition will be among your best allies as you coach. To develop a coaching philosophy, you need to come to know yourself and prioritize your competitive objectives. A rich understanding of competition and its potential uses will help shape your philosophy.

Understanding Competition and Using It Constructively

A competition is a situation where an individual's or team's performance is being compared with a standard (Martens 1975). What standard will your athletes use? Comparisons can be made with three types of standards: an athlete's previous performance (**self-evaluation** focused on learning and improving); performances of other competitors (**social evaluation** focused on winning or placing high); and **idealized standards** (commonly recognized benchmarks of superior performance, such as a 4-minute mile (1.6 km), a 20-foot (6.1 m) pole vault, a triple-double in basketball, or a 100-yard (91 m) rushing game in American football). You will learn later in this text how to help athletes reduce anxiety and improve performance by focusing on self-evaluative goals rather than on winning. Are you willing to do this, even in a competitive situation? This is the type of question that your coaching philosophy will help you answer.

In addition, you'll need to think about whether competition is good or bad. How can your view of competition affect your coaching philosophy? Critics of competition point to problems such as violence between performers, coaches, officials, and spectators; development of serious participation-related physical disabilities; promotion of poor character development and distorted reasoning skills; lack of accountability in the classroom; and negative attitudes toward physical activity because of unpleasant sport experiences. Proponents, on the other hand, view competition as a constructive use of time and energy; a way to develop a sense of fair play, positive character traits, and skills that promote success in career and life; an important tool for enhancing quality of performance; and a powerful learning strategy that helps us to view problems as opportunities for achievement and fulfillment. Arguments on both sides of this debate are insightful and compelling, and it can be difficult to determine how beneficial competition really is.

When we ask our students whether they feel competition is good or bad, the overwhelming response is that it is good, although many students want to qualify their answer, having seen or experienced the negative consequences of winning being overemphasized. To us, this is a trick question, because we view competition as a neutral process, inherently neither good nor bad. Competition is not responsible for either the positive or the negative consequences so frequently highlighted by the media. The impact of competition, both helpful and detrimental, results not from competition itself but from how it is organized and conducted. As a coach, you play a major role in making sport a positive competitive experience—or not. In fact, competition can be fun, and making sport enjoyable will help your athletes stay in it longer and feel high intrinsic motivation to improve. Coaches who focus on athletes' physical, psychological, and social development, and make sport fun, normally promote high participation rates and minimize attrition. As you can see, then, the very nature of competition can affect your coaching philosophy.

This section discusses four areas of competition that your coaching philosophy must address in order to maximize the positive effects of competing. Let's look at what coaches must do to make competition a powerful motivational force, a valuable strategy for improving the quality of performance, a way to help athletes develop positive character traits, and a means of developing cooperative as well as competitive skills.

Making Competition a Powerful Motivational Force

Just as competition is used to motivate people in a variety of educational and business settings, it can be used to motivate your athletes in sport situations

as well. Your coaching philosophy needs to ensure that competition is used appropriately to enhance your athletes' motivation. You may recall situations in which competition motivated you, such as playing an archrival for the conference championship, trying to outperform a friend on a big test, or working to land a good job. But have there ever been times when competition did not motivate you, or when it even reduced your motivation? As you can see in figure 1.3, competition provides the greatest motivation when the level of challenge is moderately difficult. That is, your athletes' motivation will probably be highest when they tackle a challenge approximately equal to their current capabilities. And their motivation will likely remain high as long as challenge falls within a comfort zone ranging from just above to just below their current capabilities.

As the discrepancy between skill level and the competitive challenge increases, motivation steadily declines. Athletes normally have less motivation to compete against substantially superior or inferior opponents than against ones of similar ability. In the first case, athletes may be able to play their best and still have no chance to win, and in the second case they'll probably win no matter how poorly they perform. Neither of these situations offers much

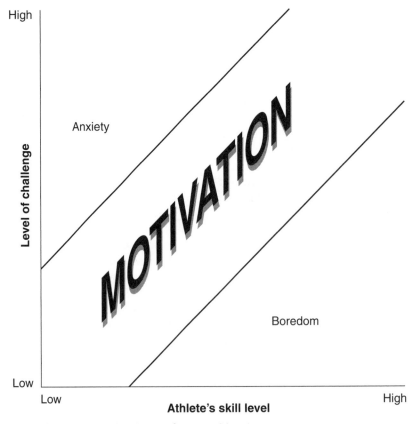

FIGURE 1.3 Relationship between motivation and competition.

motivation to perform their best. Therefore, coaches need a philosophy that encourages athletes to set process or performance goals—not focused solely on winning—with an optimal level of challenge so that they develop and maintain high motivation.

Improving Quality of Performance Through Competition

Competition can lead athletes to consistently perform their best—that is, it can improve their quality of performance. Having two players compete for a spot on the volleyball squad should lead to a better team, because each player is trying to improve as much as she can in order to make the team, become a starter, and contribute to team success. However, coaches must understand that competition doesn't automatically enhance quality, and they must learn how to counter the potential of pressure-packed situations to reduce quality or prompt performers to adopt negative solutions for reaching a particular competitive standard.

Competition can cause athletes to become short-sighted and thus hinder them from fully developing their capabilities. For example, some wrestlers become so concerned with outperforming their sparring partners that they continually rely on favorite moves instead of developing and refining new ones. Thus they perform well in practice but ultimately limit their skill development. Indeed, too much competition may be just as problematic for quality control as too little: My (Damon Burton's) work with the U.S. Ski Jumping Team showed me a classic example of the insidious effects of competition on athletes' development. Regulations from the team's executive board mandated that athlete funding and trip selection be based exclusively on performance. This system meant that every single jump—from dry-land training on plastic to on-snow training and competition—was vitally important. Every jump, each day, was a competition, prompting the jumpers to focus on maximizing their immediate results. Thus, although the system was designed to ensure equality of opportunity, it ended up inhibiting the jumpers' technical and tactical development.

Learning curves for any skill are seldom linear (see figure 1.4). Normally, when athletes learn new skills or try to correct major flaws in form, they must suffer through a temporary drop, and often subsequent plateaus, before moving on to higher performance levels. Unfortunately, the ski jumpers could not afford to go through this performance decline on their way to developing improved technique, because it could cost

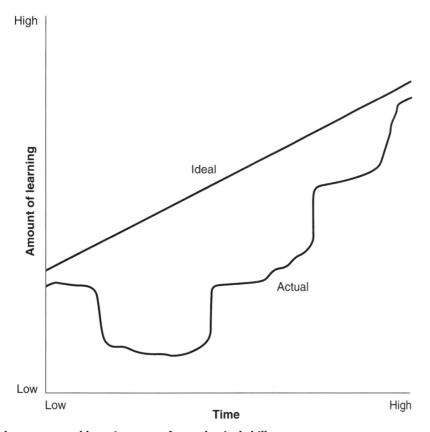

FIGURE 1.4   Ideal versus actual learning curve for a physical skill.

them funding and trips. Not surprisingly, an extensive evaluation of the jumpers' technical improvement over a 4-year period revealed minimal gains compared with those of jumpers from other countries. As a result, our jumpers had difficulty competing with opponents whose teams' selection procedures allowed them to develop their fundamental jumping techniques and tactics more normally. Competition needs to be used judiciously, so that it stimulates improvement in the quality of performance without limiting skill development. Your competitive philosophy must emphasize development, so that athletes strive to enhance quality in appropriate ways.

Competition as a Means to Develop Positive Character Traits

Your coaching philosophy must specify the importance you place on character development. Competition can play a valuable role in helping athletes develop positive character traits that will help them succeed in future endeavors. But competition does not automatically generate positive character traits, and, regrettably, competing in sport sometimes detracts from character development. Thus we believe it is essential that your coaching philosophy specify the role you will play in your athletes' character development.

Research has confirmed that athletes are less likely to participate in delinquent behavior than are non-athletes (Seefeldt & Ewing 1997). However, moral reasoning and good sporting behavior seem to decline as athletes progress to higher competitive levels, in part because of the increased emphasis on winning (Beller & Stoll 1995). Thus winning can be a double-edged sword in teaching character development. Some athletes may want to win so much that they lie, cheat, break team rules, and develop undesirable character traits that can enhance their ability to win in the short term. However, when athletes resist the temptation to win through unscrupulous means, they can develop positive character traits that last a lifetime. Character is a learned behavior, and a sense of fair play develops only if coaches plan to teach those lessons systematically, along with strategies for transferring the lessons and values to future life experiences.

Consider the character development possibilities in the following scenarios where a tennis player, Bob, could call his opponent's shot, a would-be winner, in or out because no one else could tell for sure where it landed:

- Bob and his roommate John are tied at 6 in the final-set tiebreaker of their friendly match. In addition to bragging rights, the two have a cold drink wagered on the outcome.

- Bob and his archrival are tied at 6 in the final-set tiebreaker of the state tennis championship. A possible college scholarship is also at stake.

It's easy to make the honest call in the first situation, playing against a friend with little riding on the outcome, but the response may have only minimal impact on Bob's long-term character development. However, if Bob makes the right call in the state championship match, with so much riding on the outcome, it is a lesson that can positively shape his character for the rest of his life. The value that athletes place on competitive success makes sport a domain for teaching integrity and character development, which can have long-lasting effects on personal growth. But these positive outcomes occur only when coaches make character development a high priority.

Teaching Athletes How to Cooperate as Well as Compete

We live in an extremely interdependent and cooperative society. In our everyday lives, we may go days at a time without competing, but we cooperate in many ways each day—from collaborating with others at work and home to purchasing products made by others (or creating products for others to purchase). Thus, in our modern society, learning how to cooperate is just as important for our young athletes as learning how to compete. This may become part of your coaching philosophy. Competition and **cooperation** are often depicted as opposing processes, even though they are actually complementary. Sport sociologist Gunther Luschen (1970) has described the relationship between competition and cooperation in terms of what he calls **association**—the ways that individuals or teams must cooperate in order to compete effectively.

Most of us can readily identify one type of association in that athletes in team sports must cooperate with each other in order for the team to perform cohesively. Such within-team cooperation is essential to a team's success. But *between*-team cooperation is necessary for competition to even occur. Teams have to agree on a time and place to compete. They also have to agree to a set of rules to govern their competition and promise to abide by them. Finally, competition assumes that all competitors or teams are going to give their best effort, or at least establish a mutually agreed upon level of commitment and effort. At its best, then, competition should involve a quest for excellence between evenly matched opponents who are giving maximal effort. Will you make it part of your philosophy to teach your athletes how to cooperate with each other—and with opposing teams—so that competition is the best it can be?

Final Thoughts on Competition

When administrators, coaches, parents, and fans understand competition and are committed to helping young athletes get the most from their competitive experiences, competition is viewed almost universally as positive. However, when members of any of these important adult groups, particularly coaches, lose perspective and fail to put the welfare of young athletes first, competition can become a negative experience. Your coaching philosophy provides the foundation for ensuring positive sport experiences for your athletes.

SUMMARY

1. Coaches must develop a coaching philosophy to help them make the right decisions at critical times during practice and competition. A well-developed philosophy will help you make decisions that you believe in, even in the heat of the moment.

2. Developing a coaching philosophy involves enhancing self-awareness and prioritizing the coaching objectives of winning and athlete development. The motto "Personal excellence—the foundation for success!" suggests that both objectives are important but that personal excellence should become a higher priority.

3. The true competitor prioritizes personal excellence ahead of winning and focuses on the journey rather than the destination. True competitors thrive on challenge and understand that they will achieve personal excellence only when pushed to do so by competitors performing at the top of their game.

4. To effectively shape your coaching philosophy, you must understand competition and how it affects your philosophy.

5. Competition involves comparing performance to a standard: an athlete's previous performance, the performance of other competitors, or an idealized standard (e.g., a recognized level of excellence). Your athletes need to know what standard is being used and whether they have met the standard.

6. Getting the most out of your coaching philosophy requires understanding that competition is neither good nor bad; it is simply a process. Coaches and other adults play a major role in determining whether competition turns out to be a positive or negative experience for athletes.

7. For competition to be a powerful motivator, teams or competitors must be evenly matched. The motivational impact of competition declines when the discrepancy between skill level and competitive challenge increases.

8. Competition can enhance performance quality because both within-team and between-team competition pushes athletes to develop their skills more fully and execute them more effectively under pressure. Competition must be used judiciously, so that it helps athletes improve their performance without becoming an impediment to their development.

9. Competition can enhance character development. When competition is conducted properly, with an emphasis on good sporting behavior, sport is a great arena for developing positive character traits. However, in many cases, competition hurts character because of poor role models and coaches' failure to emphasize character development over winning.

10. Competition and cooperation work together, and coaches must help their athletes learn to cooperate as well as compete.

11. Despite its problems, competition remains an essential process in sport and society. Coaches must develop philosophies that help them maximize the benefits and minimize the costs of competition for young athletes.

KEY TERMS

association   idealized standard   self-evaluation

coaching philosophy   personal excellence   social evaluation

competition   self-awareness   true competitor

cooperation

REVIEW QUESTIONS

1. What is a coaching philosophy?

2. Why is it important to develop a sound coaching philosophy?

3. What are the key steps in developing an effective coaching philosophy?

4. How can competition be used to facilitate athletes' development?

5. Is competition good or bad?

PRACTICAL ACTIVITIES

1. Develop an initial personal coaching philosophy. Identify your strengths and weaknesses as a coach. Prioritize winning versus development and provide a rationale to justify why you prioritized these objectives as you did.

2. Critique yourself based on how you use competition to enhance athletes' development. How well do you use competition to increase athletes' motivation, improve their skills, enhance their character development, and help them develop cooperative skills?

2

Communication

After reading this chapter you should be able to

- understand what communication is and why it is important,
- know how to send effective messages and provide instructional feedback,
- understand how to receive messages through effective listening skills, and
- describe how to effectively resolve conflicts through effective confrontations.

Communication skills may be the best predictor of coaching success. The life of a coach is filled with a steady flow of communication: Coaches talk, read, write, gesture, listen, teach, console, persuade, demonstrate, and observe. Beyond their interaction with athletes, they spend a great deal of time communicating with parents, administrators, officials, other coaches, the media, booster club members, and support staff. So it is no secret that your success as a coach will depend on your ability to communicate effectively. You need strong communication skills to instruct your athletes clearly, motivate them, and inspire confidence. Communication skills are the foundation for creating rapport with your athletes and developing team harmony. Being a good communicator can pave the way to a rewarding coaching experience, while communication breakdowns can lead to conflict, frustration, stress, and job dissatisfaction. Indeed, effective communication skills transcend sport. They are important in every area of life, and improving them will make your life richer and more fulfilling.

Despite their importance, communication skills are often taken for granted. In the face of communication breakdowns, we tend to believe that our communication efforts are fine and that the problem lies with the people we are trying to communicate with. The reality is that we are not always effective communicators. Have you ever made a comment you regretted? Do you sometimes unintentionally expect others to be able to read your mind? Do you find yourself talking more than you listen? Have you ever expected athletes to respond well to constructive criticism while not being open to feedback yourself? Most of us can relate to these scenarios. If you can, this chapter is for you.

Becoming an effective communicator is not an easy task. Like any other skill, it takes education, hard work, and practice. Part of the challenge in developing communication skills is that ineffective communication patterns are often so ingrained that it is difficult to become aware of them and let them go. The first step in improving your communication skills is to realize their importance and become aware of your communication style. This chapter helps you identify your strengths and weaknesses as a communicator and provides you with foundational knowledge you can put into action to improve your communication skills.

What Is Communication?

Communication is the act of expressing (or transmitting) ideas, information, knowledge, thoughts, and feelings, as well as understanding what is expressed by others. The communication process involves both sending and receiving messages and can take many forms. Verbal communication is the spoken word, while **nonverbal communication** involves actions, facial expressions, body position, and gestures. Communication can occur in one-on-one or group settings, and in written formats (e.g., printed materials) or in visual formats (e.g., pictures, videos, and observational learning). And it involves not only the content of a message but also its emotional impact, or the effect the message has on the person receiving it.

Sending and Receiving Messages

The very word *coach* suggests that individuals in this profession send many messages. Coaches need to be able to clearly communicate expectations, goals, standards, and feelings to their athletes. They instruct, encourage, discipline, organize, and provide feedback. And although we tend to think of effective communicators as being able to send clear messages that are interpreted as intended, communication is a two-way street that also involves receiving messages. For a coach, this means listening attentively. Athletes need to be able to communicate their goals, frustrations, and feelings to their coach.

Nonverbal and Verbal Channels

As a coach, you can say a lot without uttering a word: A frown, a look of disbelief, a disgusted shake of your head, or a smile can communicate quite a bit. In fact, communication experts suggest that between 65% and 93% of the meaning of a message is conveyed through tone of voice and nonverbal behaviors (Johnson 2003). Thus, in addition to becoming aware of the words you use, it is essential that you become aware of your tone and nonverbal behaviors so that you understand the messages you are sending to athletes.

Lou Holtz tells a revealing story about his coaching experience at Notre Dame that highlights the importance of developing self-awareness in becoming an effective communicator. His recruiting coordinator developed a video to send to potential recruits. Holtz thought it did a great job of selling the program but wished it included some clips of him having positive interactions with his players. The recruiting coordinator said he had looked and looked but could not find any. This comment took Holtz completely by surprise because he prided himself on being a positive coach and sending positive messages (Janssen & Dale 2002). This experience helped Holtz become more aware of his interactions with his players and discover a pathway for becoming a more effective communicator. Like Holtz, many coaches are often unaware of the messages they send nonverbally.

By the same token, athletes also communicate nonverbally, and coaches can learn to be more effective listeners by becoming astute observers of athlete's nonverbal communications. Understanding the nonverbal messages athletes send is a passport to greater understanding of the athletes you are coaching.

Content and Emotional Impact

When communicating, coaches tend to focus on the content or the substance of the messages they send: "Run hard"; "Follow through strongly on your shot"; "Fake before you pass"; "Practice with intensity." In doing so, they believe that the information is objective and that athletes will always receive the message as intended. That belief is far from the truth. When receiving messages, athletes may not share the same perception or hear the same message the coach thought she was sending. For example, by saying, "Tomorrow we are going to make sure to get this defense down," a coach may mean, "We're going to focus on the technical aspects of the defense to perfect our execution," but an athlete may interpret it as, "Tomorrow's going to be a physically tough practice." Communication problems arise if a coach assumes athletes are interpreting a message exactly as the coach intended. Thus effective communicators focus not only on message content but also on how a message might be interpreted by—and might affect—the receiver.

Beyond message content, then, communication also involves the emotional impact of the message on the athlete. How do your athletes perceive and react to the content of your messages? Failure to recognize the effect the message has on the athlete is all too common. For instance, a coach could intend "Run hard!" as a positive note of encouragement, whereas the athlete could interpret it negatively: "He never thinks I run hard enough." Effective communicators give equal weight to message content and emotional impact on the receiver. The challenge in effective communication is to be clear both about what you say and about how you say it by becoming more aware of the impact your messages have on your team.

Sending Effective Messages

Effective communicators are able to send messages that clearly convey the intended content and are received in the desired way. The most important judg-ment you need to make is whether a message needs to be sent. Some coaches talk too much, rambling on about things that bore others or distract athletes during practice. Some coaches talk too little, assuming that others know what they think or want. We've listed some guidelines for sending effective messages in figure 2.1. Read each guideline and then honestly rate whether this is a communication strength or weakness for you by circling the appropriate number. Be sure to rate yourself objectively and take action to improve any deficiencies. Rest assured that we all have communication strengths and weaknesses!

Effect of Your Messages

Smoll and Smith spent hundreds of hours observing coaches and evaluating their impact on athletes (Smith 2001, Smoll & Smith 2006). In all, they observed more than 70 coaches, coded more than 80,000 behaviors, and surveyed nearly 1,000 athletes. They found that athletes responded positively to coaches who provided

- positive feedback after a good performance effort,
- corrective instruction and encouragement after a performance mistake, and
- technical instruction and a moderate amount of general encouragement unrelated to performance quality

In contrast, Smoll and Smith found that athletes responded unfavorably to coaches who failed to notice or reinforce good performance efforts, criticized mistakes, or provided instruction after a mistake in a critical fashion.

The positive characteristics noted by Smoll and Smith are evident in great coaches such as legendary coach John Wooden, who won 10 NCAA Men's Basketball Championship tournaments during his tenure at UCLA. He spent 50% of his communication time providing verbal instruction on what to do and how to do it, 13% encouraging players to hustle and intensify effort, 8% providing constructive criticism, 8% praising (verbally or nonverbally), 7% in simple statements of displeasure, and the balance in miscellaneous infrequent behaviors (Gallimore & Tharpe 2004). Similar findings have been noted for other successful coaches. Unfortunately, most of us can think of coaches who have a negative coaching style—yelling, screaming, and relying on punishment to motivate athletes. On a positive note, Smoll and Smith found that most youth sport coaches did not fit the negative profile, and that, in all, only 3% of

Guidelines for Sending Effective Messages

1. Messages should be direct.

Coaches who are weak on this quality avoid straightforward, direct communication. Their athletes may not know where they stand. These coaches assume others know what they expect, want, or feel. Rather than expressing their message directly, they hint at what they have in mind or they expect others to be mind readers. In other cases, they may tell someone else, hoping the message will get to the intended recipient indirectly. The problem is that indirect messages are often distorted and misperceived.

How strong are you in sending direct messages?

1	2	3	4	5
Weak				Strong

2. Own your messages.

Use "I" and "my," not "the team," or "we" when referencing your messages. You disown your messages when you say, "The team feels . . .," or "Most people think you are . . .," when it is really what you believe. Using others to bolster what you have to say implies cowardice in expressing your own messages and a failure to take ownership.

How strong are you in owning your messages?

1	2	3	4	5
Weak				Strong

3. Messages should be complete and specific.

Tell the whole story without leaving out important information. Provide the person with whom you are speaking all the information he or she needs in order to fully understand your message. Watch for leaps in logic, unknown assumptions, and unstated intentions.

How strong are you in making your messages complete and specific?

1	2	3	4	5
Weak				Strong

4. Messages should be clear and consistent. Avoid double messages.

Coaches who say one thing one day and then something else on another violate this principle as do coaches who send contradictory messages. "I really want to play you, but I don't think this is a good matchup for you." "I think you're a fine athlete, but you'll just have to be patient." This example of a double message (acceptance and rejection) leaves the athlete confused and probably hurt. Double messages have contradictory meanings, and usually are sent when you are afraid to tell the person directly something that may offend him or her.

How strong are you in sending clear and consistent messages?

1	2	3	4	5
Weak				Strong

(continued)

FIGURE 2.1 Use these guidelines to rate your strengths and weaknesses in sending messages.

5. Messages should clearly state needs and feelings.

Because our society frowns on those who wear their emotions on their sleeves, we tend not to reveal our feelings and needs to others. Yet revealing our needs and feelings is a foundation for developing close relationships and opening the communication channels. Sharing needs and feelings opens the door for the other person to do the same. Unexpressed needs and hidden feelings result in unfilled expectations.

How strong are you in clearly stating your needs and feelings?

1	2	3	4	5
Weak				Strong

6. Messages should separate fact from opinion.

State what you see, hear, and know, and then clearly identify any opinions or conclusions you have about these facts. You say to your son when he returns home late one night, "I see you've been out with the Williamson kid again." In the context in which it is spoken, your son receives the message, but he is not certain exactly what your concern is about the Williamson boy. A better way to send this message would be (a) "That was the Williamson kid, was it not?" (verifying a fact); and then (b) "I'm concerned that you spend so much time with him. I worry that he will get you into trouble" (stating your opinion). Although your son may not be pleased with your opinion, this message is far less ambiguous than the first one.

How strong are you in separating fact from opinion in your messages?

1	2	3	4	5
Weak				Strong

7. Messages should be focused on one thing at a time.

Focus your message on one topic or issue at a time. Jumping from topic to topic only confuses the listener. Are your messages frequently disjointed thoughts because you don't take the time to organize your thinking?

How strong are you in focusing your messages on one thing at a time?

1	2	3	4	5
Weak				Strong

8. Messages should be delivered immediately.

When you observe something that upsets you or that needs to be changed, don't delay sending a message. Sometimes holding back can result in your exploding later about a little thing. Responding immediately also is a sound principle for giving effective feedback. However, if your emotions are clouding your judgment, it is sometimes better to wait until a better time to deliver your message.

How strong are you in delivering messages immediately when you see the need to do so?

1	2	3	4	5
Weak				Strong

(continued)

FIGURE 2.1 *(continued)*

9. Messages should not contain hidden agendas.

This principle means that the stated purpose of the message is identical with the real purpose. Hidden agendas and disguised intentions destroy relationships. Ask yourself these two questions to determine if your message contains hidden agendas: Why am I saying this? Is it because I want him or her to hear it or is there something else involved?

How strong are you in avoiding messages that contain hidden agendas?

    1   2   3   4   5
Weak   Strong

10. Messages should be supportive.

If you want the other person to listen to your messages over time, you cannot deliver them with threats, sarcasm, negative comparisons, or any type of judgment. Eventually the person will avoid communicating with you or will simply tune you out whenever you speak. Your cumulative messages need to demonstrate support for the person.

How strong are you in sending supportive messages?

    1   2   3   4   5
Weak   Strong

11. Verbal and nonverbal messages should be congruent.

You tell your player it was OK to make the error, but your negative body gestures and facial expressions contradict your words. The two conflicting messages confuse your player and hurt your credibility in future communication.

How strong are you in making your verbal and nonverbal messages congruent?

    1   2   3   4   5
Weak   Strong

12. Messages should be redundant. (That is, you should repeat the message. Get the point?)

That's correct. Repeat the key points in a message to reinforce what you are saying. Preview what you are going to tell them, tell them, and then review what you just told them. However, be aware that too much repetition results in the other person not listening, so you must be discrimininating in your redundancy. You can create redundancy by using additional channels of communication to bolster your message. For example, show a picture or video along with explaining the skill.

How strong are you in making your messages optimally redundant?

    1   2   3   4   5
Weak   Strong

13. Messages should be at the receiver's level and frame of reference.

Speak at the level of the receivers in a way that they can readily understand. Your messages can be much better understood if you tailor them to the experiences of the people with whom you are communicating. For example, it is inappropriate to use complex language when speaking to young athletes who do not have the vocabulary to understand what is being said. Make sure the message being sent is understandable given athletes' age, development, and experience

How strong are you in sending messages that are appropriate for the receiver's level of readiness and understanding?

    1   2   3   4   5
Weak   Strong

(continued)

FIGURE 2.1 *(continued)*

14. Messages should be checked for understanding.

Look for verbal and nonverbal evidence that the person with whom you are speaking is receiving the message as you intended. If you are unsure of the person's understanding, ask him or her to summarize the main points of the message or ask questions to assess comprehension. Athletes may be hesitant to ask questions if they do not understand for fear of appearing stupid in front of others.

How strong are you in obtaining feedback to make certain the person understands your message?

1 2 3 4 5

Weak   Strong

15. Messages should be attention grabbing.

You need to hook people into listening. Grab their attention by using their names or by explaining why it is important for them to understand the information you are communicating.s

How strong are you in sending attention grabbing messages?

1 2 3 4 5

Weak   Strong

16. Messages should consider each athlete's learning style.

Some athletes are visual learners, others are auditory learners, while yet others learn through doing (i.e., kinesthetic learners). Messages will be more easily comprehended if they accommodate an athlete's learning style.

How strong are you in considering each listener's learning style in sending messages?

1 2 3 4 5

Weak   Strong

Total you ratings and see where you fall in the following subjective scale:

67-80	Excellent
55-66	Good
43-54	Average
31-42	Weak
30 or less	Help!

FIGURE 2.1 *(continued)*

comments by coaches were aversive in nature and only 20% of mistakes were responded to in a negative fashion. Though infrequent, the negative comments had a strong effect on athletes. A few misplaced comments can do great damage.

Can coaches learn to be more effective communicators? Smoll and Smith developed training guidelines intended to help coaches do just that, then compared coaches who had received the training with those who had not. Athletes who played for trained coaches had a more positive sport experience than those who played for untrained coaches. They rated the coach as a better teacher, had more fun, and felt less pressure. In fact, only 5% of the athletes who played for trained coaches dropped out of sport, compared with 26% who played for coaches who had not been trained.

Consider this a pep talk to motivate you to reflect carefully on your own communication with athletes and to make improving your communication skills a priority. You *can* strengthen your skills, and doing so will benefit your athletes. The next section provides concrete strategies you can use to send effective messages.

Using Reinforcement

Although coaches do a lot of instructing, organizing, and encouraging, they also spend a great deal of time providing feedback to athletes. Successful coaches use feedback to reinforce athletes for things they have done well. A positive reinforcer is a pleasant consequence or outcome that encourages the athlete to try to repeat the desired behavior. **Reinforcement** has a strong influence on athletes' behavior, and if it is not used correctly it can be detrimental. Imagine a point guard whose role is to run the offense but not score a lot of points. In an important game, she happens to score 30 points and receives a great deal of positive feedback from the media and her parents and friends. Her pride in scoring many points, coupled with praise from others, could serve as a strong reinforcer for shooting. As a result, she might try to score a lot in the next game and, in the process, fail to run the offense effectively. Good coaches realize the power of reinforcement and use it to their advantage by reinforcing desired behaviors in an appropriate manner.

Shaping: Reward Successful Approximations

Although many athletes find mastering a complex skill to be reinforcing, the learning process itself is not always reinforcing as it can be painstakingly slow and frustrating. Coaches can help athletes work through this process by using a principle called **shaping** to reinforce successive or closer approximations to the desired behavior. In using this principle, coaches reinforce small improvements rather than waiting until the athlete performs the entire skill correctly. For example, teaching a basketball player to shoot accurately might start with getting the elbow directly under the ball. Regardless of other aspects of technique, or whether the ball goes in the basket, good elbow position is rewarded. Once this aspect of technique has been mastered, step 2 requires good elbow position and a high release point in order to receive reinforcement—and so on, until, step by step, the player masters good shooting form. At each step in the process, the coach initially gives reinforcement immediately and every time. As the proper technique becomes ingrained, reinforcement can be delayed and intermittent.

Reward Effort and Performance, Not Just Outcomes

It is crucial to reward effort, improvement, and technique, but it is common to see coaches rewarding only the outcome of a performance (say, getting a hit in baseball or softball), even if the skill is executed poorly (as when the ball comes off the end of the bat). Alternatively, coaches may fail to recognize a good performance (such as a good swing) if the outcome is poor (line drive to the shortstop). Achieving a desired outcome, even if it is executed poorly, is often intrinsically rewarding to athletes, so it is important for coaches to reinforce effort and form, which are key to long-term success but may be less intrinsically reinforcing.

Reward Social and Emotional Skills

As a coach, you will have the opportunity to help athletes develop as individuals. If you truly buy into the personal excellence philosophy, you will want to reinforce athletes for demonstrating positive emotional and social skills. For example, if you value team communication, you would reinforce athletes for being strong communicators in the heat of action. If you value fair and ethical behavior, you would reward athletes who act with integrity. If you value emotional control, you would reward athletes who demonstrate mental toughness.

Reward Good Behavior and Use Punishment Sparingly

Coaches who are masterful at using reinforcement also use it to minimize undesirable behaviors. Rather than punishing athletes for misbehaving or making mistakes, they reinforce the opposite good behavior. For example, rather than punishing athletes who are late for practice, they make it a point to reinforce athletes for being punctual. Rather than reprimanding athletes for being critical of one another on the field, they reward them for being supportive and encouraging of one another. By using reinforcement, you can create a positive environment that reduces the need for punishment. This does not mean that you should never use punishment, but simply that you should rely more on reinforcement.

Strive to use **punishment** sparingly. Perhaps the best approach is to prevent misbehaviors from occurring in the first place. To do this, it is essential that athletes understand which behaviors are appropriate, which are inappropriate, and what is expected of them. Setting forth clear expectations—and consequences for violating them—should minimize your need to nag or threaten athletes to keep order. Athletes respond favorably to clear expectations and guidelines, but they do not respond well to being regimented. Thus, you should strive to maintain order by clarifying expectations but keep things in balance by not becoming a controlling coach who micromanages. Some coaches find it effective to involve athletes in developing consequences for violating team rules. It gives the athletes ownership and helps them develop responsibility.

There will be times when punishment is necessary. In deciding whether to punish an athlete, keep in mind that performance mistakes should not be punished if they were made while giving good effort. Performance mistakes are a natural part of the learning process and form the stepping stones to success. Punishment should be reserved for misbehavior and violation of team rules. Here are some simple guidelines for maximizing the effectiveness of punishment when you do use it:

- Consequences need to be seen by team members as being fair and appropriate for the misbehavior.

- For each team rule, it is helpful to have a list of consequences, arranged in order from least to most severe. That way you can provide more severe consequences for more severe violations and for repeated offenses.

- Punishments should consist of logical consequences that follow naturally from the misbehavior. If a player arrives late for a trip, a logical punishment is for the bus to leave. If an athlete is late for practice, a logical punishment is to have the athlete arrive early for practice the next day to help set up equipment.

- Develop team rules and consequences that you are willing to enforce when the need arises.

- Be consistent by giving everyone, whether starter or reserve player, similar punishment for breaking similar rules.

- Punish the behavior, not the person. Let the athlete know that it is her behavior that needs to change.

- Make sure the punishment is not a reward for athletes who simply desire attention.

- Impose the punishment impersonally and with respect. Do not make an example of an athlete or embarrass him in front of the team. Likewise, do not yell or berate the athlete. Simply administer the punishment.

- Use punishment calmly rather than reactively. Do not punish out of anger, and don't respond in haste when you are not sure what the appropriate consequences should be.

- Rather than adding something aversive, take away something desirable. This type of punishment creates less resentment and is often more effective.

Providing Feedback

One of the primary ways coaches reinforce athletes is through their use of feedback. Although feedback has the potential to be a powerful reinforcer, using it effectively is an art. Effective coaches have mastered that art; they provide feedback in a way that motivates and inspires athletes to reach their potential.

Responding to a Good Performance Effort

This section describes how to respond when athletes try hard, improve their skills, and perform well. The next section addresses how to give instructional feedback when athletes make mistakes and perform poorly.

Nonreinforcement—At times, coaches are so focused on helping athletes improve that they take good performance efforts for granted. **Nonreinforcement** means failing to acknowledge athletes' effort, skill execution, and performance improvements. Have you ever failed to point out the positives because you were so focused on identifying what athletes needed to do to improve? It's an easy trap to fall into. Coaches who fail to reinforce when it is warranted assume that athletes know their work is noticed and appreciated. In reality, when you fail to acknowledge strong effort and performance, this communicates a negative message to athletes, leaving them to question whether their effort and improvement are recognized and valued.

Reinforcement—Coaches who are effective communicators create a positive team culture by reinforcing athletes either verbally or nonverbally for improving, executing a difficult skill, or trying hard. They may make encouraging comments, such as, "That was a great effort," "Way to look the ball into your glove," or "You got a fast start out of the blocks." In addition to a verbal comment, a simple smile, pat on the back, or thumbs-up can go a long way in communicating that an athlete's effort and performance are appreciated. Providing positive feedback creates an atmosphere of catching athletes doing something right (rather than wrong) and motivates them to continue trying.

General versus descriptive positive feedback—Not all positive feedback is equally effective. In providing general feedback, coaches may say something like, "Well done," "Way to go," or "Keep it up." This type of positive feedback does not have a significant effect on athletes. It may even come across as being insincere, and it is easy for athletes to discount. A better approach is to give **descriptive feedback**, where you describe the performance and what exactly the athlete did well: "You made a great move to get open"

Is More Always Better?

Conventional wisdom suggests that the more positive feedback coaches provide, the better. But is this always true? Some researchers have found that athletes who received the most praise and encouragement had lower confidence than those who received less praise but more corrective instruction. Sound counterintuitive? On close inspection, the athletes who received the most praise were given praise that actually communicated negative expectations from the coach because it was general and did not depend on the quality of athletes' performances. These athletes may have received a lot of general encouragement and praise for success at easy tasks, rather than descriptive feedback for success at challenging tasks. In providing feedback, quality matters. Insincere or unthoughtful praise may backfire. Telling an athlete she did a good job when she knows she did not perform well communicates only that you are trying to make her feel better. Saying "well done" on an easy task actually communicates that you are not confident in the athlete's abilities. Rather than simply providing more positive feedback, coaches should strive to provide higher-quality feedback that is appropriate to the skill level of the athlete (Allen & Howe 1998, Horn 1985).

or "Great job—you kept your head up and back straight throughout the lift." This type of feedback has a positive effect on athletes; its specificity marks it as sincere and make it more likely to be internalized. When you are giving feedback, remember that specific is terrific—let athletes know exactly what they did well.

Provide Encouragement and Instructional Feedback, Not Constructive Criticism

Although it is crucial to catch athletes doing something right, it is also important to learn how to respond effectively to mistakes, poor performance, and lack of effort. Athletes will make mistakes and they will have poor performances. It's a natural part of the learning process. Coaches are aware of this and, with good intentions, often give **constructive criticism** to help athletes improve, but in reality constructive criticism can backfire and make athletes feel belittled. So what is the best way to respond to an athlete who makes a mistake?

Encourage, encourage, encourage—Coaches should encourage athletes after a mistake because that is when they need it the most. If athletes know how to perform the skill, then simple encouragement may be enough. The coach might say, "Tough game out there today—keep up the effort." If the mistake results from a lack of effort, it is appropriate to let the athlete know you are displeased, but be sure to aim comments at the lack of effort rather than the athlete as a person. You might say, "I'd like to see you hustle more" rather than commenting that the

athlete is lazy. If the mistake is due to the athlete's not knowing how to perform the skill, or needing to refine it, then corrective feedback is warranted. The key to giving **instructional feedback** is to recognize poor performance in a positive way that is encouraging and helps athletes improve.

Make instructional feedback action oriented—Action-oriented feedback does not punish; rather, it is descriptive and helps athletes focus on their future attempts. Never provide instructional feedback in a negative, demeaning, or sarcastic fashion. Punishment is not simply a matter of yelling—it can be implied by tone of voice, a look of disgust, and a variety of other nonverbal expressions. Whatever its form, punitive feedback often results in athletes becoming frustrated and developing a resentful attitude. It destroys, rather than builds, communication bridges.

Thus it is important to learn how to give instructional feedback that motivates and inspires athletes. As with positive feedback, instructional feedback works best when it is descriptive. This kind of feedback clearly and objectively describes the behaviors the coach observed. It is not criticism. Criticism might sound like this: "How many times do I have to tell you to catch the ball with two hands?" Descriptive feedback, on the other hand, does not seek to label an athlete's performance as poor. Instead it seeks to help the athlete look more clearly at his or her behavior. The coach might say, "Remember to look the ball all the way into your hands." This type of feedback helps athletes learn while maintaining their confidence. In the two examples of descriptive feedback listed below, circle the response that you think is most effective in each pair.

> "Great effort but you are still starting your flip turn too far away from the wall."

> "Great effort. Next time start your flip turn closer to the wall."

> "You are still not bending your knees enough."

> "Next time bend your knees even more and you'll do even better."

What do you see as the main difference? You may have noticed that the first example in each pair of feedback statements focuses on the past and what the athlete did wrong, whereas the second is future oriented and focuses on what the athlete needs to do to improve. Instructional feedback focuses on the future and is action oriented—it addresses what athletes need to accomplish, not what they should avoid. Rather than saying, "Don't hit the serve long," "Don't bend your back," or "Don't take your eye off the ball," effective feedback directs athletes' attention to what they need to do to succeed: "Swing through the ball," "Back straight," or "Arms up and high." Focusing athletes' attention on what they should avoid can actually program them to do the very thing you are trying to prevent. To illustrate: Whatever you do right now, do not think of a pink elephant. Just block out any thought of a pink elephant. How successful were you? You probably immediately thought of a pink elephant. Be sure to give feedback that encourages athletes to focus on what you want them to do, not on what you want them to avoid. And remember to provide visual demonstrations to illustrate your positive verbal instruction.

Enhancing Athletes' Receptiveness to Feedback

How can you determine whether an athlete received the feedback as you intended? The answer is easy— the athlete will respond in the way you hoped. You can facilitate such responses by taking deliberate steps to help athletes be receptive to your feedback. First, try not to become so focused on message content that you forget the emotional impact of the message on the athlete. You can increase athletes' receptiveness by starting with something positive. For example, in describing how he provides instructional feedback, former NBA coach Rudy Tomjanovich says, "Correcting mistakes is one of the most important parts of coaching. . . . The majority of things a coach says to a player involve correcting him, and the manner in which you do so is vitally important. I feel a good way to change a negative is to add a positive to the formula" (Janssen 1999, p. 117).

An effective strategy for casting corrective feedback in a positive tone is to sandwich it between positive comments (figure 2.2). This approach works well because it builds athletes' confidence while also providing information about what they can do to improve. It takes the sting out of corrective feedback. One caveat: Avoid using the word *but*. Everything you say before this word gets discounted, and everything you say after it gets magnified: "You had a great setup for the double-leg takedown, but you did not lead with your hip." All the athlete will hear is "you did not lead with your hip." With the sandwich approach, you'd say, "You had a great setup on the double-leg takedown. Next time lead with your hip. Keep working hard and it'll come." In the heat of the action, when time is limited, phrase your abbreviated feedback positively.

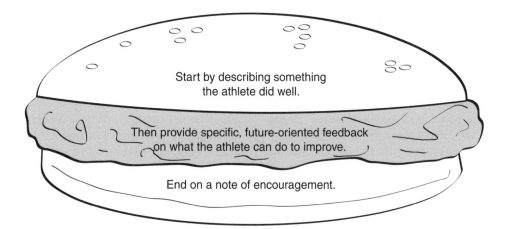

Start by describing something the athlete did well.

Then provide specific, future-oriented feedback on what the athlete can do to improve.

End on a note of encouragement.

FIGURE 2.2 In the sandwich approach, positive comments are provided before and after instructional feedback.

Adapted, by permission, from C.A. Wrisberg, 2007, *Sport skill instruction for coaches* (Champaign, IL: Human Kinetics), 119.

Athletes will not receive feedback with an open ear if they are embarrassed in front of their peers. Strive to provide corrective feedback individually instead of in front of the group. When John Wooden was asked if he did anything differently during his last 12 years of coaching (when he won 10 NCAA basketball championships) compared with his first 17 years, he reported that he made a conscious effort to pull athletes aside and give them corrective feedback individually.

Attentive Listening

Communication involves not only sending effective messages but also listening attentively. Great coaches recognize the importance of listening intently to their athletes. The legendary Pat Summitt, coach of the University of Tennessee's women's basketball team, states:

> You have to listen to develop effective, meaningful relationships with people. . . . As a coach I need to know a lot about them, and a lot about their families, their goals, and their dreams. You can't do that by talking. You do that by listening. What I have learned is, coaching is not all about me going into a locker room and telling them everything I know about basketball. It's a matter of knowing how they think and feel and what they want and what's important in their lives. Listening has allowed me to be a better coach. (Janssen & Dale 2002, p. 175)

We all realize the importance of effective listening. When others listen closely to you, it's flattering, because it tells you that they think what you have to say is important and they care about you. When you are a good listener, people enjoy talking with you, and they feel satisfied that they have been heard and understood. When you are a good listener, you don't miss out on information that may be important to you.

Many of us spend the majority of the day engaged in language-based communication—reading, writing, speaking, and listening. Yet we sometimes listen with only half an ear, or hear but don't really listen. When communication breaks down, we seldom realize that the problem may stem from our own poor listening skills. Do you ever find that you forget what someone just said, or get distracted while trying to listen to someone? Maybe you hear only part of what a person says, selectively tuning in only to what you want or expect to hear. Do you ever find yourself listening for and responding only to statements you disagree with? Do you find yourself thinking of what you want to say next rather than really hearing what the person who is speaking is actually saying? If any of these situations sound familiar, then you, like many of us, can improve your listening skills.

Evaluating Your Listening Skills

Good listening is hard work; it requires intense concentration and does not always come easily. What, then, is the key to improving your listening skills? The answer should be a familiar theme at this point in the chapter: Become aware of your strengths and weaknesses as a listener and practice effective listening skills. You can develop increased awareness of your listening skills by asking significant others, peers, administrators, and athletes to share their perceptions of your listening skills. You can also achieve some insights by completing figure 2.3, which lists 14 common causes of poor listening. Think about your general patterns of listening and indicate the frequency with which you encounter each of these blocks by circling the appropriate response.

Improving Your Listening Skills

Which listening skills do your responses to figure 2.3 suggest you need to work on? Two skills that can help improve many problem areas are **empathetic listening** and **active listening**. Let's take a closer look at each.

Empathetic Listening

By far the most useful tool for improving listening is empathy, which means understanding a person from his or her frame of reference. Empathetic listening, then, involves hearing what others say, with the intent of deeply and completely understanding their point of view. Empathetic listeners not only attend to the words being spoken; they are also attuned to the total delivery of the message, including feelings, intent, and meaning. They listen with their ears to content of the message, with their eyes to the body language, and with their heart to the feelings being expressed.

Coaches who are empathetic listeners pay attention with an open mind and are intent on understanding their athletes and other coaches. Through empathetic listening, you are able to see the world through the speaker's eyes and can put yourself in his or her shoes. You aren't concerned with making your own viewpoints understood or preparing to speak. Your first goal is to understand the other person. Being an empathetic listener does not mean you necessarily agree with the other person. Rather, it means you genuinely attempt to understand the other person's perspective. This type of listening builds communication bridges.

Listening Skills Test

Rating Scale:	Never	Seldom	Sometimes	Often
	1	2	3	4

1. You find listening to others uninteresting. ____

2. You tend to focus attention on the speaker's delivery or appearance instead of the message. ____

3. You listen more for facts and details, often missing the main points that give the facts meaning. ____

4. You are easily distracted by other people talking, chewing gum, rattling paper, and so on. ____

5. You fake attention, looking at the speaker but thinking of other things. ____

6. You listen only to what is easy to understand. ____

7. Certain emotion-laden words interfere with your listening. ____

8. As you hear a few sentences of another person's problems, you immediately start thinking about all the advice you can give. ____

9. Your attention span is very short, so it is hard for you to listen for more than a few minutes. ____

10. You are quick to find things to disagree with, so you stop listening as you prepare your argument. ____

11. You try to placate the speaker by being supportive through head-nodding and uttering agreement, but you're really not involved. ____

12. You will change the subject when you get bored or uncomfortable with it. ____

13. As soon as someone says anything that you think reflects negatively on you, you jump in to defend yourself. ____

14. You second-guess the speaker, trying to figure out what he or she really means. ____

15. You direct the conversation back to yourself.

Now add up your score. The following subjective scale will give you some help in determining how well you listen.

15-24	Excellent
25-34	Good
35-44	Fair
45-54	Weak
55 +	Can you hear me in there?

FIGURE 2.3 Use this test of listening skills to evaluate how well you listen to others.

Active Listening Skills

Although some coaches are naturally more skilled at expressing empathy than others, empathetic listening is a skill that can be developed with practice. The best way to learn it is through active listening, in which you participate purposefully in the communication process as a listener rather than just passively hearing what is being said. You can become an active listener by practicing these skills:

- *Develop a mind-set for listening.* Stop whatever you are doing and give your full attention to the other person.

- *Use encouragement.* Simple affirmations such as "I see," "Uh-huh," and "Yeah," perhaps along with a nod of your head, convey that you are listening actively and thus encourage the speaker to continue sharing.

- *Paraphrase content and reflect feelings.* State what you've heard in your own words, summarizing the core message and addressing the emotional implications. You might use a lead-in such as, "What I hear you saying is . . . " or "What you are telling me is . . ." or "It sounds as if you're excited about . . . ."

- *Ask questions for clarification and elaboration.* Asking questions communicates that you are listening and are genuinely trying to understand the speaker's perspective. Try to ask open-ended questions (ones that cannot be answered by a mere yes or no): "That's interesting—would you tell me more about it?" "What happened next?" "What would you do differently next time?" Also avoid questions that start with the word *why,* which can evoke defensive responses.

- *Check your perceptions.* You might say, "Let me make sure I understand" or "Just to clarify, did you say . . . ?" This approach communicates that you are listening and seeking to understand the other person, and it gives the speaker a chance to correct any misconceptions.

- *Convey interest nonverbally.* You can ask a question without ever saying a word, with a cast of your eyes, a tilt of your head, or an inquiring lift of your shoulder. Body language can invite or discourage the other person's talk, and effective listeners use it to communicate their readiness to listen. Face the person squarely, use an open posture, lean gently forward, make eye contact, and use a relaxed posture (Egan 1990).

Athletes also communicate a great deal of information without talking. Effective coaches pay attention to athletes' tone of voice and body language. Astute coaches realize that these nonverbal behaviors sometimes communicate more than athletes' words do and can be key to understanding what players are thinking and feeling. For example, NBA coach Phil Jackson states, "Over the years I've learned to listen closely to players—not just to what they say, but also to their body language and the silence between words" (Janssen 1999, p. 118). Duke basketball coach Mike Krzyzewski adds, "People talk to you in different ways—through facial expressions, moods, mannerisms, body language, the tone in their voice, the look in their eyes. As a coach, I must be able to read my players, to recognize those different things and then take appropriate action" (Janssen & Dale 2002, p. 170).

After reading about active listening, you may have concluded that it takes time and energy. If so, you are absolutely correct. Active listening is not easy, but it pays big dividends, and it does not take nearly as much time as attempting to correct misunderstandings and restore rapport that has been destroyed. If you can fully understand the unique situations and feelings of your athletes through active listening, then motivating, influencing, and leading them should be easier. Athletes will be more receptive to your ideas and more likely to listen to you.

Practicing Active Listening Skills

To practice **paraphrasing**, the next time you are talking with a person about a problem or personal issue, restate the meaning of their message before stating your opinion or giving advice. You can also help your athletes practice active listening. For example, in the heat of a competition it is not uncommon for an athlete to be looking right at the coach, yet not hear a word that is being said. One strategy is to have athletes summarize the message's main idea back to you. This creates a mind-set that encourages active listening.

On Advising

Coaches are often quick to give advice; after all, that is what a coach does. But advice given without understanding the other person's perspective can fall on deaf ears and even create communication barriers. Athletes occasionally approach coaches with personal or school problems, and it is tempting for coaches to give advice, hoping to help resolve the issue. Although well-intentioned, this advice may create communication barriers, especially if the athlete's goal was simply to express emotions and vent frustration, discouragement, or confusion. When athletes express themselves emotionally, the best course of action is to use active listening skills to convey your understanding of their perspective. Simply providing advice may cause an athlete to feel like you are minimizing an issue important to him or her. As the athlete's communication becomes more logical and task focused, he or she will become more receptive to your counsel.

Conflicts and Confrontations

Some people believe successful teams are completely harmonious and that a good coach–athlete relationship never involves conflict. This just isn't true. The reality is that most, if not all, teams will experience conflict and disagreement. As a coach, you will experience conflict with athletes throughout your coaching career. Although never pleasant, conflict can be a growth opportunity when handled with care, but failure to handle disagreement in a constructive way can destroy relationships. Thus, it is vital that you learn the skills to resolve conflicts constructively.

Conflicts

Conflict is inevitable in coaching because many people are involved and the environment is competitive. You might be tempted to handle conflict in whatever way comes naturally to you, perhaps combined with what you have learned from others. This approach does not guarantee success. You can learn new and better ways of managing conflict. The first step is to carefully assess how you typically manage it now. In *Reaching Out* (2003), David Johnson describes five conflict-management styles based on one's responses to two key questions in any attempt to resolve a conflict:

1. How important is it that you achieve your personal goals and get what you want?
2. How important is your relationship with the other person?

Your answers exert a strong influence on how you deal with conflict. To help you gain awareness of your current approach, consider which of the following styles you typically use.

- *Turtle (withdrawing)*. When facing conflict, turtles withdraw into their shells. In doing so, they sacrifice their goals and damage the relationship. Turtles fear confrontation or believe that it will be useless in solving the problem and thus find it easier to withdraw.

- *Shark (attacking)*. Sharks faced with conflict try to get their own way no matter what the cost. They focus on achieving their goals and do not worry about the needs and feelings of others. Sharks consider a conflict a game that one person wins and the other loses, and they plan to win by intimidating, attacking, and overpowering if necessary.

- *Teddy bear (smoothing)*. Teddy bears believe conflicts should be avoided in favor of harmony. They believe conflicts harm relationships, and because of their great need to be accepted and liked, they avoid jeopardizing the relationship by sacrificing their personal goals. Teddy bears are good at keeping a team together but give in to what others want at the expense of their own needs and interests.

- *Fox (compromising)*. Foxes are concerned with both achieving their goals and maintaining relationships, at least to a moderate degree. They prefer a compromise in which both sides gain something. They are willing to give up part of their goal and attempt to persuade others to give up part of theirs. They are willing to accept some strain on the relationship to find agreement for the common good.

- *Owl (collaborating)*. Owls place high value both on their goals and on their relationships. They view conflict as an issue to be solved and are satisfied only when they are able to achieve their goals and also help others get what they want. Owls believe conflict has the potential to strengthen relationships and are not content until tension and negative feelings have been resolved so that both parties find a win–win solution.

When selecting a conflict-management style, remember the two initial questions: How important is the issue? How important is the relationship? You may have realized that successful coaches focus both on meeting goals and on maintaining relationships. No single style is appropriate for every relationship or conflict—select the best strategy for handling each situation. Most people have one or two dominant conflict-management styles, but coaches need to be skilled in using any of the five depending on the situation and the people involved. The best way to choose a style for a particular conflict is to go back to the original two questions and evaluate how much weight you place on achieving your goals and maintaining the relationship.

- When the goal or issue is unimportant and you care nothing about the relationship, use the turtle style. For example, a fan comes out of the stands and is verbally abusive to you after the game. Being a turtle is usually wise.

- When your goal is important, but the relationship is not, you may wish to be a shark. This situation does not occur very often on a team, but you may need to use the shark approach if a harsh confrontation will accomplish your objective and you are not particularly concerned about the impact it may have on the relationship. If someone is behaving in a manner that endangers your players, shark behavior might be called for.

- When the goal is of little importance to you but the relationship is highly valued, being a teddy bear works best. Say a number of players' parents want to set up an advisory group to consult with you regularly about team activities. Even if you view the contact as relatively inconsequential, you might find it more important to retain a positive relationship than to resist the parents' desire.

- When both the relationship and your goal are of moderate importance, and meeting both will be difficult, then compromise is appropriate and it makes sense to be clever like a fox. Compromise in conflict situations is often necessary to maintain a relationship, and the compromise may be positive for you as long as it does not

require you to compromise your values. One example would be letting players decide some team rules, which gives them part of what they want, as long as you can dictate key provisions such as the drug and alcohol policy.

- When both the goal and the relationship are highly important, you will want to be an owl. Typically, to resolve this type of conflict, a tactful confrontation is necessary. In this case, finding a win–win solution for all involved groups is necessary. If you wish to alter a team procedure without damaging team cohesion or morale, for example, an owl approach may be best.

Confrontations

Confrontations are used to resolve conflicts. In a **confrontation**, you directly express your views and feelings about the conflict, and you invite the other parties to express theirs, too, in order to negotiate a mutually beneficial solution. Confrontations are a big part of sport, and you will have your fair share of them as a coach. Yet confrontations need not be heated arguments that produce hostility. This section helps you develop your confrontation skills, so that you can resolve conflicts assertively and positively.

Why Confront?

If an athlete, assistant coach, or parent behaves in a way that concerns you, you should not keep it bottled up inside. At the same time, not every little issue requires confrontation. You have to decide for yourself whether the issue is important enough to warrant confrontation. Pick your battles carefully. Consider the following situations:

- You have good reason to suspect that one of your players is responsible for vandalizing the locker room.

- You can no longer remain silent after repeated poor calls by the official.

- One of your player's parents continues to interfere with your coaching by being a sideline coach and providing instruction to his daughter when you are working with other athletes. While you welcome the parent's intent, his coaching is often incorrect.

- A coach from another team breaks league rules by not playing all team members in each half of the game.

These are but a few of the situations in which a coach may have good reason to initiate a confrontation. The purpose of a confrontation is not to put others in their place, but to get them to examine their behavior and its consequences in an attempt to seek constructive solutions. If handled poorly, a confrontation can create arguments and escalate feelings of hostility. If avoided, the problem may never get solved. With some effort, however, you can develop better confrontation skills, which will help you in your coaching and in all of your social interactions.

How to Confront

Developing good conflict-resolution skills involves learning to be assertive, to stand up for your rights and the things you believe in, without attacking or degrading others. Being assertive means expressing thoughts, feelings, and ideas in an honest, straightforward, and appropriate way. See table 2.1 for some dos and don'ts of confrontation.

There are four steps to a successful confrontation:

1. *Think.* Before you yell at officials, blurt out a put-down, or scream commands at a player, think. Consider whether what you are about to say will result in a successful confrontation—one in which you get the other person to examine his or her actions, and one in which you achieve your goal without damaging the relationship. Or will your actions escalate the conflict? If the athlete's emotions are running high, it might not be the best time to confront. Likewise, don't let your own emotions control the situation. Sometimes taking time to calm down before confronting can make the difference

between a successful and unsuccessful encounter. Also remember that confronting an athlete in front of teammates risks causing embarrassment, shame, and a resentful attitude.

2. *Understand.* Seek to accurately understand the other person's perspective. This requires you to practice empathy. When you confront others, let them know that you are trying to understand their position. Then be true to your word and do it. For example, Phil Jackson has stated, "In my work as a coach, I've discovered that approaching problems from a compassionate perspective, trying to empathize with the player and look at the situation from his point of view, can have a transformative effect on the team" (Janssen 1999, p. 130.)

3. *Describe your perspective and feelings.* Express your views and feelings openly and directly, but do it with assertive "I" statements rather than aggressive "you" statements. For example, rather than saying, "You are wrong" or "You make me so mad when you . . . ," say instead, "I'm not sure I agree" or "I feel upset when you . . ." Success at this step will result in the other person understanding your perspective. It will also create an open atmosphere that encourages the other person to examine his or her own behaviors, and their consequences, rather than simply trying to defend and justify them.

4. *Seek action.* Suggest desired changes or express interest in working together to develop a mutually beneficial solution. Tentatively communicate what you would like to see happen in response to the confrontation. Being tentative helps the

TABLE 2.1

How to Confront

Don't	Do
Do not label, accuse, or insult the person.	Do describe the other person's actions and behaviors. Focus on issues and on behaviors that can be changed and not personality issues.
Do not view conflict as a win-lose situation.	Do view conflict as a problem to be mutually solved.
Do not describe the other person's action in a general way.	Do define the conflict and describe their behaviors in a specific and limited way as possible.
Do not expect the other person to be a mind reader.	Do describe your feelings and reactions to the other person's behavior.
Do not expect the resolution to fall only on the other person's shoulders.	Do describe your actions (what you are doing and failing to do) that contribute to the conflict and what you can do to help resolve the conflict.

Created from data in D.W. Johnson, 1981, *Reaching out: Interpersonal effectiveness and self-actualization*, 2nd ed. (Englewood Cliffs, NJ: Prentice Hall), 219-223, 240.

other person consider what you are saying more easily. Avoid the temptation to demand change, which is coercive and can lead the other person to feel attacked. Especially if you are confronting an athlete, invite the athlete to partner with you to discuss the issue, and encourage the athlete to come up with a solution on his or her own terms.

Coaches often are too quick to tell athletes what they must do, which usually prompts them to rebel. Offer a solution only when the athlete cannot come up with one and is receptive to your input. If you happen to think many things need to change, then proceed gradually, dealing with one specific behavior at a time.

SUMMARY

1. Although the importance of developing communication skills is often overlooked, becoming an effective communicator is essential in coaching.

2. Communication involves sending and receiving messages through verbal and non-verbal channels. Both the content and the emotional aspect of the message should be considered.

3. Coaches spend a considerable amount of time sending messages. We've provided 16 guidelines you can use to assess your strengths and weaknesses in sending effective messages.

4. Coaches can send messages more effectively if they use reinforcement, provide feedback, and help athletes learn how to be receptive to feedback.

5. In providing reinforcement, you should use shaping, reward effort and performance rather than just outcomes, reward the use of social and emotional skills, and reinforce good behavior rather than simply punishing undesirable behavior.

6. In providing feedback, reinforce athletes by providing specific, descriptive feedback following a good performance effort and instructional feedback following performance errors.

7. After a performance error, provide instructional feedback, not constructive criticism. That is, give encouragement and action-oriented feedback, which is descriptive and future oriented.

9. Although coaches often communicate via sending messages, it is just as important that they learn to become effective listeners. You can improve this skill by being empathetic and developing active listening skills.

10. In the coaching profession, conflicts and confrontations are inevitable. How you choose to deal with a conflict depends on the importance of your goals and the relationship involved.

11. Confrontations are useful for resolving conflicts when used appropriately. Confrontations can be handled skillfully when you follow the four guidelines: think, understand, describe your perspective and feelings, and seek action.

12. If one of your coaching objectives is to facilitate athletes' development, then you will want to teach your athletes effective communication skills.

KEY TERMS

active listening

communication

confrontation

constructive criticism

descriptive feedback

empathetic listening

instructional feedback

nonreinforcement

nonverbal communication

paraphrasing

punishment

reinforcement

shaping

REVIEW QUESTIONS

1. What types of behaviors should coaches reinforce?
2. How should a coach respond to a good performance?
3. How should a coach respond to a performance mistake?
4. Describe the active listening skills coaches can use and why those skills are important.
5. What is the sandwich approach to providing feedback?
6. What are the five conflict styles that Johnson (2003) describes?
7. What are the steps for effective conflict resolution?

CRITICAL THINKING QUESTIONS

1. As an assistant coach, you disagree with the head coach on the game plan for your next competition. What conflict style would you use in this situation and why?
2. You are giving a talk at a coaching convention on how to communicate effectively. What recommendations would you provide?
3. One of your athletes broke a team rule, and you decide you need to confront him about his behavior. Describe what you would do and what principles you would apply to maximize the chances of an effective confrontation.
4. As a coach, what would you do if interpersonal conflicts developed between team members and interfered with your team's cohesion and on-field performance?

Introduction to Mental Skills Training

After reading this chapter, you should be able to explain

- the role that psychological factors play in sport performance;
- how mental skills training can improve performance, enhance enjoyment, and help athletes develop life skills;
- how your athletes can use mental training tools to develop mental skills;
- myths surrounding mental skills training; and
- the three phases in teaching mental skills.

Sport success is determined in part by physical conditioning, skill, and preparation. But it is also influenced by psychological factors such as self-confidence, motivation, concentration, and emotional control. How important do you think psychological factors are to the success of your team, as compared with physical factors? In short, how much of sport do you think is mental, and how much is physical?

_____ % physical

_____ % psychological

Yogi Berra is often quoted as saying, "Baseball is 90% mental; the other half is physical." The numbers don't add up, but his point is well taken. Like Yogi Berra, you may believe that mental factors play a big role in sport. Most coaches agree. You've probably watched games where athletes make clutch plays in the closing seconds to propel their team to victory—or choke under pressure. You may have heard coaches agonize over "practice athletes," those physically talented players who perform well in practice but seldom have a great performance in competition. On a more positive note, coaches also see athletes with a knack for performing well under pressure even though they may have only average physical talent. Despite experiences such as these that illustrate the importance of psychological factors, it is not uncommon for coaches to spend little or no time teaching athletes how to improve and master the mental game. If mental aspects of the game account for 90% of the outcome, or 50%, or even only 10%, doesn't it make sense to devote at least some time to mental training?

Fortunately, conventional wisdom is changing, and today many coaches are carving out time to work on the mental game to gain a competitive edge. Still, some coaches shy away from the mental aspect because they simply do not know how to help athletes learn mental skills. Perhaps you are comfortable with teaching athletes the physical skills and strategies of the game but feel as if you are exploring uncharted territory in attempting to help athletes become mentally tough competitors. This chapter provides an overview of an effective approach to mental skills training (MST) that you can use to help your athletes improve their mental game and more fully realize their potential.

Psychological Factors and Performance Excellence

In recalling their most memorable sport performances, most athletes remember a time when everything seemed to click and they had a peak performance. Athletes use a variety of terms to describe these almost magical moments, such as being in **flow** or "in the zone," or having "the hot hand." These special moments occur when athletes are both physically and mentally prepared and everything falls into place for them (see Bill Russell's Experience of Flow).

Like Bill Russell, athletes in flow have complete **confidence** and trust in their skills, which enables them to perform effortlessly and automatically, without conscious thought. It is like they are on automatic pilot. Csikszentmihalyi, the guru of flow, studied the flow experiences of performers across a wide variety of settings and found remarkable consistency across their experiences. (Csikszentmihalyi 1990, Csikszentmihalyi 1997, Jackson & Csikszentmihalyi 1999). Athletes in flow are completely focused and absorbed in their performance, and their heightened focus makes them aware of everything going on around them that relates to their performance. Potential distractions such as crowd noise simply fade into the background. Because of their confidence and focused attention, athletes in flow feel they have complete control and that they can do no wrong. They may sense how the action will enfold ahead of time. Sport execution comes naturally and easily: A gymnast sees the balance beam as larger than normal, and concerns about falling disappear. A batter sees a baseball pitch or cricket delivery as being the size of a beach ball and may even follow the seams of the ball as it turns. A soccer player feels the game is moving in slow motion, giving her the luxury of time to read and react to what is happening on the field.

Although flow provides some of the most memorable experiences in sport, it can be somewhat elusive. Flow happens only when athletes let it happen, rather than trying to make it happen. The harder one tries to get into flow, the more elusive it is. This fact makes some coaches believe that flow is uncontrollable. They think such experiences are magical moments that just happen and that there is not much athletes can do to increase the likelihood of experiencing flow. It is certainly not possible to offer a guaranteed plan for achieving flow every time athletes take the playing field. However, you can set the stage for flow by helping athletes develop their mental as well as their physical skills. Top athletes believe that effective mental preparation is necessary to achieve peak performance, and many elite athletes believe they can set the stage for flow through strong physical and mental preparation (Jackson 1995).

If you are still not convinced that MST can facilitate flow, then consider this: You may recognize that mentally tough athletes experience flow more

Bill Russell's Experience of Flow

"Every so often a Celtics game would heat up so that it became more than a physical or even mental game, and would be magical. That feeling is difficult to describe. . . . When it happened I could feel my play rise to a new level. It came rarely, and would last anywhere from five minutes to a whole quarter or more. . . . Then the game would just take off, and there'd be a natural ebb and flow that reminded you of how rhythmic and musical basketball is supposed to be. I'd find myself thinking, 'This is it. I want this to keep going.' And I'd actually be rooting for the other team. When their players made spectacular moves, I wanted their shots to go into the bucket; that's how pumped up I'd be. . . . At that special level all sorts of odd things happened. The game would be in a white heat of competition, and yet somehow I wouldn't feel competitive—which is a miracle in itself. I'd be putting out the maximum effort, straining, coughing up parts of my lungs as we ran, and yet I never felt the pain. The game would move so quickly that every fake, cut and pass would be surprising, and yet nothing could surprise me. It was almost as if we were playing in slow motion. During those spells I could almost sense how the next play would develop and where the next shot would be taken. Even before the other team brought the ball in bounds, I could feel it so keenly that I'd want to shout to my teammates, 'It's coming there'—except that I knew everything would change if I did. My premonitions would be consistently correct, and I always felt then that I not only knew all the Celtics by heart but also all the opposing players, and that they all knew me. There have been many times in my career when I felt moved or joyful, but these were the moments when I had chills pulsing up and down my spine. But these spells were fragile. An injury would break them, and so would a couple of bad plays or a bad call by a referee. . . . Still, I always suffered a letdown when one of those spells died, because I never knew how to bring them back; all I could do was to keep playing my best and hope. They were sweet when they came, and the hope that one would come was one of my strongest motivations for walking out there."

SECOND WIND: THE MEMOIRS OF AN OPINIONATED MAN © 1979 by William Russell and Taylor Branch (Random House, New York). Reprinted with permission of the author.

often than others do, and you may wonder why. The answer is simple. Mentally tough athletes have more than just physical skills; they also have tremendous ability to psych themselves up for competition, manage their stress and remain in control of their emotions, concentrate intensely, and set challenging but realistic goals. They have the ability to visualize themselves being successful and then do what they visualized. Simply stated, they have superior **mental skills** (Krane & Williams 2006).

Although the key physical skills and attributes differ from sport to sport, the mental skills required to achieve excellence and flow are similar across sports. These include attributes related to motivation, energy management, attentional skills, stress management, and self-confidence.

Motivation

Motivation is an important ingredient of any successful team. Most coaches have had the pleasure of working with athletes who were highly motivated. They worked hard, persisted in the face of adversity,

and viewed challenging tasks as opportunities. Most coaches have probably also had the frustrating experience of working with athletes who were less than optimally motivated. They did not consistently train hard and seemed to focus their efforts on everything but sport. Highly motivated athletes set high standards for themselves, elevating the level of play and inspiring their teammates.

Energy Management

Another skill necessary to develop mental toughness is **energy management**—the ability to get into an optimal energy zone, the psychological state that helps athletes perform their best. Optimal performance can be disrupted by an arousal level that is too high or too low. Unfortunately, it is not uncommon for athletes to report that they were too nervous or excited to have a great performance. Other athletes may comment that they could not get into the game because they felt flat due to low energy. Top athletes are aware of their ideal energy zone and are able to get into that zone and stay there.

Attentional Skills

Athletic success depends in part on the ability to focus on the task at hand and block out all distractions. This is easier said than done. A tennis player needs to determine where an opponent's shot is going, evaluate the speed and spin on the ball, and determine what type of return shot is optimal—all within a fraction of a second. A skilled quarterback needs the ability to focus his attention broadly to read a defense and check his receivers, then narrow his focus in order to throw an accurate pass. After the play, he must shift focus again, directing his attention inward to evaluate the current situation and call the next play. Because even momentary lapses in concentration can have dire consequences, athletes must sharpen and make full use of their attentional skills.

Stress Management

Sport is an inherently stressful endeavor, full of intense physical demands and psychological pressures. Most people can manage the stress of participating in a recreational league, but it takes a mentally tough person to stroke a 20-foot (6-m) putt in the Masters with big money at stake and a viewing audience of millions. To reach their potential, athletes need to develop strong skills in stress management.

Self-Confidence

Great athletes invariably mention that believing in themselves is key to their success, and they back it up by exuding self-confidence in their play. Some athletes may know the importance of self-confidence, and see it in others, but find it elusive in themselves. Coaches recognize that success builds confidence, but also that self-confidence is needed to succeed. Champion athletes have the ability to get on the success–confidence spiral in which confidence breeds success and vice versa. And when they are performing poorly, champions also have the ability to stop the corresponding failure–lowered confidence spiral.

Using Sport Psychology to Your Advantage

Most athletes have developed core mental skills to a sufficient degree that they can function well in day-to-day situations or even in low-level competitive events. But when confronted with more demanding, pressure-packed situations, they may falter. This can be most frustrating to athletes—and their coaches—because they know they have the potential to perform well. Not recognizing that the performance problems are due to a lack of mental skills, coaches may encourage athletes to work even harder on their physical skills. A gymnast may spend extra time on an apparatus. A basketball player may spend extra time shooting free throws after practice. Distance runners may pound their bodies even harder, sometimes to the point of overtraining. Indeed, some performance problems might stem from physical issues, such as inadequate training or poor biomechanics. However, in many cases inadequate mental skills could be the cause.

A coach who does not know how to help athletes develop the necessary mental skills usually does one of three things: tries to support the athlete with empathy and encouragement; selects another athlete who may be less talented physically but can perform better under pressure; or aggravates the problem by placing more pressure on the athlete to begin performing up to his or her capability. The alternative, of course, is to capitalize on advances in sport psychology. Coaches from all sports are increasingly recognizing that athletes can learn and improve the mental skills needed to achieve excellence in sport. Rather than leaving mental skills development to chance, top coaches are increasingly taking responsibility for helping their athletes develop these essential skills by incorporating MST into their athletes' training programs.

Does MST Work?

The idea that **mental skills training** can improve performance is not new. Even before the growth of sport psychology, some athletes were using MST techniques (see The Billy Mills Story). Today's coach recognizes that even small adjustments may have a huge impact on competitive outcomes. For example, in sports where time is a factor, a fraction of a second can make the difference between a first- and last-place finish, between a great and subpar performance. Mental skills training may be what it takes for athletes to shave that fraction of a second. The record-breaking performances of the future will be achieved not by athletes who only train harder physically, but by those who also train smarter mentally.

Researchers evaluating the effectiveness of MST programs draw the same conclusion: Mental training can improve performance across a wide variety of sports. In fact, as many as 85% of the studies conducted to evaluate MST showed positive performance effects (Greenspan & Feltz 1989; Meyers, Whelan, & Murphy 1996; Vealey 1994; Weinberg & Comar 1994). In general, the consensus of sport psychology researchers, coaches, and athletes is that mental skills training can enhance performance.

The Billy Mills Story

In the 1964 Tokyo Olympics, Billy Mills was a surprising gold medal winner in the 10,000-meter race and the first American to win it since 1908. Although the Billy Mills story is remarkable in and of itself, the dramatic way he won the gold medal and his use of mental training techniques make this story even more noteworthy, especially because sport psychology was not nearly as popular then as it is today. Mills had conceived his dream of winning the gold in 1962. At the time, it had seemed farfetched even to him, because he had never won a national championship and had thus far put together a sporadic career. Undeterred, he set his goal and wrote in his workout logbook, "Gold medal. 10,000 meter run. Time 28:25" (Mills 1990, page 36).

Mills initially set a training goal of running 100 miles (160 km) a week to increase his strength and endurance but soon realized this was unrealistic in light of injury problems. Rather than scaling back his training goal, however, he extended the standard training week to 10 days to give himself a sense of success and provide sufficient recovery time. In addition to goal setting, Mills also used imagery. Before the Olympics, he had competed in only four 10,000-meter races, but he had run the race hundreds of times in his mind. He also used a type of self-talk called affirmations to build his inner strength and confidence, telling himself: "I am truly a great distance runner. God has given me the ability. The rest is up to me" (Mills 1990, page 36).

Mills anticipated that to win gold he would have to outkick Ron Clarke from Australia, the world-record holder at the time. During training runs, Billy imagined catching and passing Clark, as well as any other runner who might be in contention, during the final lap. Incredibly, the final lap transpired much as Billy Mills had rehearsed it: He won the gold medal in breathtaking fashion, running the race in 28:24.4, a half second under his goal. And as in his imagery, he outran Ron Clarke and future Olympic champions Mohammed Gammoudi and Mamo Wolde in a furious race to the finish.

Improved Performance

A primary goal of MST is to help athletes consistently perform closer to their potential and avoid subpar performances. MST will help your athletes consistently execute the skills they perform in practice in pressure-packed competitions as well. A good way to conceptualize the goals of mental training is to picture a target with four rings. Most athletes can vividly recall both good and bad performances. Just as their eyes light up when discussing flow experiences, athletes may wince as they describe their worst performances. The range of performance quality is illustrated on the target in figure 3.1. The bull's-eye represents those magical moments when everything fell into place and the athlete performed extraordinarily well. Although it would be nice to hit the bull's-eye with every future performance, that is of course impossible. Instead, the goal of mental skills training is to help athletes perform more consistently near the center of the target, or at least to avoid hitting the outer rings too often.

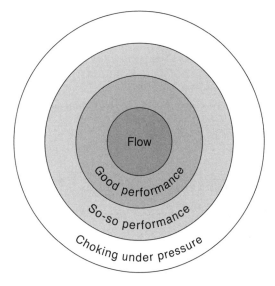

FIGURE 3.1 Mental skills training will help your athletes reach peak performance and flow more often.

Enhanced Enjoyment

In addition to improving performance, MST can be a great tool for increasing athletes' enjoyment and enhancing their ability to find satisfaction and fulfillment in their demanding sport activities. Training can be difficult, and athletes may experience excessive stress or struggle with the pressure of competition. Learning mental skills can help athletes handle competitive stress and feel self-confident, thus enhancing both their performance and enjoyment of their sport. If one of the tenets of your coaching philosophy is for athletes to enjoy their sport experiences, MST can help.

Strong Life Skills

Mental skills training also facilitates athletes' personal development. Remember when we discussed competitive philosophy in chapter 1 and argued for a coaching philosophy focused on athletes' development? Mental training lends itself well to a philosophy aimed at athletes' growth and development—physical, mental, social, moral, and emotional. In fact, mental training is training in life skills such as learning how to set goals, how to handle pressure and criticism, and how to stay focused on the task at hand. These skills can enhance sport peformance, but they can also improve performance in any achievement area—school, music, theater, or career. Those who believe deeply in the value of sport often claim that it can help teach young people how to become leaders, to be more self-confident, to develop better interpersonal skills, and to exercise self-discipline. But these potential benefits of sport participation do not happen automatically; coaches must structure athletes' sport experiences to help athletes gain these psychological benefits. Mental training provides a framework for the development of athletes' life skills.

The MST Approach

We've discussed the importance of psychological factors and the benefits associated with MST but have yet to describe mental skills training. In this section, we present an overview of a highly effective mental skills training approach that provides the foundation for the rest of the book. MST is the systematic and consistent use of mental training *tools*—goal setting, imagery, relaxation and energization, and self-talk—to build the mental *skills*, or psychological attributes, that coaches want their athletes to have—motivation, energy management, attention, stress management, and confidence. The fundamental premise behind MST is that using mental training tools or techniques can enable athletes to develop the desired mental skills (see figure 3.2). Stated another way, mental skills are the end products we are trying to achieve to enhance mental toughness and create a flow state of mind. **Mental training tools** are the methods used to develop athletes' mental skills (Vealey 1988). We discuss mental training tools at length in part II of this book and mental training skills in part III.

Table 3.1 illustrates a few of the potential applications of each mental training tool and how it affects several mental skills. For example, athletes who find it hard to maintain motivation during off-season training can use goal setting to provide a sense of direction and purpose in their workouts. Goal setting may also help them develop other mental skills. As they make progress toward attaining their goals, their self-confidence increases. During the season, they may begin to set goals to improve not only their physical skills but also their mental game. As they become proficient at goal setting, their personal goals become the standards by which they evaluate success and failure. Setting goals based on improvement and skill mastery—rather than judging success and failure

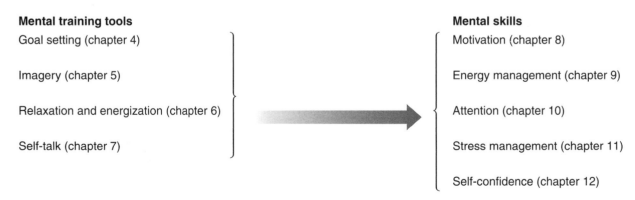

Mental training tools

Goal setting (chapter 4)

Imagery (chapter 5)

Relaxation and energization (chapter 6)

Self-talk (chapter 7)

Mental skills

Motivation (chapter 8)

Energy management (chapter 9)

Attention (chapter 10)

Stress management (chapter 11)

Self-confidence (chapter 12)

FIGURE 3.2   **You and your athletes can use mental training tools to develop mental skills.**

TABLE 3.1

Using the Four Mental Training Tools to Develop Athletes' Mental Skills

GOAL SETTING
Setting realistic but challenging short-term goals provides a sense of direction, thereby increasing **motivation** as reflected in increased effort and persistence.
Challenging, realistic goals help athletes get into their **optimal energy zone** and direct that energy to the task at hand.
Effective goals direct athletes' **attention** to what they need to focus on to succeed.
Although striving to win is important, focusing on winning can create excessive **stress**. When athletes perceive the challenge not as winning but as achieving their own realistically set performance goals, the challenge will always be near the athlete's present skill level and will create an optimal skill–challenge balance.
Consistent goal attainment raises **self-confidence**.

IMAGERY
Teaching athletes to imagine themselves attaining their goals can help raise their **motivation**.
By imagining previous strong performances, athletes can identify their optimal energy levels and strategies for getting into an **effective energy zone** prior to performing.
Using imagery effectively requires the ability to focus on desired images and thus can be used to develop **attentional skills**.
Imagery can be used to help athletes manage **competitive stress**. Athletes are less likely to experience elevated stress if they have imagined themselves dealing effectively with obstacles and unanticipated events that create stress.
Visualizing oneself succeeding can raise **self-confidence**.

RELAXATION AND ENERGIZATION
Learning to energize when feeling flat, and developing the ability to relax when overaroused, can help build **motivation**.
Relaxation and energization techniques can help athletes consistently enter and stay in their **optimal energy zone**, which is crucial to performing consistently at their peak.
Being either over- or underaroused hurts athletes' ability to direct their **attention** to the task at hand. Relaxation and energization techniques help athletes improve their concentration skills.
Learning to purposefully relax when experiencing **stress** can help athletes manage their emotions. And energizing techniques can be used when athletes feel that low-level stress is preventing them from getting into their ideal mental state for performing.
By learning to control their energy levels through relaxation and energizing, athletes will develop a sense of control, which in turn enhances **self-confidence**.

SELF-TALK
Athletes can use self-talk to help **motivate** themselves.
Self-talk can either **raise or lower energy**. Athletes can use effective self-talk strategies to reach their ideal mental state before competing.
Focusing on task-relevant cue words can help athletes focus their **attention**, or regain focus if they are momentarily distracted.
Stress level is strongly influenced by athletes' perceptions and interpretations of events that happen before and during competition. Athletes can use self-talk to develop a positive outlook on events that normally result in elevated stress.
Positive self-talk can be used to raise **self-confidence**, whereas negative self-talk can lower it.

exclusively in terms of winning and losing—may help dissipate some of the pressure athletes feel when competing.

Expanded Potential

The MST approach is based on a model of excellence and personal growth centered on helping athletes reach their full potential. Think of your athletes' behavior on a continuum from abnormal to supernormal, with normal somewhere in between (see figure 3.3). You can use MST to help your athletes move from normal to the right on the continuum, toward supernormality or excellence. Athletes are placed into demanding competitive and training environments that require extraordinary mental skills to perform optimally. The "normal" person would have a difficult time handling the demands and pressures of being an athlete. MST helps psychologically normal athletes develop the supernormal mental skills needed to excel.

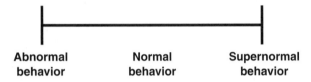

| Abnormal | Normal | Supernormal |
| behavior | behavior | behavior |

FIGURE 3.3   MST helps athletes develop supernormal mental skills.

At times, however, athletes experience personal issues that interfere with their sport performance. When athletes have profound psychological problems that interfere with everyday life functioning, their behavior falls to the left of normal. You will likely encounter such athletes. They may be dealing with eating disorders, substance abuse, identity issues, or a family crisis. Such issues fall beyond the scope of the MST approach. When athletes' behavior falls left of normal, a clinical or counseling psychologist is the appropriate professional to provide assistance.

A Skill-Oriented Approach

Much like physical skills, mental skills can be taught and learned. No great athlete, no matter how physically talented, ever achieved success without endless hours of practice. From junior high to the professional level, athletes spend roughly 1 to 6 hours per day training because they know it takes practice to learn, improve, and master the physical skills necessary to excel in a given sport. You probably readily acknowledge that physical skills need to be learned and mastered through well-developed learning progressions and countless practice repetitions. The same

is true for MST. Learning mental skills takes time, effort, and patience. MST is a skill-oriented approach that requires systematic practice.

It was not long ago that athletes did not train under any systematic program. They just went out and played the sport. Over time, coaches and sport scientists have learned how to design training programs to maximize athletes' skills and physical performance abilities. As a result, record after record has fallen. Feats once thought impossible, such as running a mile (1.6 km) in less than 4 minutes, or a marathon in less than 2 hours and 20 minutes, are now commonplace. Coaches have learned the benefits of systematic practice. MST is now where physical training used to be: Although many coaches are beginning to work on the mental game with their athletes, it is not uncommon for the approach to be haphazard. They dabble with goal setting, try a little imagery, and encourage their athletes to get themselves mentally ready to compete. However, while something is better than nothing, systematic practice is most effective. In this book, we lay out a plan for the systematic practice of mental skills.

Roadblocks and Myths Surrounding MST

If MST is effective in helping athletes perform better, enjoy their sport, and develop life skills, why is it often neglected? Let's clear the air about a variety of roadblocks and myths surrounding the mental game.

Myth: MST Takes Too Much Time

Coaches identify time as the biggest roadblock to implementing mental skills training. You may feel that you barely have time to develop and refine your athletes' physical skills, let alone add work on mental skills. Undoubtedly, working on the mental game takes time. Devoting 15 to 20 minutes several days per week may be most effective in introducing new mental training tools. However, as little as 5 to 10 minutes a day can be beneficial. A good way to implement MST is to integrate it into practice. That way it does not take extra time and has another benefit—it enhances practice quality. Developing athletes' mental skills such as motivation and attentional focus is the foundation for a high-quality practice. Using mental training tools such as goal setting, imagery, self-talk, and energization can help increase practice quality. Rather than simply going through the motions, athletes will perform practice activities with intensity and focused attention.

Myth: Mental Skills Are Innate

It is easy to believe that mental toughness is an innate characteristic that cannot be taught. You may believe that athletes are either blessed with these strong mental skills (as part of their personality or genetic makeup) or have learned them through experience. Either way, you may feel that there is little coaches can do to improve athletes' mental toughness. That is a myth. It is true that we are all born with certain physical and psychological predispositions and that mental skills are shaped and developed through the experiences of everyday life. Being motivated, staying calm under pressure, and maintaining confidence in the face of adversity are not simply innate qualities. They are mental skills that great athletes have learned through experience or through MST. MST is a more efficient way of developing these skills than waiting for athletes to pick them up through the trial-and-error process of experience.

Myth: Mental Skills Training Is Only for Psychological Problems

Many coaches and athletes believe that only those with deep-rooted psychological problems need to work on their mental game. Some athletes also perceive a stigma associated with sport psychology, thinking that those who need to work on their mental game are weak and have some sort of psychological problem that is going to be analyzed by a "shrink." Because of this, some athletes are reluctant to work on their mental game because they believe that they may be chastised and labeled as a head case. To the contrary, MST can benefit all athletes. Many of the most talented athletes use some form of MST, even as it is clear that they do not have deep-rooted psychological problems.

Myth: Mental Skills Training Provides a Quick Fix

Coaches and athletes recognize that physical skills take countless hours of practice to develop, but some expect mental skills to provide a quick fix. On occasion, coaches will ask me (Tom Raedeke) to talk to their team a few days before a big competition to get them mentally ready. This reflects a misconception about mental skills training. The short period just before competition is not the time to work on one's mental game. Ideally, mental training begins in the off-season, or at least at the beginning of the season. Would you advise coaches to have their athletes change their physical game plan shortly before competition? Probably not, because you realize that after countless hours of practice, athletes can perform a skill automatically without conscious thought. Introducing a new skill may cause them to start thinking about how to perform the skill and thus disrupt their performance. The same is true for mental skills training. It takes time and effort and is not a magical, quick-fix program.

Myth: Mental Skills Training Creates Performance Miracles

Another myth surrounding MST involves unrealistic expectations. Mental skills training will not help turn an average player into a superstar. Some coaches and athletes feel that MST will help athletes perform beyond their physical capabilities. In reality, mental skills training is designed to help athletes perform more consistently at or near their potential.

Similarly, some athletes and coaches expect incredible results from minimal effort. Athletes try a little relaxation training, imagery, or goal setting, then quit after a few sessions because nothing miraculous has happened. These same athletes would not expect to become superstar after a week or even a year of physical training; they would expect to improve only after putting in the necessary time and effort. As with physical training, mental skills training will help athletes perform at or near their performance capabilities only with consistent practice.

Myth: MST Is for Elite Athletes Only

Some coaches erroneously believe that MST can only help perfect the performance of highly skilled competitors. As a result, they shy away from MST, rationalizing that because they are not coaching elite athletes, mental skills training is less important. It is true that mental skills become increasingly important at high levels of competition. As athletes move up the competitive ladder, they become more homogeneous in terms of physical skills. In fact, at high levels of competition, all athletes have the physical skills to be successful. Consequently, any small difference in mental factors can play a huge role in determining performance outcomes. However, we can anticipate that personal growth and performance will progress faster in young, developing athletes who are given mental skills training than in athletes not exposed to MST. In fact, the optimal time for introducing MST may be when athletes are first beginning their sport. Introducing MST early in athletes' careers may lay the foundation that will help them develop to their full potential.

Developing MST

At this point, you understand the key premises behind an MST approach to improving performance, and you may be convinced that MST can improve your team's chances of success. However, you are probably still unsure how to implement an MST program. In this section, we provide an overview of how to develop an MST program tailored toward your team's needs, as well as your role in implementing it. This chapter, then, provides the foundation, and the rest of the book provides the knowledge you need to implement a well-rounded MST program.

The process of developing mental skills is similar to teaching the physical tools and skills of your sport: You begin by building the fundamentals and then work to practice and apply them in competitive situations. As with the teaching of physical skills, MST involves a three-phase process: education, acquisition, and implementation. These are shown in Figure 3.4.

Education Phase

The first step in the MST education phase is to conduct a needs assessment to determine which mental skills are the most important to develop and which mental training tools must be used to develop those skills as well as the best way to sequence them. A key goal at this point is to help athletes become aware of their strengths and weaknesses in the mental tools and skills that are critical to success in their sport. A golfer who experiences too much muscle tension due to nervousness has different needs than the golfer who pushes his putt because he is distracted by fans talking in the gallery. As with becoming an excellent coach, becoming a mentally skilled athlete depends greatly on coming to know oneself. Athletes need to become aware of their mental strengths and weaknesses. Increasing awareness will help you and your athletes identify which mental skills they need to develop and, in turn, which mental training tools to use.

Athletes in the **education phase** also receive instruction to help them understand how mental factors affect their performance, adopt the mind-set that mental skills can be learned, and learn how to develop these skills. An effective way to start this process is to sell your athletes on the importance of MST and how it can help improve their performance. One of the biggest mistakes coaches can make in implementing MST is failing to set the foundation for working on the mental game by gaining athletes' commitment to it. As a coach, you'll need to create the expectation that mental skills can be learned and that athletes will take responsibility for sharpening

---

Phases of Mental Skill Development

1. Education Phase: Awareness Focus

- Develop awareness of mental strengths and weaknesses
- Provide a rationale for learning skill
- Provide information about what skill is and how it's developed

2. Acquisition Phase: Learning Focus

- Develop skill basics

3. Implementation Phase: Overlearning and Execution Focus

- Extensive practice to overlearn skill
- Simulate competitive situations to practice skill transfer
- Simulate adversity to practice overcoming problem situations using mental tools and skills
- Integrate mental skills training concepts in competitive situations
- Effectively deal with adversity and obstacles
- Systematically evaluate and revise mental skills training program

FIGURE 3.4 Three phases of mental skill development.

their mental game to improve performance. If athletes do not believe in MST, no program, no matter how sound it is, will be effective.

Acquisition Phase

In the **acquisition phase** of MST, the goal is to help athletes acquire desired skills. As with physical skills, mental skills are best developed through a structured training program, starting with development of the basics of a given skill. As athletes become more proficient, you can begin teaching them how to use the skills as part of their mental game plan. Although well intentioned, simply instructing athletes to "relax," "stay loose," "don't choke," or "focus" is a limited approach. In most cases, athletes recognize the debilitating effect of being overly anxious or unable to concentrate, and vague instructions do not teach them how to make a change. What athletes need is specific instruction on how to relax or focus so they can perform better. In the acquisition phase of MST, you will teach athletes the skills they need to improve their mental game.

Implementation Phase

As with physical skills, mental training tools and skills are maximally effective only when athletes have overlearned them to the point they become habit and can be used automatically without having to consciously think about when and how to use them. Thus, the **implementation phase** of MST involves helping athletes practice using the tools and skills to the point of overlearning, and only then teaching athletes to apply mental skills to actual performance situations. To do this, athletes use the tools and skills in simulations, scrimmages, and low-level competitions that gradually become more and more like full competition. Adverse situations can be simulated in practice settings to help prepare athletes to handle such occurrences during competition. By creating situations that gradually increase competitive stress, the implementation phase helps athletes learn to incorporate mental skills into their game plan and deal effectively with problems and obstacles. During this stage, the mental skills training program is continually monitored to assess its effectiveness,

and necessary revisions are made to improve it. The mental skills training needs of athletes vary across a season and the MST must be modified to accommodate these changing needs.

Your Role

The ultimate key to success with MST is you, the coach. You must not only believe in the value of this type of training but also understand it thoroughly, just as you must understand the skills and tactics of your sport in order to teach them. Then you must be willing to make MST a regular part of your formal training program. Ideally, you will teach and refine mental skills on a daily basis, just as you do with physical skills.

In launching an MST program, you are not filling the role of a psychologist; rather, you are teaching athletes the mental skills necessary to achieve success in sport and life. When you encounter athletes dealing with significant life or personal issues, you will need to wisely counsel them (or their parents) that professional help may be in order. Even after you have mastered the contents of this book, you are not equipped to provide the clinical assistance such athletes may need. Your role is to educate your athletes about how they can develop specific mental skills, and to refer those who need more psychological assistance to appropriate professionals.

After reading this chapter, we hope that you are convinced MST works and that you are excited about the possibility of implementing an MST program with your team. Understanding the MST approach equips you with information crucial to becoming a better coach. You may recognize that you are already using some of the mental training tools to help your athletes develop their mental skills. If so, that is great. The remaining chapters provide information that can help you become even more effective at MST. You may also feel a bit overwhelmed by the whole MST process. This is understandable. The main purpose of this chapter was to introduce you to MST and the steps involved in developing an MST program. In the remaining chapters, we share ideas on how to implement a systematic MST program to teach athletes the specific mental training tools to develop their mental skills.

Launching an MST Program

Coach Smith decided to launch an MST for his wrestling team. After a team discussion and consultation with team captains, he decided to start with goal setting to enhance practice quality. During a team meeting, the athletes discussed the importance of goal setting and how to set effective goals. After that, the wrestlers were responsible for setting daily practice goals to improve mat skills and strategies. As the wrestlers became more proficient at goal setting, they began to set goals for improving their mental skills.

On evaluation of the team's mental strengths and weaknesses, Coach Smith realized that several of the athletes on the team experienced high anxiety before competition, which interfered with their performance. After a team meeting addressing the importance of learning to relax in order to lower arousal and handle stress, he taught athletes how to relax. After a practice session, athletes were encouraged to relax in a quiet environment at home on a daily basis for 2 weeks to develop the skill. To reinforce the importance of developing relaxation skills, Coach Smith continued to integrate relaxation training into the practice setting. As athletes became more proficient, he abbreviated the relaxation sessions. He also created practice situations designed to increase anxiety and encouraged athletes to use short relaxation techniques (e.g., a deep breath) to lower arousal to the desired level. The athletes were then encouraged to use relaxation (as appropriate) as part of their mental readiness plan.

Coach Smith knew that the use of imagery would also help his athletes manage their anxiety. But rather than simply instructing them to use imagery at home and before competition, as he had done in past years, he integrated it into the practice setting. In the beginning, he had the team imagine performing skills they had already mastered in order to get them used to using imagery. Then he had the athletes use imagery for new techniques before actually performing the skill. If athletes made a mistake, Coach Smith would encourage them to imagine the proper form before correcting the error. In practice activities in which athletes were waiting their turn to wrestle, he would have them watch others and try to imagine how they would react to the situations they observed. As athletes developed more proficiency at using imagery, he created scenarios that they might experience in upcoming matches and had them imagine how they would respond. He noticed that this helped the athletes make better decisions on the mat. He also used imagery and practice simulations to help athletes learn to regain emotional control and attentional focus when facing adversity in a match.

As part of the ongoing evaluation of his MST program, Coach Smith realized that some of the younger athletes were still defeating themselves mentally when facing a challenging opponent or when they fell behind in a match. At this point, he decided to incorporate self-talk strategies to raise confidence, focus attention, and reduce stress, using the three-phase model of MST.

SUMMARY

1. Most coaches and athletes recognize that mental factors play a huge role in influencing competitive outcomes yet devote little time to learning and mastering the mental game. Athletes believe that sport is 50 to 90% mental, depending on the type of sport and the level of competition.

2. In recalling their most memorable performances, athletes describe a state called flow. Achieving flow can be elusive, but mental skills training can help athletes reach this special state more consistently.

3. Core mental skills include motivation, energy management, attention, stress management, and self-confidence.

4. Increasing research demonstrates that mental skills training works—but consistent and systematic practice is necessary to maximize its effectiveness.

5. Some athletes learn the mental game through trial and error, but mental skills training is a much more efficient way of learning.

6. Mental skills training is the systematic application of mental training tools to improve athletes' mental skills. MST is a comprehensive, systematic, skill-oriented approach to developing mental toughness and creating a flow frame of mind.

7. The core mental training tools used to develop athletes' mental skills include goal setting, imagery, relaxation and energization, and self-talk.

8. Although improving performance is undoubtedly an important goal of mental skills training, other valuable outcomes include increased enjoyment of sport and the development of life skills.

9. Some coaches are reluctant to try MST techniques because of time pressure or myths about sport psychology even though they recognize the importance of the mental game.

10. Coaches are encouraged to facilitate athletes' development of mental skills but should avoid trying to act as clinical or counseling sport psychologists for athletes facing important life issues outside of sport. These athletes should be referred to a psychologist or counselor.

11. Mental skills training involves a three-phase process: education, acquisition, and implementation. Athletes develop awareness of their strengths and weaknesses, acquire basic competence in using mental training tools and skills, and then overlearn and incorporate them into competitive situations.

KEY TERMS

acquisition phase
confidence
education phase
energy management

flow
implementation phase
mental skills

mental skills training
mental training tools
motivation

REVIEW QUESTIONS

1. Can athletes control whether they get into flow?

2. Aside from improving their team's performance, how else can coaches justify investing in mental skills training?

3. You hear a coach say that the key to the mental game is selecting athletes who are motivated and cool under pressure because mental toughness is just a gift that some athletes are born with. How would you respond?

4. What is the distinction between mental skills and mental training tools?

5. Can a person trained in sport psychology meet with athletes on a one-time basis before an important competition and get them mentally ready to compete? Why or why not?

6. How can you determine whether an athlete needs outside counseling or MST?

PRACTICAL ACTIVITIES

1. Describe one of your flow experiences. In what ways is it similar or dissimilar to Bill Russell's experience and to the description of flow provided in the chapter?

2. Suppose a member of your coaching staff is resistant to the mental skills training concept. What are some of the possible reasons? For each reason, describe at least one solution for getting past that roadblock.

3. Despite the potential benefits of sport psychology, many coaches continue to neglect MST or address these skills inconsistently. Suppose that, because of your expertise in sport psychology, you have been asked to speak to high school coaches at a national clinic. Prepare a statement that

   • emphasizes the importance of psychological factors in sport performance,

   • highlights the key psychological factors thought to influence performance, and

   • describes how coaches can incorporate mental skills training into their overall coaching plan by using the three-phase model of MST.

4. For each of the mental skills described in this chapter, describe strategies you could integrate into practice to help athletes improve those skills.

PART II

Developing Mental Training Tools

Part II includes four chapters designed to teach you about mental training tools, the techniques you use to help your athletes develop crucial mental skills that influence their sport enjoyment, performance, and personal development. Chapter 4, Goal Setting, teaches the importance of using goals, identifies the types of goals that athletes should set, and explains key steps in the goal implementation process. Chapter 5, Imagery, provides a general understanding of imagery and offers a blueprint for using it. Chapter 6, Relaxation and Energization, provides a basic understanding of these two companion skills and their benefits, lays out a systematic model for developing total and rapid relaxation and energization, and offers guidelines for using these skills effectively. Chapter 7, Self-Talk, demonstrates why self-talk is effective, identifies the dangers of negative thoughts, provides a systematic approach to reprogramming self-talk and countering negative thinking, and concludes with step-by-step guidelines on how to help athletes develop their self-talk skills.

Goal Setting

When you finish reading this chapter, you should be able to

- understand what goals are and the benefits that athletes get from setting them;
- understand why you and your athletes should make process and performance goals a higher priority than outcome goals;
- describe the characteristics of effective goals, including specific, moderately difficult, positive, short- and long-term, individual and team, and practice and competitive goals;
- understand how to make goals work by employing a systematic goal implementation process; and
- teach your athletes how to set goals through a program that incorporates education, acquisition, and implementation phases.

etting goals is not new to coaches and athletes: Athletes have set goals for themselves since ancient times. Almost all athletes set goals, yet most rate their goals as only moderately effective (Burton, Weinberg, Yukelson, & Weigand 1998; Weinberg, Burton, Yukelson, & Weigand 1993, 2000). Why? Consider these two examples. Ray loved volleyball but was average in height and jumped poorly. Ray's coach convinced him that he would grow and could become a strong player by following an off-season physical conditioning regimen of weight training and plyometrics. Sold on the goal of improving his jumping skills, Ray nailed a measuring stick to his garage wall and measured his vertical jump every 2 weeks. Ray was committed to his program, which he believed would help him become a good volleyball player, and over time his hard work paid off. Many of his test sessions revealed improvement in his vertical jump, if only a few centimeters. Ray grew more confident about reaching his long-term goal and more motivated to train even harder. It wasn't long until he made his provincial team, and, aided by a timely growth spurt, he became a two-time Olympian. Ray's experience is a classic **goal setting** success story.

Tracy was a promising swimmer who set several age-group records when she was 12. She became a star in her small community and was frequently compared to past Olympic swimmers. Tracy's parents and coach set challenging goals for her based on their lofty expectations, but instead of motivating her to train harder and building her confidence, these ambitious goals put pressure on Tracy and made it difficult for her to live up to everyone's expectations.

Even when she swam well, it never seemed enough to satisfy her coach or parents, prompting Tracy to doubt her ability. As the self-doubts mounted, her performance suffered, until she was more afraid to fail than motivated to win. Tracy's goal-induced failure suggests the problems that can develop from poorly designed goal-setting programs.

What was the difference between Ray's and Tracy's experiences with goal setting? The answer is simple. Ray's goals were realistic and motivating, while Tracy's were set by others and were so lofty that they were demotivating and stress inducing. Athletes can reap tremendous benefits from setting goals—but only if coaches help them learn to do it well. This chapter is intended to help you understand how to help your athletes set goals effectively, minimizing undesirable side effects and maximizing the benefits.

What Are Goals and Why Use Them?

Ed Locke, America's most prolific goal-setting researcher, defines a goal simply as "what an individual is trying to accomplish; it is the object or aim of an action" (Locke et al. 1981, p. 126). In a more passionate description, Lessin suggests that "goals are like magnets that attract us to higher ground and new horizons. They give our eyes a focus, our mind an aim, and our strength a purpose. Without their pull, we would remain forever stationary, incapable of moving forward. . . . A goal is a possibility that fulfills a dream" (Kennedy 1998, p. 25).

Using Goals to Create a Positive Team Climate

Several years ago, one of Damon Burton's former students began coaching a women's collegiate cross country team. After the first week of practice, she called for advice on how to deal with the extreme negativity hindering the team's practices. The runners complained about everything—type and length of workouts, quality of training, and lack of support from teammates and coaches. When the team didn't run well in its first meet, everyone was pointing fingers and looking for scapegoats.

To counteract these problems, a goal-setting program was implemented, and the atmosphere changed right away. The coach emphasized how each workout fit into the season-long training plan and would help the runners achieve individual and team goals. This gave workouts a positive focus. As runners became engrossed in attaining their goals, the griping, negativity, and finger pointing no longer had fertile soil for growth. Everyone enjoyed running, which enhanced workout quality and improved long-term performance. In fact, this more positive focus prompted runners to provide greater encouragement and support for each other in the quest to reach their practice and competitive goals.

Goals give athletes purpose and direction and provide a standard for measuring progress. As we saw in the story about Ray, well-designed goals promote self-confidence, motivation, and effective performance. They also provide a variety of other benefits, many of which are listed in figure 4.1. Goals are also instrumental in fostering a more positive and cohesive team climate, as illustrated in Using Goals to Create a Positive Team Climate. And for experienced and skilled goal setters, the process can ultimately become more important than the product. Goals are the beacon, but the journey is the joy. Bill Russell, captain of one of the most successful dynasties in sport history, the Boston Celtics of the 1950s and '60s, says that he profited more from striving for excellence than from winning 11 NBA titles in 13 seasons. He emphasizes that challenging goals prompt us to strive to our fullest and give our lives purpose, whether we reach them or not, as long as we give our best effort. The same can be true for your athletes.

Perhaps the most critical question about goal setting for most coaches is, "Does it work?" The answer is a resounding yes! Accounts from successful coaches and athletes and from sport psychology research strongly confirm that goal setting enhances performance, increases enjoyment, and helps us feel better about ourselves (Burton & Naylor 2002, Burton & Weiss 2008). In fact, the evidence is so overwhelming that goal setting may be the most effective performance enhancement strategy in sport. More than three-quarters of the published studies on goal setting in sport and physical activity found that it yields positive results. The key is to do it right.

Characteristics of Effective Goals

Goals motivate athletes by helping them focus attention on specific tasks, increase effort and intensity, and persist in the face of adversity and failure (Locke 1996). Setting and attaining goals also boosts athlete's self-confidence and motivation, but all of these benefits depend on formulating goals with the right characteristics. Thus this section of the book examines the basic question of whether goals should be focused on process, performance, or outcome, then addresses proper emphasis on six other goal characteristics in order to maximize athletes' performance.

Process, Performance, and Outcome Goals

We believe that focusing on process and performance rather than outcomes is fundamental, and perhaps the most important concept in all of sport psychology (Burton 1989; Kingston & Hardy 1994, 1997). **Process goals** focus on improving form, technique, and strategy. **Performance goals** address overall personal performance, such as running a faster time, throwing farther, or shooting a lower score. **Outcome goals** emphasize outperforming other competitors, as well as the objective outcome—that is, placing high or winning. You can see, then, that outcome goals require athletes to attain performance goals, such as shooting a golf score of 74 or running the 100 meters in 10.22 seconds. To attain these performance goals, athletes must achieve a series of process goals that focus on improving form, technique, knowledge, or strategy, such as improving one's putting, hitting more greens in regulation, or getting a good start

---

Benefits of Goal Setting

- Goals enhance focus and concentration.
- Goals boost self-confidence.
- Goals help prevent or manage stress.
- Goals help create a positive mental attitude.
- Goals increase intrinsic motivation to excel.
- Goals improve the quality of practices by making training more challenging.
- Goals enhance playing skill, techniques, and strategies.
- Goals improve overall performance.

FIGURE 4.1 Goal setting may be one of the most effective performance enhancement strategies in sport, as suggested by its many benefits.

out of the blocks. In fact, these three types of goals might best be conceptualized along a continuum (figure 4.2), with outcome goals on the product end of the continuum (at the right), process goals on the opposite end, and performance goals in between.

Outcome goals represent our ultimate destination, and performance and process goals are the paths for getting there. Disaster awaits if we focus too much on outcome without developing the **action plan** to achieve it. When Steve Nash sinks a 3-pointer with the game on the line and defenders in his face, he's not thinking, "I have to make this shot to win the game." His thinking is much more process oriented: "Stay relaxed, square up, good rhythm, strong follow-through." In sport, where highly complex skills require years of practice to master, process goals should function as the stepping stones to achieving the performance levels that will ultimately lead to desired outcomes (such as placing high and winning).

Why Emphasize Process and Performance Goals?

In sport, achievement is usually measured by one criterion: Winning is success, and losing is failure. Even the youngest athletes quickly learn this lesson. But when athletes base their self-confidence on winning rather than on attaining process and performance goals, their self-confidence is likely to be very unstable—in any contest or competition, there is only one winner. You have probably seen athletes who become overconfident after a win or two, only to have their bubble burst by a loss. Such instability becomes a source of uncertainty, anxiety, and frustration. Athletes who base their self-confidence on winning usually feel helpless to do anything about their unstable self-confidence. They have become so convinced that winning is the only criterion for evaluating their competence that they are unable to separate their performance from its outcome (see The Problem With Outcome Goals for an example).

So how do you help athletes achieve stable self-confidence and feel competent regardless of whether they win or lose? The answer lies in setting realistic process and performance goals. Success must be redefined as achieving process standards—following through on a jump shot or making solid contact with the baseball—and exceeding personal performance goals rather than surpassing other competitors. Phil Niekro, the ageless knuckleballer, understood this concept well:

> I don't try to explain it. Some days I feel like I have great stuff and I get knocked out in the third inning. Other days I have lousy stuff before the game, and when I'm pitching I will throw the ball right into the batter's power zone, but the batter pops it up rather than hits a home run. I don't try to work out the problems of winning and losing. I don't have any control over it. (Martens 1987, p. 159).

Thus you will want to make sure that athletes don't base their self-worth on factors beyond their control. It makes no sense for them to perform well, reach realistic process and performance goals, yet consider themselves failures because they lost; nor does it make sense for them to perform poorly, win because of luck or a weak opponent, yet consider themselves successful. Great athletes avoid evaluating themselves on the basis of every win or loss. They set long-term objectives and measure their progress by evaluating their own performances in light of the quality of the competition, regardless of whether they win or lose. Athletes who use process and performance goals instead of outcome goals play with less anxiety and more self-confidence, concentrate and perform better, and feel more satisfied with their participation (Burton 1989, Pierce & Burton 1998, Sharples 1992).

Incorporating Control and Flexibility

You can increase your athletes' success in setting goals by building control and flexibility into them, and process and performance goals can help. Let's look at the control factor first. Goals should allow athletes to exert control over their own success, so that when they achieve a goal they can take credit for it. Process and performance goals identify specific behaviors the athlete is to achieve, and attaining these goals does not depend heavily on others. But outcome goals, especially winning, are only partially controllable.

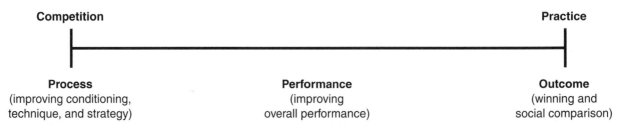

FIGURE 4.2 Continuum of process, performance, and outcome goals.

The Problem With Outcome Goals

My (Damon Burton's) epiphany about the complexity of goal setting came in my final year as a high school basketball coach. The community's expectations were high: "Best team since the state championship club 5 years ago," said the regulars at the drugstore. Conference coaches made us the preseason favorite, and I caught the fever, too, fully expecting this team to bring our community another state title. However, because I was concerned that these lofty expectations would breed overconfidence and complacency, our team set only one goal for the season—to win the Central Prairie League Championship.

During the first 4 weeks of the season, the team played better than any I had ever coached. Although somewhat undersized, this team was talented, played well together, understood what we wanted to do offensively and defensively, and executed with tremendous confidence and aggressiveness. Our record at winter break was 6-1, with our only loss coming on the road in double overtime to the third-ranked team in the state. Then a funny thing happened on our way to a dream season. Our team was decimated by a nasty flu strain, and for over 3 weeks we had at least two starters out of every game. The kids confronted this adversity head-on, practicing harder and competing more intensely than ever, but we still lost six of the next seven games. Suddenly, our single goal for the season was unrealistic, and the players fixated on this failure. For several weeks, my assistant coach and I did nothing but put out brush fires, talking with players individually and as a team about putting our problems behind us and making the best of the remaining games. We also instituted a substitute goal—qualifying for the state tournament—but for some reason commitment to that new goal was moderate at best.

We lost only four more games the rest of the year—all by small margins—and nearly qualified for the state tournament, but we were not the same team. We recovered physically and continued to improve our execution, but the psychological damage was irreparable. We had lost that confidence and mental toughness that had allowed us to play with poise, aggressiveness, and composure. Now our play was punctuated by timidity, indecision, and mental lapses. The close losses were particularly frustrating, because the team that had played with such confidence before the break almost assuredly would have won those games. Once our self-confidence was shattered, we just couldn't put it back together again.

What should we have done differently? Setting outcome goals is an important motivational strategy, and the long-term goal of winning the conference championship was not necessarily the problem. However, I should have broken that outcome goal into the process and performance goals that would serve as the action plan for becoming conference champs. We should have set three to five performance goals to allow the team to maximize its chance of winning, along with several process goals to ensure top performance. These goals would have maximized our chances of winning even as they provided benchmarks for success when illness prevented us from winning. More important, they would have raised the athletes' intrinsic motivation to strive for personal excellence.

Think of all the variables that determine whether an athlete wins a competition: Their own performance is, of course, important, but so are those of teammates, other competitors, officials, and coaches. Outcomes are also determined by situational factors such as equipment, playing fields, weather, and even luck (which is discounted by many coaches and athletes but often plays a major role).

Try to set goals that are as personally controllable as possible. For example, it is much more within a gymnast's control to meet a goal of practicing her routine at least six times daily for the next week than it is to achieve the goal of receiving a certain score on her floor exercise—which, in turn, is more controllable than the goal of winning the event. Yet even the training goal is not completely controllable. She could become sick during the week, sprain an ankle, or lose focus due to final exams. But the process-oriented training goal is more controllable than winning. And if the gymnast achieves her goal of running through her routine six times daily and then also places well at the meet, she can more readily take credit for her success than if it happened by chance. Thus she becomes a more self-confident athlete.

In addition to controllability, the best goals are flexible so that they can be raised or lowered to create the optimal level of challenge. Typically, the more difficult the challenge, the higher the motivation. However, if goals become unrealistic, then athletes will no longer be confident of reaching them, and the resulting stress may lower their motivation as well as their ability to perform. As a coach, you have to find the right balance between creating the highest feasible level of challenge and maintaining a realistic opportunity to succeed. Outcome goals offer little flexibility. Opponents are normally determined by competition schedules, making it virtually impossible to adjust the difficulty of the goal to create an optimal level of challenge. At the other end of the continuum, process goals make it much easier to adjust goals. If you find that taking good, open shots 90% of the time is too challenging, you can drop the difficulty to 85%. Conversely, if 90% is too easy, you can raise the goal to 95%.

Choosing the Right Kind of Goals

In addition to prioritizing process and performance over outcome, you will need to understand six other goal characteristics that promote the greatest performance gains. They are summarized in figure 4.3 and discussed next.

Set Specific, Measurable Goals

Goals range from vague and intangible ("Do your best!") to specific and measurable (running 100 meters in 10.8 seconds or scoring 15 points in a basketball game). With do-your-best goals, athletes never fail because they can always say they did their best. But this vagueness is also a shortcoming of general goals, which are not in fact goals but objectives—things athletes continuously strive to do. Specific, measurable goals are more effective at improving athletes' consistency and quality of performance because they identify a criterion that defines success, establish clear expectations for athletes, and focus athletes' attention on what they need to do to succeed. They foster accountability. See figure 4.4 for examples of specific, measurable goals for various sports.

In setting specific goal standards, keep in mind these three concepts:

- Emphasize both quantity and quality of performance (e.g., improve the number of good shots taken by 10%).

- Use both **objective and subjective performance measures**: for example, a basketball player improving her free throw percentage (objective), or a player improving her footwork from, say, a 3 on a 10-point scale to a 4 or 5 (subjective).

- Measure abstract elements such as effort and being a good sport by setting goals based on specifically defined behaviors that demonstrate such qualities.

Guidelines for Setting Effective Goals

1. Emphasize process and performance goals as a higher priority than outcome goals.

2. Set specific, measurable goals rather than general or "do-your-best" goals.

3. Set moderately difficult goals that are challenging but realistic.

4. Set positively—*not* negatively—focused goals.

5. Set both long-term objectives and short-term goals, with short-term goals serving as the building blocks for reaching long-term objectives.

6. Set both individual and team goals, with individual goals becoming the role-specific steps used to attain team goals.

7. Set both practice and competitive goals, with practice goals focusing on developing skills and competitive goals geared to performing optimally.

FIGURE 4.3 Follow these guidelines when setting goals.

Examples of Specific-Measurable Goals for Various Sports

- To run the 1500-meter race on Saturday in 3:57.
- To keep the man I'm guarding from having more than three open shots in tomorrow night's game.
- To shoot at least five takedowns in the first period against Wally Davis.
- To make solid contact with the ball 80% of the time in batting practice this week.
- To block the correct person every time in today's scrimmage.
- To score a 72 in the championship round on Tuesday.
- To read the defense correctly 90% of the time, and to call the correct audible when the defense is loaded against the play called in the huddle in this week's game.
- To pitch the ball to the spot called for by the catcher 80% of the time in tomorrow's game.
- To extend my concentration practice today from 5 to 6 minutes.
- To record at least 50% of my negative thoughts today and then to spend twenty minutes this evening developing and practicing use of positive-realistic counterarguments.

FIGURE 4.4   The best goals are quantifiable and identify a specific performance standard.

Set Moderately Difficult Goals

Goals need to be difficult enough to encourage great effort and persistence but easy enough to make success realistic and minimize stress. **Moderately difficult goals** promote the greatest gains in performance (Burton & Naylor 2002; Burton, Naylor, & Holliday 2001). Goals that are too difficult may threaten athletes' feelings of competence as well as their motivation (see figure 4.5). Like the rabbit in a dog race, goals should be kept just beyond one's grasp, even though the rabbit must be caught now and then. The reward of attaining a goal will motivate your athletes' pursuit of the next, slightly more difficult one.

How do you know just how challenging a goal should be? We have found it best to use athletes' most recent performances, preferably within the past week or two, as a baseline, and we highly recommend the staircase approach to goal setting (see figure 4.6). Athletes' immediate goals should be set only slightly (5%–15%) above their **current performance capabilities**, or their recent performance average, so that they can be 90% (or more) confident of attaining their goal. Then a series of steps is planned, each slightly more difficult than the one before. Athletes will seldom progress directly up the staircase—sometimes they will take a step back—but with continued commitment, they will most likely succeed in the end. It is also wise to avoid projecting goals too far into the future. Plan three or four steps, covering a

period of no more than six weeks to keep motivation and self-confidence high.

The staircase can be considerably steeper for highly confident athletes than for less confident ones. When athletes have difficulty achieving the next step in a staircase, they must consider two possibilities: that the step is too big and should be

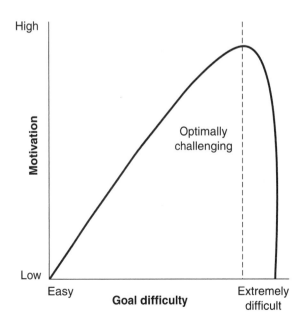

FIGURE 4.5   Relationship between goal difficulty and motivation. Notice the dramatic drop in motivation when goals become too difficult.

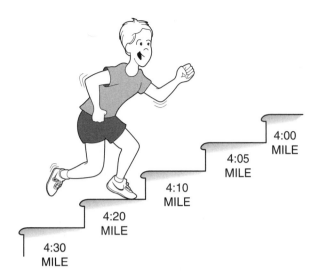

FIGURE 4.6 Goal staircase: The athlete's immediate goal is set only slightly above his or her present baseline. Each step is a little more difficult than the one before.

subdivided, or that a technical or tactical problem is hindering them. In the second case, your athletes may need to develop the requisite fundamentals before overcoming this obstacle. As you and your athletes work through the goal-setting process, you may find that goals need to be adjusted if they are to remain realistic. This should be seen as an acceptable decision, not a sign of failure. At the same time, be sure to adjust goals downward only when circumstances warrant and not to cover for a lack of motivation or a poor performance.

Set Positively Focused Goals

Goals can address either positive behaviors that you want to increase (e.g., high first-serve percentage in tennis) or negative behaviors that you want to decrease (e.g., double-fault percentage). Positively focused goals are usually more effective, particularly for new or difficult skills, because they help athletes focus on correct execution. Moreover, positive goals tend to promote greater self-confidence and intrinsic motivation. So have your athletes set goals in positive terms, focusing on what you want them to accomplish (e.g., 2 hits in 4 at-bats) rather than what you hope to avoid (e.g., going 0 for 4).

Set Both Short-Term Goals and Long-Term Objectives

As you plan, consider the roles of **short-term goals** and **long-term objectives**. An objective is not so much a standard as it is a quest for continuous improvement; it is a continuum along which athletes can progress

systematically. A goal is a point on that continuum, a specific behavior to be done. A common objective for athletes is to develop their ability to the fullest. The Olympic creed, "Citius, Altius, Fortius" (Faster, Higher, Stronger) is an objective. A goal, by contrast, is to high-jump 7 feet 6 inches (2.3 m), improve one's best time in the 100-meter dash by 0.1 second in the next meet, or focus attention on the seams of the approaching baseball on every pitch. Long-term objectives provide athletes with direction, while short-term goals get them to their destination (Burton & Naylor 2002). Long-term objectives represent the top of the staircase, and short-term goals are the steps for getting there by developing individual skills and staying motivated along the way.

While it is valuable for you to set long-term objectives extending one, two, or even more years into the future, short-term goals should not be set more than 6 weeks ahead. For example, Bernie is a high school sophomore with the long-term goal of winning a college basketball scholarship. His biggest obstacle is his mediocre shooting skills. Bernie and his coach agree that he needs to be shooting over 50% from the field, over 40% on 3-point shots, and over 80% on free throws by his senior year. Bernie's coach feels these goals are realistic if Bernie improves his shooting mechanics, and they have chosen to focus on three aspects of Bernie's technique: being on balance, with his elbow under the ball for better alignment; shooting at the top of his jump, with a high release to use more wrist and less arm; and extending fully, with good follow-through.

The action plan for making these improvements calls for Bernie to shoot 100 to 150 extra shots per day, before and after practice, at least four times per week. For year 1 of this 3-year plan, Bernie focuses on process goals, not shooting percentage. This allows the technical changes Bernie wants to make to become automatic. For year 2, he splits his goals evenly between process and performance (field goals at 45%, 3-pointers at 35%, and free throws at 72%). In year 3, Bernie works on getting and taking good shots and meeting his long-term objectives for shooting percentages. We recommend such combinations of short-term goals and long-term objectives to maximize performance gains.

Set Both Individual and Team Goals

Both team and individual goals make a valuable contribution to sport success. In fact, it might surprise you to learn that researchers have found that team goals enhance performance as effectively as individual goals (Locke & Latham 1990). Team goals offer direction for collective performance, which is then broken down into individual goals for improving the motivation and confidence of individual athletes. If you use team goals without accompanying individual goals, your athletes may reduce their effort, a phenomenon known as **social loafing** (Hardy & Latane 1988). This performance problem plagues teams because athletes working together on a task tend to exert less individual effort and perform at a lower level than when they do the same task alone. They feel they can loaf because teammates will pick up the slack. To prevent social loafing, individual goals must be set that hold each team member accountable for a specific level of performance, and athletes must view these individual goals as indispensable to the team's success. Base individual goals on the role that each athlete needs to play in order to maximize team effectiveness.

Set Practice and Competitive Goals

Goals often have different functions in practice than in competition (see table 4.1). Athletes feel less pressure during practice, so goals can be used to motivate them to work with purpose and intensity on developing complex skills (e.g., shooting in basketball, volleying in tennis). Practice goals should focus on the quantity or quality of skill mechanics and should challenge athletes to push beyond their comfort zone. They can range from moderately to very difficult, but they must be set high enough to encourage athletes to strive to improve in some way every day.

In competition, on the other hand, athletes feel more pressure because they are measured against opponents or against their own previous performances (not to mention observed by a crowd). Competitive goals that are overly ambitious or rooted in factors athletes have little control over can hinder performance by adding to the existing pressure. Thus it is best to use competitive goals to develop poise, maintain confidence, enhance mental toughness, and perform optimally. Focus on effort-based achievements and improving the quantity of specific behaviors (Riley 1996), and keep competitive goals realistic to help reduce stress and promote self-confidence.

Making Goals Work: The Goal Implementation Process

One of the biggest misconceptions about goals is the belief that you can "set 'em and forget 'em" (Burton et al. 2001). Goal setting means more than merely setting a few goals; it requires a comprehensive implementation process. We recommend that you and your athletes follow the five steps shown in figure 4.7 on page 60.

Set Goals Systematically

The first step is to set appropriate goals. The best way to make sure goals are set systematically is to have your athletes take the following actions:

1. *Create a vision.* Ask your athletes to think about where they would like their career to go over the next 3 to 5 years. What long-term achievements would they like to pursue? You might have athletes draw their vision for their sport career using crayons and butcher paper, then translate their vision into 3 to 5 written long-term objectives that spell out how they are going to improve their performance. A high school volleyball player, for example, might envision earning a college scholarship and therefore set objectives to improve her vertical jump and spiking mechanics, as well as develop a jump serve over the next 4 years.

TABLE 4.1

Differences Between Practice and Competitive Goals

Dimensions	Practice goals	Competitive goals
Goal focus	Developing skills	Performing optimally
Mental skills emphasized	Focus, concentration, and motivation	Poise, confidence, and stress management
Types of goals set	Outcome, performance, and process	Process and performance
Level of goal difficulty	Push the comfort zone	Keep realistic for current performance capabilities

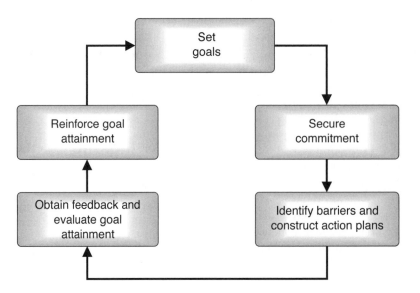

FIGURE 4.7   The five-step process for setting and implementing goals.

2. *Develop a mission statement.* A mission gives meaning to training because it defines and focuses on exactly what you want to accomplish. For example, an athlete might define her mission as being the team's defensive stopper, or a team might decide that its mission is to play the best defense in the state.

3. *Conduct a comprehensive needs assessment.* Have athletes evaluate their strengths and weaknesses, with a focus on areas to be improved. You might develop a sport-specific form to help your athletes do this. They should identify three to five areas that most need improvement or that are so important that improvement is crucial regardless of their current skill level.

4. *Prioritize and coordinate goals.* When athletes have several goals, they need to rank them in order of importance. Some goals may need to be put on hold while athletes concentrate on others. As you prioritize and coordinate goals, remember that reaching short-term goals makes it easier to achieve long-term objectives, meeting individual goals helps to attain team goals, and attaining process goals helps athletes reach performance goals, which, in turn, promotes positive outcomes.

Develop Goal Commitment

For goals to work, your athletes must be committed to achieving them. Without **goal commitment**, athletes will not give the necessary effort or use the right strategies to achieve their goals. You can do a number of things to increase your athletes' commitment to their goals (see figure 4.8). Most important, make sure that athletes have ownership of their goals. When players participate actively in setting their goals, they work harder to find ways to achieve them.

Construct Action Plans Based on Evaluating Barriers

Goals are more effective when a systematic action plan guides the athlete toward reaching them (Locke & Latham 1990). Many great athletes recognize the value of planning how they will achieve their goals. For Michael Johnson, the world-record holder at 200 and 400 meters, planning is a must:

> You must understand, I am not by nature a daydreamer. I try to control those parts of my life that can be controlled, to plan everything that I want to happen down to the most insignificant detail. I "traffic" in a world where fractions of a second separate success and failure, so I'd visualized the 1996 Olympics down to the millisecond. I'd crafted a decade of dreams into ambitions, refined ambitions into goals, and finally hammered goals into plans. (Johnson, 1996, p. xiv)

Let's say you've identified defensive rebounding as a problem for your team. The second step in developing an action plan would be to collect data on current rebounding performance by evaluating game footage. Next, you need to identify patterns that have helped or hurt rebounding effectiveness. For example, failure to make contact with opponents and lack of strength can hurt rebounding

Ways to Increase Commitment to Achieving Goals

1. Make sure athletes set their own goals, not someone else's.

2. Allow your players to participate in setting their own goals.

3. Encourage performers to write down their goals.

4. Have players tell their goals to others or post their goals.

5. Teach athletes to imagine in attaining their goals.

6. Provide players with incentives or rewards for achieving their goals.

7. Ensure that performers receive social support from coaches, teammates, and parents.

8. Help athletes earn a position on an elite team.

9. Provide players with opportunities to win a major competition or championship.

10. Help your athletes shape their goals.

11. Ensure that players make their goals competitive, primarily with themselves.

FIGURE 4.8 Tips for encouraging athletes to commit to achieving their goals.

performance, whereas strong jumping ability, good eye–hand coordination, and well-timed anticipation can help it. Then you would develop ways to correct the problem, emphasizing practicality, creativity, and individualization. Finally, you would construct a plan using the best of these solutions to accomplish your team's goals. You must keep your action plan as specific as possible, setting up practice schemes that will teach athletes how to perform the skills in simulated game conditions.

As you construct an action plan, be sure to evaluate the obstacles and roadblocks that might prevent athletes from reaching their goals (Burton et al. 2001). In order for your players to attain their goal of improving their defensive rebounding, they need to evaluate the factors currently preventing them from rebounding well. A quick analysis might show that little practice time is devoted to developing rebounding skills, that players don't have good knowledge of where they need to position themselves to rebound shots missed from specific locations on the court, and that players have insufficient upper-body strength to block out opponents or pull down the rebounds they get their hands on. Thus, you may need to develop a series of process goals to help players overcome each of these barriers and allow the team to rebound more effectively.

Give Feedback and Evaluate Goal Attainment

For athletes to reach their goals, you have to give them feedback. Using goals and feedback together yields significantly better results than using goals or feedback alone. In fact, adding feedback can raise goal productivity by an additional 17% (Locke & Latham, 1990). General principles for providing feedback are covered in chapter 3. Giving feedback related to reaching goals requires that you measure an athlete's performance. For example, offensive linemen in American football may have little opportunity to set meaningful process or performance goals and accurately evaluate their progress unless their coaches watch video of practice sessions and games and grade each player. You can maximize the effectiveness of your feedback by using logs to monitor athletes' progress toward achieving their goals (see figure 4.9 for a sample goal log). Logs can be posted publicly in the locker room, but generally we recommend that they be kept private so that those who are progressing more slowly are not threatened or embarrassed. When the goal is a common one for all members of the team and you believe some friendly competition would be helpful, then posting the feedback is recommended.

GOAL SETTING			WEEK OF:						
Goals	Current level (%)	Goal level (%)	M	T	W	Th	F	Game	Performance average
1.									
2.									
3.									

From D. Burton and T. Raedeke, 2008, *Sport Psychology for Coaches* (Champaign, IL: Human Kinetics).

FIGURE 4.9 Have athletes use logbooks to track their progress toward goals.

In addition to giving feedback, you will want to teach athletes to evaluate their progress toward reaching goals. **Goal evaluation** may be the most critical step in the goal-setting process (Locke & Latham 1990). While feedback gives athletes information on how they're doing (e.g., keeping their weight back on the breaking pitch) or what to adjust (e.g., look for a specific pitch in a certain zone when ahead in the count), evaluation provides a factual snapshot of how the athlete is moving toward a goal (e.g., batting average has increased from .360 to .385). When athletes' performance equals or exceeds a goal, it raises their self-confidence and increases their intrinsic motivation. If players' performance is improving but does not yet reach goal levels, then they will be motivated to work even harder to attain their goals.

Evaluation can also help you and your athletes know whether to adjust goals. If an athlete's performance is very close to meeting a goal, the athlete will normally be happy to keep the same goal and maintain or increase effort levels to reach it. However, if evaluation reveals a large gap between an athlete's performance and the goal, he or she may need to adjust the goal to avoid discouragement and a resulting decrease in effort. We have found that maintaining the same goals for weekly intervals, but evaluating them both daily and weekly, is better than changing goals each day. Working toward the same goals for a full week allows adequate time for athletes to demonstrate consistent goal achievement, while the daily and weekly evalutions help ensure that athletes think about and strive to reach their goals on a daily basis. Be sure to provide feedback and encourage frequent evaluation of progress toward goals. This will keep athletes' motivation and confidence high (Burton et al. 1998).

When coach Bill Snyder took over the most inept program in college football history at Kansas State, a key part of his plan for turning it into a national contender was to stress setting and evaluating goals each day in practice. "During that first season, I would go into the locker room each day, every single day after practice, and talk with virtually every single youngster and ask each one exactly the same question, 'Did you get better today?' The answer eventually became 'yes,' because they just didn't want to say no. Then I asked them to identify for me where they got better. Pretty soon everyone came to understand the concept of continually working toward improvement. I think this is a very important concept" (Shoop & Scott 1999, p. 41).

Reinforce Goal Achievement

When an athlete achieves a goal, be sure to reward him or her. Reinforcing goal achievement, or significant progress made toward achieving a goal, will help athletes continue that behavior (Locke & Latham 1990; Smith 2006) and should enhance your players' motivation to set and reach new goals. Remember that as you teach athletes a new skill, you will break the skill down into a series of realistic steps, and specific goals might be set for each of these steps. Reward athletes for attaining each of these small goals. Once athletes are reaching their goals consistently over a period of time, they need to set higher goals, and the process is repeated until they finally perform the skill proficiently (see chapter 4 for a more detailed discussion of shaping).

In summary, the goal implementation process is important to making goals work, and all five steps of this process are essential: Set goals systematically, develop goal commitment, construct action plans by evaluating barriers, provide feedback and evaluate goal attainment, and reinforce goal achievement. Now that you understand how to implement goals, how will you teach these skills to your athletes? That is the focus of the next section.

Developing Athletes' Goal-Setting Skills

The better your athletes develop their goal-setting fundamentals, the more they will benefit from using goals. Developing goal-setting skills follows the three-phase process outlined in chapter 3 for refining mental training tools and skills. During phase 1, the education phase, you teach athletes about goal setting and help them become aware of their personal goal patterns. Next, in the acquisition phase, you help your athletes acquire basic goal-setting skills. Finally, during the implementation phase, you emphasize the automation and execution of key goal-setting skills.

Education Phase

The education phase of any MST program is based on two objectives: education and awareness. And it is during this phase that you can help your athletes begin to develop a goal mentality. First, provide athletes with a general education about goals and how they work. The first part of this chapter provides the information your athletes need to know: what goals are, the evidence supporting their effectiveness, and the characteristics of effective goals. We recommend holding a team meeting to provide your athletes with this basic goal-setting information. If you have time, you might ask teammates to share how goal setting has helped them. You might share quotations from elite or pro athletes discussing how they have used goal setting to improve their skills. The second objective of the education phase is to help your athletes understand their current strengths and weaknesses in setting goals. Do they set goals too infrequently? Are their goals unrealistic? You might devise a simple form for athletes to fill out that would ask basic questions, such as what their most recent goal was, whether they met it, and why or why not. Reflecting on such questions will help athletes see what they might change as they set new goals.

Goal setting involves more than choosing the right type of goal and employing a systematic goal implementation strategy. At its best, goal setting becomes a lifestyle in which this important mental training tool helps your athletes do what they want in life. Research indicates that most athletes and coaches find goals only moderately effective. We believe this is because they set goals too infrequently and too unsystematically; because they are reluctant to put forth the time and effort required, they fail to appreciate the tremendous potential benefits (Burton et al. 1998, 2007). Effective goal setters establish dozens of goals every day, and these goals are critical components of a well-designed plan to achieve their competitive dream. Certainly, athletes must have a dream that they break down first into long-term objectives and then further into short-term goals. There is no doubt that gaining commitment, identifying obstacles, developing action plans to overcome obstacles, regular evaluation, and frequent feedback are critical steps in the process. But the secret to making goals work seems to be developing a goal mentality.

A goal mentality is a mind-set in which performers learn to love setting goals and then do so, spontaneously and systematically, in everything they do. A goal mentality develops when setting goals becomes self-fueling, prompting high levels of intrinsic motivation and steadily increasing competence. Based on our experience, developing a goal mentality requires implementing the goal-setting process daily for 8 to 12 weeks. During this time, the process needs to be conducted systematically, and athletes' progress needs to be monitored closely while they learn how to set goals effectively and build a strong history of success. This initial goal-setting stage is a difficult and time-consuming phase for coaches because they must dissolve athletes' resistance, teach them the basics of how to set goals effectively, help them develop the self-discipline to conduct the process systematically, and troubleshoot a wide variety of obstacles and problems. However, once athletes develop a goal mentality, the process becomes intrinsic and self-sustaining, so that only minimal guidance is needed. Goals then become more than a tool; they develop into a practice for lifelong success.

Acquisition Phase

This is where you work with athletes to acquire the skill of setting goals. First, guide them through defining their vision or dream and writing a mission statement. Then have them evaluate their skills by conducting a needs assessment, from which they will identify three to five long-term objectives that can be broken down into specific goals. Ask athletes to write their goals in logbooks, taking care to make the goals measurable and optimally challenging. For each short-term goal, the athlete should develop an action plan that outlines the smaller steps toward reaching it. They then log their progress, noting obstacles that arise. During this phase, it is best if you review athletes' logs each week in order to ensure that goals are specific and measurable, as well as optimally challenging, and to determine whether athletes have well-designed action plans for overcoming identified obstacles. Try to meet with each athlete briefly each week to review progress toward goals, set new goals or develop new action plans if necessary, and provide support for athletes' goal-setting efforts. These meetings might last as few as 10 minutes. As athletes become good at setting goals, meetings can be held less frequently.

Implementation Phase

Experience has taught us that even when athletes learn goal-setting skills, problems develop when they try to make these skills automatic or execute them in pressure-packed competitions. During this next phase, then, you will want to build goal setting into practice and competition, adjust goals as necessary, and use social support to make goal setting more effective.

• *Build goal setting into practice and competition.* Encourage your athletes to set goals for one or two activities per practice, then record their progress in their logbooks. You can collect logbooks at the end of the week, check them over the weekend, and pro-

vide written feedback on each player's goal setting. As athletes' skills become more automated, you can cut back to biweekly meetings to evaluate goals. To transfer goal-setting skills to competition, identify the situations in which problems typically occur. For example, an athlete might lose focus under pressure or experience negative thoughts during competition. For each problem, identify goals to focus on, record performance, and evaluate goal attainment.

• *Adjust goals if necessary.* Be ready to raise goals in practice if they are not challenging enough, but in competition you are more likely to lower unrealistically difficult goals to reduce unwanted stress. You may also need to adjust goals due to illness, injury, quality of training, competition site, weather conditions, quality of opposition, point in the training cycle, and slumps. In some cases, you may even need to adjust goals based on an athlete's personality (see chapter 10).

• *Develop social support systems.* Remember from figure 4.8 that athletes who are better at setting and reaching goals tend to use social support. As athletes set goals, getting support from other people can help them feel better emotionally and even perform better. You might have athletes discuss their goals in a group setting, to share how they are doing and get reinforcement from each other. You can also set up a mentor system in which more experienced goal setters help novice teammates devise and implement a personal goal-setting program.

SUMMARY

1. Goals are the most commonly used performance enhancement strategy in sport, and a goal is defined simply as "what an individual is trying to accomplish; it is the object or aim of an action" (Locke et al. 1981, p. 126).

2. Goals have many benefits: enhancing athletes' focus and concentration; boosting their confidence; helping athletes manage stress; allowing them to maintain a positive mental attitude; motivating them to stretch their limits and perform their best; and enhancing playing skills, techniques, and strategies.

3. In setting goals, the journey is more important than the destination, because the process gives meaning to our lives and enriches us for striving to make ourselves and the world around us better.

4. Research has proven the effectiveness of goal setting. In fact, the evidence is so overwhelming that goal setting just might be the most effective performance enhancement strategy in sport.

5. Setting and meeting goals increases athletes' motivation and self-confidence.

6. Coaches and athletes should focus on process and performance goals more than on outcome goals. This is the fundamental concept in goal setting.

7. Goals should be specific and measurable, and they should emphasize both quantity and quality. Goals can use objective or subjective performance measures, and they can measure abstract concepts.

8. Goals should be moderately difficult to create an optimal level of challenge. Typically, goals should be set 5% to 15% above current performance capabilities so that athletes are 90% confident of success.

9. Goals should focus on positive behaviors you want to increase or include, rather than negative behaviors you want to reduce or avoid.

10. Coaches and athletes should set both short-term goals and long-term objectives.

11. You can use team and individual goals in a coordinated fashion to enhance both collective and individual performance. Team goals must be broken down into individual goals so that each performer is held accountable for performing his or her role effectively.

12. Goals should differ for practice and competitive settings. During practice, goals are used to increase concentration and motivation so that complex skills can be improved. Practice goals should be difficult enough to stretch athletes' comfort zones. During competition, goals should emphasize mental skills such as poise, confidence, and mental toughness. Base competition goals on effort and set them realistically so that they don't create stress.

13. The goal implementation process is a systematic five-step routine: set goals systematically, develop goal commitment, construct action plans by evaluating barriers, obtain feedback and evaluate goal attainment, and reinforce goal achievement.

14. Developing athletes' goal-setting skills involves a three-phase process: education, acquisition, and implementation. Use this process to help athletes develop a goal mentality.

KEY TERMS

action plan
current performance capabilities
goal commitment
goal evaluation
goal setting

long-term objective
moderately difficult goals
objective performance measure
outcome goals
performance goals

process goals
short-term goal
social loafing
subjective performance measure

REVIEW QUESTIONS

1. What are goals?
2. What are the benefits of setting goals?
3. What are the advantages of process and performance goals versus outcome goals?
4. What are the characteristics of effective goals?
5. What are the best implementation strategies to ensure that goals are optimally effective?
6. How should coaches set up a goal-setting program for their team to maximize its effectiveness?

PRACTICAL ACTIVITIES

1. Develop a long-term goal for your team and an action plan for overcoming potential obstacles and achieving the goal. Next, break down that long-term goal into a daily or weekly goal that you'll use to start the season. Also develop the format for a logbook that you can use with your athletes to record performance and evaluate goal attainment.

2. Critique the daily goal you identified in question 1 on three criteria: Is it specific and measurable? (That is, does it provide a performance standard that can be counted or rated?) Is it flexible, so athletes can raise or lower the goal in order to create optimal difficulty to maximize motivation? Is it controllable, so that success is predominantly under athletes' personal control, allowing them to take credit for their success and raise their self-confidence?

5

Imagery

After reading this chapter, you should be able to

- explain what imagery is and how it improves performance,
- describe the factors that influence the effectiveness of imagery,
- discuss the key steps in helping athletes learn to use imagery effectively, and
- develop a sport imagery program you can implement with your team.

Many athletes and coaches today recognize the power of imagery. In fact, athletes from most sports attribute at least part of their success to their use of imagery. Legendary golf great Jack Nicklaus, for example, believes that an effective shot is 10% swing, 40% setup, and 50% the mental picture of the optimal swing (Nicklaus 1974).

> I never hit a shot, even in practice, without having a very sharp, in-focus picture of it in my head. It's like a color movie. First I "see" the ball where I want it to finish, nice and white and sitting up high on the bright green grass. Then the scene quickly changes and I "see" the ball going there; its path, trajectory, and shape, even its behavior on landing. Then there is sort of a fade-out, and the next scene shows me making the kind of swing that will turn the images into reality (Nicklaus 1974, p. 79).

Swimmer Amy Van Dyken, winner of multiple Olympic gold medals, also views imagery as a key to her success. Van Dyken did not swim competitively until about age 14, and she believes her ability to use imagery helped compensate for her lack of experience. Before the 1994 NCAA national championships, she imagined swimming the 50-meter freestyle from start to finish in less than 21.6 seconds. In reality, she finished in 21.7, setting a new American record (Van Dyken 1995).

Former Chicago Bulls and current Los Angeles Lakers coach Phil Jackson also uses imagery. He believes that one of his strengths in preparing for a game is his ability to image ways to short-circuit an opponent's offensive schemes. He recognizes that the ability to use imagery did not come overnight, but is an ability he developed through years of practice (Jackson & Delehanty 1995).

What is the magic in imagery that helps a golfer shoot a below-par round, a swimmer attain personal goals, and a basketball coach win championships? It's not magic at all. It is a human capacity and mental training tool that most of us have not developed to the fullest extent possible. In this chapter, we introduce you to imagery and provide evidence that it works to improve performance. We discuss key considerations in using imagery effectively, and we conclude by outlining a framework for implementing imagery training with your team.

What Is Imagery?

Imagery means using the senses to create or re-create an experience in one's mind. Imaging a sport skill is similar to performing the skill, except that athletes experience the action only in their minds. Though they do not actually see a tennis ball, feel the racket in their hand or the sensation of their muscles moving, or hear the sound of the racket hitting the ball, they do experience all these sensory cues in their mind.

Using Imagery to Replay or Create New Experiences

In essence, imagery is a product of your memory system. Your brain recalls and reconstructs pieces of information stored in your memory to build a meaningful image. Through imagery, athletes can recall previous experiences in great vividness and detail: A tennis player may recall what it feels like to serve an ace. A golfer may visualize the path a ball needs to travel and then imagine the type of putt needed to send the ball on that path at the optimal speed. Athletes can also create images of events yet to occur by piecing together bits of information already stored in their memory. A skier can imagine skiing a new course by combining memories of previous runs. A wrestler can prepare for a new opponent's moves by analyzing video footage, then imaging how he would handle situations likely to develop during the match. A softball player can watch a skilled pitcher's form and imagine throwing strikes with that same form.

Imagery—More than Visualization

Visualization is picturing, or seeing, yourself, but imagery is not limited to vision. It can involve multiple senses: sight, feel (how muscles feel as they move), touch, sound, smell, and taste. Imagery may also include the emotions associated with the experience being imagined. A golfer might visualize the lie of the fairway and image herself making the perfect drive. Not only can she see herself make the perfect swing, but she can also feel the sensations in her muscles as she executes the drive in her mind. The feel of her grip on the club and the glove against her skin are vividly etched in her memory. As she hits the ball, the sweet sound of the perfect drive resonates in her mind. She is also aware of the smell of fresh-cut grass, and perhaps even a faint taste of salty sweat on her lips if she is imaging a hot summer day.

In thinking of your sport, what senses seem most critical for athletes to incorporate into their imagery? You probably recognize the importance of sight and **kinesthetic feel**—the sensation of bodily position, presence, or movement that arises from the stimulation of sensory nerve endings in muscles, tendons, and joints. A hockey player uses his visual sense to read the defense and focus on the puck, and a tennis player uses vision to watch the ball and her opponent's location on the court. A gymnast relies on what it feels like to perform the perfect balance beam routine, and a golfer might rehearse the feel of a perfect swing before stepping onto the tee. Other senses are also important in certain sports. For example, tactile sensory information is crucial in wrestling. Auditory information is important in many team sports and in tennis, where shots hit with top spin sound different from those that are sliced. Even if you do not view a particular sensory modality as important in your sport, it is best to incorporate as many of the senses into imagery as possible, for one simple reason: It is easier to create a more vivid, lifelike image if most of the senses are involved.

Imagery Works!

If you remain somewhat skeptical about the power of imagery, consider that athletes of all skills levels are increasingly harnessing the power of this mental training tool (Hall 2001, Murphy & Martin 2002). Successful and highly skilled athletes are more likely than less accomplished athletes to use imagery regularly (Cumming & Hall 2002); in fact, studies have found that more than 90% of surveyed U.S. and Canadian Olympic athletes used imagery (Murphy, Jowdy, & Durtschi 1990; Orlick & Partington 1988). On average, these athletes engaged in imagery practice about 4 days a week for 10 to 15 minutes at a time, and some spent 2 to 3 hours using imagery to prepare for their event at the Olympics.

If this isn't proof enough, more than 200 hundred studies show that imagery is effective in improving performance across a wide variety of sports (Martin, Moritz, & Hall 1999). When carefully scrutinized, the bulk of the evidence clearly supports the idea that a combination of physical practice and imagery is more effective than physical practice alone. Imagery by itself is less effective than physical practice, but better than no practice. Imagery works best when it supplements, not replaces, physical practice (Hird, Landers, Thomas, & Horan 1991). In addition to augmenting physical practice, imagery can be used to maintain sport skills when athletes are unable to practice physically. Imagery is an effective learning strategy for fatigued athletes, because it allows them to practice mentally with good form rather than physically with poor form. Injured athletes can use imagery to keep their game skills sharp so that they are better able to play with confidence upon their return. And because imagery can be done almost anywhere at any time, it can even be used when bad weather rules out physical practice.

Imagery works because in many ways the mind cannot distinguish an image from the real thing. The central nervous system processes imagined information much as it does an actual experience, thus clearly imagined events produce effects that are similar to, if somewhat weaker than, the effects produced by actual experiences (Marks 1977). Imagery works by helping athletes create a blueprint for performing a skill. A basketball player can use imagery to create a blueprint of what it looks and feels like to execute a jump shot. The blueprint may include the body position, sequencing, and timing of steps used in the shot (e.g., position of the shooting arm relative to the nonshooting arm at the start of the jump). Developing a strong mental blueprint helps make the skill automatic, which allows the athlete to perform the skill without having to think about technique. Imagery can also be used to program an automatic response to various situations that may arise.

Factors Influencing the Effectiveness of Imagery

Although using imagery can improve performance, it does not do so automatically. Some athletes benefit more than others. Here are several reasons.

Imagery Ability

Athletes who are able to create accurate and lifelike images benefit more than those who can create only a blurry, fleeting image (Isaac 1992). Athletes with strong imagery skills are able to create vivid and controlled images. Increasing **imagery vividness** is like focusing a camera—a vivid image contains sharp, clear details. But athletes also need to be able to manipulate the content of their imagery to create images that do what they want them to do. Without strong **imagery control**, athletes, especially those low in self-confidence, may find themselves repeating mistakes in their imagery. A tennis player may unintentionally imagine choking on a critical match point, a softball player might see herself making a critical error, or a runner might experience an overwhelming sense of fatigue in the last leg of a race. Such negative images are counterproductive, serving only to hurt performance (Beilock, Afremow, Rabe, & Carr 2001; Short et al. 2002).

Athletes' Skill Level

Although both novice and skilled athletes benefit from using imagery, experienced athletes, who can draw on personal experience to create a vivid, lifelike image of their performance, benefit more. It is harder for novice athletes to create real life images because of their unfamiliarity with the skill being practiced. For example, it would be difficult for a novice kayaker to image the sensations of completing a roll to right a capsized boat if she has never experienced the feeling of the crisp hip snap necessary to do so. Nonetheless, novice athletes do benefit from using imagery, and it does help them improve their performance, just not as much as for experienced athletes. They can use imagery to acquire a basic idea of what it is like to perform a movement, whereas skilled athletes can use imagery for other reasons such as to refine their form, develop strategy, and get themselves mentally ready to perform.

Imagery Perspective

Athletes using imagery can take an internal or external perspective. With an internal perspective, athletes experience the event, seeing it through their own eyes and feeling the movements as if actually performing the skill. With an external perspective, they experience a performance from outside their body, seeing and hearing the image as if watching themselves on screen. Recent evidence suggests that both **internal and external imagery** perspectives are effective but at different times for different reasons (Hall 1997, Hardy 1997, Hardy & Callow 1999, Holmes & Collins 2001). In deciding which imagery perspective to use in a given situation, athletes should choose the perspective that helps them create the most vivid image possible. Internal and external imagery each have unique advantages.

Athletes may find that an internal imagery perspective provides them with a greater kinesthetic feel than is possible with external imagery. It is difficult to feel the movements associated with perfect skill execution when viewing an external image. Internal imagery is effective in sports where the competitor must respond to a constantly changing environment, such as ski racing or football, because it allows athletes to imagine changing environmental conditions and the exact timing at which various movements need to be initiated. A soccer goalie might use an internal perspective to prepare to respond to a shot from a particular location and angle, seeing himself time his dive (or jump) perfectly to make the save.

External imagery is well suited to evaluating and refining form. Athletes are able to see their entire body and the position of various body parts in relation to one another. In sports where form is critical, an external perspective allows the performer to image and rehearse the precise movements and positions used in a skill with greater detail than would be

possible from an internal perspective. External imagery also enables athletes to see the big picture. For example, a basketball player can image the entire court, including the positions of both teammates and opposing players as well as the flow of the play. This can help athletes develop decision-making skills and determine which strategies and moves to use in various situations. Finally, some athletes like to step out of their body and review an outstanding performance to enhance their confidence and motivation. Using external imagery can be like watching a highlight film without the actual footage.

In summary, both internal and external imagery are effective in enhancing performance, and many athletes report that they switch back and forth between the two. Thus, it is beneficial to help athletes learn to image using both perspectives.

Using Imagery Effectively

We hope we've piqued your interest in learning more about how to help athletes maximize the benefits of using imagery. The next section discusses three key steps in doing so: convincing athletes of the effectiveness of imagery, helping them develop their imagery skills, and using imagery to improve physical and mental skills.

Convince Athletes of the Effectiveness of Imagery

The most important part of motivating athletes to use imagery is to convince them that doing so can enhance their sport performance. As with any mental skills training program, it is crucial that athletes make the commitment to practice the skills systematically. In fact, imagery training is more successful when athletes expect it to be helpful, so you must encourage athletes to bring a positive attitude, an open mind, and patience. One strategy used by many coaches and sport psychology consultants is to discuss highly successful athletes who have used imagery. You may also find it useful to have a team discussion where athletes describe how they currently use imagery, setting the stage for you to discuss how a systematic program will make their use of imagery even more effective. This strategy works well if some athletes on your team are already using imagery on their own, especially team leaders. Although it is important to create positive expectations about imagery, those expectations also need to be realistic. Some athletes are eager to use imagery but expect to achieve miracles, and of course this is unreasonable.

Develop Athletes' Imagery Skills

For many athletes, images will seem fuzzy, unfocused, or even blank, especially when they first start using imagery. Few people are fortunate enough to start with vivid, clear images, but all athletes can improve their imagery powers through systematic practice. The first step in developing athletes' imagery skills is to assess their current ability, using a simple imagery test (figure 5.1, pages 72-73). The test helps you assess the vividness of athletes' imagery for visual, auditory, and kinesthetic senses, as well as their emotional state, for a series of four sport situations. It also helps you assess how well athletes can control their images. Assessing your athletes' imagery ability will help you determine the type of imagery training they need.

Athletes who report that they cannot create a clear, detailed, vivid, lifelike image or who cannot control what happens in their imagery will benefit from practicing some simple imagery exercises. As with physical skill acquisition, learning imagery works best by starting with simple images, then gradually progressing to more complex ones. You could start by simply having athletes view a sport photograph and try to recall the photo in as many details as possible. Or you could have athletes start imaging simple skills that they know well. If they can create a vivid image of those simple skills, progress to more difficult movement patterns and skills. For example, start with stable movement patterns like serving or free-throw shooting and gradually progress to more reactive environments such as game play or running a fast break. Figure 5.2 (pages 74-75) provides an example of exercises designed to help athletes develop their imagery skills.

Coaches can use several strategies to help athletes create clearer and more controllable images. These strategies are particularly helpful for athletes with low imagery ability but can also help those with high imagery ability get the most out of their imagery practice.

Involve All Senses

Including only one sense, such as vision, seldom produces a lifelike image. The more senses athletes stimulate during their imagery, the more vivid and lifelike the image will be. Encourage athletes not only to see themselves performing, but also to create the feel of the movement in their mind and include the other senses as well. For example, ask a soccer player who is only seeing himself dribble to make the image more vivid by including the sound and feel of the ball against his foot as he dribbles and passes.

Develop Sensory Awareness

Athletes who are aware of their internal and external sensory experiences while performing a skill have an easier time creating a vivid image than those who are less mindful. You can help athletes develop **sensory awareness** by designing practice activities to help them become more aware of their sensory experiences as they perform. Athletes need to notice the position of their bodies, the footwork, the timing, the flow of movement, the change of direction, and the preparatory movements before the actual striking or hitting of an object. They need to become more aware of their own visual, kinesthetic, and auditory senses as they participate in their sport. The more athletes see, feel, and hear—and the more they become aware of their mood and emotions—the easier it will be for them to create vivid images. For example, to help a wrestler become more aware of kinesthetic feelings, a coach can have him practice blindfolded, helping him to focus on what a move feels like rather than relying solely on vision. Whatever the sport, you can design practice activities to help athletes develop sensory awareness by tuning into all of the sensory stimuli they experience while performing.

Another technique we have found to create greater awareness is **mindfulness**. This process essentially directs athletes' attention toward cues where greater awareness is desired by asking them to become more mindful of their sensory experience while performing a skill. A sample exercise to develop mindfulness is illustrated in figure 5.3 (page 75); this exercise will help you and your athletes tune in to the sensations associated with the simple act of walking. Before reading the figure, close your eyes and create an image of what it is like to walk.

After completing the mindfulness exercise, close your eyes and imagine yourself walking before you read the rest of this paragraph. You probably observed that you could create a more vivid image of walking after completing the mindfulness exercise. Likewise, coaches can help their athletes become mindful of their behaviors and of what they experience as they participate in their sport. You can adapt the mindfulness exercise to any sport. Simply break the skill into phases and observe the sensations (sights, sounds, feelings, and so on) of each phase. Of course, sport skills also involve timing, as in, for example, shooting a free throw in basketball. Break the skill into phases for observation, including the feel of the ball in the hands, raising the arms, cocking the wrist, extending the arms, releasing the ball, and following through. The athlete can focus on timing by being mindful of the rhythm of shooting free throws, thereby developing greater ability to create a vivid image of it.

Evaluating Imagery Ability

Directions: Below you will read descriptions of four general sport situations.

After you read each general description, think of a specific example of it—the skill, the people involved, the place, and the time. Close your eyes and take a few deep breaths to become as relaxed as you can. Put aside all other thoughts. Keep your eyes closed for about one minute as you try to imagine the situation. If you have distracting thoughts, gently redirect your attention to the scene you are imagining.

There are, of course, no right or wrong images. Your accurate appraisal of your images will help you to determine what skills you need to focus on in the development of your imagery-training program.

After imaging the situation, rate the following imagery dimensions by circling the appropriate number.

- Visual
- Auditory
- Kinesthetic
- Mood and emotion
- Control

Situation 1: Select a specific skill or activity in your sport. Imagine yourself performing the activity in the place where you would normally practice, without anyone else present. Now close your eyes for about one minute and try to see yourself at this place, hear the sounds, feel the body movements, and be aware of your mood.

		Very poorly				Very well
a.	Rate how well you saw yourself performing the activity.	1	2	3	4	5
b.	Rate how well you heard the sounds of performing the activity.	1	2	3	4	5
c.	Rate how well you were able to feel yourself performing the activity.	1	2	3	4	5
d.	Rate how well you were aware of your mood and emotions.	1	2	3	4	5
e.	Rate how well you were able to control your image.	1	2	3	4	5

Situation 2: You are performing the same activity but are now practicing the skill with the coach and your teammates present. This time, however, you make a mistake that everyone notices, but you remain calm, recover quickly, correct your mistake, and perform well. Now close your eyes for about one minute and imagine making the error, correcting it, and performing well as clearly as possible.

		Very poorly				Very well
a.	Rate how well you saw yourself performing the activity.	1	2	3	4	5
b.	Rate how well you heard the sounds of performing the activity.	1	2	3	4	5
c.	Rate how well you were able to feel yourself performing the activity.	1	2	3	4	5
d.	Rate how well you were aware of your mood and emotions.	1	2	3	4	5
e.	Rate how well you were able to control your image.	1	2	3	4	5

From D. Burton and T. Raedeke, 2008, *Sport Psychology for Coaches* (Champaign, IL: Human Kinetics).

(continued)

FIGURE 5.1 Have athletes use this imagery test to evaluate their imagery skills.

Situation 3: Think of a teammate performing a specific activity successfully in a contest—for example, making a 20-foot shot, passing other runners, or making a field goal. Now close your eyes for about one minute to image watching your teammate performing this activity successfully in a critical part of the contest as vividly and realistically as possible.

		Very poorly				Very well
a.	Rate how well you saw your teammate performing the activity.	1	2	3	4	5
b.	Rate how well you heard the sounds of your teammate performing the activity.	1	2	3	4	5
c.	Rate how well you felt your own physical presence in this situation.	1	2	3	4	5
d.	Rate how well you were aware of your mood and emotions.	1	2	3	4	5
e.	Rate how well you were able to control your image.	1	2	3	4	5

Situation 4: Imagine yourself performing the same or a similar activity in a contest, but imagine yourself performing very skillfully. Spectators and teammates show their appreciation. Now close your eyes for about one minute to imagine the situation as vividly as possible.

		Very poorly				Very well
a.	Rate how well you saw yourself performing the activity.	1	2	3	4	5
b.	Rate how well you heard the sounds of performing the activity.	1	2	3	4	5
c.	Rate how well you were able to feel yourself performing the activity.	1	2	3	4	5
d.	Rate how well you were aware of your mood and emotions.	1	2	3	4	5
e.	Rate how well you were able to control your image.	1	2	3	4	5

Now add up your responses to each question and write your scores in the spaces that follow.

Dimension	Score
Visual (all "a" Items)	____
Auditory (all "b" Items)	____
Kinesthetic (all "c" items)	____
Mood (all "d" Items)	____
Control (all "e" items)	____
Total	____

Compare your scores for each dimension to the following skill categories.

Score	Rating
18-20	Good skills. Periodically do an exercise to keep yourself sharp.
13-17	Average development of skills. Spend time each week improving these skills.
0-12	These dimensions need daily attention to bring your imagery skills to a useful level.

From D. Burton and T. Raedeke, 2008, *Sport Psychology for Coaches* (Champaign, IL: Human Kinetics).

FIGURE 5.1 *(continued)*

Imagery Training Exercises

Directions: Read or tape-record the description of each of the images below. Then produce the image and rate the vividness of your images by circling the number that corresponds best to the quality of your images.

Sport Arena

Imagine yourself in the setting your normally perform your sport (gym, pool, rink, field, track, etc.). It is very quiet because nobody is there except for you. As you stand in the middle of the site look around and become aware of your surroundings. Pick out as many details as you can. What do you see? What does it smell like? What sounds do you hear? Now imagine yourself in the same setting, but this time as you prepare for competition. Your teammates and spectators are there. Imagine yourself getting ready to perform. See the spectators, your teammates, your coach, and the opponents. Become aware of the sounds. You may notice the sound of a noisy crowd, your teammates talking, your coach offering encouragement, and all the other sounds you associate with your sport (e.g., the sound of skates on ice, balls bouncing). Notice the smells you associate with your sport. Re-create the feelings of nervous anticipation and excitement that you have before competing.

	Low				High
Overall vividness	1	2	3	4	5
Visual vividness	1	2	3	4	5
Kinesthetic vividness	1	2	3	4	5
Auditory vividness	1	2	3	4	5
Emotional vividness	1	2	3	4	5

Sport Equipment

Choose a piece of equipment in your sport, whether it be a ball, racket, or stick. Focus your attention on this object. Create a detailed picture of it in your mind. Turn it over in your hands and feel the fine details of the object. Become aware of what it feels like, such as its texture. Now imagine yourself performing with the object. See yourself very clearly performing the activity. Visualize yourself repeating the skill over and over. Try to see yourself performing from behind your own eyes. Then step outside of your body and see yourself perform as if you were watching yourself on film. Now, step back in your body and continue performing. Become aware of what it feels like to perform the skill. How do your muscles feel, what is your breathing like? Next, try to hear the sounds that accompany the movement. Now become aware of all the sounds being made as you perform this skill.

	Low				High
Overall vividness	1	2	3	4	5
Visual vividness	1	2	3	4	5
Kinesthetic vividness	1	2	3	4	5
Auditory vividness	1	2	3	4	5
Emotional vividness	1	2	3	4	5

FIGURE 5.2 Imagery exercises such as these can help athletes develop their imagery skills.

Sport Skill

Pick a very simple skill in your sport that you know how to perform well. Perform the skill over and over in your mind and imagine every feeling and movement in your muscles as you perform that skill. Become aware of how the different parts of your body feel as perform the skill. Notice the stretch and pull of your muscles. Now try to combine all of your senses, but particularly those of feeling and seeing yourself perform the skill over and over. Try to imagine the total experience using all of your senses.

	Low				High
Overall vividness	1	2	3	4	5
Visual vividness	1	2	3	4	5
Kinesthetic vividness	1	2	3	4	5
Auditory vividness	1	2	3	4	5
Emotional vividness	1	2	3	4	5

Adapted from R.S. Vealey and C.S. Greenleaf, 2006, Seeing is believing: Understanding and using imagery in sport. In *Applied sport psychology: Personal growth to peak performance*, 5th ed., edited by J.M. Williams (Mountain View, CA: Mayfield Publishing), 322–323, by permission of The McGraw-Hill Companies.

FIGURE 5.2 *(continued)*

Mindfulness Exercise

To prepare for this exercise, clear a space large enough to allow you to take several steps—forward, backward, and sideways—without bumping into anything. Remove any potentially distracting items from the area. You can either record the following and play it back or have someone read it to you.

Walking Script

Begin to walk slowly in a large circle. Direct all of your attention to your feet (pause 10 seconds). Notice the sensations associated with each step. You lift your foot (wait 5 seconds); you place it on the ground in front of you (wait 5 seconds); and you put your weight onto that foot (wait 5 seconds). Concentrate on the sensations of each phase: the lift . . . (pause 5 seconds), the place . . . (pause 5 seconds), and the put . . . (pause 10 seconds). Walk slowly and complete one full step before you begin the next. Become totally aware of the sensation of walking . . . (pause 10 seconds): the lift . . . (pause 5 seconds), the place . . . (pause 5 seconds), and the put . . . (pause 10 seconds).

Now close your eyes and continue walking, focusing your attention on the feeling of walking. If your mind wanders, don't worry. Gently bring it back to the task at hand—observing the sensations of walking: the lift (pause 5 seconds), the place . . . (pause 5 seconds), and the put . . . (pause 5 seconds). Lift . . . (pause 5 seconds), place . . . (pause 5 seconds), and put (pause 40 seconds). Lift . . . (pause 10 seconds), place.. . (pause 10 seconds), and put.

Adapted from D. Goleman (narrator), 1976, *Flow and mindfulness: An instructional cassette* (New York, NY: Psychology Today).

FIGURE 5.3 **Here is a sample exercise to develop mindfulness.**

A final strategy for developing sensory awareness is to use observation in conjunction with imagery. Watching (on video or in person) someone else perform a skill helps athletes become more aware of key techniques and timing issues before attempting to image that skill themselves. Observation does not create awareness of what it feels like to perform the skills, but it does enable visual and auditory sensory awareness. NBA coach Phil Jackson, for one, makes use of this technique. If he cannot develop a clear image of an upcoming opponent, he will study tapes for hours until he becomes familiar with the opposing team's style of play so he can start imaging an effective game plan.

Use Vivid Cues

Vivid cues can also help create clear images, and some coaches keep a notebook listing cues that help athletes experience what it looks and feels like to perform a skill. For example, a dancer or gymnast might imagine her back against a cold steel wall to create the image of a straight body during a routine. Creative golf professionals help players image their arms as a pendulum to create the feel of swinging from the shoulder during putting; they might also envision skipping a rock to create the feel of a golf swing or dragging a mop across the ground to develop the sensation of one's hands leading the club head through the hitting area (Rotella 1997). Coaches can also use short words to focus attention on key elements of performance during imagery, such as "quick bat" in baseball or softball or "plant and square up" in basketball. Vivid cues help trigger a vivid image of the desired form or technique.

Include Both the Situation and Responses

Images consist of two parts—the description of the situation and the athlete's response to it (Lang 1979). A soccer player preparing for an important competition might create a scenario in her mind by imagining the stadium, the crowd noise, and various tactical situations she could face during the game. The image should also address how she will respond, including actions, physiological feelings, and emotions. She might imagine the feel of the soccer ball against her foot, the sensation of fatigue and heaviness in her legs, and the feelings of excitement as she prepares to execute a clear shot on goal during the closing minutes of the game. If you are helping athletes create an image, describe the situation in very vivid terms, but also provide guidance as to how they should respond in specific situations.

Ensure Relaxed Attention

When athletes are first learning imagery, they have an easier time focusing when relaxed in a quiet environment away from distractions. Those who are highly skilled can use this mental training tool in almost any setting, whether at home, during practice warm-ups, on the bus ride to a competition, or in a noise-filled stadium. Few athletes possess such skill, however, so most need initially to practice imagery in a quiet setting. Another key to creating lifelike images is to allow the image to happen, rather than trying to make it happen. Using imagery is a passive process that requires relaxed attention. Remind athletes to relax and let the image develop. If they lose focus, instruct them to gently redirect attention back to their image.

Use Props

Some athletes find it helpful to use a prop or object involved in their sport to help them initiate or focus on their image. Basketball players may find it useful to hold a ball when they play the game mentally. Bruce Jenner, winner of the 1976 Olympic decathlon, reportedly kept a hurdle in his living room. When asked why, he said he would mentally jump over it whenever he was lying on the couch. Gustav Weder, a great Swiss bobsledder, took photographs of the entire course when previewing an upcoming competition. He would then lay it out at home, photo by photo, and imagine himself racing the course to develop his strategy (Murphy, 1996).

Use Partial Movements

Some athletes find it hard to create a vivid image while lying down because they do not execute their sport skills from that position. A wrestler may find it easier to create a vivid image by getting into a position similar to that used when actually wrestling. Many athletes also find that performing partial movements makes it easier to create vivid images. A volleyball player might move her arms as though she were serving, and a snowboarder might move as though carving a turn.

Use Imagery to Develop Physical and Mental Skills

In addition to appreciating the merits of imagery and developing their imagery skills, athletes should recognize that imagery has nearly countless applications and potential uses (Hall 2001; Munroe, Giacobbi, Hall, & Weinberg 2000; Orlick & Partington 1988; Murphy & Martin 2002). Given that, in several respects, the mind interprets a vivid image and a real sport experience similarly, imagery can be used to develop any skill or strategy that can be practiced physically. It can also be a powerful tool for mastering the mental game.

Using Imagery to Learn and Master Physical Skills

Learning physical skills is one of the more commonly known uses of imagery. Athletes can mentally rehearse anything from shooting free throws to driving golf balls to performing gymnastics routines in order to learn, fine-tune, or automate these skills. As a coach you can help athletes use imagery to improve their physical skills by integrating imagery into practice. For example, after listening to a coach's instructions or observing a demonstration, athletes can imagine themselves performing a desired skill before physically practicing it. Immediately after executing a skill effectively, athletes can create a vivid image of their performance while it is fresh in their memory, thus helping etch the mental blueprint into the mind. After a practice session, they can use imagery to review key points.

Imagery can also be used to help athletes correct mistakes and refine their form. Here are several strategies: Have athletes imagine what their form looks like and then imagine what the ideal or desired form looks like. By comparing the two, athletes develop awareness of what they need to do to correct their form. Athletes can also watch video of someone else performing a skill, or watch a teammate who is technically sound, then imagine themselves performing the skill with the desired form before practicing it physically. You can also have athletes imagine a skill they are struggling with. If they make a mistake or perform the skill incorrectly in their mind, instruct them to stop the image and redo it correctly.

Using Imagery to Learn and Master Strategy

Imagery can be used to help athletes learn and master the strategic aspect of their sport. For example, mountain bike racers benefit from imagining a particular course and how they will respond to difficult sections of it; in doing so, they begin to form a strategy for competition. Golf pros recognize that one key to success is to recognize situations and pick the smartest shots, a process they call "course management." Thus golfers may play a course in their mind as they practice, envisioning various scenarios and the shots they would need to make in each one. They then select a club and hit the appropriate shot. In team sports, visualizing what might occur during a game, and

how they would respond, enables athletes to react without hesitation, without thinking, because they have already seen it happen in their mind.

Coaches can help athletes learn the strategic side of their game by using imagery in conjunction with chalkboard illustrations, video analysis, and walk-throughs. When viewing chalkboard illustrations, athletes find that imaging the Xs and Os as players, rather than as symbols on the board, makes the scenario more lifelike and meaningful. Before or after walking through a play, athletes can image their role in the effective execution of that play. Imagery sessions also provide a great bridge between video sessions and practice. Rather than just watching video, using imagery helps athletes become more actively involved in developing strategy. For example, they can watch video of an opponent, then image how they would respond to the opponent's style of play. Even while sitting on the bench, athletes can imagine playing in the game and responding to various situations; this not only helps them improve their strategy but also keeps them in the flow of the game.

Using Imagery to Improve Mental Skills

So far, we have discussed how athletes can employ imagery to enhance their physical skills and use of strategy. It can also help them improve their mental game by developing self-awareness, enhancing self-confidence and motivation, managing stress and energy, and improving focus and concentration.

Developing Self-Awareness—Recall from chapter 3 that increasing self-awareness is a building block in helping athletes improve their mental game. Imagery can help athletes become more aware of the psychological states they experience when competing. Ask athletes to recall times when they played very well, when concentration was automatic and events flowed easily, when self-doubt was nonexistent. Have them investigate these feelings and use the resultant images as cues to create the feeling they want as they enter competition. This process makes them more aware of what mental state helps them perform best and which strategies help them enter that frame of mind. Athletes can also use imagery to help themselves develop key skills and qualities for becoming the type of performer they want to be: taking a calm, cool, collected approach to competition; developing the ability to maintain composure after mistakes; or demonstrating the demeanor required of a team leader. In this way, athletes can develop awareness of specific actions and attitudes to help them move toward their ideal image.

Using Imagery to Plan Race Strategy

Murphy and Jowdy relate how a three-time Olympian used imagery to plan his race strategy.

It's as if I carry around a set of tapes in my mind. I play them occasionally, rehearsing different race strategies. Usually I imagine the race going the way I want—I set my pace and stick to it. But I have other tapes as well—situations where someone goes out real fast and I have to catch him, or imagining how I will cope if the weather gets really hot. I even have a "disaster" tape where everything goes wrong and I'm hurting badly, and I imagine myself gutting it out. (Murphy & Jowdy 1992, p. 242)

You can also ask athletes to recall previous sport experiences that provoked anxiety or anger. This exercise helps athletes become more aware of factors that throw them off their mental game plan, so they can develop strategies for responding more effectively. For example, a hockey player tends to become angry and lose his cool when the opposing team takes cheap shots or when officials miss calls. Through imagery, the athlete is taught to become aware of the specific situations that cause him to lose his composure and of his mental state before and after such events. Next, the coach teaches the player how to use mental training tools such as self-talk and deep breathing to manage his emotions and focus his attention. The player is then taught to imagine various negative events, and he imagines remaining focused and performing well by using self-talk to direct his anger to the task at hand.

Enhancing Self-Confidence and Motivation—Some athletes find it difficult to sustain their motivation when faced with several weeks of practice without an important competition. For them, imagining themselves playing in front of a cheering audience and seeing themselves perform well can invigorate and sustain their motivation. Athletes find replaying outstanding performances or imagining themselves attaining goals to be motivational and confidence inspiring. Here are a few other possibilities: Create a highlight video capturing those perfect moments when athletes are performing well and achieving their goals. After athletes view the highlight video, instruct them to imagine themselves playing with confidence in an upcoming competition. Before practice, you can have athletes visualize their goals, the steps they will use to reach them, and the successful attainment of their goals. Such goal programming can increase motivation and help athletes focus their attention during practice. After practice, if athletes did not accomplish their goals, have

them use imagery to solve problems and develop action plans to help them attain the goals in the next practice.

Managing Stress—It is not uncommon for athletes lose their poise in the face of adversity or when a competition does not go as planned. Imaging things that might go wrong or factors that could throw off their game plan enables athletes to develop an action plan for overcoming such obstacles. It also gives athletes confidence to know that they have prepared for the unexpected. Here is a classic example from Al Oerter, four-time Olympic gold medalist in the discus throw:

I used to imagine that it was the day of the Olympic trials, the day that I had spent the last four years preparing for, and that it was raining. Pouring rain. The throwing area was slippery, conditions were atrocious, and I had to go out and throw anyway. And I imagined myself throwing well. I visualized myself throwing strongly, with good technique despite the rain. Or sometimes I would imagine that I was down to my last throw in the Olympic finals. The Russian was competing right ahead of me, and with his last throw he set a world record. So to win the gold medal, I now had to set a new world record! On my last throw of the Games, I would imagine that I did just that; I would see myself setting a new world record. Those were the things I visualized. I thought about what might go wrong, and I imagined responding to the challenge. (Murphy 1996, p. 67)

Energy Management—Imagery can be used to help athletes manage their arousal and achieve their ideal energy level before competition. Some athletes find it effective to imagine themselves in a place they associate with calmness and tranquility—a mountain meadow, a beach, or another place they associate with relaxation (see chapter 6 for more details). NBA coach Phil Jackson has used an imagery exercise called the safe spot. He found that players were so keyed up that they could not concentrate on what he was saying during time-outs, so he had them spend a few seconds imagining themselves in a place where they felt secure. This reduced their anxiety and focused their attention on the task at hand when they returned to the court (Jackson & Delehanty 1995).

On the other hand, an athlete feeling flat or fatigued needs to increase arousal and energy levels, and one way to do so is through the use of energizing images. For example, triathletes may visualize themselves as an efficient machine, a train that is unstoppable, a fish that glides effortlessly through the water, or a greyhound that moves quickly and efficiently. Others energize themselves by imagining themselves starting up their energy shoes or running effortlessly on a conveyor belt while everyone else is running in sticky tar. The key is for athletes to find an image that brings them to an energized state of readiness.

Focusing Attention—Imagery can be used to focus athletes' attention on the task at hand. Before practice, athletes can review their goals and focus on what they want to accomplish. During practice, they can use imagery to focus before executing a skill. A tennis player might imagine the perfect serve, or a baseball pitcher the perfect slider. Athletes can also use imagery as part of their mental preparation routine before competition (see chapter 13).

Developing an Imagery Training Program

You now know what imagery is and are aware that it is effective in improving performance. You have also learned keys to using imagery effectively. But one ingredient is still missing: the steps involved in designing a systematic imagery training program. Imagery training should not be viewed as something extra athletes need to do, rather it should be an integral part of the sport experience. Incorporating imagery into practice sessions on a regular basis ensures that athletes achieve its full benefits and learn to transfer it to competition preparation. This final section outlines a training program you can use to help your athletes develop this essential mental training tool through the three-step process of education, acquisition, and implementation.

Education Phase

The first step is to introduce imagery to your athletes. Your goal is to get them interested in this mental training tool by creating a strong belief in the power of imagery. You can use information from the earlier parts of this chapter, testimonials from some of your more experienced athletes who have successfully used imagery, and published accounts from elite or professional athletes, some of which are included in this chapter. The second step in the education phase is to evaluate athletes' strengths and weaknesses in creating vivid and controlled images that incorporate all the senses. You can have athletes complete figure 5.1 to assess their imagery skills, then discuss the results to highlight strengths and target areas that can be improved with practice. Although athletes should be encouraged to use imagery outside of practice sessions, it is critical that coaches teach them how to do so.

Acquisition Phase

The primary goal in the acquisition phase is to help athletes develop the ability to create vivid and controlled images. Including all the senses helps create the most lifelike and effective images, but the visual and kinesethic senses are especially important in most sports. In developing athletes' imagery ability, start with simple sport skills and gradually build up to more complex skills as athletes become more proficient at using imagery. The imagery program does not need to take a great deal of time. In fact, a few minutes a day can be beneficial, and in the beginning athletes should only focus on imagery for a short time so that the experience is appealing and user friendly. During this phase, help your athletes develop their imagery skills by involving all the senses, using vivid cues, focusing on the situation and the performer's response, using props, and doing partial movements as part of their imagery. Integrate the use of imagery into practice but also encourage athletes to practice it on their own to further sharpen their skills.

Implementation Phase

Once your athletes have developed basic imagery skills, your goal is to help build imagery into their daily routine by incorporating it into practice and competition. You can use some of the techniques described earlier in the chapter to incorporate imagery into practice sessions: If athletes execute a skill well, encourage them to take a moment to form an image of that execution, so that it is etched in their mind. Before practice, encourage athletes to create images of themselves accomplishing their goals for the session. If an athlete is bringing a lot of life stress into practice, have him or her imagine a calm place (e.g., a field, beach, or mountain) in order to relax and get mentally prepared for practice.

Imagery practice must be systematic to achieve desired benefits. Athletes often fall short on this. They may use imagery 1 or 2 days before competition but not on a regular basis. Although they may realize some benefits from haphazard use, imagery is most effective when practiced systematically. Initially, imagery practice should primarily involve rehearsal of physical skills and strategy. Then have athletes gradually move into using imagery to develop mental skills, such as confidence, motivation, stress management, and attention, depending on their specific needs. After athletes have practiced using imagery during practice sessions, gradually introduce it during competition. Encourage athletes to use imagery in the locker room before competition and on the bench during competi-

tion. You might use it for arousal control before competition or during time-outs. Athletes who compete in individual events can use imagery between events to manage stress, create the best arousal level, and imagine accomplishing their performance goals.

Periodically evaluate the imagery program to assess its effectiveness. As part of this process, evaluate the vividness and controllability of athletes' images by simply asking them to rate these qualities of their image on a scale of 1 to 5. As part of the evaluation process, some athletes benefit from keeping an imagery log or journal, in which they describe what they imagined, the session's goal, the vividness and controllability of the image, and the effectiveness of the session.

SUMMARY

1. Using imagery is more than just visualization. It means involving all of the senses to create or re-create an experience in your mind.

2. Increasing evidence suggests that imagery is effective in improving performance.

3. Imagery is most effective as a supplement rather than a replacement for physical practice, but it can also be used when athletes are unable to practice physically due to fatigue, injury, or lack of access to facilities or equipment.

4. In many respects, the mind cannot distinguish between a vivid image and a real experience. Imagery can be used to improve any skill that can be practiced physically as well as to help develop mental skills.

5. Although all athletes benefit from imagery, skilled athletes gain more than less skilled athletes, and those who have strong imagery skills benefit more than those with less developed imagery skills.

6. Imagery ability consists of being able to create vivid and controlled images.

7. Both internal and external perspectives are effective. Athletes should choose the perspective that results in the most vivid images but practice using both perspectives as each has unique advantages.

8. Three keys to helping athletes get the most out of imagery are convincing them of its effectiveness, helping them develop their imagery ability, and helping them recognize that imagery has nearly countless applications.

9. To help athletes create vivid and controlled images, encourage them to involve more than one sense in their imagery, develop sensory awareness, use vivid cues, include both situational and response characteristics in imagery, practice imagery when relaxed, and make use of props and partial movements.

10. An imagery training program should be founded on the three-phase approach to developing and using mental training tools: education, acquisition, and implementation.

11. To achieve full benefits from imagery, athletes need to practice it on a consistent basis, and you can help by regularly integrating imagery into practice settings.

KEY TERMS

external imagery

imagery

imagery control

imagery vividness

internal imagery

kinesthetic feel

mindfulness

sensory awareness

REVIEW QUESTIONS

1. Is imagery the same thing as visualization? Why or why not?

2. What is the distinction between internal and external imagery perspectives? What would you see in your favorite sport if using imagery from an internal perspective? From an external perspective? Is one perspective more effective than the other? Why or why not?

3. Although physical practice is generally more effective than imagery, when would using imagery be more beneficial than physical practice?

4. Why do experienced athletes benefit more from imagery than novice athletes?

5. How can imagery be used to help athletes manage stress?

PRACTICAL ACTIVITIES

1. As a coach, you believe in the power of imagery and want your athletes to start using it. Describe some ways you could incorporate imagery into practice sessions.

2. Imagine that you are coaching a high school track team. One of your high jumpers possesses great talent but has recently plateaued. After discussing imagery with her, you realize that she could create only a weak and incomplete image of a jump. How can you help her create vivid, lifelike images?

3. You are coaching a physically gifted athlete who plays well in practice and during the early parts of a game. Toward the end of a game, however, he tends to play tentatively—"not to lose" rather than to win. At these times, he tends to lose focus and is easily distracted by events that he cannot control (e.g., calls that go the other team's way, lucky shots by the other team). Design a specific imagery program for this athlete.

4. You have an injured athlete who will miss at least 1 month of practice time. How could the athlete use imagery while injured to facilitate the transition back to competition?

5. Some athletes on your team are hesitant to use imagery. What would you say and do to convince them that imagery can help them perform better?

6. Develop an imagery script that an athlete could use in your sport to help learn a physical skill or to help prepare mentally for competition.

Relaxation and Energization

After reading this chapter, you should be able to

- understand what relaxation is and differentiate between total and rapid relaxation,
- explain the benefits of total and rapid relaxation and describe some of the common relaxation techniques,
- describe the basic guidelines for choosing a relaxation technique and conducting relaxation practice,
- understand energization and describe how to develop both total and rapid energization skills,
- explain the benefits of energization and describe several energization strategies,
- describe the basic guidelines for choosing an energization technique and conducting energization practice, and
- understand how to help athletes develop and automate relaxation and energization skills.

No doubt you have coached athletes who were so tense or "freaked-out" that it prevented them from performing their best at key times, such as attempting a game-winning free throw, penalty kick, or field goal. You have probably also watched athletes run out of gas late in a contest, get outhustled by a fresh opponent, or fail to push through the fatigue barrier during long, grueling training sessions. Any of these athletes would benefit from developing the mental training tools of **relaxation** and **energization**.

These tools are important to success in most sports, but in some they are absolutely essential. Biathlon, for example, requires athletes to both relax and energize effectively as well as to switch quickly between the two behaviors. Biathlon performers ski a challenging cross-country course, often at high altitude, that tests the bounds of energization capabilities. On each loop, skiers stop at the shooting range and must relax enough within a few seconds to accurately shoot five targets before skiing another demanding cross-country leg. Not every sport places such extreme demands for relaxation and energization, but athletes who want to perform their best in any sport must be competent at both. For example, an outside hitter in volleyball must bring high energy for power skills, such as executing a stuff block or hitting high off the blocker's hands, while at the same time relaxing effectively to execute precision skills such as passing or tipping over the block.

Coaches readily recognize the importance of relaxation and energization in competitive success, often encouraging athletes either to relax or to "psych up" if they want to perform successfully. Most athletes, however, have never been taught the requisite skills and simply don't know how to relax or energize on command. This chapter teaches you how to help your athletes learn relaxation and energization fundamentals, as well as how to automate these important mental training tools.

What Is Relaxation?

To relax is to decrease unwanted muscular tension, reduce excessive activation of the sympathetic nervous system (associated with adrenaline and elevated heart rate), and calm the mind by keeping it productively occupied. When the sympathetic nervous system is activated, athletes experience the fight-or-flight response—they feel anxious and experience physical symptoms of stress, such as increased heart rate, goose bumps, butterflies in the stomach, and perspiration. A number of relaxation techniques have been adapted for use in sport to elicit the "relaxation response" that relaxes tense muscles, lowers unwanted arousal, and calms the mind.

In creating the relaxation response, the mind and body function as an integrated system. **Muscle-to-mind techniques** such as **diaphragmic breathing** and progressive muscle relaxation (PMR) are designed primarily to relax the body, which in turn calms the mind. In contrast, **mind-to-muscle techniques**, such as imagery and meditation, focus on calming the mind in order to relax the body (Martens, 1987). Both approaches can be useful to athletes. A basketball player may find that alleviating unwanted muscular tension before he shoots a crucial free throw helps calm his mind and boost his confidence; his tension is triggered physically, but using a muscle-to-mind technique also helps him relax mentally. A softball pitcher who tenses up before a big pitch may discover that the mind-to-muscle technique of imagery relaxation enables her to feel comfortable emotionally and thus to relax physically.

Some muscle-to-mind techniques aim to reduce muscular tension, while others focus on lowering excessive activation, and some do both. A sprinter might use strategies targeting muscular tension in order to reduce the hamstring tightness that reduces stride length and slows turnover. A place-kicker might use strategies designed to reduce excessive arousal to slow his pounding heart and get his butterflies to fly in formation before he attempts a game-winning field goal. The most effective techniques simultaneously reduce unwanted muscular tension and lower excessive arousal, and they work even better when they combine physical and mental strategies. Progressive muscle relaxation, for example, combines tension-relaxation cycles (to reduce unwanted muscular tension) and diaphragmic breathing (to reduce excessive activation) with imagery or cue words (to calm the mind). This chapter addresses the physical aspects of relaxation, and the next chapter (Self-Talk) focuses on mental relaxation.

Basic Relaxation Model

Although relaxation is a valuable and versatile mental training tool, it can be misused if athletes do not distinguish between and master both **total relaxation** and **rapid relaxation**. For example, a high school basketball coach I worked with had a talented player named Terry who got extremely stressed when he played, seldom demonstrating in competition the extraordinary skills he showed in practice. The coach taught Terry how to do PMR, but, not understanding the difference between the two approaches, he taught only the total relaxation technique. Terry was transformed from nervous, distraught, and hyperactive to lethargic, sluggish, and passive. Even if athletes develop the ability to relax off the field, court, or track—when they have plenty of time and little interference—they often can't relax quickly before and during competition when faced with a multitude of distractions. To be effective, then, coaches need to help athletes develop relaxation skills that work quickly in practice and competition.

Our relaxation model develops both total and rapid relaxation (see figure 6.1). Total relaxation is a lengthier strategy (10–20 minutes or more) that helps athletes relax as completely as possible, whereas rapid relaxation is an abbreviated form that allows optimal relaxation in a few seconds. Total relaxation can be used to help athletes alleviate chronic stress and anxiety and to recover from workouts and injuries. Learning total relaxation techniques can also help athletes develop rapid relaxation skills. Most sport situations don't allow 10 minutes for relaxation, so rapid relaxation techniques need to work on the spot (generally, in 3–5 seconds) in order to be useful to athletes. In fact, as in the case of Terry, employing total relaxation during practice or competition is usually counterproductive, because it overrelaxes athletes, leaving them flat, lethargic, and unable to perform their best. Athletes need techniques they can use on the fly, either while performing or during momentary breaks in the action.

Total Relaxation and Energization

- The objective is to attain maximal relaxation or energization.
- Take as long as needed to reach a deeply relaxed or energized state (8 or above on a scale from 1 to 10, with 10 being the most relaxed or energized).
- Use diaphragmic breathing with any effective relaxation strategy.
- Use "psych-up" breathing with any effective energization strategy.

Cued Relaxation and Energization

- This technique links total relaxation or energization with rapid relaxation or energization.
- Pair your relaxation cue word with a deeply relaxed state and your energization cue word with a highly energized state.
- Repeat your relaxation cue word each time you exhale, focusing on breathing and how relaxation feels.
- Repeat your energization cue word after every 3 psych-up breaths, focusing on breathing and how energization feels.

Rapid Relaxation and Energization

- Rapid relaxation and energization are designed to develop optimal relaxation and energization levels in practice and competitive situations.
- For rapid relaxation, take 1 or 2 diaphragmic breaths and repeat your relaxation cue word after each exhalation.
- For rapid energization, take 3 to 6 psych-up breaths and repeat your energization cue word after exhalation on every third breath.

FIGURE 6.1 Relaxation and energization development model.

No technique will get used by athletes if it works too slowly or creates too much or too little relaxation. When a basketball player steps to the line for the game-winning free throw, he has to be able to relax rapidly by taking one or two diaphragmic breaths while repeating his cue word. In those few seconds, rapid relaxation should lower tension and activation to optimal levels. Phil Jackson used the rapid relaxation idea with the Chicago Bulls, having his players relax physically and elicit mental calm during the first 15 to 30 seconds of time-outs so they could increase their focus before discussing strategy (Jackson & Delehanty 1995). The next two sections review the benefits of total and rapid relaxation.

Benefits of Total Relaxation

Total relaxation helps athletes in at least four ways: alleviating chronic stress to help them enjoy life more fully, promoting recovery from workouts and injuries, improving sleep, and developing rapid relaxation skills.

- *Alleviates chronic stress.* Estimates suggest that 20% to 30% of athletes suffer from chronic stress that, if not managed properly, reduces their capabilities. And all athletes experience periods of stress caused by major life crises such as breaking up with a longtime boyfriend or girlfriend, battling for playing time with a close friend, or experiencing academic problems. Stress can also result from an accumulation of smaller stressors that are difficult to resolve. In any of these cases, practicing total relaxation on a daily basis can help reduce stress to manageable levels.

- *Promotes recovery from workouts and injuries.* Half of training is recovery. Each tough workout takes a toll on the body due to minor tissue damage and accumulation of lactic acid in the muscles. Active regeneration techniques such as relaxation and massage promote recovery by stimulating dilation of blood vessels to supply more oxygen to fatigued or injured muscles, enhancing disposal of waste products, and speeding up the repair process.

- *Improves sleep.* Sleep is deeper and more restful when a person is relaxed. Athletes who sleep poorly often suffer from tension or excessive arousal problems that are magnified when traveling or on the night before competition. Sleep problems before a game can stem from positive excitement or negative nervousness, as well as extensive cognitive concerns about doing well. Taking time to relax promotes better sleep by lowering tension, reducing excessive activation, and calming the mind.

- *Develops rapid relaxation skills.* Total relaxation is essential in developing rapid relaxation skills. Rapid relaxation requires first experiencing deep levels of total relaxation, then pairing those feelings and related breathing cues with a cue word that can be used to trigger relaxation when needed during practice and competition. Athletes must first learn what complete relaxation feels like in order to trigger optimal relaxation when needed during competition.

Benefits of Rapid Relaxation

Rapid relaxation is an abbreviated technique designed to help performers relax optimally in a few seconds. This practical technique enhances performance by reducing tension, promoting better arousal control, breaking the stress spiral, promoting an unconscious trusting attitude, conserving energy, and increasing enjoyment.

- *Reduces muscular tension.* Rapid relaxation reduces tension in antagonistic muscles, giving athletes greater range of motion and better rhythm, timing, and feel. A classic example of excessive tension in antagonistic muscles occurs when a basketball player air-balls a crucial free throw. Since muscles can only contract, they are arranged in pairs: The first muscle contracts to initiate a movement, then its antagonistic muscle contracts to return the joint to its original position. When a muscle contracts at the same time as its antagonistic partner, the two muscles fight each other, hindering rhythm, timing, feel, and range of motion. In the tense free-throw shooter's arm, muscles are fighting each other, and she fails to go through a full range of motion, thus leaving the shot well short. Although this is clearly one type of "choking," its cause is more physical than mental. Rapid relaxation reduces or eliminates excessive tension in antagonistic muscles so that movement patterns remain smooth, fluid, rhythmic, and well timed.

- *Controls arousal.* Athletes who fail to control their arousal level can experience excessive activation—the fight-or-flight response—which causes physical and mental symptoms of stress. Overaroused performers can use relaxation to lower activation levels and reduce physical anxiety, thus enabling them to attain the optimal arousal level needed for top performance (see chapter 9 for more on arousal management).

- *Breaks the stress spiral.* Acute (short-term) stress is a problem for many athletes, especially in terms of handling pressure and letting go of mistakes. Under stress, athletes' minds begin to race; they lose awareness of what's going on around them, and they often panic and feel overwhelmed. Rapid relaxation can help your athletes lower their arousal to a more effective level, slow down, let go of excess tension, and think more constructively. Relaxation also reduces feelings of pressure and promotes expectations of success. Although mistakes can take athletes out of their game by causing them to focus on negative thoughts, rapid relaxation promotes feelings of control that help athletes let go of mistakes.

- *Promotes an unconscious trusting attitude.* When athletes experience flow, they operate at an unconscious level where they completely trust their bodies to execute skills. Relaxation can provide an important bridge between conscious preparation (e.g., selecting what play to call or identifying how you want to play the next point) and unconscious performance. Athletes use rapid relaxation in conjunction with imagery to trigger automated performance rather than trying too hard. For example, a volleyball player serving a critical point uses rapid relaxation to let go of her fears of serving poorly so she can trust her body to execute automatically with the match on the line.

- *Conserves energy.* Relaxation can play an important role in endurance-based performance. Demanding endurance events such as marathons require runners to develop relaxation skills that enhance mechanical efficiency to maximize energy reserves and maintain a faster pace (Ziegler, Klinzing, & Williamson 1982). Multiday events such as wrestling tournaments can also become endurance tests, and performers need the ability to conserve energy and maximize recovery time so they can continue to perform aggressively during the later stages of the competition.

- *Increases enjoyment.* Performing while you're tight or stressed is no fun. Relaxation can dramatically increase your enjoyment of sport by reducing muscular tension and excessive activation symptoms (e.g., butterflies).

Relaxation Strategies

Remember that relaxation is best accomplished through both the total and rapid approaches. Total relaxation strategies take longer and lead athletes to a completely relaxed state. Athletes must be able to achieve total relaxation on a consistent basis before they will be able to accomplish the rapid relaxation that is needed in the heat of competition.

Common Total Relaxation Strategies

Numerous total relaxation strategies have been used to enhance sport performance. We focus here on five strategies we've found most effective and easiest for coaches to implement: diaphragmic breathing, **imagery relaxation**, **progressive muscle relaxation**, **self-directed relaxation**, and music. Regardless of the technique chosen, athletes should follow these guidelines: Select a quiet and comfortable setting with minimal distractions; take a passive attitude that focuses on breathing and letting go of worries and concerns; choose a comfortable but serious practice environment; and find a comfortable position, preferably sitting in a comfortable chair, with arms supported, feet uncrossed, and eyes closed. (Lying down might not be the best choice because it often promotes falling asleep.)

Diaphragmic Breathing

Deep diaphragmic breathing was developed to facilitate hatha yoga and involves fully filling the lungs by expanding the diaphragm, the thin muscle that separates the lungs from the abdominal cavity. Inhaling through the nose causes the diaphragm to move down slightly, pushing the abdomen out and creating a vacuum that allows the lungs to be filled from the bottom up in three distinct phases. First, as your diaphragm expands and your abdomen is pushed outward, you can feel the area under your belly button enlarge as your lower lungs are filled. Next, the middle portion of your lungs is filled by allowing your rib cage to expand. Finally, your chest and shoulders are raised slightly and the upper third of your lungs is filled. The inhalation should be followed by a healthy pause, then a slow and complete exhalation through the mouth. The inhalation should be slow and deliberate, taking about as long as the exhalation. Some experts recommend a slight sigh at the end of the exhalation to maximize the amount of air expired. Diaphragmic breathing should be used in combination with an athlete's preferred relaxation strategy to help reduce excessive activation.

Imagery Relaxation

In imagery relaxation, athletes imagine taking a minivacation to a place where they feel relaxed and comfortable—strolling through a peaceful wood, sitting by a fire in a remote cabin, lying on a beach under the warm sun as a cool breeze blows and waves rhythmically lap the shore (see the sample script on pages 88-89). In fact, they can go anywhere they find relaxing, including their bed at home. What is important is imagining a place that they already find deeply relaxing.

Imagery relaxation is based on the simple idea that if you can't change the environment prompting your stress, you can still change the environment in your mind. This ability is one of the magnificent qualities of the human mind, yet it is rarely used. Athletes can think of their relaxation place, the spot where they always feel comfortable and safe, to trigger deep relaxation. Athletes should picture themselves in their special place as vividly as possible—hear the sounds, smell the air, feel the sand, use all their senses to envision the place. The more they can feel themselves to be in this special place, the more relaxing it will be. They should regularly practice imaging this place, until they can create it in their mind's eye quickly and feel the associated relaxation. My (Damon Burton's) relaxation place is a secluded beach on the Big Island of Hawaii. I can easily conjure up the image of its black lava fields, white sand beaches, blue water, and breathtaking sunsets to feel far away from deadlines, problems, and concerns. When I feel muscle tension and other arousal-related stress symptoms, I go on a minivacation to relax in my special place. I have taught this simple technique to many athletes who now use it productively.

Sample Imagery Relaxation Script

This technique is called imagery relaxation and it's used to help you relax by going on a minivacation to a place that you find very restful and relaxing. You may choose to go to the beach, a secluded mountain lake, a peaceful meadow, a glade in the woods, or even your bedroom at home. Where you go is unimportant, as long you find it relaxing.

Now listen to the sound of my voice as I guide you through the process of letting yourself relax. Start out with several deep, diaphragmic breaths, breathing in deeply through your nose, feeling your diaphragm expand under your belly button, expanding your chest completely, holding your breath briefly, then exhaling slowly through your mouth. Each deep diaphragmic breath brings in invigorating and refreshing oxygen and breathes out tension and stress. Concentrate on your breathing and make sure that the length of your inhalation is approximately equal to the length of your exhalation.

With imagery relaxation, you will use your imagination to achieve deep relaxation. Let's begin. Allow yourself to imagine that you are in a large two-story house, standing at the top of a long flight of stairs. Allow yourself to be in any type of house you like and allow the staircase to be any style you want it to be. Reach out and grab the banister. Notice the cool, smooth feel of polished wood under your hand. As you begin to feel comfortable, just allow yourself to begin to slowly descend the staircase, one step at a time. Each step you take down the stairs takes you deeper and deeper into relaxation. As you descend, allow yourself to go down, down, down, deeper and deeper into relaxation. Each step allows you to relax more deeply and completely. You totally control how deeply relaxed you get, so whenever you feel comfortably relaxed all you have to do is stop. Concentrate on your breathing as you descend. With each step, you inhale invigorating, refreshing oxygen and exhale tension and stress.

Whenever you feel comfortably relaxed, just open the door off the stairs and enter into your special place. Your special place is anywhere you choose to go where you can feel totally relaxed. It can be a beach, with the warm sun shining down on you and the waves gently lapping the shore. It can be the mountains, where the cool, crisp air invigorates you and the beauty and serenity bring you peace. It can even be your bedroom at home, where your mind and body go to recuperate each night. Wherever your special place is, allow yourself to relax, be yourself, feel totally comfortable and secure, and feel calm and at peace. Your special place should be somewhere without negative thoughts or concerns, schedules or deadlines, obstacles or problems, failure or adversity. It is a place where you can let your hair down and totally be yourself. You don't have to worry how you dress or act. Your only objective is to relax totally, get away from it all, and enjoy those feelings of relaxation. Use your breathing to help enhance those feelings. Relaxation is an ongoing process, and the more you work at it, the more your muscle fibers will loosen up, smooth out, unwind, and relax.

Notice how calm and peaceful your mind feels and how loose and limp and heavy and relaxed your body feels. Allow yourself to become aware of your thought patterns. You'll notice that you aren't thinking much, as worries and concerns disappear because you have no problems to solve or deadlines to meet. If an occasional stray thought or concern enters your mind, you just let it go, let it float away like a butterfly flittering slowly and effortlessly out of your mind. Just take a passive approach to your thoughts and simply let them go while you focus only on being relaxed and on feelings associated with total relaxation. Concentrate on those feelings of deep relaxation and help them to get stronger and stronger. Allow your mind to feel very calm, peaceful, tranquil, and comfortable. Your mind is at peace with who you are, what you do, and all your surroundings. You are feeling very, very relaxed, mentally and physically. Your mind is totally focused on your deep, diaphragmic breathing and the total relaxation throughout your mind and body.

In this deeply relaxed state, we now will conduct conditioned relaxation. For 15 to 20 breaths, each time you exhale, repeat your relaxation cue word (e.g., *relax*, *calm*, or *chill*) to yourself. Your attention should be focused totally on your deep, diaphragmic breathing and on the feelings of deep relaxation throughout your mind and body. Conditioned relaxation means attempting to develop a strong association between your cue word and these feelings of deep relaxation, so your cue word can be used later to elicit rapid relaxation when needed in daily life. That is, when you notice that you are too tense while taking an exam, giving a speech, interviewing for a job, or trying to win a tight ball game, you will be able to relax enough to achieve your optimal energy level so you can develop and maintain a flow mentality and perform your best. This quick relaxation response is possible only if you've developed a strong association between your cue word and a state of deep relaxation during this conditioned relaxation process.

Your special place is a great location for a minivacation that allows you to develop deep and complete relaxation. It is also a great place to do imagery, think more clearly, solve major problems, and make critical decisions. This is your all-purpose getaway where you can go to either enjoy a little rest and recovery or to have a productive work environment in order to practice imagery, solve problems, and make decisions. You can come here as often as you like, and stay as long as you like, and when you get ready to leave, all you have to do is simply retrace your steps. Thus, you open the door, exit your special place, and move back onto the stairs. This time, as you slowly begin to ascend the stairs, one step at a time, each step will allow you to become more aware of your mind and body and your surroundings in the room. Each step will allow you to reorient yourself to feelings in your legs, trunk, arms, neck, and head, regaining normal sensation in each of these body parts. Similarly, each step will help your mind get in touch with reality and heighten awareness of where you are and what's going on in the room around you. Each step you take in ascending the stairs brings you more in touch with how your body feels, heightens your sense of the reality of what's going on around you, and reacquaints you with your conscious mind. As you reach the top of the stairs, you find it comfortable to open your eyes, adjust to your surroundings, and be consciously aware of the world around you. You feel rejuvenated and refreshed, as if you had just gotten up from a short but invigorating nap. Your body feels very loose and limp and heavy and relaxed, but energized and ready. Your mind feels very calm, peaceful, tranquil, and comfortable, but also sharp and focused and ready to accomplish all the goals that you've set for yourself. You are relaxed but invigorated and ready to overcome all obstacles and achieve all goals.

From D. Burton and T. Raedeke, 2008, *Sport Psychology for Coaches* (Champaign, IL: Human Kinetics).

Progressive Muscle Relaxation

Progressive muscle relaxation (Jacobson 1938) is a more elaborate relaxation strategy that is most effective for athletes with limited body awareness. Over time, PMR has been modified extensively to better diagnose minute muscular tension levels and teach performers how to let go of this tension. PMR is based on the premise that initially tensing the muscles fatigues them, prompting deeper relaxation than could be reached by just passively releasing the tension. Tension is built up gradually, held for 5 to 7 seconds (to enhance diagnostic effectiveness), then released all at once, whereupon the focus shifts to letting the muscle group relax as completely as possible for 20 to 60 seconds.

Jacobson's original PMR procedure involved 16 muscle groups, practice times of nearly an hour per session, and several months to fully master the skill.

Contemporary PMR starts with 16 muscle groups, then, as the skill is mastered, simplifies first to 7 groups and then to 4, thus greatly speeding up relaxation time (Bernstein, Borkovec, & Hazlett-Stevens, 2000). We have found that athletes' heightened body awareness typically allows them to start at the more advanced 4-group stage of PMR, reducing session length to 15 to 20 minutes and mastery time to 2 to 3 weeks. A sample PMR script can be found in Appendix B on page 257. Athletes who don't get effective results within several days using 4 muscle groups can switch to the more basic 7-group approach (see table 6.1).

Self-Directed Relaxation

Self-directed relaxation (SDR) is an abbreviated form of PMR that involves guiding yourself through relaxation of the four major muscle groups while eliminating the contractions and emphasizing slow, diaphragmic breathing. Self-directed relaxation teaches athletes to focus on a muscle group, allow the muscles to relax, and feel them respond. SDR is most effective for athletes who are skilled at systematically identifying muscular tension and letting it go. Because most athletes know their bodies well, they should readily be able to develop SDR skill, but those who become easily distracted are better candidates for the more active PMR approach. A sample SDR script can be found in Appendix B on page 259. Some athletes find it useful to combine imagery with self-directed relaxation. For example, one athlete goes through SDR while lying in his special place at the beach. Another visualizes a little man with a broom sweeping away the tension from specific muscle groups, one at a time. And a third imagines tension as autumn leaves, with each breath acting like a strong wind that blows tension off her muscles while she enjoys her relaxation place.

Music

Most athletes already make use of music to help themselves relax. Whether or not they listen to the lyrics, the rhythm and tempo of music work at a subconscious level to promote relaxation. Athletes can think of a rhythm or beat that has this effect and use it to trigger relaxation at critical times during a contest or at specific points during a race. For example, a distance runner might keep his tempo consistent with the beat of a favorite song, a golfer might mentally replay a tune that helps keep her swing smooth and fluid, and a skier might use an upbeat song to synchronize his body with the terrain and keep it flowing powerfully, but fluidly, from gate to gate.

Cued Relaxation: The Link Between Total and Rapid Relaxation

Of all the rapid relaxation strategies that have been used in sport (including centering, body scans and differential relaxation, and Benson's relaxation response [1975]), we recommend **cued relaxation**. This rapid relaxation strategy works in conjunction with any total relaxation technique, is quick and easy to master, helps almost all athletes, and is fast enough to trigger the relaxation response in a wide range of sport settings. To use it, athletes develop a strong association between a chosen cue word and deep levels of relaxation (refer back to figure 6.1 on page 85). With sufficient practice, the cue word triggers a relaxation response.

To develop this skill, performers first get deeply relaxed by using the total relaxation technique of their choice. On a 10-point scale (with 1 indicating "most tense I've ever been" and 10 indicating "most relaxed I've ever been"), your athletes need to reach a level

TABLE 6.1

Contraction Cycles for Progressive Muscle Relaxation

Seven muscle groups	Four muscle groups
1. Dominant shoulder, arm, and hand	1. Both shoulders, arms, and hands
2. Nondominant shoulder, arm, and hand	
3. Head	2. Head and neck
4. Neck	
5. Chest, back, stomach	3. Chest, back, stomach
6. Dominant hip, thigh, calf, and foot	4. Both hips, thighs, calves, and feet
7. Nondominant hip, thigh, calf, and foot	

of relaxation that corresponds with a score of 8 or above. Second, a relaxation cue word (e.g., *relax, calm, peaceful,* or *chill*) is selected and paired with feelings of deep relaxation for 15 to 20 repetitions. Each time they exhale, athletes repeat the cue word. Then, when needed, athletes use cued relaxation to stimulate rapid relaxation by taking 1 or 2 diaphragmic breaths and repeating their cue word with each exhalation. Cued relaxation works in 3 to 5 seconds and allows performers to relax as much as needed to perform their best. Many athletes build this type of rapid relaxation into their preperformance routines (e.g., before shooting a free throw or hitting a putt). Some athletes also use it during the flow of competition, such as runners or swimmers relaxing certain tight muscle groups during a race or a soccer player letting go of tension when the ball is at the other end of the field.

Choosing a Relaxation Strategy

No single strategy is equally effective for all athletes. An athlete's preferences may hinge on subjective criteria, including comfort level, personal effectiveness, ease of use, and personal enjoyment. Relaxation strategies are most effective when personalized to meet individual needs, so we recommend that athletes choose their own total relaxation technique. Many athletes use multiple techniques that they mix and match depending on the situation. For example, a golfer may use imagery relaxation and diaphragmic breathing as her primary total relaxation strategy, yet also practice PMR enough that she can tense and relax her shoulders and arms to remove tension in antagonistic muscle groups before putting.

What Is Energization?

Energization is the opposite of relaxation and involves the activation of the body to help prepare for optimal performance. It requires that athletes learn how to speed up heart rate and respiration, stimulate greater blood flow to muscles, and enhance brain activity. It requires development of both total and rapid energization skills (as shown in figure 6.1 on page 85). Like relaxation, energization is a versatile mental training tool that can be used in sport a variety of ways. Energization skills allow athletes to get more out of practice, where low energy can reduce concentration and motivation. Low-energy problems are less common in competition, except late in games, as energy reserves are depleted, and in times of hardship, adversity, and failure. When athletes can draw on their energy reserves during such times, it gives them a decided performance edge. The benefits of

energization include controlling arousal, enhancing concentration, and boosting confidence.

- *Controls arousal.* Athletes often become lethargic and underaroused in practice situations and late in competitions, lacking the energy to perform aggressively. Rapid energization techniques help lethargic athletes energize on the spot to attain optimal arousal and perform their best (see chapter 9 for specific arousal control strategies).

- *Enhances concentration.* When performers' energy levels are too low, they tend to focus too broadly, causing them to be easily distracted. As athletes raise their arousal level closer to their optimal range, attention should narrow, reducing distractions and helping them focus on important performance cues. An underaroused basketball player may find that energizing helps her ignore distractions (e.g., the crowd, scouts in the stands, or her plans for after the game) in order to concentrate on how to reach her personal goals and help her team execute its game plan. (See chapter 10 for a more complete description.)

- *Elevates confidence.* Energization skills enhance athletes' confidence in their ability to perform more successfully when tired, during the later stages of competitions, and under difficult circumstances. It is a big confidence booster for athletes to know they can draw on their energy reserves in times of need and control their arousal level in pressure-packed situations.

Energization Strategies

As with relaxation, athletes need to learn total energization strategies before they can accomplish rapid energization in competitive situations. Once they are proficient at total energization, then you can introduce rapid energization as the next step.

Common Total Energization Strategies

The nature of competition—dynamic, fluid, pressure packed, and time limited—requires that energization strategies be fast, effective, and personalized. We'll focus on five techniques: psych-up breathing, imagery energization, energy machine, healing white light, and music.

Psych-Up Breathing

Psych-up breathing is similar to the breathing patterns used by many strength, power, and speed athletes when preparing for an all-out effort. Psych-up breathing involves quick, shallow breathing to rapidly transport as much oxygen as possible to the working

Sample Imagery Energization Script

This technique will help you energize yourself by using your imagery skills to reexperience an energizing event or competition from your past. Now tune out all the distractions around you and listen to the sound of my voice as I guide you through the process of energizing yourself. Start with several deep, diaphragmic breaths, breathing in deeply through your nose, feeling your diaphragm expand under your belly button, then expanding your chest completely, holding your breath briefly, and exhaling slowly through your mouth. Each deep diaphragmic breath brings in invigorating and rejuvenating oxygen and expels tension and stress. Imagine yourself at the bottom of a long staircase in a large house. Reach out and grab the polished wood banister under your hand and begin slowly climbing the staircase, smoothly and effortlessly. With each step, you become more and more energized. Feel more strength, power, stamina, and energy as you ascend, very smoothly and very effortlessly, until you finally reach a point where you feel as energized and as vital as you want to be.

At that point, open a door and enter a large room that looks like an art gallery. However, instead of containing paintings and sculptures, this room is your personal Hall of Fame, with many large-screen video monitors replaying great practice or competitive performances. Browse through the Hall of Fame, watching your athletic successes being brought to life before your eyes. Select the monitor that is replaying the practice or competitive performance where you had the highest and most positive energy level. Watch the experience first on the monitor. Once you've relived the situation on the video, put yourself at the site and re-create the event, noticing the other people involved and getting in touch with your thoughts and feelings about the moment. Allow your body to develop a highly positive energy level, as much like the one in your previous performance as you can achieve. Reexperience the feelings in your muscles, the strength and power and energy in your arms, legs, shoulders, back, and stomach. Your muscles are tingling with strength and power and stamina and energy. Your breathing is quick and powerful and invigorates and rejuvenates your muscles, even if they are tired, sore, or injured. Each breath rejuvenates the reservoir of power and strength and energy within you. Your mind feels keen and sharp and ready to learn. You're psyched, focused, and confident. You're not concerned about problems, roadblocks, or obstacles because you trust yourself and know that you'll find some way to overcome the difficulties and achieve success. No problem is too large, no obstacle too great, because you're exuding the strength and confidence that comes from knowing that your mind and body are ready to perform at your best. You feel a tremendous inner strength and power engulfing your mind and body. You know that you can harness this personal power to meet challenges and overcome roadblocks. In this frame of mind, anything is possible if you let it happen. Let the inner strength and power surround you and carry you to great things. If you are feeling energized to a level of 8 or above, then go through the conditioned energization process by focusing on your quick, powerful breathing and on the feelings of energization throughout your mind and body. Take three quick, shallow, powerful breaths, and after the third one emphatically repeat your energization cue word. Repeat the process (three breaths, cue word) until you have counted a total of 15 to 20 repetitions. This process will allow you to pair the feelings of energization in your mind and body with your chosen cue word so that you can use that cue word to trigger rapid energization when you need it.

Once you've completed the conditioned relaxation process, you simply need to retrace your steps, going back out of your Hall of Fame and down the stairs, meticulously retracing your steps until you get to a more relaxed state where you are highly energized, focused, confident, and ready to go out and accomplish any goal, solve any problem, and overcome any obstacle.

From D. Burton and T. Raedeke, 2008, *Sport Psychology for Coaches* (Champaign, IL: Human Kinetics).

muscles. A weightlifter might use this breathing pattern before a max lift, a defensive lineman before an important fourth-and-goal play, and a sprinter before the start of a 100-meter dash. The Lamaze method taught to facilitate natural childbirth is based on the same principle. The quicker breathing rhythm requires athletes to breathe more shallowly, with the lungs rather than with the diaphragm, and psych-up breathing is particularly effective in elevating arousal.

Imagery Energization

In **imagery energization**, athletes imagine themselves reliving a competitive experience in which they were highly energized, experienced little fatigue, and demonstrated great stamina while performing successfully (as in the sample energization script on page 92). For imagery to promote total energization, athletes must vividly recall what they saw, heard, felt, tasted, smelled, and touched, as well as their predominant mood and emotions. The focus is on recalling performances that help them feel energized rather than ones selected only for performance quality. The key is to feel the adrenaline pumping. If athletes imagine those type of events vividly and often enough, they will develop the ability to energize to similar levels.

Energy Machine

This imagery strategy allows athletes to imagine receiving an energy transfusion from a powerful outside source—a sophisticated energy infusion machine—that energizes their mind and body. **Energy machine** is especially effective when athletes are skilled imagers and prefer to imagine their energy coming from an external source. A sample energy machine script can be found in Appendix B on page 261.

Healing White Light

Athletes can use this imagery technique to imagine a personal power source that both heals and energizes their body. The source of the **healing white light** is the athlete's own mind, but the technique allows him or her to self-energize by harnessing cognitive powers in new, more powerful ways to promote recovery and top performance. This technique is particularly powerful for athletes recovering from a tough workout, illness, or injury. A sample healing white light script can be found in Appendix B on page 262.

Music

Most athletes already make use of music as an energization technique. The beat of up-tempo music provides an energizing effect regardless of the song's lyrics. Rhythm and tempo work at a subconscious level to enhance energy levels, and a particular rhythm or beat may be used as a cue to trigger energization at key points of a competition as an athlete plays the song mentally. For example, a distance runner might use the tempo of an upbeat song to pick up the pace during a midrace push or a strong finishing kick, a weightlifter might mentally replay a tune that helps him feel powerful and explosive while completing a difficult clean workout, and a tennis player might use a fast-paced song to draw on her energy reserves during the tie-breaker of a grueling match.

Cued Energization: The Link Between Total and Rapid Energization

We recommend **cued energization** as the primary rapid energization strategy because it works with any total energization technique, is easily learned by most performers, and works in a wide range of sport settings. Cued energization repeatedly pairs a cue word with high energy levels in order to develop a strong association between the two. The cue word can then be used with psych-up breaths to trigger a rapid energization response (see figure 6.1). Cued energization is generally easy to master in three basic steps: The athlete first performs any total energization technique that works for him or her, then pairs the cue word with feelings of being highly energized, repeating it after each third psych-up breath for a total of 15 to 20 repetitions. The cue word should have a strong energizing connotation (e.g., *energize, push, strong, powerful,* or *mojo*). Finally, the athlete uses cued energization to promote rapid energization in 3 to 5 seconds by taking 6 quick psych-up breaths and repeating the cue word after each third breath. Once athletes master this technique, they can energize enough to play their best in a few seconds.

Choosing an Energization Technique

We encourage athletes to try several energization techniques and select the one that works best for them. Each player must choose a technique that is fast, personalized, comfortable, effective, easy to use, and enjoyable. Athletes should feel free to personalize any of these strategies in ways that enhance their effectiveness. In fact, many athletes use multiple energization techniques as circumstances warrant. For example, a volleyball player might choose a combination of music, psych-up breathing, and energizing imagery as her predominant strategy in practice and competition. She might also use healing white light to promote recovery from a tough workout or injury, and energy machine as a backup strategy when having trouble with personal control or adjusting her energy levels.

Midrace Energization Strategies for Endurance Athletes

Success in many endurance sports, such as distance running, cross-country skiing, cycling, and triathlon, requires athletes to manage their energy reserves and draw from the well at critical times. Every endurance athlete has come to that decision point in a race when lactic acid builds up and pain escalates dramatically. The performer can energize and fight through the pain, or reduce pace to lower lactic acid buildup. Competitors have found a number of strategies for focusing on energizing images instead of pain and fatigue.

Well-proven energization images include imagining yourself as an efficient machine (e.g., sports car) or animal (e.g., cheetah) with incredible grace, speed, power, and energy. Other helpful images include a powerful locomotive, a shark gliding effortlessly through the water, or a sleek greyhound. If you can imagine yourself as a locomotive, then it should be easier to maintain a steady, controlled pace at decision time. Becoming a greyhound allows you to move smoothly and effortlessly when your muscles begin to tire and tighten. Other possibilities include starting up your "energy shoes" or running effortlessly on a moving sidewalk. You can imagine drinking energy instead of water, adding high-octane energy at your personal pump, or using healing white light to surround you and provide an energy transfusion while you run, bike, or ski. You can imagine siphoning energy from spectators, fellow competitors, or the sun or wind.

You can also energize by using imagery to eliminate your fatigue. Imagine your feelings of fatigue being transferred into the ground with each step or poured into a pitcher. Exhale tension and fatigue with each breath, and inhale revitalizing oxygen that energizes you. Draft behind your opponent like an auto racer, while you run more efficiently, save and build energy, and get ready to slingshot past.

Energization strategies have an important place in endurance competition. Try these strategies until you find one or more you like and then practice it systematically until you can use it effectively in competition. You will perform better and enjoy your race more.

Developing Athletes' Relaxation and Energization Skills

Helping your athletes learn how to use relaxation and energization skills to enhance their performance is critical to sport success. The process involves the same three phases used to develop any mental training tool (see chapter 3). The education phase provides your athletes with a general and personal education about relaxation and energization and how they enhance performance. The acquisition phase helps your athletes acquire both total and rapid relaxation and energization skills. And in the implementation phase, you help your athletes learn to use relaxation and energization skills automatically to maximize development and performance.

Education Phase

This phase provides athletes with a good general understanding of relaxation and energization and helps them assess their strengths and weaknesses in each area. We recommend first holding an hour-long meeting to teach your students about relaxation, then having a second meeting to address energization. The meetings should conclude by taking athletes through several techniques for developing skills in total relaxation and energization, respectively.

Next comes self-assessment. Athletes are notoriously inaccurate in understanding their typical relaxation and energization patterns. Many competitors simply don't pay enough attention to how relaxed or energized they are prior to or during competition, so they have no idea if they are too high or low. Developing such awareness can have a huge impact on their performance. Have your athletes monitor their tension and energy patterns for several days, identifying circumstances associated with high tension and low energy. We recommend developing a simple logbook for your athletes that includes a form for assessing their personal tension and energy patterns (see figure 6.2). Identify several key times during practice when you want

Tension and Energy Log

Week of:						
TENSION	**RATING: (MOST RELAXED) 1 2 3 4 5 6 7 8 9 (MOST TENSE)**					
Situation	M	T	W	Th	F	Notes
1.						
2.						
3.						
4.						
5.						
ENERGY	**RATING: (LEAST ENERGY) 1 2 3 4 5 6 7 8 9 (MOST ENERGY)**					
Situation	M	T	W	Th	F	Notes
1.						
2.						
3.						
4.						
5.						

From D. Burton and T. Raedeke, 2008, *Sport Psychology for Coaches* (Champaign, IL: Human Kinetics).

FIGURE 6.2 Athletes can use a log to record their tension and energy levels for assigned situations as well as other situations in which they feel too tense or too relaxed. They can use the notes section to record specific thoughts or triggers during each situation.

your athletes to monitor their tension and energy levels, and after practice have them record how they felt at those times. Ask them also to monitor and record any other times during practice when they felt tense or lethargic.

Stress often builds up gradually. If it is diagnosed early, while stress is low, most competitors have the relaxation skills to reduce or eliminate unwanted tension. But many athletes have trouble recognizing their own mounting tension, so they tend to ignore the warning signals until tension gets so high that it becomes difficult to manage—that is, they reach the **threshold level** (see figure 6.3). The lower the tension when diagnosed, the easier it is to manage, and as long as tension remains below the threshold level, relaxation skills can be used to effectively reduce or eliminate it. But once tension level exceeds the threshold, even the most skilled athletes have difficulty reducing it. Thus, diagnosis is important in learning to control unwanted tension before it gets too high.

Acquisition Phase

This is where you help athletes develop their own skills. Although relaxation and energization can be developed at different times, we recommend teaching them simultaneously, so that athletes can use them to raise and lower arousal levels as needed to reach and maintain an optimal state.

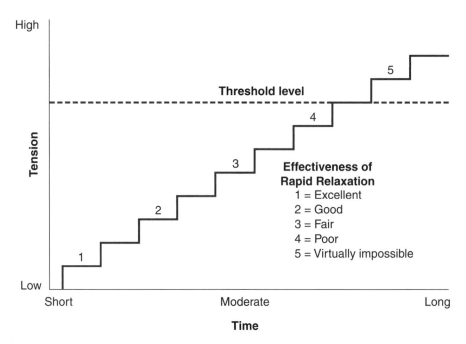

FIGURE 6.3 Impact of tension level on stress management: Beyond a certain level of tension, it is virtually impossible to reduce on demand.

Developing Total Relaxation Skills

Athletes can learn total relaxation skills by practicing them at home when they have sufficient uninterrupted time to attain deep relaxation. When practicing on their own, your athletes should try several strategies and choose the one that works best for them. The technique chosen and time required are unimportant as long as athletes reach the goal of an 8 on a 10-point relaxation scale. You can use the sample scripts given in this chapter and in Appendix B for imagery-based, self-directed, and PMR total relaxation to make an audio recording that includes each technique. Athletes can then use the recording to practice relaxation on their own. To make effective recordings, start in a conversational voice, then gradually slow your speaking tempo and soften the volume to heighten the effects of relaxation.

Music is also a great relaxation strategy, whether used by itself or in conjunction with another strategy. Because musical tastes vary widely, let athletes select their own relaxation music. If your athletes find a piece of music they like, we suggest combining it with one of the other total relaxation techniques. Have athletes select a practice time and location that will minimize distractions and give them the best chance to master this skill. Normally, athletes perform total relaxation once a day, but they can enhance the process with a second total relaxation practice session. We recommend practicing total relaxation as a team once or twice a week—after practice, so that relaxation

doesn't interfere with practice intensity but facilitates cool-down and recovery from the workout. Try to find a comfortable spot where athletes can lie down on mats. Two or three weeks of sessions should help your athletes master these skills, after which you can probably cut back to weekly sessions for maintenance.

Make sure your athletes conclude each total relaxation practice with the conditioning process designed to bridge the gap between total and rapid relaxation. Because they should pair their cue word only with deep levels of relaxation, they should never perform conditioning with a relaxation level below 8. Rapid relaxation problems can often be traced back to athletes' failure to get deeply relaxed during total relaxation practice, so you may choose to have your athletes record their total relaxation results in a section of their log to ensure that they are consistently reaching level 8.

Developing Rapid Relaxation Skills

Rapid relaxation is simply the ability to quickly relax one's body during practice and competition to promote optimal performance. Once your athletes have practiced total relaxation for several days, identify three times during practice when relaxation may be necessary and give your team a few seconds at those points to relax and reduce their tension levels. As depicted in figure 6.4, a score of 5 denotes optimal activation, 1 represents extreme relaxation, and 9 indicates extreme tension. To conduct rapid

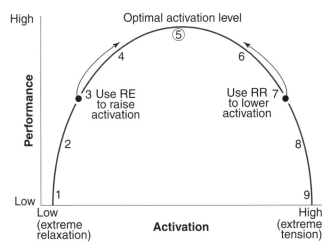

FIGURE 6.4 Optimal activation level: Athletes can employ rapid relaxation (RR) or rapid energization (RE) to achieve the optimal level.

relaxation, have your athletes take one or two deep breaths and repeat their cue word silently each time they exhale. After 5 seconds, have them assess the level of relaxation they attained. Within several days, they should begin to see rapid improvement in their ability to lower their tension. Ask your athletes to try to consistently reach level 5 (optimal activation), or the relaxation level that corresponds with best performance for them. Their optimal activation level must be low enough that tension does not interfere with performance, yet high enough to have sufficient energy. Normally, within several weeks, most athletes can learn to relax to their optimal level in 3 to 5 seconds regardless of their initial tension level.

Developing Total Energization Skills

Athletes learn total energization skills through a similar process, with several notable exceptions. Practice is normally conducted early in the day, when athletes have sufficient uninterrupted time to attain a highly energized state. Performers can use any energization technique they choose, as long as they consistently reach an energization level of 8 or above. You are encouraged to make audio recordings of scripts for the energization techniques. Up-tempo music can be used, either by itself or in addition to another strategy; let athletes select their own music.

Athletes normally perform total energization once a day (twice if they want to accelerate the process), and, to help them energize for practice, we recommend using it as a team once or twice a week, before practice, for several weeks. Energization differs from relaxation in two ways: Athletes should select a cue word capable of triggering a highly energized state, and they should use a shorter, quicker breathing pat-

tern. After becoming highly energized, your athletes should repeat their cue word 15 to 20 times following each third psych-up breath, being careful to pair cue words only with energization levels reaching level 8 or higher. Athletes can record their total energization practice in their log. Remember that pairing cue words with inferior energization levels causes many of the problems that athletes have with rapid energization. It will pay off to help your athletes consistently reach their total energization level of 8.

Developing Rapid Energization

Rapid energization is the ability to energize one's body at any time, regardless of how low energy levels may be. After your athletes practice total energization for several days, identify three times during practice when energy levels are low and give your team a few seconds to energize and assess the results. Within several weeks, athletes should be able to rapidly attain their optimal energization level on a consistent basis.

Implementation Phase

During the implementation phase, your objectives are to help your athletes automate their rapid relaxation and energization skills and integrate them into practice and competition. Normally, once your athletes have spent 2 to 3 weeks on heightening their awareness of tension and energy problems, and developing their rapid relaxation and energization skills, you should move to a maintenance schedule, with relaxation and energization checks once or twice during each practice. Each night, your athletes should go over tension or energy problems and try to understand why their relaxation or energization skills were ineffective. If an athlete identifies a consistent problem, he or she may need to develop a plan to deal with it. Athletes can reduce the frequency of total relaxation and energization sessions as their skills develop (e.g., practicing three times a week instead of seven). They should use the effectiveness of their relaxation and energization techniques as an indicator of how often to practice them, increasing the frequency if their skills begin to lose efficacy.

Rapid relaxation and energization skills are important components of any plans for mental preparation, performance, or recovery. Systematic practice of these skills dramatically reduces tension- and energy-related problems in practice and competition. When something does go wrong, have your athletes quickly identify the problem and use their rapid relaxation or energization skills to solve it. You may want your athletes to keep a list of situations that cause the most problems and encourage them to use imagery to practice resolving them. Then set up similar situations in practice to further rehearse use of the skills in competition. As athletes' skills develop, have them practice their skills during increasingly stressful situations (e.g., scrimmages and less important competitions). For example, a volleyball coach might put athletes through conditioning drills for a few minutes, then have each team member execute one serve. If less than 80% of the serves hit the target, the drill is repeated. This pressure-filled exercise offers a great chance to use relaxation and energization skills. Eventually, rapid relaxation and energization should become powerful weapons for creating a flow mind-set and maximizing performance.

SUMMARY

1. Sport places demands on athletes' ability to relax and energize, particularly when competitors have to adjust their activation level quickly and substantially. To perform their best, athletes must learn how to relax and energize quickly.

2. Relaxation means decreasing unwanted muscular tension, reducing excessive activation of the sympathetic nervous system, and calming the mind by keeping it productively occupied.

3. Relaxation strategies elicit the relaxation response through muscle-to-mind techniques (e.g., progressive muscle relaxation) and mind-to-muscle strategies (e.g., imagery).

4. Total relaxation is a longer strategy that helps athletes relax completely, whereas rapid relaxation is an abbreviated technique that uses a cue word to relax quickly.

5. Total relaxation alleviates chronic stress, promotes recovery from workouts and injuries, enhances sleep quality, and develops rapid relaxation skills. Rapid relaxation reduces tension, controls arousal, breaks the stress spiral, promotes an unconscious trusting attitude, conserves energy, and increases enjoyment.

6. Total relaxation strategies include diaphragmic breathing, imagery relaxation, progressive muscle relaxation, self-directed relaxation, and music.

7. Cued relaxation associates a cue word with deep relaxation to stimulate optimal relaxation in 3 to 5 seconds. It works with any total relaxation strategy, is easy to master, and rapidly relaxes athletes in most sport settings.

8. Energization involves activation of the body to help prepare for optimal performance. Total energization is a longer strategy designed to get athletes as energized as possible, whereas rapid energization allows athletes to use a cue word to quickly energize in 3 to 5 seconds.

9. Energization helps athletes control arousal, enhance concentration, and elevate confidence, particularly when they are tired, encountering adversity, or dealing with low energy levels.

10. Effective total energization strategies for sport include psych-up breathing, imagery energization, energy machine, healing white light, and music.

11. Cued energization associates a cue word with feelings of high energy in order to stimulate optimal energization in 3 to 5 seconds. It works with any total energization strategy, is easy to master, and rapidly energizes athletes in a wide range of sport settings.

12. Developing athletes' relaxation and energization skills employs the same three-phase process used to develop all mental training tools and skills: education, acquisition, and implementation.

13. The education phase provides athletes with basic knowledge of relaxation and energization and enhances their self-awareness of their relaxation and energization patterns.

14. The acquisition phase helps athletes develop their skills in the total and rapid versions of relaxation and energization.

15. In the implementation phase, athletes learn to automate relaxation and energization and implement these skills in practice and competitive settings.

KEY TERMS

cued energization

cued relaxation

diaphragmic breathing

energization

energy machine

healing white light

imagery energization

imagery relaxation

mind-to-muscle techniques

muscle-to-mind techniques

progressive muscle relaxation

psych-up breathing

rapid relaxation

relaxation

self-directed relaxation

threshold level

total relaxation

REVIEW QUESTIONS

1. What are total and rapid relaxation?

2. What are the benefits of total and rapid relaxation?

3. What are the guidelines for choosing a relaxation strategy and conducting relaxation?

4. What are total and rapid energization?

5. What are the benefits of total and rapid energization?

6. What are the guidelines for choosing an energization strategy and conducting energization?

7. How should coaches set up a program to help their athletes develop and automate skills to relax and energize effectively?

PRACTICAL ACTIVITIES

1. Select a total relaxation strategy and practice the technique to see what level of relaxation you are able to attain. Also try out one energization strategy.

2. In order to gain experiential understanding, pick either a relaxation or an energization strategy to try out for six days. Perform the strategy once or twice daily, pairing a cue word with the appropriate breathing pattern for 20 repetitions after you reach the desired state (deeply relaxed or highly energized). For the last 2 days of the project, try out your rapid relaxation or energization skills by pairing your breathing with 2 repetitions of your cue word to see what effect you get in 3 to 5 seconds.

Self-Talk

After reading this chapter you should be able to

- understand what self-talk is and how it works;
- explain eight strategies to program positive thinking;
- describe the types of negative thinking used by your internal critic;
- explain how to optimize self-talk; and
- understand how to accomplish the three phases of developing athletes' smart-talk skills: education, acquisition, and implementation.

Self-talk is the steady stream of thoughts and internal dialogue in our minds. Used purposefully, it can be a versatile and powerful technique for improving performance. Although self-talk occurs constantly, it becomes more extensive—for coaches and athletes—in more important situations, so we tend to engage in abundant self-talk in our most important competitions. Here is a collegiate runner's self-talk in preparation for an important competition (notice the blend of positive and negative thoughts):

> I am standing in the paddock where everyone must stand thirty minutes prior to their race without any warm-ups on. There are 40,000 spectators surrounding the track and 15,000 athletes competing, including most of the nation's best collegians. The temperature is cold, about 40 degrees, the wind is blowing, and sprinkles are beginning to fall. I am extremely excited to be at such a big meet. At the same time, I have butterflies and nervous feelings. I also feel lots of anxiety. I am tired of waiting. I want to get out there and run. Positive as well as negative thoughts run through my mind. There are so many people watching. It is so cold. The wind is blowing strong. The competition looks fast and strong. Everyone has to run in these conditions. I need to relax. All I can ask is to do the best I can. I am prepared to run. I know I can run a fast leg. . . . I need to run well so I don't let my teammates down. This is our biggest meet next to nationals. . . . Why do we have to stand for half an hour? I'm not going to be loose. Hey, I can't control those things—let them go. If we don't qualify for nationals, it does not mean we will never qualify. If I don't run as fast as I am expected, it is hardly the end of the world. All I can do is give my best. If we don't run well in this relay, it doesn't mean we are a bad relay team.

Did you notice the two distinct voices going back and forth as this runner waited to compete? One voice is rational and supportive, and it will help the athlete stay positive to perform her best. The other voice is the **critic**, our self-doubting side that focuses on negatives and worries about performing poorly. To make self-talk work for you and your athletes, you want to increase positive thoughts and decrease negative thoughts. This chapter shows you how to design self-talk programs to do just that. You and your athletes can master your own thoughts and use your improved competitive mind-set to perform better.

What Is Self-Talk?

Human beings think almost every waking moment. Have you ever tried to turn off your thoughts? Try it! For the next 30 seconds, try to think about absolutely nothing. Eliminate all thoughts and empty your mind of all conscious activity. How did you do? Was it tougher than you thought? Most of us find this a virtually impossible task. Any effort to empty the mind usually prompts a flood of thoughts to rush in and fill the void, often causing us to think about the worst possible things at the most inopportune times. This continuous stream of thoughts, positive or negative, is self-talk, and it plays an important role in determining mood and emotions. Have you noticed how much happier you feel when the sun is shining than you do on gloomy days? The external environment plays a big role in altering your mood and emotions. But your internal environment—what's in your head—often influences your mood even more.

As you might expect, then, self-talk can affect sport performance. The more a thought gets repeated, the more automatic it becomes. Both positive and negative thoughts can be repeated enough to become **beliefs**. Playing in front of a large, hostile crowd on the road may prompt you to feel anxious because you want your team to play well, impress these fans, and show them you're a top coach. If this worry is repeated often, it may lead to a belief that causes you to feel anxious whenever your team plays in front of large road crowds, even though you may no longer be aware of specific thoughts that trigger your anxiety. Your athletes can experience the same process—thoughts (positive or negative) get automated and lead to beliefs. Recall from chapter 3 that flow is an almost magical state of concentration that results in complete absorption in the game. Athletes describe it as being "in the zone" or completely caught up in the activity without interference from outside thoughts. Notice the differences between positive and negative self-talk in table 7.1. Positive self-talk leads to a flow mind-set in which athletes excel. Negative self-talk leads to a choking mind-set in which irrational thoughts cause athletes to underachieve.

How Self-Talk Works

Most coaches and athletes believe that emotions and behavior are the products of the situations in which they compete. Put yourself in the following situations and think about how much you feel the situation determines your emotions and behavior: You call a blitz on third and long, and your opponent completes a long pass for the winning touchdown. Your best player misses a free throw with three seconds to go, and your team loses the state title by one point. Your favorite athlete pulls a hamstring that threatens to keep her out of the Olympics after training with you for seven years.

TABLE 7.1

Positive Versus Negative Self-Talk

Positive	Negative
positive and optimistic	negative and pessimistic
logical, rational, and productive	illogical, irrational, and unproductive
boosts confidence	deflates confidence
heightens focus/concentration on the task at hand	reduces focus and increases distractions
focuses on the present	focuses on the past or future
stimulates optimal arousal where energy is high, positive, and process-oriented	stimulates under- or overarousal
motivates you to push your limits	motivates you to give up easily
appraises problems as a challenge or opportunity	appraises problems as threats to be eliminated
attributes (credits) success to replicable internal factors	attributes success to external factors that are not replicable
attributes (blames) failure to surmountable factors	attributes failure to insurmountable factors
alleviates stress	promotes stress
minimal process-oriented thinking	extensive product-oriented thinking
performance enhancing	performance debilitating

Each situation represents a unique competitive challenge, but does it automatically dictate stress or confidence, choking or flow? No. In the ABCs of self-talk (Ellis, 1996), the situation represents A, the **activating event**. This is whatever happens to you or your athletes, such as needing to make a critical defensive adjustment or having to defend against a potentially game-winning penalty kick in the state championship. The C represents the consequences—how you feel or what you do in response to the situation. In the example shown in figure 7.1, negative consequences might include emotions (e.g., stress, anxiety) and disruptive behaviors (e.g., poor concentration in seeing the kick come off the opponent's foot and slow reaction to the ball). Beneficial consequences would include positive emotions (challenge, excitement) and helpful behaviors (good concentration, anticipation, quick reaction, and a secure trap).

Finally, the B in the figure represents your beliefs about the situation, or what you are thinking between points A and C. This is your interpretation of the situation, and it determines your emotions and behavior to a much greater extent than does the situation itself. Positive thoughts ("I've prepared well for this moment. I know how this guy kicks the ball in pen-

alty situations. Despite the pressure, I'm confident I can defend against this kick.") should lead the athlete to feel positive emotions and perform skillfully.

Negative thoughts, on the other hand, can lead to unproductive consequences. Negative thinking ("This is their best shooter—I don't stand a chance against him") will probably prompt negative emotions, leading to tense muscles and slowed reaction. Destructive thoughts ("No one will think I'm as good a goalie as Boggs if I let them score here") will probably cause different unproductive emotions, such as anger or frustration, which can lead to tunnel vision and reduced anticipation. The basic principle of self-talk is that we can't always control what happens to us, but we can control how we respond to uncontrollable events. You and your athletes can do this by learning self-talk skills.

Positive Versus Negative Thinking

To enhance self-talk, it is important that you fully understand positive thought patterns that facilitate performance and how they compare with negative thought patterns that impair it.

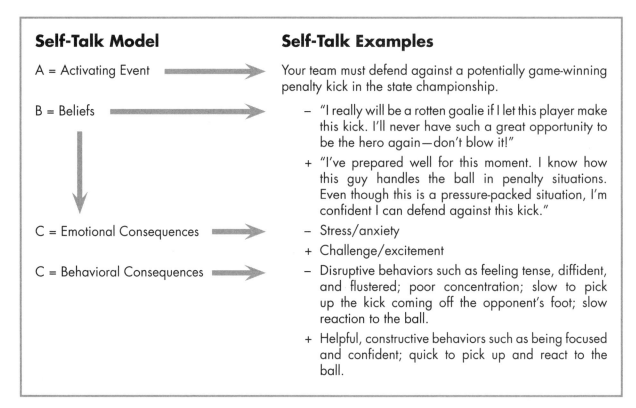

FIGURE 7.1 The ABC model of self-talk.

Positive Thought Patterns

Positive thought patterns help create a flow mind-set by boosting confidence, maintaining an optimistic attitude, promoting concentration at crucial moments, enhancing motivation to push your limits, creating an optimal level of arousal, and ensuring poise and mental toughness when confronting failure or adversity. To develop these positive thought patterns, which we term **smart-talk**, you must become familiar with eight strategies that help us use self-talk proactively and effectively. We call these the "smart-talk commandments":

• *Be an optimist, not a pessimist.* Self-talk is always a choice—it can be positive or negative. Be a good role model for your athletes and focus on the positives in every situation. Concentrate on what your athletes can do rather than what they can't. Emphasize your athletes' strengths, correct their weaknesses, and help them see every success as a building block to reaching longer-term objectives. Smart-talk always favors the optimistic choice.

• *Remain realistic and objective.* Self-talk must be more than just "thinking positively" in a way that confuses reality with daydreams. Quickly translate dreams and visions into specific goals and action plans. Not everyone will be an Olympic athlete, but with careful planning, realistic goals can be achieved. Smart-talk keeps our thoughts well grounded and realistic.

• *Focus on the present, not the past or future.* We perform better and enjoy it more when our attention is focused totally in the present (see chapter 3). Past failures cannot be changed, and we cannot guarantee future victories, such as hitting two homers in the championship game next week. The present is the only time that any of us can act. Athletes who fixate on a poor play or a missed opportunity can become so distracted or panicked that they make more mistakes. Smart-talk forgets the "if only's" and "what if's" and concentrates on staying in the moment and enjoying the here and now.

• *Appraise problems as challenges rather than threats.* Athletes who view problems as challenges bring out the best in themselves; they remain motivated and perform up to their capabilities. Help athletes avoid seeing problems as threats, so that they don't become consumed with avoiding failure, feel stressed out, and perform poorly. With your team down 6 points with 54 seconds to go, you want them to view the situation as a challenge and be motivated to go all out. Smart-talk casts problems as challenges rather than threats, helping athletes maintain an optimistic, competitive outlook.

• *View successes as replicable and failures as surmountable.* When athletes believe that their success is due to ability and effort, rather than luck, they see the success as replicable (something they can do again). Likewise, help athletes attribute failure to factors they can control, such as effort level ("I'll work harder next practice"), skill development ("I can learn to read defenders better"), and mental preparation ("next time I'll improve my focus"). Smart-talk focuses on replicable reasons for success and surmountable causes of failure.

• *Concentrate on process, not product.* Focus self-talk on process goals—hard work, mental preparation, skill and strategy development—that help us achieve desired product goals. With the game riding on his hitting both one-and-one free throws, Matt uses the time-out designed to ice him to focus instead on relaxing and going through his preshot routine using imagery. At the line, Matt faithfully follows his routine, concentrates only on "a good, high release point and a strong follow-through," and calmly hits both shots to win the championship. Smart-talk focuses on process, secure in the knowledge that as skills improve, so do athletes' and teams' chances of attaining valued product goals such as winning.

• *Concentrate on things you can control.* This may be the most important aspect of self-talk. We create stress for ourselves by trying to change people and events beyond our control, but when we focus self-talk on things that can be controlled, our emotions and behavior remain positive and constructive. We cannot control an opponent's behavior and performance, but we *can* control our own. We cannot control officials' decisions, playing conditions, or luck, but we *can* control how we react to these situations. Smart-talk keeps self-talk focused on what you can control rather than what you can't.

• *Separate your performance from your self-worth.* Your worth as a human being has nothing to do with how you perform as a coach or an athlete. It has everything to do with who you are, particularly your values. Help your athletes see that they are unique human beings with their own gifts to offer the world, regardless of their sport performance, and apply this view to yourself as well. Every coach was a worthwhile human being before starting to coach and will remain worthwhile long after hanging up the whistle. Smart-talk reminds us that we are not our behavior or performance—our self-worth is innate, not earned.

Negative Thought Patterns

Negative thought patterns interfere with athletes' flow mind-set and create a failure mentality by deflating confidence, promoting pessimism, reducing concentration and motivation, disrupting optimal arousal, and weakening the mental toughness needed to deal with failure or adversity. To recognize and change negative thought patterns, you must become familiar with five types of distorted thinking and five common **irrational beliefs** that your inner critic uses to promote negative thinking and a failure mind-set.

The Critic

"The critic" is the term that psychologist Eugene Sagan used to describe the inner voice that attacks and judges you (McKay & Fanning 1992). **The critic** blames you when things go wrong and negatively compares you to others; sets impossible standards of perfection, then blasts you for falling short; and maintains an album of your failures but ignores your successes. The critic has your life planned out in detail and castigates you whenever you break one of the unwritten rules you're supposed to live by. The critic calls you names (*stupid, untalented, slacker, weak, slow, selfish*) and tells you they're true; reads others' minds and tells you they consider you wanting because they are bored, frustrated, threatened, or unhappy around you; and exaggerates the size and impact of your weaknesses. If you miss an easy shot, the critic says, "A good player never misses a shot like that!" And the critic sometimes uses your values against you: "Great players always play hurt," the critic says, even though it's not true.

In short, the critic is the most negative part of each of us, and it hits you where it hurts, where your self-esteem is low. To develop effective smart-talk, then, we must be able to silence the critic and focus on more positive thought patterns. The next two sections expose some of the critic's weapons—distorted thinking and irrational beliefs.

Distorted Thinking

Distorted thinking involves drawing incorrect inferences based on inadequate or incorrect information, or failing to separate fantasy from reality (Beck 1976). Five common types of distorted thinking are catastrophizing, overgeneralization, blaming, "mustification," and polarized thinking. As you read about each, think about whether it affects your own or your athletes' thought patterns and about what **counterarguments** might help.

• **Catastrophizing** means expecting the worst and exaggerating the consequences of real or imagined negative events. To counter catastrophizing, ask yourself what really is the worst thing that can happen in this situation. Generally, even though your worst-case scenario may not be pleasant, it's something that you've lived through before and can again if necessary.

- **Overgeneralization** is the process of erroneously forming conclusions based on an isolated incident while ignoring broader facts. For example, a basketball player who misses a crucial free throw may in the heat of the moment come to believe that she chokes under pressure, even if in fact she has hit two game-winning shots for every one she has missed. To counter overgeneralization, help your athletes take the time to accurately assess the big picture and understand where this event fits into the larger scheme of things. You might also look at statistics over an extended time (e.g., a season) or even at game footage to see if the generalization is supported by facts.

- **Blaming** involves holding others responsible for negative events in your life. Blamers have myriad excuses for their failings and shortcomings, and they lay blame on coaches, players, parents, and officials. Blaming others lessens the threat of failure, but it also allows little hope for future success. To counter this distortion, help your athletes recognize that they must accept the blame for failure in order to make positive changes that will bring more success next time. You can model this as a coach as well. Clearly, coaches must accept their fair share of the blame for their athletes' or team's failures, and you can use this as a chance to view the causes of failure as surmountable, then concentrate on what you can do to be more successful in the future.

- **Mustification** involves one of two beliefs: that life should be lived according to a rigid set of rules that everyone must or should follow without deviation, or that things in your life *have* to be the way you want them to be. Athletes who take this approach usually end up feeling frustrated, angry, or indignant when things don't go their way. To counter "must thinking," help athletes recognize that life is often unfair and that we simply have to accept this fact and make the best of it. Model this attitude by not escalating your personal preferences into musts. Of course you would prefer that your team carry its high quality of play in practice this week over to the conference tournament tomorrow, but don't feel that the team *must* be at its best, because teams often underachieve and encounter adversity in major competitions.

- **Polarized thinking** frames things in all-or-nothing terms—black or white, good or bad. Polarized thinkers take extreme positions and give themselves little room to be human and make mistakes. They see themselves as either stars or flops, and this self-labeling in absolute terms can directly affect performance. To counter this distortion, help athletes recognize that there is much gray in the world and that it is okay to adopt a more pragmatic position somewhere between the extremes.

Which of these types of distorted thinking do you see in your own self-talk or that of your athletes? Use counterarguments to reduce or eliminate them. The next section examines how irrational beliefs can fuel the critic and contribute to negative emotions and subpar performance.

Irrational Beliefs

Irrational beliefs can be detrimental to your own and your athletes' performance. In fact, they may be at the core of anxiety, depression, and stress (Ellis, 1996), so it is important to learn to recognize and reframe them. Irrational beliefs involve cognitive distortion—in the form of unsound evidence and questionable logic—but are even more highly seductive because they are also based on partial fact. **Reframing** often requires intense debate to convince athletes of the irrational nature of their thinking. Let's look at five irrational beliefs detrimental to sport performance:

- **Perfectionism**. "I should be thoroughly competent in every aspect of my game at all times, never have ups and downs or make mistakes." How many flawed game plans, poor adjustments, or faulty decisions did John Wooden make in coaching UCLA to 10 national championship in 12 years? How many turnovers, defensive lapses, and missed shots did Michael Jordan have in his Hall-of-Fame career? How many times did Babe Ruth strike out? Champions expect mistakes and failure, and they are committed to learning from them without fearing them. John Wooden believes the team that makes the most mistakes usually wins, because aggressiveness prompts mistakes but also is key to winning. Help your athletes develop excellence thinking, where criticism is used to learn and improve, and self-esteem is based on performing up to one's capabilities, not on winning. Use these counterarguments to reframe perfectionist thoughts:

  - Mistakes are a normal part of learning. Only performers who are content not to get better can avoid making mistakes.
  - Mistakes are stepping stones to future success.
  - The world's best performers make just as many mistakes as you do; they are just more subtle and harder to notice.
  - Don't fear your mistakes—learn from them. It's better to be aggressive and accept mistakes as the price of improving than to stagnate because you're afraid to make mistakes.
  - Strive to keep your self-talk focused on excellence, not perfectionism.

- **Fear of failure**. "I'm worried my team won't play well today." "I'm afraid I won't make this shot." "We must win this tournament." Whenever you or your athletes say such things, you fall victim to an irrational fear of failure. Some fear of failure is normal, but when your concern about failing overwhelms your enthusiasm to succeed, it is irrational. Use these counterarguments to reframe your thoughts:

    - When you say something must occur, you really mean that you won't be able to endure if it does not happen. In fact, while an undesired outcome might be inconvenient or even unpleasant, it's not beyond endurance.

    - Everyone plays poorly sometimes, but playing poorly does not leave you without friends, give you a life-threatening disease, or ruin your love life.

    - What is the worst thing that can happen? It may not be pleasant, but you've probably already survived something similar before.

- **Social approval**. "I must win the approval of others and impress everyone who sees me perform." "I can't face my players if this play doesn't work." "They won't think I'm a good athlete if I can't shut my opponent down." Do you recognize these thoughts in yourself or your athletes? Everyone wants social approval, but when coaches and athletes overfocus on pleasing others or fearing disapproval, their desire has become irrational. Use these counterarguments to reframe your thoughts:

    - You can't control what others think or how they behave.

    - People can find fault even with Hall of Famers. Critics have called Joe Torre too laid-back, Phil Jackson too touchy-feely, and Vince Lombardi too hard-nosed. If people can pick at the greatest coaches in history, they can find fault with anybody.

    - Accept the fact that what others think about you can't hurt you.

    - Please yourself and have fun coaching or performing. Make sure you can feel good about facing the person you see in the mirror every morning.

- **Equity**. "Life should be fair, and if I diligently work at my craft, I should improve, play well, and get the rewards I deserve." Coaches and athletes who irrationally believe that everything in life should be fair make statements such as, "We should be improving more with all the hard work we're putting in," "It's unfair for a bad call to cost us this game," or "It's not right that one bad race cost Jill a chance at the state finals." Wanting equity is normal, but it becomes irrational when we insist that life always be fair and follow our preferences. Use these counterarguments to reframe your thoughts:

    - Life is often unfair.

    - Improvement is not steady or predictable. Quality of performance tends to spurt, oscillate, and plateau. Even if improvement is not visible, you are often laying the groundwork for future growth.

    - Forget about what you can't control and concentrate on doing your best on what you can control. Persistence does pay off! Inequities usually even out in the long run.

- **Social comparison**. "The behavior and performance of other competitors is important to me and can destroy my game." Social comparison is one of the most insidious irrational beliefs in sport, and it is operative in comments such as, "We never play well against this team," "They really put the pressure on us with that big inning," or "Winning is the only thing that matters." Social comparison places too much importance on largely uncontrollable outcomes, such as winning and outperforming others, rather than concentrating on controllable factors, such as playing your best. Use these counterarguments to reframe your thoughts:

    - Winning is ability-limited. You often can't win even if you play your best. You should have no regrets if you've made your best effort and performed up to your capabilities.

    - The real goal in sport and life is to pursue excellence by making the most of the talent you have.

    - You have no control over how others perform, nor can they control your performance unless you let them. Concentrate on playing your best and sticking with your game plan.

Optimizing Self-Talk

Making your self-talk more positive can improve your performance, and the process of optimizing self-talk is relatively simple. Athletes must first develop a solid understanding of their current self-talk patterns (both positive and negative), then use a variety of strategies to proactively increase the quantity and quality of their positive thoughts. Finally, they must correct any remaining negative thoughts. Let's briefly review each of these steps.

Heighten Awareness of Current Self-Talk Patterns

Athletes can choose from a number of strategies to become more aware of their self-talk patterns. Possibilities include imagery recall of good and bad performances, **negative thought counts** in practice, and keeping postpractice and competition logs.

Imagery Recall of Good and Bad Performances

Ask athletes to use imagery to recall a competition in which they played very well. After they reexperience this successful competition for several minutes, ask them to write down specific thoughts they had during that performance—that is, self-talk they used to help themselves succeed. Then repeat the process using a poor performance. After athletes have recorded their thought patterns from both good and bad experiences, have them compare the two lists and identify positive and negative self-talk patterns that most affect their performance.

Negative Thought Counts

Another way to become more aware of self-talk patterns is to count your negative thoughts. Some athletes find this more enlightening than examining their self-talk patterns. The best way to conduct a practice-related negative thought count is to video-record it and play it back to stimulate athletes' recall of their negative thoughts. Some coaches and athletes, however, need to conduct their negative thought count for an entire day because problems in daily life intrude on their sport performance. To perform an all-day count, we suggest putting a number of paper clips, pennies, or sunflower seeds in a pants pocket. Each time you catch yourself using a negative thought, move one item to a different pocket. Totals for athletes will vary based on how vigilant and picky they are (we have seen counts range from 5 to 150), so it is unimportant how their counts compare with each other. What matters is whether negative thoughts decrease with the use of smart-talk.

Postpractice and Competition Logs

Athletes can probably best identify their sport-related patterns of self-talk by completing logs after practice and competition. Postpractice logs can be kept daily, several days a week, or occasionally, when you want to highlight certain situations in which athletes need to control their thoughts. Competitive logs can be completed after every competition or only after selected ones. You can have athletes start by completing the Self-Talk Log Form (figure 7.2) for a few practices and at least one competition. Have athletes select up to three positive and three negative situations from each practice or competition. A positive situation is any event in which athletes execute correctly, show improvement, demonstrate team unity and cohesion, or have fun. In the log, athletes briefly describe each situation, highlighting its positive nature, then record a predominant positive emotion for each situation (e.g., happiness, satisfaction, excitement,

or pride). Next, they identify and record the specific positive thoughts they recall. In learning a new play, an athlete's thoughts might include, "I got it! My hard work paid off. I'm excited to try it against our rival next week."

Next, athletes repeat the process for up to three negative situations, in practice or competition, in which they or the team played poorly and experienced negative emotions. They briefly describe each negative situation, record their predominant negative emotion for each one (e.g., sadness, dissatisfaction, anxiety, anger, or embarrassment), and identify the specific negative thoughts they had during the experience.

If athletes have trouble getting an accurate overall picture of the practice or competition by assessing only individual positive and negative situations, encourage them to record an overall **positive mental attitude** (PMA) score for each day. Rate PMA from 1 to 10, with 1 being the most negative day of your life, 5 an average day, and 10 the most positive day of your life. The PMA score should represent the quality of the overall day across a number of situations. It reflects one's overall mind-set. Now that you understand the first step in optimizing self-talk—developing awareness of self-talk patterns—let's look at how to use this information to program positive thoughts.

Program Positive Thoughts

Most athletes can make significant changes in their self-talk by focusing on positive thoughts and repeating them frequently. This can be done by **programming** positive thoughts, and athletes can use this mental training tool to increase confidence, improve concentration and focus, enhance motivation, control stress, and, of course, perform optimally.

One way athletes can proactively program positive thoughts is to use **positive affirmations**, team mottos, and motivational slogans to remind themselves of their skills and abilities: "I'm a talented athlete with the skills to get the job done." As a coach, you can use a positive affirmation, motto, or slogan (e.g., "Footwork is the key to success!") to focus players' attention on a key team goal for a practice or competition. Or you can use a slogan on an ongoing basis to emphasize a characteristic or goal of the team: "Suffocating defense!" or "Tradition never graduates." Another way to program positive thoughts is to use **cue words**, quick reminders (often closely linked to goals) of how you want to focus your thoughts at a particular time. Cue words help trigger automatic responses. They can be used with mental skills such as relaxation (e.g., "relax"), concentration

Self-Talk Log

Daily PMA _____   Day _____

Positive Situations	Predominant Emotions	Positive Thoughts	Times Script Read or Played
1.			1.
			2.
2.			3.
			4.
3.			5.
			6.

Negative Situations	Predominant Emotions	Negative Thoughts	Counterarguments
1.			
2.			
3.			

From D. Burton and T. Raedeke, 2008, *Sport Psychology for Coaches* (Champaign, IL: Human Kinetics).

FIGURE 7.2   Athletes can use a log form such as this one to keep track of their positive and negative thoughts.

General Self-Talk Script From a High School Volleyball Player

I like school because of the opportunity it gives me to learn. I learn things that will help me in my job and in other areas of life. Because I have had these experiences, I know I will be successful. When I am having problems, I know I have great friends to help me out. They care about me and want me to succeed. I like to be with my friends, but I also like spending time alone—I am my best friend. This time by myself gives me a chance to relax and enjoy life, not stressing out about school or who to impress. I don't need to impress anybody because I like the way I am.

I like to go to weights because they make me feel good and strong. I know they will help me be a better volleyball player in the fall. Hard work pays off! If I work hard, I will be successful and have fun. I love the way I feel after a hard-fought match, knowing I gave it my all. When I get tired during practice or during a match, I want to push harder because I will gain more from it and will be a good example to my teammates. I am a good example and constantly try to help my younger teammates.

I am an assertive person. I have no need to be shy and quiet. I have confidence that people want to know what I have to say and what I think. My opinion or input is important because I am an intelligent person and everyone knows that.

I have time to get everything done because I have the capability to manage my time. My life is very busy because I can handle it. I like being busy and accomplishing many things because it makes me a better, well-rounded person.

("one play at a time"), and confidence ("we play well every time we take the floor"). Encourage your athletes also to develop performance-related cue words that focus attention on aspects of technique ("smooth tempo") and strategy ("stick with what's working") to promote automated execution.

While motivational slogans and cue words are helpful, we believe the best way to program positive self-talk is to develop a **self-talk script** that can be read or played four or five times a day. Scripts can be quite short (one or two sentences) or somewhat longer (up to 3–5 minutes), and they often include positive affirmations and cue words along with other types of positive thoughts. Scripts can be general, for use in a variety of situations, or highly specific, for a particular game or a specific purpose such as prepractice readiness. We focus here on developing a general self-talk script, but you can customize self-talk scripts to reduce stress, heighten concentration, adjust arousal, increase motivation, enhance self-confidence, or perform optimally. To develop a general script, follow these steps: Decide the purposes of your script; identify specific thoughts to include for each purpose; arrange the thoughts to facilitate flow and strengthen the impact of each section; arrange the sections to create the best overall flow and impact; and develop a catchy introduction and a powerful conclusion.

To walk your athletes through these steps, have them use the Smart-Talk Script Development Form (figure 7.3) and the Purposes and Thoughts for Smart-Talk Scripts handout (figure 7.4). Athletes should identify the purposes from the handout (section 1) that they want to include in their script and write them in separate sections on the blank form. Next, for each purpose, they write specific thoughts that capture its essence (the handout suggests specific thoughts, affirmations, and counterarguments, but athletes can also use their own or borrow from song lyrics or famous quotes). Athletes then arrange the specific thoughts for each section to achieve optimal flow, placing the most powerful ideas first or last to maximize their impact. They can place numbers in the parentheses before each thought to reflect their order in the script. Now athletes should arrange the overall sections, putting the most powerful purposes first and last, and placing numbers in the parentheses before each purpose to indicate final order.

The next step is to develop an effective introduction and conclusion. Both should be short, powerful, and memorable. Introductions might include such phrases as these: "I hold the secret to winning the 5000 meters at the conference championship." "Making my move into the starting lineup is just a few thoughts away." Scripts might close with something memorable such as these statements: "Now that I've got my plan in

Smart-Talk Script Development Form

Directions: Step 1 is to identify the purposes of your smart-talk script. Look at the accompanying Purposes and Thoughts for Smart-Talk Scripts (figure 7.4) and select one or more of the seven purposes for developing a self-talk script. Write each of the purposes you choose on a separate section of this form (i.e., write your first purpose in Section 1, your second purpose in Section 2, etc). **Step 2** is to study the form and select one or more specific thoughts to convey each purpose and record them under the Specific Thoughts that correspond to each purpose. Sample thoughts are listed for each purpose, but you may also make up your own thoughts or borrow them from other sources. **Step 3** is to number the specific thoughts in each section in the order that maximizes the flow of your script and strengthens its impact. Place a numerical ranking reflecting the order you want thoughts listed on your script inside the parentheses provided at the beginning of each thought. **Step 4** is to reorder each section to create ideal flow for your script and heighten its impact by placing a ranking inside the parentheses at the beginning of each purpose. Finally, develop a catchy introduction and a powerful conclusion that will maximize the effectiveness of your smart-talk script.

Example:

Purpose (1) <u>Reminders of strengths and assets</u>

Specific Thoughts:

(1) <u>I have the ability, dedication, and work ethic to excel in whatever I do.</u>

(2) <u>I am a talented person with skills and abilities that allow me to be successful in life.</u>

Section 1 Purpose (1) _____

Section 1 Specific Thoughts:

(1) _____

(2) _____

(3) _____

(4) _____

(5) _____

Section 2 Purpose(2) _____

Section 2 Specific Thoughts:

(1) _____

(2) _____

(3) _____

(4) _____

(5) _____

(continued)

From D. Burton and T. Raedeke, 2008, *Sport Psychology for Coaches* (Champaign, IL: Human Kinetics).

FIGURE 7.3 With guidance, athletes can use this form to develop a personalized smart-talk script.

Section 3 Purpose (3) _____

Section 3 Specific Thoughts:

(1) _____

(2) _____

(3) _____

(4) _____

(5) _____

Section 4 Purpose (4) _____

Section 4 Specific Thoughts:

(1) _____

(2) _____

(3) _____

(4) _____

(5) _____

Section 5 Purpose (5) _____

Section 5 Specific Thoughts:

(1) _____

(2) _____

(3) _____

(4) _____

(5) _____

Catchy Introduction: _____

_____

Powerful Conclusion: _____

_____

From D. Burton and T. Raedeke, 2008, *Sport Psychology for Coaches* (Champaign, IL: Human Kinetics).

FIGURE 7.3 *(continued)*

mind—just do it." "The best is yet to come now that I am confident; I am thinking the right way." Have athletes do a final check of the script for length and vivid language. Scripts should be short enough to be read frequently (1.5 to 3 minutes is recommended) and specific enough to trigger images of the desired performance or the type of person the athlete wants to be. Finally, athletes write out the script and make a self-talk audio recording. Many athletes like to add background music to create the right mood, to incorporate an appropriate rhythm to help adjust their arousal level, or to provide another way to cue positive thoughts during practice and competition.

Self-talk scripts are a powerful way to program positive thoughts, and we encourage you to use this technique with your athletes and even on your own as a coach. Scripts vary in length and language and can be adapted to specific events or contests. Thus far, then, to optimize self-talk, athletes have heightened their awareness of their self-talk patterns and increased their positive thoughts. Now they need to deal effectively with any remaining negative thoughts.

Purposes and Thoughts for Smart-Talk Scripts

Directions: Select the main purpose for your smart-talk script from section 1. You may select one purpose, all seven, or any number in between. Next, for each purpose, select from section 2 any of the specific thoughts, affirmations, or counterarguments that convey the nature of that purpose for you. You can also use your own thoughts or borrow ideas from other sources. Write a smart-talk script based on these thoughts.

Section 1: Purposes for Script Development

1. Remind yourself of your assets, strengths, and desirable personal qualities.

2. Establish priorities and goals as well as action plans for how to achieve them.

3. Recall past successes, particularly in similar situations or when overcoming obstacles, failure, or adversity.

4. Emphasize the quantity and quality of your preparation.

5. Appraise all situations as challenges rather than threats and implement effective problem-solving strategies.

6. Reframe negative thoughts.

7. Attribute success to hard work and improving ability and failure to internal/controllable/unstable factors such as the need to try harder, to improve your mental preparation, or to develop your skills more fully.

Section 2: Sample Positive Thoughts, Affirmations, and Counterarguments

1. Reminders of Assets, Strengths, and Desirable Personal Qualities

a. I'm a talented person with skills and abilities that allow me to be as successful as I want to be in life.

b. Ultimately I'll be judged by who I am, not by what I accomplish.

c. I have the ability to make myself into a better performer who can help my team in many ways.

d. I have rich, rewarding relationships with my close friends and family.

e. I like who I am and enjoy being me. I like the person I see in the mirror.

2. Priorities and Goals Plus Action Plans to Achieve Them

a. I have a dream or vision of what I want in life.

b. I have set my goals, established my priorities, and developed action plans to make them a reality.

c. Dreams become reality through hard work and sacrifice.

d. I have the time, energy, and wisdom to accomplish all my goals.

e. This is a "can do," "will do," and "get things done" day.

(continued)

From D. Burton and T. Raedeke, 2008, *Sport Psychology for Coaches* (Champaign, IL: Human Kinetics).

FIGURE 7.4 Once they've clarified the purpose or purposes of their script, athletes can select the positive thoughts that are most meaningful and effective for them.

3. Remember Past Successes in Similar Situations or How You Overcame Adversity

a. I have been very successful in similar situations in the past.

b. I have overcome difficult obstacles in the past and I can do it again.

c. Failure makes me stronger by helping to identify areas where I need to improve.

d. I know it's only a matter of time until my hard work pays off and I become successful.

e. Overcoming failure and adversity requires a commitment to work even harder and an effective plan to get better and eliminate my weaknesses.

4. Recall the Quantity and Quality of Preparation

a. Nobody works harder than I do, and at crunch time, I'll be in better condition and more willing to pay the price than my opponent.

b. My physical, mental, technical and tactical training were carefully designed to prepare me perfectly to excel in this competition.

c. My coach has taught me to understand my opponent's game and to counter these tactics successfully.

d. I have prepared myself well to maximize my strengths and minimize my weaknesses.

e. I get a little bit better every day in practice and move a step closer to being the best I can be.

5. Appraise Situations as Challenges, Not Threats, and Problem-Solve Effectively

a. Everyone encounters failure and adversity. Champions rise above adversity by viewing problems as opportunities for excellence.

b. I recognize that mistakes are a normal part of learning. As long as I'm learning and trying to get better, mistakes are inevitable. I will look at each mistake as an opportunity to learn and grow as I strive for excellence.

c. I will approach each problem as a challenge—an opportunity to learn and get better as a person and as an athlete.

d. No matter how bleak the outlook or how difficult the obstacle, I will accept the challenge to perform my best and come up with a strategy that will allow me to be successful.

e. I take constructive criticism well, using that feedback to make myself a better person and athlete.

6. Reframe Negative Thoughts

a. I'll concentrate on doing my best right now because I can't change what has happened in the past or what may happen in the future. All I can do is to strive for excellence at this moment.

b. I accept what I can't change or control. I can't control what others think of me or how they play, I can't control my God-given ability or how fast I learn skills. I can't control official's decisions, playing conditions, or luck. I can control my own effort level, attitude, mood, and performance. I'll concentrate on what I can control and not worry about what I cannot control.

c. Life is often unfair, and that is OK. I will continue to work hard because persistence pays off in the long run.

d. I can't control what others think and how they behave. People can find fault with even Hall-of-Fame performers. I will strive to please myself and enjoy competing. The person I have to answer to is the one in the mirror.

e. Playing poorly is disappointing but not awful or unbearable. My life will go on, even if I don't play well. I will try to learn from my mistakes so that I can be more successful in the future.

(continued)

From D. Burton and T. Raedeke, 2008, *Sport Psychology for Coaches* (Champaign, IL: Human Kinetics).

FIGURE 7.4 *(continued)*

---

7. Attribute Success to Hard Work and Failure to Low Effort or the Need to Develop Skills

a. Working hard and developing my skills will allow me to continue to achieve success as I progress up the competitive ladder.

b. I know my hard work and consistent practice have paid dividends and allowed me to achieve the success I've had.

c. This failure is temporary and can be overcome with hard work and persistent skill development.

d. All failure is surmountable with enough time, patience, hard work, and careful planning.

e. When confronted with failure, I focus on the things I can control such as trying harder, getting better prepared mentally, developing my skills more fully, and enjoying the opportunity to test my skills.

From D. Burton and T. Raedeke, 2008, *Sport Psychology for Coaches* (Champaign, IL: Human Kinetics).

FIGURE 7.4 *(continued)*

Reframe Negative Thinking

No matter how effective smart-talk programming is at enhancing positive thinking, some negative thoughts will remain, and they can lead to negative emotions and subpar performance. Correcting negative thoughts is more complicated than just substituting positive thoughts for negative ones. Typically, three steps are required, and we call them the three Ds of reframing: Detect negative, unproductive, or irrational thinking; disrupt negative thoughts by means of thought stopping or thought changing; and dispute negative thoughts by using effective counterarguments. First, athletes must learn to detect, or notice, their distorted or irrational thoughts. These thoughts can be difficult to spot since they are often automatic and lightning fast, and athletes differ in their ability to notice them. Encourage athletes to look for the thoughts that precede feelings of stress or other negative emotions.

Once aware of negative thoughts, athletes can act quickly to disrupt or alter them through thought stopping or thought changing. Thought stopping is a self-talk technique that forcefully disrupts the stream of negative thinking before replacing it with more constructive thoughts. Stopping negative thoughts requires using a sudden, intense stimulus that grabs your attention, such as saying "Stop!" to yourself. Athletes may also incorporate an intense color or image (e.g., a stop sign, red flag, or flashing red lights). Some athletes have better luck stopping their "stinkin' thinkin'" with behavioral cues, such as snapping their fingers or wearing a rubber band and snapping themselves at each negative thought.

Thought changing works like a television remote control to simply change the channel from one with negative thoughts to another that is more positive and productive. Whichever strategy is employed, it is important to disrupt the negative thought quickly and forcefully.

Athletes complete the reframing process by disputing negative thinking with counterarguments. In this step, athletes use logic to establish that a negative thought is irrational and counterproductive, then develop a better way of looking at things (Ellis 1996). Athletes can use figure 7.5 to learn how to reframe negative thoughts. We discussed counterarguments to negative thoughts earlier in the chapter. Unlike positive thinking, which tends to simply hide negative thoughts, counterarguments are solutions, not cover-ups. They function like a good attorney, putting faulty beliefs on trial; refuting them with logical arguments; and identifying logical, realistic, productive thoughts to take their place. If Mary wants more playing time, she can't worry about her coach not liking her. A counterargument will reduce her anxiety: "I can't control what my coach thinks or how much she decides to play me. I need to concentrate on what I can control and play my best by focusing on footwork and positioning off the ball." Counterarguments promote problem solving, thus reducing or eliminating threats. By detecting, disrupting, and disputing negative thoughts, athletes can become more positive and productive.

You have now learned a lot about self-talk skills. But how do you work these concepts into practices and competitions to help athletes develop their smart-talk skills?

Worksheet for Reframing Thoughts

Champions reframe situations in ways that motivate them to perform their best. They proactively create a positive mind-set that promotes excellence rather than allowing the situation to dictate how they think and feel. For this worksheet, list situations in the box on the left that interfere with personal excellence, and reframe those situations more constructively by asking yourself the questions from the box on the right.

Situations

Situations I dislike or complain about that prevent me from performing my best.

Reframing Strategies

How can I reframe this situation as a positive challenge?

What are the positives/benefits of this situation?

How might I benefit from this opportunity?

What can I learn from this situation?

Adapted, by permission, from K. Ravizza and T. Hanson, 1995, *Heads up baseball: Playing the game one pitch at a time* (Indianapolis, IN: Masters Press), 3d, by permission of The McGraw-Hill Companies. From D. Burton and T. Raedeke, 2008, *Sport Psychology for Coaches* (Champaign, IL: Human Kinetics).

FIGURE 7.5 Athletes can use this worksheet to learn how to reframe negativity and produce a flow mind-set.

Developing Athletes' Smart-Talk Skills

Smart-talk represents our best effort to combine scientific findings and practical experience into a program to enhance athletes' self-talk skills. Smart-talk skills are developed through the same three phases used for other mental training tools: education, acquisition, and implementation. Throughout the process, help athletes remember the self-talk dos and don'ts listed in table 7.2.

Education Phase

In this phase, your athletes should learn about self-talk and become aware of their current self-talk patterns. In general terms, they need to know what self-talk is, understand how specific beliefs dictate their emotions and behaviors, and learn the difference between positive and negative thinking. They also need to know how to optimize self-talk by programming positive thoughts and reframing lingering negative thoughts. We recommend holding one or two team meetings to provide your athletes with general self-talk information. You should also distribute handouts that highlight key self-talk principles and application strategies. To help your athletes become more aware of their current self-talk patterns, have them complete self-talk logs after practice for several days (see figure 7.2 on page 109) and conduct one negative thought count. The focus of keeping a baseline log is to identify the types of self-talk that help and hurt performance, so that performers can build on their good patterns and change their negative ones.

TABLE 7.2

Self-Talk Dos and Don'ts

Dos	Don'ts
BEFORE PRACTICE OR COMPETITION	
Focus on positive self-perceptions and strengths.	Don't focus on negative self-perceptions and weaknesses.
Focus on your effective preparation.	Don't focus on inadequacy of or problems with preparation.
Remind yourself of previous successes.	Avoid thinking about previous failures.
Focus on positive expectations and goals.	Avoid unrealistic expectations and negative goals.
Reframe any irrational beliefs using effective counterarguments.	Don't allow irrational beliefs to go unchallenged.
DURING PRACTICE OR COMPETITION	
Limit thinking and rely on automated skills.	Don't think too much, overanalyze, or try to make it happen.
Focus on the present, not the past or future.	Don't dwell on past mistakes or potential future problems.
Focus on process, not product, using effective cue words.	Avoid thinking about the product too much.
Appraise the situation as a challenge, and maintain positive expectations and goals.	Don't appraise the situation as a threat.
Reframe negative thoughts, and use effective problem-solving strategies.	Avoid haphazard reframing or unsystematic problem-solving.
FOLLOWING PRACTICE OR COMPETITION	
Attribute success to internal, controllable factors such as effort and mental prep that will increase perceived competence.	Don't attribute success to external factors or failure to stable, internal ones that will reduce perceived competence.
Develop positive future expectations and goals, complete with action plans for how to achieve them, and minimize oversights.	Avoid negative expectations and goals.

Acquisition Phase

We recommend holding another group session to launch planning and implementation of the smart-talk program. The goal of smart-talk is to help players make positive changes in the quantity and quality of their current self-talk patterns. This involves two steps: programming thought patterns to make them as positive and productive as possible, and using counterarguments to reframe any remaining negative thoughts.

Programming simply means repeating thoughts frequently enough that they become automated, eventually developing into beliefs. Self-talk scripts are an excellent way to program positive thoughts. Athletes can use the process described earlier (and figures 7.3 and 7.4) to develop their own scripts with minimal input from coaches, making this a manageable process to implement. They should start by reading or playing their script four or five times a day. When they report memorizing their script, they are beginning to reach the automated stage. Prime times to read or play scripts include first thing in the morning, last thing at night, on the way to class, during study breaks, while waiting for appointments, and before and after practice. Even after your athletes program their smart-talk, they will have to deal with lingering negative thoughts. Remember the three Ds of the reframing process: Develop an awareness of your negative self-talk patterns so you quickly *detect* negative thoughts. Use thought stopping or thought changing to *disrupt* negative thoughts. Then use effective counterarguments to *dispute* each negative thought and replace it with one that is more positive and productive.

Be sure to monitor self-talk patterns periodically. After a few weeks, collect several more days of data using the self-talk log. Monitor positive and negative situations, emotions, thoughts, counterarguments, and positive mental attitude score. If possible, conduct a second negative thought count using a video of practice to stimulate recall. Normally, with increasing practice, athletes use smart-talk programming to create a more positive mind-set and use counterarguments more effectively to resolve negative thoughts that still arise. Athletes should see an increase in PMA and a decline in the frequency and severity of negative thoughts.

Implementation Phase

Monitoring and programming can be streamlined during this phase. In addition, athletes can start practicing smart-talk skills in imagined, practice, and competitive situations.

Advanced Self-Talk Monitoring and Programming

Once you've acquired basic smart-talk skills, how do you automate and maintain them? Encourage your athletes to continue using the self-talk log, but in a more limited way. If an athlete handles a negative event ineffectively, he or she can use the log to describe the situation and identify effective counterarguments. Athletes also continue to monitor their PMA each day. Any time athletes' PMA dips below level 5, they should identify any problematic negative situations and generate effective counterarguments. Similarly, any time PMA drops below 5 for three or more days, athletes should keep the log for the next three days to identify any new negative thoughts that may be causing problems. Finally, athletes may reduce how often they read or play their self-talk script (from, say, 4 or 5 times daily to 2 or 3 times), as long as positive thoughts remain automated.

Imagery Practice

We encourage athletes to keep a list of negative situations that they have difficulty reframing. Several times per week, they should spend a few minutes imagining recent situations from their list. For each situation, they should intensely imagine the problem and experience the corresponding negative emotions before using reframing skills to counter their faulty thinking. Athletes should practice reframing their thoughts until the situation ceases to cause problems. They might build counterarguments for situations that are particularly problematic into their smart-talk scripts.

Using Smart-Talk in Practice and Competition

If programming is effective, the incidence of self-talk problems in practice and competition should decline. When problems do arise, have athletes detect, disrupt, and dispute negative thoughts as quickly as possible. (Refer back to table 7.2 for self-talk dos and don'ts.) They can also add these situations to their list after practice and begin developing appropriate counterarguments as time permits.

SUMMARY

1. Self-talk is the steady stream of thoughts and internal dialogue that goes on in our heads almost constantly. Your thoughts have a major impact on your mood, emotions, and performance.

2. The ABCs of self-talk describe how thoughts affect emotions and behaviors. The A is the activating event or whatever happens in the situation. The C is the consequence—how you feel and act afterward. The B is your belief or interpretation of the situation, and it determines your emotions and behavior to a much greater extent than the situation itself does.

3. The eight positive self-talk commandments are be an optimist, not a pessimist; remain realistic and objective; focus on the present, not the past or future; appraise problems as challenges rather than threats; view successes as replicable and failures as surmountable; focus on process, not product; concentrate on things you can control; and separate your performance from your self-worth.

4. The critic is the inner voice that attacks and judges you, blaming you when things go wrong and negatively comparing you with others. The critic sets impossible standards of perfection and blasts you when you fall short of them. It exaggerates your weaknesses and minimizes your strengths. Smart-talk can be effective only if it silences the critic.

5. Successful self-talk requires recognizing and changing negative thoughts—particularly distorted thinking and irrational beliefs.

6. The five most common types of distorted thinking are catastrophizing, overgeneralization, blaming, mustification (must thinking), and polarized thinking.

7. Irrational beliefs are highly seductive negative thoughts based on partial fact, unsound evidence, or questionable logic. Five common irrational beliefs in sport are perfectionism, fear of failure, social approval, equity, and social comparison.

8. You can combat distorted thinking and irrational beliefs by using counterarguments to reframe your thoughts.

9. Optimizing self-talk involves becoming aware of current self-talk patterns, programming positive thoughts, and reframing remaining negative thoughts.

10. Athletes can heighten awareness of their self-talk patterns by using imagery recall of good and bad performances, video replay to stimulate accurate negative thought counts in practice, and postpractice and competition logs to investigate the quality of thought patterns.

11. Coaches can teach their athletes to program positive thoughts through self-talk strategies, including positive affirmations, team mottos, and motivational slogans; cue words; and self-talk scripts.

12. The best way to program positive self-talk is to develop a smart-talk script. Scripts should be kept short so that they can be read or played often, up to four or five times daily.

13. Reframing negative thoughts involves using the three Ds: *detecting* negative, irrational, or unproductive thoughts; *disrupting* negative thoughts using thought stopping and thought changing; and *disputing* unproductive negative thoughts by using effective counterarguments.

14. Developing athletes' smart-talk skills involves three phases: education, acquisition, and implementation. First, athletes learn the concept of self-talk and evaluate their current self-talk patterns. Second, they start programming positive thoughts, reframing remaining negative thoughts, and monitoring improvement in self-talk patterns. Finally, they build thought control into normal sport practice and competition.

KEY TERMS

activating event

beliefs

blaming

catastrophizing

counterarguments

(the) critic

cue words

distorted thinking

equity

fear of failure

irrational beliefs

mustification (must thinking)

negative thought count

overgeneralization

perfectionism

polarized thinking

positive affirmations

positive mental attitude

programming

reframing

self-talk

self-talk script

smart-talk

social approval

social comparison

REVIEW QUESTIONS

1. What is self-talk?

2. How does self-talk work?

3. What are eight strategies for proactively programming positive thinking?

4. What is the critic, and what are the five types of distorted thinking it uses?

5. What are the five predominant irrational beliefs common to sport?

6. How does self-talk programming work?

7. What is the three-Ds process for countering negative thoughts?

PRACTICAL ACTIVITIES

1. Develop a script to program your self-talk. Use the Smart-Talk Script Development Form as well as the Purposes and Thoughts for Smart-Talk Scripts handout to facilitate your work.

2. Identify three to five negative or irrational thoughts that athletes in your sport have and provide several counterarguments for each one.

PART III

Enhancing Mental Skills

This section comprises five chapters that demonstrate how to use mental skills to enhance performance. Chapter 8, Motivation, teaches the critical aspects of motivation and shows how to motivate your athletes. The ninth chapter, Energy Management, gives you an understanding of arousal and its impact on performance and shows you how to teach athletes the fundamentals of arousal control. Chapter 10, Attention, helps you understand what to focus on and how to maintain concentration in an easy-to-use and systematic program for developing athletes' attentional skills. The eleventh chapter, Stress Management, teaches basic skills for managing stress and shows you how to develop those skills in your athletes. Finally, chapter 12, Self-Confidence, provides a basic understanding of this essential mental skill, how it influences performance, how it develops, and how you can systematically enhance athletes' confidence.

8

Motivation

After reading this chapter you should be able to

- understand motivation and debunk the myths about it;
- describe how you can structure sport to sustain intrinsic motivation by meeting athletes' needs;
- describe how extrinsic rewards can undermine as well as build intrinsic motivation, depending on how they are structured;
- understand the motivational differences between mastery-oriented, success-seeking, and failure-avoiding athletes; and
- use your knowledge of motivation to create an effective team atmosphere that maximizes athletes' motivation.

Think of an athlete who has dominated your favorite sport, such as Annika Sorenstam, Cal Ripken Jr., Lance Armstrong, Rafael Nadal, Tiger Woods, or Mia Hamm. All are talented, to be sure, but they are also known for their incredible work ethic and drive. Without motivation, talented athletes do not reach their full potential. And athletes who are not particularly talented can achieve a great deal of success with strong desire and motivation.

Despite their best efforts, most coaches can vividly recall the frustrating experience of working with athletes who were less than optimally motivated. The exasperated coach may exclaim, "I just cannot understand why I can't get these athletes to consistently train hard. They seem to focus their efforts on everything else but sport. I've tried everything but just can't motivate them." Most coaches have also had the pleasure of working with highly motivated athletes—they worked hard and persisted even in the face of adversity. Their commitment stemmed from their love of the game and the satisfaction they derived from working toward their goals. After working with such an athlete, the coach may comment, "I've never known a more persistent competitor. I wish I knew what drives her to excel; I'd package it and give it to every member of my team."

Motivating athletes to sustain hard training, compete aggressively, and focus their energies toward specific goals is indeed a challenge. It's one thing to develop athletes' motivation when things are going well; it's a whole new challenge to keep them motivated in times of adversity or during the off-season. Motivation is influenced by so many factors that it would take several volumes to consider them all in depth, but the most vital components are few and easy to understand. When we talk with coaches, they ask two questions:

Why are some athletes so much more motivated than others?

How do I motivate the athletes I coach?

Coaches want the secrets to motivation. There is no quick fix or simple solution. If it were that easy, you would have learned the secrets to motivation long ago. Instead, we recommend that you develop an understanding of the principles that underlie motivation. This chapter helps you do that. Rather than focus on simple how-to approaches, which tend to oversimplify, we focus on understanding *why* athletes are motivated. Armed with that understanding, we can then turn our attention to *how to* motivate athletes through the ups and downs of a season.

What Is Motivation?

How do we know that athletes are motivated? They act like it. And how does the motivated athlete act or behave? Motivation is reflected in three behaviors:

- *Choice.* Motivation shows in the choices athletes make—choosing to play sport, to practice, to set challenging goals, and to train even in the off-season.
- *Effort.* Motivation is also reflected in how much effort athletes give—how intensely they train, compete, and strive to achieve their goals.
- *Persistence.* Motivation level can be seen in how long athletes persist at striving to attain their goals, even in the face of adversity and obstacles.

We can better understand what motivation is by debunking some motivation myths.

Motivation Myth 1: Athletes Are Either Motivated or Not Motivated

Some coaches believe that motivation is simply a personality trait, a static internal characteristic. They believe that an athlete either has motivation or doesn't—end of story. They don't believe motivation is something coaches can develop. For these coaches, the key to having a motivated team is to find and recruit athletes who have the right personality. If this were true, little could be done to inspire athletes who were not highly motivated. However, while some athletes are, in fact, more motivated than others, this view does not provide any direction or guidance on how coaches can help develop and sustain athletes' motivation. The fact is, coaches *can* help athletes develop motivation.

Motivation Myth 2: Coaches Give Athletes Motivation

Other coaches view motivation as something they can inject into their athletes on demand, like a flu shot, by means of inspirational pep talks or gimmicks. They may use slogans, posters, and bulletin board quotes from upcoming opponents. These strategies may be helpful, but they are only a small piece of the motivation puzzle. There is much more to the story—motivation is not something coaches can simply give their athletes.

Motivation Myth 3: Motivation Means Sticks and Carrots

Some experts suggest that effective motivation means using carrots (rewards) and sticks (punishments) to drive athletes to do things they would not do on their own. This may seem innocuous, but think about it on a deeper level. It assumes that athletes don't want to do something, so the coach will provide motivation to make them do it through punishments or rewards. Coaches who emphasize the stick, in the form of chastising, criticizing, yelling, coercing, and creating guilt, often find themselves swimming upstream. No matter what they try, they meet resistance and negative attitudes. Not only is this approach ineffective, it saps the enjoyment out of sport. There is also more to the motivation puzzle than the carrot (reward) approach. Coaches must understand athletes' needs in order to create a team culture that naturally motivates them.

Athletes' Needs and Intrinsic Motivation

Great coaches know that they don't give athletes motivation. Rather, they create the conditions or team climate in which athletes motivate themselves. Coaches do this by recognizing the importance of **intrinsic motivation**, which stems from the sheer pleasure and inner satisfaction athletes experience from participating in sport. Intrinsically motivated athletes play for the love of the game. They enjoy the process of learning and mastering difficult sport skills and play for the pride they feel when working hard toward accomplishing a challenging goal. They also find sport stimulating and feel exhilarated when engaged in it.

So what is the secret to cultivating athletes' intrinsic motivation? The answer is simple: Understand what athletes need from sport. Like anyone, athletes are motivated to meet their needs. Structuring sport in a way that meets athletes' need fosters intrinsic motivation, and failure to meet athletes' needs lowers it. What do athletes need from sport? Evidence from a variety of sources suggests that athletes seek to fulfill four primary needs: to have fun and experience stimulation and excitement, to feel accepted and belong to a group, to exercise control and autonomy, and to feel competent.

The Need for Fun and Stimulation

If you asked athletes why they participate in sport, what do you think they would say? In a survey of nearly 10,000 athletes, the most common reason given was to have fun (Ewing & Seefeldt 1990; Seefeldt, Ewing, & Walk 1992;). Having fun and developing skills were rated as more important than even winning. When former athletes are asked why they quit sport, they typically say something along these lines:

"I found other activities more interesting."

"I would rather do other things than play sport."

"Sport was no longer fun."

"I burnt out on sport."

Do you see the connection between the reasons athletes play sport and the reasons they drop out? Motivation comes naturally and easily when athletes are having fun. Lack of fun makes sport seem like a boring job, lowers motivation, and even causes athletes to drop out. If sport is not fun, coaches find that motivating athletes is difficult, if not impossible.

Sport is much more enjoyable when athletes find practice activities stimulating, challenging, and exciting. A youth sport coach came to see me (Tom) in complete frustration because her team was not motivated. On arriving early to watch the team practice, I noticed a group of youngsters playing an intense game of basketball outside on a bent hoop without a net. It turned out that these were her players, but once inside the gym, true to the coach's word, they were totally unmotivated. The practice was intense, highly structured, and monotonous. The drills were either boring or beyond their skill level. The kids often appeared antagonistic to the coach, who constantly threatened and administered discipline. The coach had failed to realize that most of these kids wanted to play basketball for fun and to learn skills in a way that was enjoyable, not to do drills and calisthenics all day. Nor did they want to be yelled at. When the coach left at the end of practice, many of the players stayed behind and played pickup basketball. The entire atmosphere changed, everyone hustled, and there was a lot of laughter and intense play. Because the coach had deprived the players of attaining one of their major goals for joining the team—to have fun—they met their need outside of practice.

Most athletes are intrinsically motivated when they first start playing. One of your greatest challenges as a coach is to avoid destroying your athletes' intrinsic motivation to play sport. Some coaches erroneously believe that fun means easy workouts, frivolous games, and countless team parties. But challenging practices, intense workouts, and focusing on skill development can be fun. In fact, fun is maximized when athletes experience optimal stimulation and excitement. No one finds it fun to lose or fail constantly, so build in some success. Most athletes are also bored by being underchallenged while performing tedious drills. Thus coaches should strive to fit the difficulty of the skill to the ability of the athletes. Coached this way, athletes feel challenged but not overwhelmed, because they have the ability to meet the challenge (see figure 8.1).

Wise coaches have long known that meeting athletes' need for fun enhances motivation. Yet they also know that athletes must practice to learn and improve skills. The creative coach can find ways to facilitate skill development in a way that is fun for athletes. Here are a few examples:

- Use developmental progressions to create an optimal skill–challenge balance.

- Keep practices stimulating by varying the activities.

- Teach fundamentals by means of action-packed, gamelike activities that use the targeted skills.

- Keep everyone active. Don't give players time to get bored by having them stand in long lines.

- Set aside time in each practice when athletes can just play the game, without receiving evaluation or feedback from the coach.

Structuring sport to be fun is key not only to motivation but also to helping athletes develop their skills. If athletes enjoy sport, they become more motivated. If they are more motivated, they improve. As they improve, they enjoy sport more. And so it goes.

Athletes who are motivated primarily by their need to have fun may present discipline problems for coaches who have sapped the fun out of sport. As these athletes try to find creative ways to have fun, they may be seen as goof-offs or discipline problems. Some coaches assume that athletes are not motivated when they balk at doing everything the coach's way. In reality, such players are often highly motivated to play—just not according to the structure and methods dictated by the coach.

The Need for Acceptance and Belonging

The second basic need athletes strive to fill through sport is for acceptance and belonging. This need can be met if athletes feel they fit in and are accepted by others on the team. In fact, some athletes play sport primarily because they enjoy being with their friends and being part of a team, and coaches can use this need as a powerful motivator. Here are some guidelines:

- Recognize that these athletes are usually responsive to team goals. Although performing well and winning may not be as significant to them as is identifying with the team, they will internalize team goals because of their desire to be part of the group.

- Arrange activities that allow athletes to get to know each other and spend time together. Social activities are a good way to help fulfill the need for acceptance and belonging.

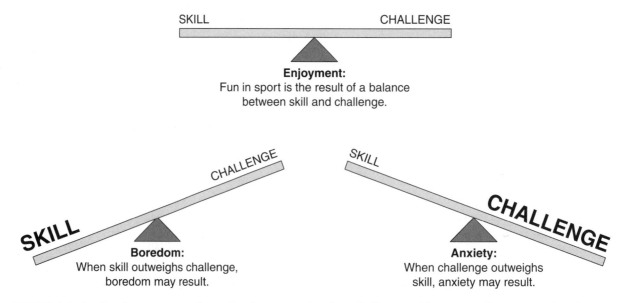

Enjoyment:
Fun in sport is the result of a balance between skill and challenge.

Boredom:
When skill outweighs challenge, boredom may result.

Anxiety:
When challenge outweighs skill, anxiety may result.

FIGURE 8.1   To develop an atmosphere that fosters motivation, challenge athletes enough to excite them but not enough to overwhelm them.

Adapted from M.E. Ewing and V. Seefeldt, 1990, *American youth and sports participation: A study of 10,000 students and their feelings about sports* (North Palm Beach, FL: Athletic Footwear Association), by permission of the Sporting Goods Manufacturers Association (SGMA).

- Include team building activities to help build cohesion. By working together toward a common goal that is not directly related to sport, athletes can learn to appreciate previously overlooked strengths in themselves and their teammates.

- Create an atmosphere on the team where athletes feel they are playing with each other rather than against one another.

- Have returning athletes serve as mentors to new athletes

- Ensure that all athletes feel they are important members of the team and that their roles are important and valued.

The Need for Control and Autonomy

This need is important but easily overlooked. In fact, one of the most basic human needs is to develop autonomy, and this is especially true among adolescents on their journey to adulthood. Filling this need requires that athletes have control over their own lives and determine their own course of behavior. Once they choose to participate in a sport, they need to have ownership and feel they have a say in decisions affecting their involvement. Otherwise, they feel pressured or obligated to act, think, or feel a certain way. High autonomy encourages wanting to participate, whereas low autonomy means having to participate.

One of the best ways we can enhance motivation is to help athletes develop personal responsibility. Pressure to win, scholarships hanging over athletes' heads, and the apparent necessity to conform to coaching demands may cause athletes to feel controlled by coaches, reducing motivation. A wealth of scientific evidence (Deci & Flaste 1996) has come to the same conclusion: Deny people the right to control their own lives and you destroy intrinsic motivation, sense of achievement, self-responsibility, and self-worth. Grant people the opportunity to control their own lives and nurture their personal development, and you enhance these motivational qualities. Nurturing personal responsibility not only enhances autonomy and motivation, it also promotes athletes' personal development. Most coaches agree that sport should help athletes learn responsibility, but find it difficult to give them the opportunity to demonstrate responsibility. The problem is clear: When athletes are given responsibility, they do not always use it wisely. They do not always make the best decisions, and these errors can hurt the team's performance. Coaches who feel society's pressure to win, or who coach for their own ego enhancement,

may be quick to withdraw such responsibility if it threatens their team's chances of winning. You can use several strategies to help athletes develop a sense of ownership and responsibility. When appropriate, involve athletes in decision making, provide choice, and request their input. You can do this, for example, by giving them a say in their training regimen. You can teach athletes how to develop their own training program, giving them more and more responsibility as they learn more about effective training principles. Encourage athletes to take as much responsibility as you judge they have the maturity to handle. Provide structure and guidance, giving more control as athletes demonstrate the wise use of responsibility. When athletes err in using their responsibility, constructively help them better understand how to act responsibly. Athletes should neither expect nor be given free rein, but they should be given choices within a structured environment.

The coach who facilitates this type of graduated responsibility development is not necessarily a democratic coach in every respect. Not all decisions are voted on—many are the sole responsibility of the coach. But by shifting some control to athletes, it is possible to develop a disciplined team where athletes feel a strong sense of ownership.

In summary, to meet athletes' need for control and autonomy, you should make sure they feel a sense of ownership over their sport involvement. Ways to do this include the following:

- Provide a rationale for your decisions.

- Ensure that athletes feel they are responsible for their own fate and are not merely pawns.

- Solicit athletes' input and provide choices whenever possible.

- Involve athletes in developing practice plans and game strategies, evaluating practices and competitions, developing team rules and a team covenant or mission, and selecting captains.

The Need to Feel Competent and Successful

The need to feel competent is one of the most important components of motivation. **Perceived competence** means having positive perceptions of one's skills and abilities and feeling capable of succeeding in sport. It is doubtful that athletes will work hard, or even stay in sport, if they feel like failures. Athletes use many sources to judge their skill and success at sport. Even the simple act of choosing up sides can influence athletes' feelings of competence. Always getting picked first by one's peers contributes to feeling competent, thus enhancing motivation, whereas routinely getting picked last may cause an athlete to feel incompetent and walk away from sport.

Athletes' perceived competence can be raised through success at challenging tasks, positive feedback from a coach, and approval from parents. Effective coaches spend a lot of time and energy structuring sport in a way that makes each athlete feel competent. Indeed, you as a coach are responsible for ensuring that athletes develop positive perceptions of their skills and abilities and feel successful at sport. You can use the strategies listed in the section on making sport fun to help your athletes' feel competent and successful. Additional suggestions are given later in this chapter as well as in chapter 12. Although experiencing success is central to feeling competent, experiencing failure is inevitable in the sport world, as in life. All athletes, no matter how talented, experience failure, adversity, and setbacks at some point. How athletes respond to failure has a huge effect on long-term motivation, and more information about preparing athletes to deal with success and failure is presented later in this chapter.

Impact of Rewards

As you strive to meet athletes' needs, it is important to understand how rewards can help and hurt your efforts to improve motivation. Even as sport has the potential to be intrinsically motivating, a wide variety of extrinsic motivators also exist. Athletes can be motivated by tangible rewards, such as awards, letter jackets, trophies, all-star recognition, and athletic scholarships. They may also work hard for intangible rewards, such as public recognition and approval from family, coaches, and friends.

Rewards (extrinsic motivators) sometimes undermine intrinsic motivation by turning play into work. In *Punished By Rewards* (1999), Kohn argues that a steady stream of research has found that rewards backfire; rather than bolstering motivation, they actually undermine it. People tend to lose interest more quickly, give up more easily, and ultimately perform worse when rewards are involved. While rewards might be effective in bringing about temporary compliance, over the long haul, they almost always backfire. When asked what he was offered by college recruiters, Hall of Famer Magic Johnson said, "I received my share of offers for cars and money. It immediately turned me off. It was like they were trying to buy me, and I didn't like anyone trying to buy me" (Weinberg 1984).

The potential of rewards to undermine intrinsic motivation is illustrated vividly in the now-classic story of how a man stopped a group of children from playing noisily in the vacant lot next to his house each afternoon. The more he hollered, the noisier the children got and the longer they played. One day, he called them to his house and told them that he liked watching them play and that he wanted to pay them to continue playing. He offered to pay each of them a dollar for each day they played on the vacant lot after school. The next day, the kids played enthusiastically and collected their money. The second day, the old man apologetically explained he could pay them only 75 cents, and on the following two days he reduced his payment to 50 and then 25 cents. By day 5, the old man told them he had run out of money but certainly hoped they would continue to play. Indignant, the children declared they were not going to play for nothing! Problem solved.

Thus, when extrinsic rewards are used in such a way that athletes feel they are being controlled or bribed, intrinsic motivation is likely to be undermined (see figure 8.2). Rewards can also lower intrinsic motivation if they diminish athletes' sense of competence. This often occurs when the reward unintentionally communicates something negative to athletes about their skill or contributions to the team. If rewards help athletes feel successful, such as when they are given as recognition for improvement, attaining a standard of excellence, or accomplishing a goal, they can raise perceived competence and intrinsic motivation. But rewards that are not based on performance accomplishments and do not communicate anything positive to athletes about their competence have no real power to build intrinsic motivation; in fact, they can lower perceived competence. Take for example, "participant" rewards in youth sport. Although well intentioned, such rewards can leave athletes feeling that the coach does not appreciate their contributions to the team—important team members received meaningful rewards, and they didn't. However, if participant rewards are personalized and specify the contributions each athlete made to the team, they have the power to increase intrinsic motivation.

Does this mean that coaches should not use rewards to motivate athletes? Certainly not. In fact, successful coaches skillfully use external rewards to build intrinsic motivation. Intrinsic and extrinsic motivation can work together to maximize total motivation if the extrinsic reinforcers are properly structured.

• Rewards can raise intrinsic motivation if they are based on meaningful accomplishments and thus raise perceived competence. Skilled coaches help athletes understand that while a trophy or medal is nice, the ultimate rewards are pride and sense of accomplishment.

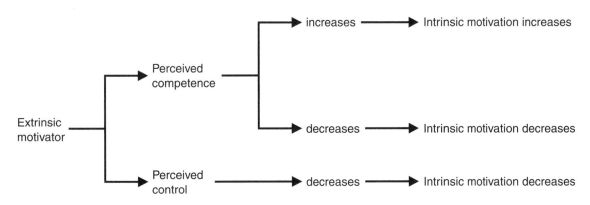

FIGURE 8.2 Rewards and intrinsic motivation.

• Sport provides many extrinsic rewards for outcomes such as winning, but coaches can use rewards to acknowledge effort, improvement, and performance quality regardless of winning and losing, thus raising perceived competence.

• Rewards can also be used to help transform extrinsic into intrinsic motivation, especially for athletes who start with low intrinsic motivation. For example, some recreational runners start participating in road races for extrinsic reasons, such as receiving a T-shirt and improving their health. Over time, a shift occurs, and they continue to run because they enjoy running and the sense of accomplishment it provides. Similarly, coaches can use extrinsic rewards to develop an athlete's initial interest in a sport, then slowly withdraw or deemphasize them as the intrinsic rewards grow.

• Rewards do not have to be big to raise motivation. The power of extrinsic motivators derives from their meaning, not their actual value. Simple rewards—such as the "glue award" for the athlete who builds team cohesion or the "nail award" for the mentally tough athlete—can reinforce feelings of pride and accomplishment and thus go a long way toward increasing motivation (Janssen 1999). In fact, small rewards are less likely to be viewed as controlling than large ones and thus are often more effective in raising intrinsic motivation.

There is an art to using extrinsic rewards to develop intrinsic motivation. The effect of rewards on intrinsic motivation is determined by the message given. If rewards raise perceived competence and are not viewed as a form of sly manipulation, then they raise intrinsic motivation. Thus it is important that rewards be neither excessive nor presented in a controlling or autonomy diminishing way. Athletes will react negatively to perceived manipulation. Give rewards for meaningful accomplishment and help athletes understand that while extrinsic rewards are nice mementos, the primary purpose for playing is the enjoyment and satisfaction derived from the experience.

Handling Success and Failure

Several pieces of the motivation puzzle are now in place. You understand that the key to developing and sustaining intrinsic motivation is to meet athletes' needs. With this knowledge, you can work to strengthen motivation and avoid undermining it. You can use extrinsic motivators to increase intrinsic motivation if you structure them properly. The next piece of the motivation puzzle is understanding how athletes respond to success and failure. Motivating athletes is much easier in success than in failure, but there is a wrinkle: Although some athletes respond to success by feeling even more motivated, others get complacent or seem unaffected.

In times of adversity, some athletes stay positive, keep trying, and never feel like they are failing. Michael Jordan puts it this way: "I've missed more than 9,000 shots. . . . I've lost almost 300 games. Twenty-six times I've been trusted to take the game-winning shot and missed. I've failed over and over again in my life and this is why I succeed." (Greenfield 1997). But other athletes faced with adversity turn negative and stop trying. Let's explore the reasons athletes respond to success and failure as they do.

Mastery and Outcome Orientations

Athletes want to demonstrate competence and to avoid demonstrating a lack of competence. In doing so they can adopt either a mastery or an outcome orientation. Take two typical athletes, Jamie and Josh. Jamie enjoys winning but focuses on the challenges of sport and seeing how much she can improve.

Josh likes to be the best and wants recognition for winning; he feels successful when he accomplishes a task that others find difficult because it makes him feel talented. Thus Jamie and Josh define success quite differently. Mastery-oriented athletes like Jamie define success based on personal standards such as effort, improvement, personal development, and task mastery. They are motivated by the satisfaction of working hard, improving, and accomplishing a personally challenging goal. Even if they lose, mastery-oriented athletes feel successful if they perform well. Ask mastery-oriented athletes to list the keys to sport success and they will say falling in love with the process of improvement, hard work, and persistence. In contrast, outcome-oriented athletes base feelings of success and failure on how they compare with others. They feel successful if they do well compared to others, and they feel like a failure if their perfor-

mance does not measure up well. Ask them about the foundation of sport success, and they'll highlight having talent and being gifted.

Mastery-Oriented Athletes and Motivation

Mastery-oriented athletes are highly motivated both in times of success and in adversity. They are likely to achieve consistent success and feel good about their accomplishments because they define success in terms of factors they can control, such as effort and improvement. They try hard to master challenging tasks and continue to work hard even in the face of failure (see table 8.1). Thomas Edison was a classic mastery-oriented person. He tried several thousand times to develop the light bulb without becoming discouraged, even though everyone around him had given up hope

TABLE 8.1

Goal Orientations: A Crash Course

Characteristics	Mastery-oriented	OUTCOME-ORIENTED	
		Success seekers	Failure avoiders
Goal-setting style	Focus on learning and personal improvement. Both those with high and low perceived ability believe they can succeed.	Focus on social comparison and winning. High perceived ability because they compare well socially. Motivated to succeed.	Focus on social comparison but fear failure. Low perceived ability because of poor social comparison. Motivated to avoid failure.
Preferred task choice	Difficult, challenging. Select learning opportunities even at risk of displaying mistakes.	Challenging but realistic. Sacrifice learning opportunities if risk of displaying mistakes is high.	Very difficult or very easy. Sacrifice learning opportunities to avoid displaying low ability.
Effort	Consistently strong effort to promote maximum learning and improvement.	Only as high as needed to demonstrate positive social comparison.	Low effort on moderately challenging tasks to avoid demonstrating low ability. High effort on easy tasks to avoid failure. May give high effort on very difficult tasks.
Response to failure and setbacks	Increased effort and persistance.	Increased effort as long as they believe they can succeed.	Give up and quit trying.
Explanations for success and failure	Success is due to effort and improvement. Failure is due to something that can be improved, such as effort and skill development.	Success is caused by talent. Failure is discounted or is due to something that can be improved.	Success is due to luck or an easy task. Failure is caused by a lack of ability.

of ever making it work. He believed that every time he tried something and it didn't work, he was one step closer to finding something that did work.

Mastery-oriented athletes thrive on challenge and respond to adversity with confidence and heightened motivation. They dig deep within themselves and remain focused on achieving success even in the face of failure. In fact, mastery-oriented athletes do not perceive failure. Although they readily recognize they have not yet succeeded, they don't see that as a failure, and this motivates them to be persistent and create strategies for succeeding. They persist because they realize their hard work will eventually pay off and their performance will improve. David Duval had 86 starts before he won on the PGA tour and led the tour in earnings and scoring in 1998. Throughout that time, he never felt like a failure, because he was always progressing and improving (Duval 1998). All athletes will experiences slumps, plateaus, and periods where they see little progress. Mastery-oriented athletes focus on striving to improve and have consistently high confidence because they feel they are always on verge of breaking out and experiencing success. Because of this mind-set, they are a joy to coach, and they fully develop their potential.

As these athletes experience success and become more confident in their abilities, their motivation continues to grow. Each improvement, no matter how small, reinforces their hard work and keeps them inspired because they know they are making progress toward their goals. Mastery-oriented athletes are drawn to challenging but obtainable goals because challenging tasks afford them the greatest opportunity to develop their skills and succeed. They take credit for their success, attributing it to internal qualities like hard work and diligent preparation, which allows them to feel pride in their accomplishment and creates positive expectations that they can succeed again in the future. Attributing success to effort and skill development motivates them to keeping working hard for weeks, months, and years if necessary to maximize long-term development.

Mastery-oriented athletes attribute failure to lack of effort, poor execution at critical points in the contest, being physically or mentally unprepared to play, or anything else that can be changed in the future. These athletes take responsibility for failure in a way that can be fixed and improved. Failure is not threatening because it is not a negative reflection on their underlying ability and self-worth. They are confident that the next game will turn out differently and that failure is a stepping stone to success. This tendency to take credit for success and accept responsibility for failure is a healthy attitude, one you want to develop in your athletes.

Success Seekers and Motivation

Success seekers are outcome-oriented athletes who are confident in their abilities to succeed. These athletes are motivated to be the best. Like Josh in the earlier scenario, success seekers feel talented and thus most satisfied when they succeed at tasks that other athletes struggle with. Success seekers typically show positive motivational qualities. Their primary goal is to demonstrate their talent by doing well compared with other athletes, and they believe they can be successful. As long as they are confident that they compare well, they will work hard and strive for success. Given a choice, they will choose challenging but realistic tasks to maximize the chances of performing well and demonstrating their ability. Succeeding at an extremely easy task does not showcase their talent and succeeding at an extremely difficult task is unlikely. Success seekers internalize success by attributing it to their ability and talent, which is confidence building in times of success.

Although success-oriented athletes generally have positive motivational qualities, they work only as hard as they need to. These athletes often have difficulty training during the off-season, because they believe talent, not just effort, is the key to success. During the season, they will sometimes use practice strategies that are ineffective in developing their potential. Occasionally, they will show off in practice and competition. Based on their views of ability, they believe that athletes who have to try hard to accomplish a task are less talented than those who can succeed without putting forth complete effort. In addition, they may focus on their favorite moves to ensure they do well rather than trying new techniques and strategies. Although this approach helps them succeed in the short run, it limits their long-term growth as athletes.

In response to an occasional failure, success seekers respond well and attribute their lack of success to something that can be fixed through skill development. However, success seekers do not always respond well to adversity, especially if it is prolonged. Anything that reflects negatively on their talent is viewed as a threat to their self-worth. These athletes have difficulty separating performance from self-worth. Rather than taking responsibility for failure, they tend to discount it by blaming their poor performance on external factors such as bad luck, poor playing conditions, the coach, or lousy officiating. In some situations, this type of response is warranted and allows athletes to save face and maintain their feelings of confidence and self-worth. But athletes who routinely blame external factors for poor performances are limiting their growth as athletes because they are not taking responsibility.

There is an even bigger motivational drawback for outcome-oriented athletes: It is hard for athletes to sustain feelings of competence based on how well they compare with others because they can give the best performance of their life and still fall short. This lack of control over success makes it difficult for outcome-oriented athletes to maintain a strong sense of ability; few athletes can outperform others on a consistent basis, particularly as they move up the competitive ladder. After all, in every competition, at least half of all competitors lose. And if success seekers start doubting their ability, they become failure avoiders.

Failure Avoiders and Motivation

Outcome-oriented athletes who doubt their abilities are called **failure avoiders**. Rather than striving to demonstrate success, they focus on avoiding failure because they doubt they can compare well with others. Take, for example, Terri, a talented first-year athlete who was a standout in high school. She is extremely dedicated and wants to become an All-American but is having trouble with the transition to collegiate play. In high school, she was always the best player on the field, and it is hard for her to handle being one among many. Lately, Terri has been in a slump, and her confidence is fading fast. She is devastated when she loses to several opponents she used to defeat with ease. She begins to experience high levels of anxiety before each competition, which breeds poor performance, which in turn causes even greater anxiety, and the downward spiral continues.

Athletes like Terri lose motivation if they begin questioning their ability. Sport clearly identifies winners and losers, and because these athletes doubt their ability to succeed, they become motivated to avoid failure (and thus avoid exposing what they fear is their low ability). Failure avoiders shy away from challenges, lose composure easily, and tend to give up in response to failure. Their self-confidence is fleeting. Even if they have a string of good performances, they might respond to one bad game with a dejected attitude and return to doubting their ability. Because of their self-doubt and anxiety, these athletes tend to avoid the challenging tasks that are necessary for long-term skill development and give up quickly in response to adversity. They focus more on avoiding failure than striving for success, and, as a result, they seldom develop their skills fully.

What is the best way for these athletes to avoid failure and protect self-worth? Avoid situations that may reflect negatively on their ability. Often these individuals choose not to participate in sport at all or to avoid competition. If they do participate, they are likely to drop out of sport. Some learn to protect their self-worth by giving a token effort, putting forth only minimal effort, so that others will not discover their feared lack of ability. Deep down, they believe that if they try hard and lose, everyone will know they lack talent. By not trying, they have an excuse for performing poorly: "I could have succeeded, but I didn't try." In the mind of the failure avoider, not trying is less threatening than having others discover their lack of ability. The tragedy in this approach is that giving only partial effort almost certainly guarantees failure in the desperate attempt to avoid it.

Other common ploys of the failure-avoiding athlete include staying armed with excuses and blaming external factors for possible failure: "I haven't felt good this week." "My ankle is acting up, so I doubt I'll do well." "The calls aren't going my way." As with the token effort strategy, these excuses are desperate attempts to protect their fragile self-worth. Failure-avoiding athletes also tend to select easy tasks, where they are guaranteed to succeed, thus avoiding a display of low ability. On occasion, these athletes will select an incredibly difficult task, where no one would expect them to succeed. If they fail, they can attribute their lack of success to the impossible nature of the task, not their lack of ability. If they pull off the impossible, they view it as a positive reflection of their talent.

It is important that you recognize the motivational characteristics associated with failure-avoiding athletes so you do not misdiagnose their motivational problems. On the surface, failure-avoiding athletes appear not to care, but in reality they care deeply. It's not that they lack motivation, they are just motivated differently, hoping to avoid failure rather than striving for success. Some coaches try to motivate failure avoiders by arranging success experiences, figuring that consistent success should help these athletes develop the qualities of success seekers. However, they often find that failure avoiders reject success. Rather than internalizing success, they discount good performances, believing that they got lucky or their opponent was having an off day (or some other external explanation). As a result, success does not provide them with positive feelings of accomplishment, nor does it raise their confidence in their ability to succeed again in the future. Thus success has little impact on their confidence or motivation because they discount it.

Although failure-avoiding athletes do not take credit for success, they do internalize poor performances, which in turn lowers their sense of self-worth. After a loss or poor performance, these athletes will hang their heads in shame because they feel they lack talent. Failure reaffirms the belief that they are too slow, uncoordinated, or unathletic to do well in sport. Motivation to try hard is thwarted. This tendency to blame themselves for failure, yet discount success, spells disaster.

Creating a Mastery-Oriented Motivational Atmosphere

After reading the descriptions of mastery-oriented athletes, success seekers, and failure avoiders, you can see that mastery-oriented athletes have the optimal motivation. They set challenging goals, put forth higher and more consistent effort, and demonstrate greater persistence in the face of adversity. Thus successful coaches have learned how to create a **mastery-oriented team atmosphere**. They recognize that this environment breeds success.

You might expect that the most talented athletes are mastery-oriented or are success seekers, and that their less skilled counterparts are failure avoiders. In reality, some of the most physically talented athletes are failure avoiders. Who are these athletes? You've probably never heard of them, unless they happen to be on your team. Without hard work and a focus on learning, they will not reach their long-term potential. Some coaches accept that a mastery-oriented team atmosphere is good for young, developing athletes but erroneously believe that high-level athletes need an **outcome-oriented team atmosphere** with a focus on winning. This is blatantly false. Legendary coach John Wooden, winner of 10 NCAA titles in 12 years, never focused on winning. Rather, he insisted that each player give the game his all, and he defined success in terms of how well prepared his team was to execute at its own level of competence. If a player walked off the court having given 100%, then he could hold his head high, no matter the outcome. These athletes were encouraged to view success as the self-satisfaction that came from striving to be the best team they were capable of becoming (Wooden 1997). Undoubtedly, Wooden's emphasis on effort, preparation, and personal improvement stacked the deck in favor of winning by creating a team atmosphere that

Thoughts from Coach John Wooden on the Meaning of Success

I informed every player who came under my supervision that the outcome of a game was simply a by-product of the effort we made to prepare. They understood our destination was a successful journey—namely, total, complete, and detailed preparation. Thus there were many, many games that gave me as much pleasure as any of the ten national championships we won, simply because we prepared fully and played near our highest level of ability. . . . The preparation is where success is truly found. . . . I was just as satisfied with my efforts in the fourteen years before we won a national championship as I was the final twelve years, when we captured ten championships. In fact, and you may have trouble accepting this, I believe we were *more* successful than in some years when we did. . . .

Winning games, titles, and championships isn't all it's cracked up to be, and getting there, the journey, is a lot *more* than it's cracked up to be. . . . Please understand that I wanted to win every single game I ever played in or coached. . . . But, I understood that ultimately the winning or losing may not be under my control. What was under my control was how I prepared myself and our team. I judged my success, my "winning," on that. . . . If we won, great; frosting on the cake. But, at no time did I consider winning to be the cake.

I had mistakes, plenty, but I had no failure. We may not have won a championship every year, we may have lost games. But we had no failures. You never fail if you know in your heart that you did the best of which you are capable. . . . And are you going to make mistakes? Of course, but it is not failure if you make the full effort. I told my players many times, "Failing to prepare is preparing to fail." If you prepare properly you may be outscored *but you will never lose*. Long before any championships were ever won at UCLA, I came to understand that losing is only temporary and not all encompassing. You must simply study it, learn from it, and try hard not to lose the same way again. Then you must have the *self-control* to forget it.

Adapted from J. Wooden and S. Jamison, 1997, *Wooden: A lifetime of observations and reflections on and off the court* (Chicago, IL: Contemporary Books), 53-55, 80, 82, by permission of The McGraw-Hill Companies.

fostered athletes' motivation and maximized their skill development.

Across sports, the most successful athletes place great emphasis on both mastery and outcome goals. Considering what it means to win a gold medal, mastery-oriented athletes have said that winning is not about beating others but about reaching into the depths of their capabilities and competing against themselves to the fullest extent. Although winning is important, the greatest inspiration for highly successful athletes is not to outdo others but to outdo themselves. Their focus on self-improvement is especially strong in practice, where the emphasis is on learning. Even golf great Tiger Woods completely revamped his swing after reaching the pinnacle of his profession, because he recognized the need for self-improvement in order to progress.

Most coaches believe that skill learning and improvement are essential precursors to competitive success, but they sometimes lose that perspective in their quest to win, inadvertently creating an outcome orientation that undermines their intended emphasis on effort and improvement. Coaches can inadvertently shift to an outcome-oriented climate by constantly emphasizing the importance of winning. The focus is transferred from learning skills to performing skills. Mistakes and errors that are a normal part of the learning process are seen as threats to be eliminated at all costs; coaches may punish the athletes who make them, or use them as sources of public embarrassment. Many coaches also fall into the habit of giving most of their attention to star athletes, and sometimes they create rivalry on their own team by pitting athletes against one another in the belief that players will be motivated to reach higher levels.

A mastery focus takes just the opposite approach. Table 8.2 describes what you and your athletes will emphasize as you develop a mastery-oriented team atmosphere, where learning is the focus. Given the fragile motivation of outcome-oriented athletes and their difficulty in sustaining positive self-perceptions based on comparisons with others, coaches should encourage all athletes to become mastery-oriented. Athletes who play for mastery-oriented coaches are highly motivated and have higher confidence and lower anxiety than athletes who play in a different atmosphere. Not surprisingly, these athletes ultimately perform better. And this is true in youth sport settings as well as higher-level sport.

How do coaches create a mastery-oriented motivational climate? In a nutshell, they make their actions consistent with their beliefs about the importance of effort and learning. They focus on skill development and foster an attitude of enjoyment by defining success in terms of effort, personal bests, and skill execution, rather than outcome. They encourage athletes to challenge themselves to improve. They create a team culture that views mistakes as a natural and necessary part of the learning process, not a reason for ridicule or a sign of failure. And they help athletes realize that even though there are ability differences between team members, each athlete plays an important role in the success of the team.

TABLE 8.2

Defining a Mastery-Oriented Motivational Atmosphere

Key questions	Mastery team atmosphere
How is success defined?	Individual progress, improvement
What is valued?	Effort, preparation, and improvement
How are athletes evaluated?	Progress, effort
How are mistakes viewed?	Part of learning
Why participate?	Develop new skills
When do athletes feel satisfied?	Successful effort, challenge, and personal bests
What are athletes focused on?	Skill learning and development
What is the coach focused on?	Skill learning and development

Adapted from C. Ames and J. Archer, 1988, "Achievement goals in the classroom: Students' learning strategies and motivation processes," *Journal of Educational Psychology*, 80(3):260-267, by permission of The American Psychological Association (APA).

Set Mastery-Related Goals

One of the most effective ways to foster a **mastery orientation** is to set goals that emphasize personal standards of success based on effort, improvement, and skill development. Such goals define success in terms of exceeding one's own standards rather than outdoing others, and this focus should allow most if not all athletes to feel successful and competent. It should also help athletes develop a positive outlook on challenges and setbacks. Refer to chapter 4 for an in-depth discussion of how you can use goal setting to help athletes become more mastery oriented.

Alter Feedback

Most coaches realize that criticism directed at a person can lower motivation. But what about praise following success? Approximately 85% of parents believe that praising children's ability is a necessary part of the process of building self-esteem (Dweck 1999). Coaches often agree; in fact, it is a widespread belief among coaches that giving athletes a great deal of praise about their talent and ability will raise their self-confidence and bolster their self-esteem, thus improving their motivation and performance. And it seems to work, at least in the short run during times of success. But what happens to athletes' motivation, confidence, and performance during hard times? Does this type of feedback sustain confidence when they are dealing with adversity and striving to overcome setbacks?

Actually, athletes who receive a great deal of praise about their talent and ability are at a clear disadvantage in dealing with adversity. Their enjoyment and motivation plummets in the face of challenges and setbacks. Why is this so? On the surface, it sounds counterintuitive. But think about it: This type of praise tells athletes they succeed because of their talent and ability. If they take this message to heart, what happens when they struggle or face adversity? They believe the reason they are not doing well is that they lack talent and ability. If athletes learn that praise for success means they are talented, they also learn that failure means they lack talent. Success and failure are opposite sides of the same coin.

So what is the solution? Following both good and bad performances, provide feedback that emphasizes hard work, preparation, effort, and development of skills and strategy. Such feedback motivates athletes to continue to work hard and seek new challenges after a good performance, and it puts them in good position to cope effectively after a bad performance. It communicates that improvement and success are right around the corner, and that mistakes, performance plateaus, and slumps are not a negative

reflection on the athlete but a natural part of skill development. This type of feedback makes it easier for athletes to separate their sport performance from their self-worth (Dweck 1999, 2006). Viewing success in terms of effort and ongoing development is beneficial not only in the world of sport, but in other achievement domains as well.

Develop a Constructive Outlook on Both Success and Failure

We have noted that consistent success is a key to raising motivation, but there is a bit more to the story than simply providing success experiences. To raise motivation, athletes need not only to experience success but also to take credit for it. How do we get athletes to take credit for success and handle adversity in a way that builds motivation? Through your leadership as a coach, you can teach athletes to internalize success by acknowledging that it was due to their effort and preparation. You can help athletes adopt a mastery-oriented view of failure—to recognize that it is often due to controllable factors such as a lack of effort or poor strategy rather than a lack of ability—and to use failure as motivation to improve (see figure 8.3).

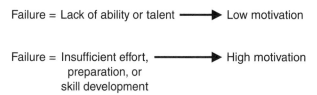

FIGURE 8.3 Reframe the reasons for failure from lack of ability or talent to the more controllable factors of effort, preparation, and skill development.

Use TARGET to Create a Mastery-Oriented Team Climate

By now, you realize that you can create a mastery-oriented team atmosphere through your leadership. What you value will be revealed in how you structure practice activities, the types of goals you focus on, the feedback you give athletes, and, ultimately, how you define success and evaluate the team's performance. Here are some final thoughts on how you can create a mastery-oriented motivational climate and raise intrinsic motivation by using the TARGET concept to structure **t**asks, **a**uthority, **r**ewards, **g**rouping, **e**valuation, and **t**ime. Although sample ideas are provided, the exact strategies you use should be customized to fit the competitive level of your players (Epstein 1988, 1989).

Task structure

Design practice activities that emphasize self-improvement and learning and that are both challenging and fun. Include variety in practice and create activities that actively involve all athletes. Have athletes set realistic short-term goals based on performance improvement.

Authority structure

Create opportunities for independence, responsibility, and self-direction by creating an autonomy supportive environment. Develop athletes' sense of responsibility, and involve them in decision-making and leadership roles. Ensure that athletes perceive a high degree of caring and social support from the coaching staff.

Reward structure

Recognize athletes' learning, effort, and improvement ahead of winning. Ensure that athletes receive positive recognition for playing well even if they lose.

Group structure

Use variety in grouping athletes to expand learning opportunities. Clearly define their roles and foster role acceptance.

Evaluation structure

Ensure that evaluation is based on concrete performance criteria, including individual skill development, progress, improvement, and mastery. Encourage athletes to self-evaluate rather than rely only on coaches. View mistakes as a natural part of the learning process, especially if they are made while trying hard.

Time structure

Adjust time allotments based on athletes' ability and on task difficulty so each player has adequate time to learn skills fully. Emphasize skill improvement and learning in each practice throughout the season.

SUMMARY

1. Intrinsically motivated athletes play for love of the game. They enjoy learning and mastering difficult sport skills and play for inner pride in working hard toward accomplishing a challenging task.

2. The four primary needs of athletes are to have fun and experience stimulation and excitement, to feel accepted and belong to a group, to have control and autonomy, and to feel competent.

3. Although a variety of strategies exist for enhancing enjoyment, one of the most effective ways is to create activities that present optimal challenges. Optimal challenges feature skills that are within the athletes' range of ability but are difficult enough that athletes need to stretch to reach them.

4. The need for acceptance and belonging can be met by making sure each athlete feels he or she has an important role on the team and by developing team cohesion.

5. Intrinsic motivation is enhanced by creating an autonomy supportive environment rather than a controlling environment. This can be done by increasing athlete ownership, providing choice, and soliciting athlete input.

6. Perceived competence is central to motivation and can be enhanced through success experiences.

7. Extrinsic rewards can be used to enhance intrinsic motivation if they raise perceived competence. But if they lower perceived competence or are viewed as manipulative or controlling, they will undermine intrinsic motivation. The key is to provide rewards that sincerely and appropriately recognize performance accomplishments and things athletes did well.

8. Mastery-oriented athletes define success based on personal standards in areas such as effort, improvement, personal development, and task mastery. These athletes are motivated

by the feelings they get when they work hard, improve, and eventually accomplish a personally challenging goal. Although mastery-oriented athletes enjoy winning, they also feel successful if they play well but lose the game.

9. Success seekers are outcome-oriented athletes who are confident in their ability to succeed. They feel talented and thus satisfied when they accomplish tasks that other athletes struggle with. They attribute success to ability and talent, which is confidence-building in times of success but undermines motivation in times of failure. Since few athletes can outperform others consistently, basing success on social comparison makes it difficult for outcome-oriented athletes to maintain a strong sense of ability.

10. Failure avoiders are outcome-oriented athletes who doubt their abilities. Rather than striving to demonstrate success, they focus on avoiding failure because they doubt they can compare well with others. These athletes have low motivation.

11. You can create a mastery-oriented motivational climate by using goal setting, providing feedback related to effort rather than ability, teaching athletes to make appropriate attributions for for successes and failures, and using the TARGET concept to shape practice and competitive environments.

KEY TERMS

failure avoiders

intrinsic motivation

mastery orientation

mastery-oriented team
atmosphere

perceived competence

outcome-oriented team
atmosphere

success seeker

REVIEW QUESTIONS

1. Describe the four needs underlying intrinsic motivation, as well as two strategies coaches can use to meet each need.

2. What effect do extrinsic motivators such as exams and homework assignments have on intrinsic motivation?

3. Would athletes playing for autocratic or democratic coaches potentially have higher intrinsic motivation? Explain your answer.

4. Under what conditions will success-oriented athletes exhibit high motivation?

5. How do mastery-oriented athletes differ from success seekers in their beliefs about the keys to success?

6. Andi is outcome oriented and wants to beat Sydney, whereas Sydney is mastery oriented. Sydney runs a personal best. Andi runs her slowest time of the season but beats Sydney. How successful does each athlete feel after the race?

PRACTICAL ACTIVITIES

1. Interview at least three athletes to find out why they play sport and what makes it enjoyable for them. Afterward, consider what insights you gained into how coaches can better meet athletes' needs and make sport participation fun.

2. Imagine that you want to implement a reward system to increase your team's intrinsic motivation. What effects do rewards have on intrinsic motivation? How will you structure rewards to raise, rather than undermine, intrinsic motivation? What types of rewards will you use and what behaviors will you reward?

3. A coach mentions that she is not comfortable involving athletes in decision making, because in the past it has caused her athletes to lose the game. How would you respond?

4. You have two athletes, Bobby and Sammy, who possess equal athletic potential but behave very differently. Bobby works hard to learn new skills and constantly challenges players at his ability level. Sammy plays hard when paired against far less skilled players but gives up quickly at the first sign of adversity.

- Is it fair to conclude that Bobby is more motivated than Sammy? Why or why not?
- Define the contrasting goal orientations of these two athletes.
- Imagine Bobby and Sammy just played in a tough game and lost. What would each athlete attribute the loss to? What effect would those attributions have on motivation?
- What strategies will you use to raise the Sammy's motivation?

Energy Management

When you are finished reading this chapter, you should be able to

- understand what arousal is and how it develops;
- explain the inverted-U relationship between arousal and performance;
- describe the major reasons why too little or too much arousal impairs performance;
- understand how individual and task differences influence optimal energy zones;
- know how to help your athletes identify their optimal energy patterns;
- explain the mental component of arousal;
- describe facilitative, debilitative, and neutral arousal, and what your athletes can do to develop facilitative arousal; and
- understand how you can help your athletes develop and use energy management skills during practice and competition.

You may be wondering, "What is energy management, and how does it affect my athletes or team?" Good question! The quick answer is that energy management has to do with helping your athletes control their **arousal,** or the energy that fuels their performance. Consider these two examples from the 2004 Olympics.

American gymnast Paul Hamm, one of the favorites for the all-around title, had a disastrous performance on the vault, seemingly knocking him out of medal contention. However, Hamm kept his composure and put together nearly flawless routines on the parallel bars and high bar to win by .012 point. Later, during the individual event finals on the high bar, Hamm's performance was delayed for more than 10 minutes while the crowd booed the mark given to a Russian gymnast. Hamm waited patiently for the crowd to settle down, then performed flawlessly, tying for the top mark on the apparatus. Paul Hamm's performance in these two intense competitive situations suggests that he has extraordinary energy management skills that allow him to perform his best when it matters most. (Hamm's all-around medal was later contested but not removed from him, and that controversy does not diminish the skill with which he managed his energy during the competition.)

In contrast, 15-year-old swimmer Katie Hoff, the favorite to win the women's 400-meter individual medley, got so nervous about her preliminary race that she couldn't sleep the night before and then experienced extreme prerace jitters. Not surprisingly, about three-quarters of the way through her race she tightened up and ran out of gas, failing to qualify for the semifinals. This story is a classic example of how poor energy management can lead to subpar performance, particularly in major competitions. Although Hoff had the physical skills and conditioning to win, she had not yet developed the energy management skills necessary to perform up to her capabilities in the pressure-packed Olympic environment.

When an athlete performs poorly, coaches may incorrectly assume that the problem is physical and try to solve it with more training and increased skill repetitions. Unfortunately, this can prompt burnout and overtraining, and it will do little to solve an underlying energy management issue. And even if you understand the mental nature of the problem, you may be unsure of how to help athletes resolve it. This chapter helps you understand how to control arousal—the physical and mental energy that fuels athletic performance—so that your athletes will thrive in competitions where everything is on the line.

Understanding Energy Management

Athletes get their energy from arousal—the general physiological and psychological activation of the body that varies on a continuum from deep sleep to intense excitement (see figure 9.1). Arousal involves both how much the body is activated and how that activation is interpreted; it is the body's way of preparing for intense, vigorous activity. You will have more or less arousal at different times of the day and in different situations. Where on the continuum would you place yourself when watching television? Moments before your team plays an important game? Right now, as you are reading this book? Some tasks require relatively low levels of arousal (e.g., lying on the beach). Other tasks, such as working out, demand higher arousal levels. The sport world has its own terminology for arousal. When athletes are trying to raise arousal, they talk about "psyching up," and when arousal is too high, they feel "psyched out." To perform their best, athletes need to find the right arousal level for each competitive situation.

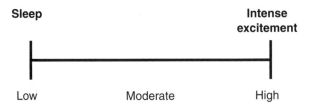

FIGURE 9.1 Arousal continuum.

The exact physiological changes that occur with increased arousal are highly complex, but here's a simplified description (Zaichkowsky & Baltzell 2001): When you are faced with a stressful competitive situation, the cortex of the brain is stimulated, triggering the activation of the **autonomic nervous system** (ANS), which controls most of the body's automated systems (e.g., organs and glands). The ANS pumps adrenaline, noradrenaline, and cortisol into the bloodstream, and these hormones spur physiological changes that prepare the body for action: Heart rate, blood pressure, and breathing increase, and muscles begin to develop tension in anticipation of work to come. Glucose is released from the liver to provide extra fuel for emergency response, while blood is shunted away from the digestive system and directed to the large muscles of the arms and legs, which will be needed for any major physical response. Decreased blood flow to the digestive system prompts athletes to experience "butterflies" in their stomach, while reduced blood flow to the extremities can leave hands and feet feeling like ice cubes. Kidney functioning is limited, and the bladder is emptied, making for plenty of trips to the restroom. Brain activity increases, enhancing alertness, and athletes begin sweating, a sign that the body is cooling itself in preparation for vigorous activity.

Arousal is triggered in response to any real or perceived demand, whether physical or mental. This activation process, often termed the **fight-or-flight syndrome**, originated as the body's way of dealing with real or imagined physical danger by readying itself to fight or run. This primitive response was probably hardwired into our prehistoric ancestors to aid in survival, and as life-threatening dangers have declined over time, arousal has been triggered increasingly by psychological demands, such as preparing for a big test, an important speech, or a big game.

Understanding arousal is important for two reasons. First, you must help your athletes accept that these physical symptoms are normal and signal readiness to deal with a competitive challenge. Athletes should not worry about physical symptoms, such as butterflies or sweating, unless they interfere with performance. Second, athletes deal with elevated arousal in various ways. Some become active, even hyperactive—pacing, talking incessantly, or screaming—to control their arousal. Others seem lethargic, yawn a lot, and may even take a nap. Both approaches can be effective. Just because you control your arousal in a particular way doesn't mean that strategy will work for your athletes. Each person responds differently, and each athlete must find an energy management strategy that works for him or her, then learn to use it systematically to attain optimal arousal in practice and competition.

How Does Arousal Affect Performance?

Picture an inverted U (figure 9.2). As arousal increases from low to moderate levels, performance improves, eventually reaching a zone where athletes perform their best. But any increases in arousal beyond this optimal zone will reduce performance quality. This is called the **inverted-U hypothesis**: When arousal is too low, athletes lack sufficient physical and mental energy to perform their best. When arousal is too high, athletes may suffer from a variety of problems related to tension, attention, motor control, and interpretation that prevent them from performing their best. Thus the inverted-U hypotheses predicts that optimal performance occurs when arousal is moderate.

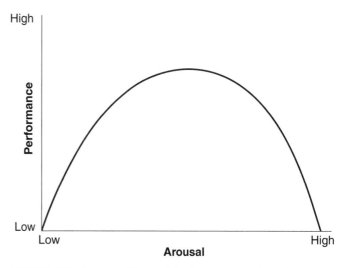

FIGURE 9.2 Inverted-U model of the arousal–performance relationship.

A practical way to look at the inverted-U relationship is depicted in figure 9.3. The left side of the inverted U, where arousal is too low, is termed the **psych-up zone**, because athletes here need to raise their arousal in order to perform their best. The right side of the inverted U, where top performance is hindered by excessive arousal, is called the **psych-out zone**. Here, athletes need to lower their arousal levels. The band in the center represents the ideal arousal range, where athletes are more likely to experience flow and perform their best (see chapter 3 for more on flow). We term this arousal band the **optimal energy zone**. It is crucial to note, however, that athletes vary in terms of their optimal energy zones: Some perform best at low arousal, others at

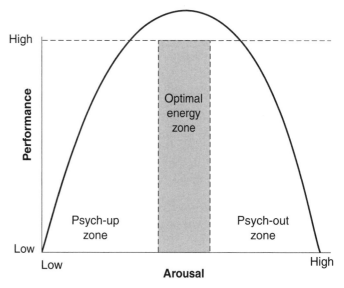

FIGURE 9.3 Psych-up, psych-out, and optimal energy zones.

moderate levels, and still others at high arousal. You may even have athletes who perform best at multiple arousal levels, and some may demonstrate no pattern at all. As illustrated by the opening stories of Paul Hamm and Katie Hoff, it is essential that you help your athletes identify their optimal energy zone and learn to control their arousal.

Why Underarousal and Overarousal Impair Performance

The inverted-U hypothesis doesn't directly address the issue of *why* athletes perform less effectively when under- or overaroused. Sport psychologists have been fascinated with this question for decades, and they have come up with several explanations.

How Underarousal Limits Performance

The physiological changes that occur when an athlete is aroused are designed to prepare the body to meet the real or perceived demands of challenging situations. The cardiovascular system pumps more oxygen to the working muscles, the body's cooling system kicks into high gear, and nonessential systems such as digestion and excretion are put on standby. Arousal also sharpens mental functions: Attention is heightened and focused, motivation increases, and processing becomes automatic (athletes can make a play or perform a move without thinking about it). When arousal is too low, these physiological changes fail to occur or fail to reach the necessary level for top performance. At optimal levels, athletes have the energy and physiological readiness to play up to their capabilities. Thus, they must be able to elevate arousal in order to play their best (without becoming so overaroused that their performance declines).

How Overarousal Hurts Performance

Sport psychologists have identified three primary explanations for why performance declines when arousal levels become too high: excessive muscular tension and coordination problems, attentional problems, and processing problems.

Excessive Muscular Tension and Coordination Problems

When athletes are overaroused, their muscles become tenser, which can cause opposing muscle groups to fight each other, leading to awkward movement patterns or limited range of motion (thus the tendency of some basketball players to air-ball a crucial free throw). Muscle tension causes coordination problems as well. A diver with leg tension might not get her normal lift off the board. A field hockey player might grip her stick tighter, changing how she receives and executes passes and throwing off the whole team's timing. Excessive muscular tension can also drain valuable energy, leaving athletes more fatigued than they should be toward the end of a five-set tennis match, 10,000-meter race, or an overtime soccer match.

Attentional Problems

When arousal increases, athletes' attention naturally narrows, allowing them to focus on the most important performance cues. This **attentional narrowing** helps athletes ignore distractions such as the crowd, the band, or the weather, making it easier to concentrate on relevant cues, such as reading defensive positioning during a fast break or sensing where teammates are when passing. However, if attention narrows too far, athletes may not even pick up on these task-relevant cues, thus hurting their performance. With excessive arousal, athletes may also lose their ability to shift attention. Athletes need to be able to shift to different **attentional styles**—that is, at various points in the competition, an athlete might need to analyze and plan, mentally rehearse a play, or focus and perform (Nideffer 1976); excessive arousal may impair the speed and timing of these attentional shifts (see chapter 10).

Controlled Versus Automatic Processing

Overarousal can also cause problems in processing, or how consciously we think about technique as we learn and perform skills. For example, athletes learning to throw a curve ball often use **controlled processing**: They think through every step sequentially, develop (slowly and clumsily) a mental blueprint of how the skill should be executed, and, as they practice, correct the blueprint until it is perfected. **Automatic processing** converts the blueprint into a single, complex image, developing a single program rather than a series of complex instructions. With automatic processing, an athlete throws the ball in one fluid motion, without thinking about the individual parts of the movement (e.g., oppositional foot and arm motion, shoulder rotation, stride length, release point, and follow-through).

When athletes are in flow, they switch smoothly between controlled and automatic processing, as the situation demands. Normally, controlled processing corrects errors and develops strategy, and automatic processing executes learned skills automatically, sometimes in creative ways. However, the two types of processing sometimes get in each other's way, and several explanations are commonly offered. First, if athletes are not concentrating on their performance, they may retrieve the wrong motor blueprint. Second, competitors might "just play" when they should be analyzing their performance. This tends to occur in practice when athletes are fatigued or bored—they go through the motions, letting automatic processing dominate. But without analysis and controlled processing, they cannot improve their skills. Only through analysis can the mental blueprint be perfected. This is why the old adage "practice makes perfect" has been replaced by the more accurate slogan "perfect practice makes perfect."

Third, and far more commonly, athletes may analyze when they should be just performing. When players overanalyze their performance, they suffer "paralysis by analysis" and use controlled instead of automatic processing. Athletes must learn to trust their bodies to do what they've been trained to do through thousands of hours of practice, without their mind getting in the way. Platform diver Laura Wilkinson, an Olympic gold medalist, calls this "diving stupid." If the term seems a bit negative, it nonetheless accurately conveys the idea that athletes cannot let their mind get in the way of their body's ability to perform. Athletes must learn to let it happen rather than constantly trying to make it happen.

Determining Optimal Energy Zones

We have seen that performance declines when athletes are under- or overaroused. When underaroused, athletes don't experience the physiological changes needed to perform at their best. When overaroused, they suffer from problems with muscular tension, attention, and overly controlled processing. So how can athletes determine their optimal energy zones? The answer involves many factors. In this section, we look first at how individual and task differences influence your athletes' optimal energy zones. Optimal arousal levels also fluctuate in response to the demands of the situation, so we shift to discussing optimal energy *patterns* rather than a single optimal energy zone. These patterns reflect ongoing arousal adjustments that athletes need to make in order to meet situational demands. Finally, we look at several proven strategies for helping athletes find their optimal energy zones or patterns.

Individual Differences

The optimal energy zone for each athlete is unique, as shown in figure 9.4. Note that the curves are asymmetrical and the height varies by player. These three players have different optimal energy zones, with different widths, and they are located in different regions of the arousal continuum. Kelli, for

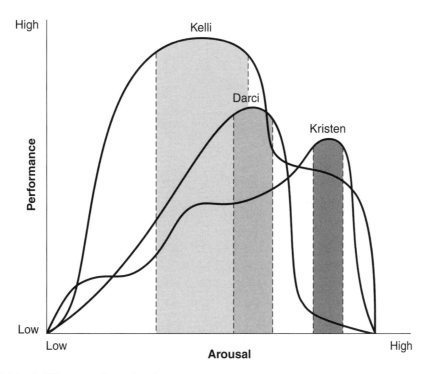

FIGURE 9.4 Individual differences in optimal energy zones.

example, has a much wider optimal energy zone than Darci, meaning Kelli can perform well at a range of arousal levels, whereas Darci needs to get to just the right level.

Athletes' optimal energy zones are influenced by various factors related to personality and athletic ability. Personality differences may explain why Kristen performs best at a higher optimal energy level than Kelli—Kristen is extroverted, whereas Kelli is mellower and more laid-back. Because Kristen has lower athletic ability than either Kelli or Darci, the height of her curve is somewhat lower than the heights of theirs. Finally, the different shapes of the curves reflect unique arousal patterns for these athletes. Kristen takes a long time to raise arousal to her optimal energy zone, but even the slightest amount of overarousal sharply reduces her performance quality. Darci gets to her optimal energy zone more quickly, but also suffers a dramatic drop in performance with even a small amount of excessive arousal. Kelli's arousal pattern is more symmetrical; she gets to her optimal energy zone the fastest and tolerates excessive arousal more effectively, experiencing only a gradual decline in performance when overaroused. Thus you can see how individual differences in optimal energy zones and arousal patterns make energy management a challenging process, with significant implications for the tradition of pep talks before competitions (see The Pep Talk).

Task Differences

Optimal energy zones also fluctuate for different kinds of tasks. Although it is impossible to tell athletes exactly which energy zone is ideal for any particular sport or task, consider how your athletes' optimal energy zone might change for these three task categories:

- *Fine versus gross motor tasks.* Fine motor skills that rely on accuracy, such as shooting a basketball and hitting a golf ball, have a narrower optimal energy zone than gross motor skills that rely on strength and power, such as shot-putting and weightlifting. As shown in figure 9.5, a shot-putter needs a higher level of arousal (farther to the right in the figure) than does a golfer, whereas a basketball player falls somewhere in between due to the need for both fine and gross motor skills (e.g., playing physical defense compared with handling the ball skillfully). Additionally, various positions or tasks within the same sport may have different optimal energy zones. A quarterback or football kicker has a lower, narrower optimal energy zone than a defensive lineman, and a golfer has a lower optimal energy zone for putting than for driving.

- *Short- versus long-duration tasks.* Events and tasks that take a few seconds to execute, such as a volleyball serve, a discus throw, or a penalty shot, require arousal to be sharply focused for the few moments

---

The Pep Talk: Is It an Effective Energy Management Strategy?

Many coaches continue to use the team pep talk, but if you've followed the discussion so far, you understand that this is an ineffective energy management strategy due to two false assumptions: that all athletes have the same precompetitive arousal level, and that all athletes are underaroused. A more accurate assumption is that your athletes fall at all points on the inverted-U curve. Some of them (Damon Burton's experience suggests about 15%) are underaroused or in the psych-up zone, some (about 65%) are overaroused and in the psych-out zone, and others (about 20%) are optimally aroused and in their optimal energy zone. So, if you emulate Knute Rockne's "win one for the Gipper" speech and inspire your athletes to raise their arousal levels, as pep talks are designed to do, you will help one segment of your athletes—those in the psych-up zone. But those already in the optimal energy zone will become overaroused, and those already overaroused and in the psych-out zone may be pushed over the line and rendered ineffective for the contest.

Thus it is far better to teach athletes how to manage their own energy. With proper guidance, athletes can find their own optimal energy zones. Separate those who need help into under- and overaroused groups. Provide a pep talk to help underaroused athletes raise their arousal. Help overaroused athletes relax, while boosting their confidence and emphasizing a process focus. Optimally aroused athletes should, of course, be left alone. They are already in a flow mind-set.

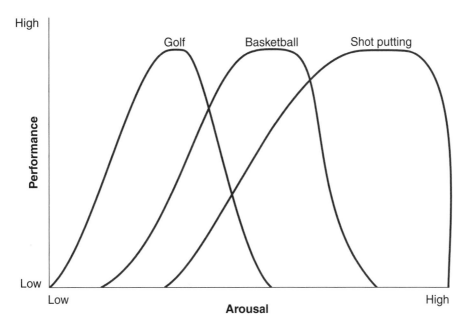

FIGURE 9.5   Sport differences in optimal energy zones.

of performance. And, not surprisingly, any amount of overarousal at the key moment can hurt performance substantially. In contrast, longer events, such as distance running, cross-country skiing, or cycling, require that athletes control their arousal to minimize energy expenditure and allow them to focus on good technique and correct pace. Brief episodes of overarousal are less harmful to these athletes because they have time to lower arousal, reenter their optimal energy zone, and begin performing well. Athletes who participate in sports with repeated short-term tasks (as in some track-and-field events and in golf, tennis, baseball, and cricket) must be able to turn arousal up when they are performing and down between shots, trials, and at-bats. Athletes who try to maintain high arousal while waiting for their next turn are more likely to suffer mental fatigue, and those who keep arousal too low may lose their focus or mental edge.

- *Simple versus complex tasks.* Athletes' optimal arousal level also varies by task complexity. Complex skills demand close attention, rapid and complicated decision making, and (due to difficult movement patterns) precise fine-motor responses. Simple skills have fewer attentional, decision making, and motor control demands. In basketball, getting up the floor quickly, playing physical defense, and pulling down a tough rebound in traffic would be simple skills, whereas shooting a three-pointer, making a pinpoint pass, or handling the ball against pressure are more complex skills. Because less skill is required for simple tasks, the optimal energy zone for performing them is

higher and wider than for complex tasks (figure 9.6). Complex tasks require a more focused arousal (a narrower optimal energy zone) and demand lower levels of arousal than simple tasks do.

Thus we have seen that athletes must adjust arousal to accommodate personality and task differences. They must also respond to situational demands that can change from moment to moment, which leads us to look at energy patterns rather than a single arousal level.

Optimal Energy Patterns

When we discuss arousal and optimal energy zones, there is a tendency to think in static terms. But in many sports, arousal demands change constantly based on the situation at the moment. Golfers must adjust their arousal from the tee to a delicate chip to a tough downhill putt. Basketball players face different arousal demands when they are playing physical defense, fighting for a rebound, handling the ball against pressure, threading a pass to a cutter, or hitting a clutch free throw. Thus, athletes' optimal energy zones are not single levels of arousal but patterns that require constant adjustment to meet situational demands. As athletes gain increasing experience and skill, they can typically create optimal energy patterns more consistently. This is crucial, because athletes who can learn to manage their arousal, adjusting it to these various demands, will perform better than those with poor energy management skills.

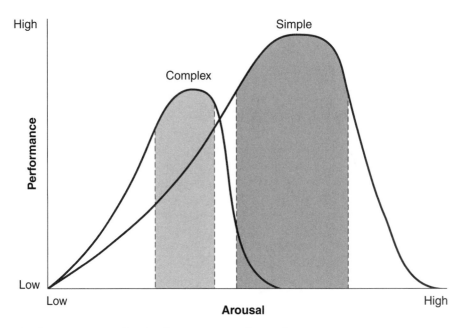

FIGURE 9.6   Optimal energy zones for simple versus complex tasks.

Finding Optimal Energy Zones

Many great athletes know what their optimal energy zone feels like. Bill Russell, leader of the Boston Celtics dynasty that won 11 NBA titles in 13 years, always felt confident that the Celtics would win a big game if he threw up in the locker room before the contest. A nervous stomach meant he was interested and excited, ready to have a great game. Similarly, here is golf great Jack Nicklaus's response when asked if he still gets nervous: "I don't know how you play well unless you're nervous. Nowadays I don't get nervous unless I'm in a major and in a position to win. If I could only learn to concentrate when I'm not nervous, so I could get in position to win, then I'd be fine" (Rotella & Cullen 1995, p. 171). The first step in effective energy management, then, is to help your athletes learn to accurately identify their optimal energy zone. We recommend that athletes think of their optimal energy zone as an **individual zone of optimal functioning** (IZOF). In the IZOF model, each athlete's optimal functioning zone is seen as a bandwidth (Hanin 1986, 2000), and arousal levels that exceed or fall short of this range are associated with less successful performance.

To help athletes determine their zone of optimal functioning, we've had good luck using the Arousal Monitoring Scale (AMS), which rates arousal on a 9-point scale, with 5 representing the optimal energy zone (best performance), 1 to 4 representing underarousal, and 6 to 9 indicating overarousal (see figure 9.7). Athletes assign themselves an AMS score repeatedly during practice or competition, and over time they discover what optimal arousal (rating of 5) feels like for them

in various situations. Generally, athletes will experience good performance at arousal levels 4 to 6 (their personal optimal energy zone or bandwidth) and feel their very best when their arousal is at level 5. Although this process is relatively simplistic, practical experience suggests it is quite effective in helping athletes learn to find their optimal energy zone and recognize when to make adjustments by means of rapid relaxation (to lower arousal) and energization (to increase arousal).

Once athletes understand how to determine their optimal energy zone, they need to understand how mental factors can affect arousal and performance. Only when they understand and can control these mental influences will they be able to manage their

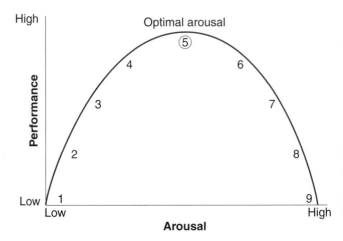

FIGURE 9.7   Athletes can use the Arousal Monitoring Scale to assess their arousal levels and learn what optimal arousal feels like to them.

energy levels successfully so they can perform to the best of their capabilities.

Mental Side of Arousal

At the beginning of this chapter, we described arousal as mainly a physiological response—faster heartbeat, increased respiration, and tense muscles preparing for physical activity. This physical part of arousal is neutral, affecting performance in a way that is neither inherently positive nor inherently negative. However, you have likely already recognized that mental factors influence arousal levels. Indeed, arousal includes how athletes interpret physiological changes: Do they view the butterflies in their stomach as a sign of excitement and anticipation of the competition to come? Or do those butterflies cause them to worry and become anxious about how they will perform? How athletes interpret their arousal has a huge effect on how they perform.

Figure 9.8 shows how the physical and mental components of arousal interact with each other. When athletes are highly focused, thinking positively, feeling prepared and in control, and imagining successful outcomes, they interpret high arousal positively and often experience it as challenge, readiness, or excitement. This facilitative arousal aids in good performance. However, athletes may interpret these same high-arousal symptoms very differently if they are worried about how they'll perform, distracted by outside factors or images of disaster, or feeling overwhelmed. This debilitative arousal hurts performance quality. Thus the same physical symptoms of arousal can accompany good performance in a flow state, or poor performance when an athlete chokes. The difference lies in how the athlete interprets the arousal.

Relationship Between Arousal and Anxiety

It is clear, then, that arousal and **anxiety** are closely related. In response to an increase in arousal, which is purely neutral, an athlete can experience anxiety, which is a negative emotional state characterized by nervousness, worry, and apprehension. Like arousal, anxiety has both mental and physical components. **Physical anxiety** refers to physiological changes: muscular tension, butterflies, shortness of breath, sweating, dry mouth, frequent urination, and increased heart rate. You might recognize these symptoms as similar to those of arousal. The difference is that with physical anxiety the athlete views them negatively, and thus they impair performance. If athletes experience **mental anxiety**, they either expect to fail or worry about negative consequences of failure, both of which impair performance. Symptoms include self-doubt, a sense of being out of control or overwhelmed, inability to concentrate, and images of failure or disaster. You can imagine how an athlete with mental anxiety may find it hard to perform well (as in the story of Katie Hoff at the beginning of this chapter).

Reconsidering the Inverted U

Although the inverted-U hypothesis provides a framework for understanding the arousal–performance

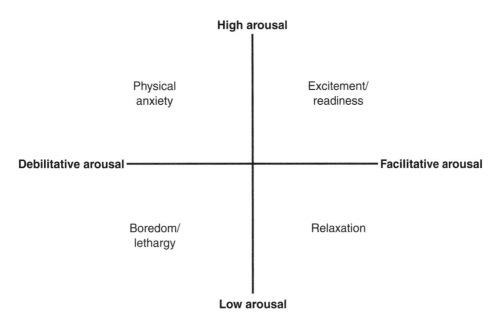

FIGURE 9.8 Physical and mental components of arousal.

relationship, it does not consider the mental side of arousal. Some newer models take into account how athletes interpret arousal, and their predictions might help you understand how to help your athletes adjust arousal levels for best performance.

Catastrophes

Have you ever worked with an athlete or team who performed well before hitting a certain arousal level, then suffered a catastrophic drop in performance? If so, you have witnessed **catastrophe theory** at work. You can see from figure 9.9 that this theory suggests much greater consequences from overarousal than the inverted-U hypothesis predicts. While identical to the inverted U on the left side of the curve, catastrophe theory shows a precipitous drop in performance quality after a certain point on the right side. Maybe you have watched one of your athletes suffer such a drop during competition. It occurs when a high level of mental anxiety accompanies high arousal.

To help your athletes prevent such catastrophes, you need to help them learn how to minimize mental anxiety when highly aroused. If they start to experience self-doubt, loss of control, or images of failure, they can use mental training tools to get themselves back on track and take a more positive approach. Imagine that your soccer team has been playing well but all of a sudden the opponent scores several goals. If your athletes begin to suffer anxiety but don't intervene to

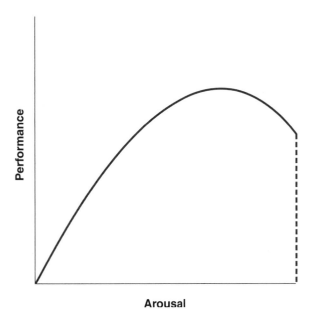

FIGURE 9.9 Catastrophe model. Some athletes experience a sudden drop in performance quality at high arousal levels due to mental anxiety.

Adapted, by permission, from J. Fazey and L. Hardy, 1988, *The inverted-U hypothesis: A catastrophe for sport psychology?* (BASS Monograph 1) (Leeds, UK: British Association of Sports Sciences and National Coaching Foundation), 21.

reinterpret their arousal, a catastrophe could occur. They need to use relaxation and self-talk skills to resolve this problem First, they relax completely (using the tools from chapter 6) in order to lower arousal to a minimal level. Then they use self-talk (chapter 7) to reinterpret their arousal constructively and rebuild their self-confidence. Next, they use energization skills (chapter 6) to raise arousal back to their optimal energy zone, while keeping thoughts about arousal and competition as positive, rational, and constructive as possible. This is a daunting task to accomplish during competition and provides a good reason to make sure your athletes have automated the mental training tools described in part II of this book.

Reversals

Athletes interpret their arousal in different ways, and even the same athlete can perceive arousal as positive or negative at different times in the same contest. Athletes often begin a contest focused on all the right things—personal performance level and meeting personal goals—and view arousal as excitement or readiness to meet a challenge. But in the heat of competition, athletes may shift their focus to outcome, become anxious (or angry about poor performance), and choke. This phenomenon, called a reversal, is laid out in **reversal theory** (Apter 1982; adapted to sport by Kerr 1989, 1993), shown in figure 9.10. When athletes interpret high levels of arousal as excitement, they perform optimally, but when they interpret high arousal as anxiety, they perform poorly (Burton & Naylor 1997). Therefore, even in the heat of competition, you want to help your athletes focus on the process and enjoy what they are doing, thus providing them with a better chance to experience flow.

So what can you do if your athletes experience a reversal—that is, start to interpret elevated arousal in a negative way? We recommend a three-step process similar to the process used to counter catastrophe. First, arousal must be lowered, because it is very hard to change perspective when arousal is elevated. Second, athletes must reverse their motivational style to be process oriented, so they can interpret their arousal positively. Finally, they must gradually reelevate their arousal, taking pains to view heightened arousal as excitement and readiness. To do this, of course, athletes must be highly skilled at relaxation, energization, and self-talk as discussed in part II.

Integrated Arousal–Performance Model

The inverted U explains arousal and performance without taking into account mental anxiety. Catastrophe theory explains sudden drops in performance under high levels of arousal due to high mental

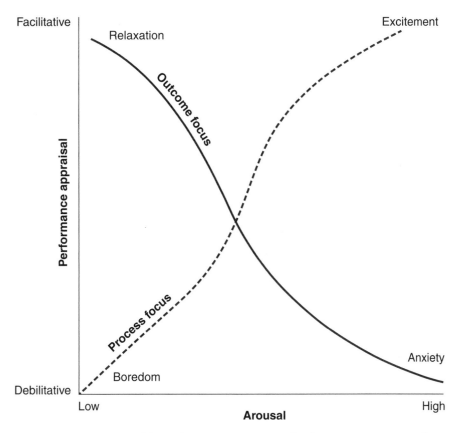

FIGURE 9.10 Reversal model: When athletes focus on process goals, they appraise arousal positively and perform well. But in competition a reversal often occurs, and athletes begin to focus on outcome, appraise arousal negatively, and suffer a drop in performance.

anxiety. Reversal theory explains similar drops in performance but focuses on athletes' motivational state—are they focused on process or outcome? We have developed a comprehensive approach by integrating concepts from all three theories to develop a new picture of the true relationship between arousal and performance. Our integrated arousal–performance model is shown in figure 9.11. This model offers separate predictions for the arousal–performance relationship in three types of conditions: facilitative, neutral, and debilitative.

Athletes perceive arousal as facilitative (figure 9.11a) when their mental anxiety is low, their self-confidence is high, and they are focused on the process or performance rather than the outcome. **Debilitative arousal conditions** (figure 9.11c) occur when mental anxiety is high, self-confidence is low, and athletes are focused on product or outcome instead of process. Falling between these two extremes, **neutral arousal conditions** (figure 9.11b) include moderate mental anxiety, moderate self-confidence, and some combination of focus on process (or performance) and product (or outcome). Under debilitative arousal conditions, athletes' per-

formance will likely decline dramatically, even with only minor overarousal. In neutral arousal conditions, athletes' performance should demonstrate the classic inverted-U relationship, in which performance declines gradually as overarousal increases, reflecting a mixed interpretation of arousal. Finally, when athletes experience **facilitative arousal conditions**, their performance should be best at high levels of arousal.

Our integrated model makes three other predictions. First, although each component of the model predicts an optimal energy zone where athletes perform best, the *magnitude* of performance will be highest under facilitative conditions and lowest under debilitative conditions. Thus, under facilitative conditions, not only do athletes perform optimally with much higher levels of arousal, but the overall magnitude of their performance is higher as well. This is when you see swimmers set new personal bests, basketball players make almost every shot, and teams perform "in the zone." Conversely, under debilitative conditions athletes' optimal energy zones occur at a lower level of arousal and overall performance is lowest of the three conditions.

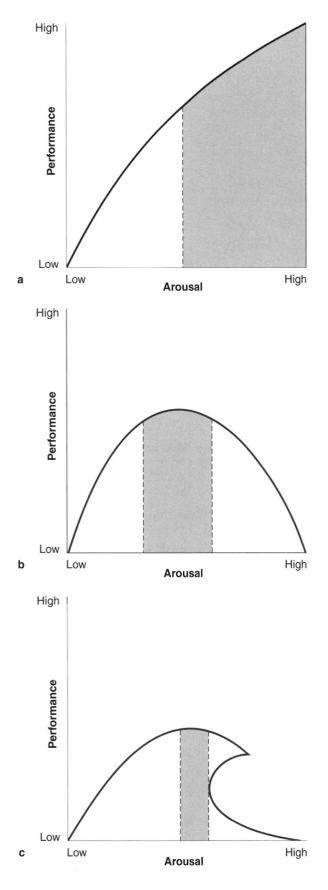

FIGURE 9.11 Integrated arousal–performance model for (a) facilitative, (b) neutral, and (c) debilitative conditions.

Second, the bandwidth for athletes' optimal energy zone is widest for facilitative conditions, and arousal cannot be too high as long as athletes interpret it positively. This means athletes can perform at their best under a wide range of arousal. Under debilitating conditions, however, the optimal energy bandwidth is narrow, and the penalty for over-arousal severe. Neutral arousal conditions produce a moderate bandwidth for optimal energy and good performance.

Finally, we believe that fluctuations in arousal conditions are a primary cause of momentum changes in sport. Arousal conditions fluctuate constantly as athletes respond not only to their external environment but also to the internal environment of their thoughts and **appraisals**. We believe that changes in momentum occur, in part, because of the ebb and flow of performers' or teams' arousal—from facilitative to neutral to debilitative conditions—due to changes in appraisal. Read the example in Table 9.1 of the fluctuations in arousal appraisal between Mark, a 9-to-2 favorite, and Steve as they compete in a racquetball game. This example should help you better understand how your players' arousal conditions might fluctuate throughout a match, as well as the role that appraisal plays in that process.

Mark had the upper hand at 12–0 but backed off and gave Steve a chance to get his game together and grab the momentum. Even though Steve began the match worried about losing, he moved into a facilitative arousal condition when he became certain that he would lose, because his goal shifted from winning to trying to perform well. When Mark saw Steve's comeback, he raised his arousal slightly, but more importantly he began to worry and to press harder, resulting in a negative appraisal, which prompted debilitative arousal conditions that hurt his game.

What factors affect athletes' level of arousal and how they interpret it? The list includes physical and mental fatigue, current performance quality (their own and that of the opponent), officials' calls, fans' reactions, injuries, anticipation of defeat or victory, and positive or negative feedback from coaches or fellow players. To help your athletes manage arousal successfully, then, you must help them become familiar with how these factors influence their arousal and performance and encourage them to use mental training tools such as relaxation, energization, self-talk, and imagery. In summary, the integrated arousal–performance model brings together many of the themes you have heard throughout this chapter. For athletes to perform to the best of their capabilities even as their arousal reaches very high levels, they need to keep their mental anxiety low, maintain high self-confidence, and focus on process and performance goals instead of worrying about outcome.

TABLE 9.1

Example of Changes in Momentum Based on Arousal Conditions

SCORE		
Mark	**Steve**	**Changes in arousal conditions**
0	0	Mark is full of self-confidence, knowing he is the favorite. He has high facilitative arousal.
		Steve knows he is the underdog, so he has moderately high debilitative arousal.
12	0	Mark now sees this as an easy match and lowers his facilitative arousal to a moderate level.
		Steve feels he is out of it and decides he cannot win but tries to play well to improve his game. He experiences moderately high facilitative arousal.
14	6	Mark's arousal is unchanged.
		Steve is encouraged by his play. Facilitative arousal is now high.
15	11	Mark begins to get concerned. He has moderate debilitative arousal as he entertains the possibility of Steve's making a comeback.
		Steve now feels his game is flowing and experiences high facilitative arousal.
17	17	Mark realizes he is struggling to get back in the game and tells himself to fire up. He still has moderately high debilitative arousal.
		Steve feels in full control of his game, experiencing high facilitative arousal.
19	21	Mark has very high debilitative arousal, because he is angry at himself for letting the game get away from him.
		Steve continues to have high facilitative arousal. He is ready for the next game.

Developing Athletes' Energy Management Skills

Developing energy management skills consists of the same three phases we've used to develop other mental training tools and skills. Through the three phases of education, acquisition, and implementation, you will lead your athletes from general knowledge and awareness to mastering skills that will help manage their energy, and then to using those skills effectively and automatically in practice and competition.

Education Phase

This phase consists of two primary objectives: educating athletes about the mental training skill and developing awareness of their strengths and weaknesses in performing that skill. For energy management, you will want to make sure that your athletes understand what arousal is, how it affects performance, and the importance of being able to adjust their arousal levels to promote the best conditions for a good performance. Have athletes think about the task they

perform and whether it requires high or low arousal. Ask athletes to consider their own personality and how that might affect what level of arousal is best for them. Have them recall competitions in which their performance seemed to fluctuate depending on what they were thinking and feeling. Explain some of the basic principles of adjusting arousal levels.

Your athletes must also become aware of their energy management patterns, which means recognizing both how arousal affects their performance and how frequently their arousal deviates from optimal energy zones. One strategy is to use the Arousal Monitoring Scale (AMS). For 3 to 7 days, identify three instances during each practice when athletes' tension levels are high and three times when energy levels are low. Stop practice for 30 seconds at each predetermined checkpoint and have players monitor their arousal level using the 9-point scale depicted in figure 9.7 (page 146), in which 1 represents low energy (with poor performance), 9 indicates high tension (with poor performance), and 5 denotes optimal arousal (enabling excellent performance). Have your athletes record their arousal levels on a version of the AMS that you copy on a note card. Once you've monitored arousal for several days, have athletes look for patterns in their data. Do they have frequent problems with underarousal? With overarousal? Which portions of practice create arousal control concerns? Why? This information, combined with similar data collected during competition, can be used to help athletes create an arousal control plan.

Acquisition Phase

Objectives for the acquisition phase include developing fundamental energy management skills and learning how to adjust arousal to stay within the optimal energy zone. In chapter 6, we introduced total and rapid relaxation and energization skills and described a systematic program for developing each skill. You can use that program to help your athletes develop the basic relaxation and energization skills they will need to master energy management in sport. Players will need to be able to use these tools to create neutral or facilitative arousal conditions.

To reach their optimal energy zone before practice, athletes typically need to energize to reach optimal arousal, whereas before competition, when players are normally overaroused, they need to use rapid relaxation to lower arousal to optimal levels. To adjust arousal *during* practice or competition, they need to be able to use rapid relaxation and energization as demand requires to achieve optimal arousal for neutral conditions. Your athletes can use the AMS to practice developing their basic arousal control skills, taking it one step further than during the education phase. For each of the AMS checkpoints during practice, give your team 30 seconds to monitor arousal levels, then give them a moment to use rapid relaxation and energization skills to adjust their arousal as needed.

Within several days, your athletes should begin to see significant improvement in their basic arousal control skills. Ask them to try to consistently reach and maintain their personal optimal arousal level (i.e., level 5) that corresponds with good performance. Remember that personal optimal arousal varies across athletes, activities, and situations. It must be low enough that tension and attentional problems do not interfere with performance, but high enough that the athlete has the energy necessary to perform his or her best. Normally, within two weeks

most athletes can learn to adjust their arousal to an optimal level for neutral conditions in 3 to 5 seconds, regardless of how high or low their starting point was. Having developed this ability, athletes can begin working to reach optimal facilitative arousal.

Implementation Phase

Monitoring arousal on a regular basis and adjusting it as needed will help your athletes gain skill at controlling their energy levels. Initially, they should monitor their arousal level multiple times daily and practice adjusting it whenever they're not already in their optimal energy zone. You can simulate competition during scrimmages and have your athletes check and adjust arousal as needed during each break in the action. For endurance athletes, who need to be able to adjust arousal while they perform, help them practice these skills during workouts. As athletes' arousal control skills develop, have them practice during increasingly stressful situations, such as scrimmages and minor competitions. For example, to add pressure to serving practice, a volleyball coach might condition athletes for a few minutes and then have each team member execute one serve. If fewer than three-quarters of the team members hit the target, the process is repeated. This pressured serving drill provides an excellent opportunity for athletes to learn to monitor and adjust their arousal level to attain optimal arousal, first under neutral conditions and subsequently under facilitative arousal conditions.

Once your athletes have developed basic arousal control skills, how do they keep these skills sharp and further automate them without the process becoming tedious? Normally, once your athletes have spent sufficient time heightening their awareness of arousal levels and learning to systematically adjust their arousal, you can discontinue regular use of the AMS. However, athletes shouldn't quit self-monitoring completely. Each night, your athletes should review arousal control problems that they failed to handle effectively and attempt to understand why their attempts were ineffective. If they begin to experience ongoing arousal problems, athletes should begin keeping the AMS for a few days to identify causes. Coaches should remain vigilant for arousal control problems during practice and competition and conduct debriefings as needed to help athletes make necessary adjustments.

SUMMARY

1. The energy athletes use in practicing and competing comes from arousal, which is the general physiological and psychological activation of the body designed to prepare performers for intense, vigorous activity. Arousal varies on a continuum from deep sleep to intense excitement and has a significant effect on performance.

2. The body goes through a number of complex physiological changes when it becomes aroused, including activation of the autonomic nervous system (ANS), which pumps adrenaline into the bloodstream, thus increasing muscle tension, heart rate, blood pressure, and breathing.

3. Arousal can be triggered by physical and mental stress—a process known as the fight-or-flight syndrome because it is the body's way of preparing to fight or run.

4. Arousal is a normal part of readying for competition. Athletes respond to elevated arousal in different ways, from lethargy to extreme agitation.

5. The inverted-U hypothesis predicts that as arousal increases from low to moderate levels, performance improves until some optimal point is reached. Further increases in arousal, from moderate to high, reduce performance quality. The band in the center of the model represents the arousal level where performance is best, and it is termed the "optimal energy zone."

6. Underarousal limits performance because the body has not activated itself enough to create the physiological changes necessary for optimal performance. Overarousal, in contrast, hurts performance by means of excessive muscular tension and coordination problems, attentional issues, and too much controlled (versus automated) processing.

7. Athletes have different optimal energy zones, causing individual differences in the shape of the inverted U.

8. The optimal energy zone is also affected by task differences. Fine-motor actions and complex tasks have a lower and narrower optimal energy zone than do gross-motor skills and simple tasks. Short-duration tasks require arousal to be sharply focused for the few moments of performance, whereas long-duration tasks allow more opportunity to adjust arousal levels not initially in the optimal energy zone and still perform successfully.

9. Optimal energy zones are dynamic and can be characterized most accurately as optimal energy patterns. As competitive demands change, athletes must systematically adjust their arousal levels.

10. Athletes should be able to identify their optimal energy zone, which can be thought of as an individual zone of optimal functioning (IZOF). Athletes can use the Arousal Monitoring Scale (AMS) to rate their arousal on a 9-point scale, with 5 representing optimal arousal. Athletes learn what an arousal level of 5 feels like to them, even though any score between 4 and 6 (their optimal bandwidth) will typically prompt good performance.

11. Mental factors reflect how athletes interpret arousal. If they interpret it positively, as challenge, readiness, or excitement, they are positioned to experience top performance and flow. If they interpret it negatively, they are likely to perform poorly.

12. Catastrophe theory suggests that if mental anxiety is low, performance will demonstrate the traditional inverted-U relationship with arousal, but that if mental anxiety is high, overarousal will spur a catastrophic drop in performance.

13. Reversal theory suggests that athletes perform their best when they are focused on process and their arousal is maximal.

14. The integrated arousal–performance model makes separate predictions for three conditions: facilitative, debilitative, and neutral. Under facilitative conditions—when the athlete is self-confident, has low mental anxiety, and is focused on process—performance increases as arousal increases. Under neutral conditions, the arousal–performance relationship should

follow a traditional inverted-U model. Under debilitative conditions, the catastrophe model typically occurs, and overarousal has an extremely negative effect on performance.

15. Use the three-phase process to help athletes develop their energy management skills. In the education phase, athletes learn about energy management and become aware of their personal arousal patterns and optimal energy zone. In the acquisition phase, athletes master energy management skills and learn how to find and maintain their optimal energy zone. In the implementation phase, athletes learn to automate arousal control and build these skills into their game.

KEY TERMS

anxiety	catastrophe theory	mental anxiety
appraisal	controlled processing	neutral arousal conditions
arousal	debilitative arousal conditions	optimal energy zone
attentional narrowing	facilitative arousal conditions	physical anxiety
attentional styles	fight-or-flight syndrome	psych-out zone
automatic processing	individual zone of optimal functioning (IZOF)	psych-up zone
autonomic nervous system (ANS)	inverted-U hypothesis	reversal theory

REVIEW QUESTIONS

1. What is arousal and how does it develop?

2. What is the inverted-U relationship between arousal and performance?

3. What are the major reasons that too little or too much arousal impairs performance?

4. How do personality and task differences influence athletes' optimal energy zone?

5. How do mental factors influence the impact of arousal on performance?

6. What is the relationship between arousal and performance under facilitative, debilitative, and neutral conditions?

PRACTICAL ACTIVITIES

1. Develop a plan for how you can help your athletes identify their optimal energy zone during practice, including any log forms you might use.

2. Develop a systematic program for helping athletes use their relaxation, energization, and self-talk skills to develop optimal arousal before practice and maintain it during practice.

Attention

When you finish reading this chapter, you should be able to

- describe why focusing on the task at hand, blocking out all distractors, and maintaining that focus is challenging but critical to sport success;
- explain attentional capacity and its implications for effective coaching;
- describe selective attention and how it can be used to help athletes focus on the right things and block out external distractors; and
- define concentration and discuss strategies for improving it.

In describing outstanding performances, athletes invariably highlight that their **attention** was completely focused on the game and that they were unaware of outside distractions. They may report that they were so focused on their performance that they did not hear the thunderous cheering of the crowd. Others report that they were aware of everything around them, but that potential distractors, such as crowd noise, just faded into the background as they maintained their task focus.

On the surface, the keys to attention seem simple: Just go out and focus on the task at hand and block out all distractions. But that's easier said than done. Many coaches lament that getting their athletes to focus can be incredibly difficult, and you hear comments like this from teams who did not perform well: "We just weren't focused enough and made too many careless mistakes." How often have you heard coaches instruct their athletes to focus and concentrate, without teaching them how? The coach may yell at performers, instructing them to get their head in the game, and the athletes grit their teeth and try even harder to concentrate. Athletes may stare intently and continually tell themselves to focus, but the harder they try, the more elusive an effective state of concentration becomes.

Like the other mental skills discussed in this book, attentional skills are essential for achieving excellence. How many times have you seen an athlete lose focus and make a big mistake? Even a momentary lapse in attention can have dire consequences. One of the primary goals of mental skills training is to help athletes improve their ability to focus on the task, block out all distractors, and sustain their focus over time.

Understanding Attention

Attention is a complex phenomenon. To help you understand it, we'll discuss the nature of this mental skill, why the seemingly simple act of focusing on the task at hand can be such a challenge, and how attention is linked to sport success.

What Does it Mean to Pay Attention?

Attention is the process that directs our awareness to information available through our senses. We continually receive information through our senses about our external and internal environments. In fact, at any moment, our senses are bombarded with stimuli. If you stop reading for a moment and redirect your awareness from this book, you might notice a radio or TV playing or hear people talking in the background. You might also become aware of internal stimuli such as what you are thinking or whether you are hungry or tired. It is impossible to become aware of, or perceive, all the sensory information coming into your central nervous system. Once you notice certain sensory information, you must decide what action to take, and that process requires attention. Thus attention involves perceiving sensory information and using it to make decisions and choose responses (see figure 10.1).

Attentional Dimensions

Each sport is unique in the sensory information that needs to be attended to for optimal performance, but some aspects of attention are common across sport. Attentional demands can be viewed along two dimensions: width (broad or narrow) and direction (internal or external), as shown in figure 10.2. Attentional width refers to how many stimuli or cues athletes need to attend to at any given moment. In some sports or situations, athletes must be aware of many stimuli almost simultaneously, whereas others require them to narrow focus to a few cues. A broad attentional focus is needed when a quarterback reads a defense and looks for open receivers or when a basketball point guard runs a fast break. A narrow focus is critical when a goalie makes a save or a basketball player shoots a free throw. Attentional direction, on the other hand, refers to whether the athlete is focusing inward on thoughts and feelings or outward on events happening around him or her. An internal attentional focus is important for analyzing what is happening in the game, planning strategy, and read-

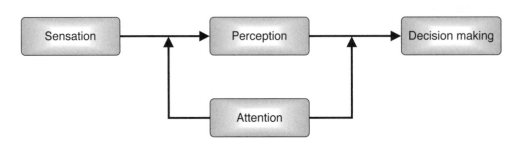

FIGURE 10.1　The role of attention in perception and decision making.

Broad

Analyze and Plan	Assess
• Quarterback calling a play • Pitcher deciding on the type and location of the next pitch	• Rock climber surveying the climb route • Linebacker reading the play as it unfolds
Mentally Rehearse	Focus and Perform
• Skier focusing on breathing to relax • Golfer imagining the perfect putt	• Rock climber focusing on a foothold • Batter focusing on the pitcher's release point

Internal — External

Narrow

FIGURE 10.2 Two-dimensional model for understanding attentional demands in sport.

ing one's body (i.e., monitoring bodily responses and feeling states). An external focus is needed in order to assess a situation and execute sport skills and strategies.

The Attentional Challenge

Across all sports, the essence of attention is focusing on task-relevant cues or stimuli and ignoring all others. Think of the attentional challenge a running back faces in American football: taking the ball from the quarterback, watching the blocking develop, determining if the planned hole is open, seeing all potential tacklers, protecting the ball, and making cuts that allow him to run to daylight is an extraordinary feat in attentional skills. Now consider the attentional challenge a blocker in volleyball faces: She must anticipate where the spike will come from, but, in an attempt to disguise the direction of the kill attempt, the opposing team will, over the course of a match, fake sets and spike the ball from various positions while calling for sets of various heights and speeds. Amidst all this, the blocker has only a fraction of a second to determine which direction the attack will come from and then react.

Beyond focusing on task-relevant cues, athletes also need to block out all internal and external distractors. The ability to block out distractors and sustain focus is called **concentration**. Think about the concentration required to hit a baseball. Many great baseball players say that the key to hitting is to see the ball. Because focusing on anything else complicates the batting process and results in ineffective concentration, they attempt to keep only that one thought in mind when they are at the plate. Sound simple? Imagine how difficult it is to quiet your mind and block out all distractors under normal conditions. Now imagine how much harder

it is with a grandstand full of fans yelling as you try to drive in the game-winning run with two outs and a full count. Imagine too that the pitcher throws an incredible fastball, giving you only a fraction of a second to determine whether to swing and, if so, to initiate the appropriate swing.

To compound the attentional challenge, the exact cues an athlete needs to focus on change, often very quickly. Thus, athletes must able to switch focus depending on the demands of the task. For example, a golfer must use a broad external focus to survey a fairway, shift to internal focus to plan her shot and select the appropriate club, then shift again to a narrow external focus to execute the swing. Or consider a quarterback: At first, he needs internal focus to analyze the situation, choose a play, and rehearse it as he walks to the line. Behind the center, he must shift to a broad external focus to read the defense and find the open receiver. And finally, to throw an accurate pass, he must narrow his focus of attention to the receiver.

Does Attention Affect Sport Success?

Research on the psychology of excellence makes one thing strikingly clear: Attention-related factors are crucial to sport success. Researchers have shown that highly successful athletes are better able to maintain focus on the task at hand throughout competition than are their less successful counterparts. They report being less distracted by irrelevant stimuli, and when they become distracted they quickly regain focus with minimal effort (Krane & Williams 2006).

Further support of the important role attention plays in sport comes from research examining differences between expert and novice performers (see Abernathy 2001; Moran 1996; Starkes, Helsen, & Jack 2001). You've probably noticed that very skilled

Choking Under Pressure: Attention Pitfalls

Most athletes can recall a time when they choked. Suzie, a gymnast competing in a lead-up to the nationals, was giving one of her all-time best performances but failed to stick her vault landing, dropping her several places in the standings. It was still possible for her to finish high, if she gave the performance of her life on the final event—the uneven bars. As the time neared, she started to feel a great deal of pressure, noticed a "tight" feeling, particularly in her shoulders and neck, and felt her breathing get shallow and rapid. She started to feel like she was in a daze, and her mind raced: "I have to stick this routine. Why did I blow my vault? That was such a stupid mistake. Everyone is going to be so disappointed with me if I mess this event up. I just need to relax. Why can't I relax?"

Normally, Suzie mentally rehearsed her routine using cue words before competing, but this time she was so preoccupied that she forgot to do so. During her performance, she had a hard time concentrating, and everything felt rushed. She made an early mistake on an easy element, and her mind raced even faster. She began to think about the mechanics and how to perform the skills. Rather than trusting her skills and training, she instructed herself through the routine, focusing consciously on her body mechanics and movements. But the harder she focused, the shakier she felt and the worse she performed. You probably realize that Suzie's choking was caused in part by attentional problems. She directed her attention inward, focusing narrowly on her thoughts and feelings rather than on the task at hand. Instead of trusting her skills and training, she became analytical, began to think about mechanics, and tried to talk herself through the skills step by step. She let her mind get in the way.

---

athletes make sport look easy: running backs with an uncanny ability to see the entire field when making cuts that shred the defense, tennis players who always seem to be in the right spot at the right time, golfers who seem to narrow their focus almost to the point of playing in a trance. It is easy to attribute this quality to superior reaction time, vision, depth perception, or other physical attributes. But research suggests that expert athletes perform in a superior fashion only on tasks specific to their sport. An increasing body of evidence suggests that a primary difference between expert and novice athletes lies in attention–related, sport-specific skills (see Abernathy, Wann, & Parks 1998; Ericsson & Charness 1994). Expert performers are better able to attend to, extract more information from, and sustain their focus on task-relevant cues than novice athletes. Clearly, attention-related factors are crucial to sport success.

Attentional Capacity

Before discussing how to teach your athletes to attend to the right cues, block out distractors, and sustain their focus, we need to recognize that there are limits to attention. We can think about only so many things at a time, and trying to do more spells disaster. In many cases, just focusing on more than one thing causes poor performance (e.g., if a receiver tries to run before catching the ball). When attentional demands exceed athletes' ability to handle information, they suffer **attentional overload**, which hurts performance and skill learning. An underloaded attentional system also causes trouble—a lack of focus and a lackluster practice environment.

As long as task requirements do not exceed athletes' **attentional capacity**, they can perform several tasks at once. Remember when you first learned to drive? You probably kept your hands glued to the steering wheel and your eyes straight ahead, because driving took all of your attention. However, with time and practice, you automated the process so that driving under normal circumstances requires less conscious thought and active attention. You can now probably drive while enjoying the scenery, listening to the radio, and carrying on a conversation with a passenger. But if you are driving in heavy rain on a winding road while trying to read road signs, conversation is much harder because driving itself demands more of your attention.

Watch a person learning a new sport skill; it is clear that executing the skill demands attention. When an athlete is first learning to play basketball, dribbling requires full focus. Attempting to do anything else at the same time might cause a novice to lose the ball. Consequently, an inexperienced player has no spare attention for reading the defense. With time, however, dribbling becomes less attention demanding, allowing the athlete to dribble with either hand and simultaneously protect the ball from defenders, notice where teammates and defenders are on the court, and hit an open teammate who is cutting to the basket for a layup (see figure 10.3).

Controlled Versus Automatic Processing

Why is it that performing sport skills requires less attention with time and practice? Remember from chapter 9 that in the early stages of learning a skill, athletes use controlled processing, which requires conscious attention to and awareness of the actions involved in the skill. This type of focus is slow, deliberate, and attention demanding. After countless hours of practice, however, athletes develop the ability to perform basic skills automatically, without conscious thought. They shift to automatic processing, also known as **skill automaticity**. This is the type of focus that occurs with flow. Athletes do not think about their performance; they just perform and let it happen. Because automatic processing is not attention demanding, it allows performers to focus on other tasks while executing basic skills and to do several tasks at the same time. Not only do athletes need to be able to perform basic skills without conscious thought, they need to be able to make smart decisions automatically as well. A skilled racquetball player knows what shot to make based on court positioning, a skier knows how to respond to various snow conditions, and a shortstop knows where to throw the ball in any given situation.

Developing Decision-Making Skills

You can use video to help athletes learn to choose appropriate responses quickly, with minimal conscious thought, in the heat of competition. Pause a video depicting a game situation at a critical moment and have your athletes articulate the best response before watching how the scenario actually unfolded. For example, a soccer coach could show a video depicting typical attacking situations and have players indicate as quickly as possible whether they would shoot at the goal, dribble, or pass to a teammate. Such exercises help athletes automate their response selection.

Coaching Tips Based on Skill Automaticity

The challenge of teaching athletes new skills is to recognize that their attentional system is easily overloaded. A youth basketball coach complained that she could not get her athletes to focus in practice and wondered if I (Tom Raedeke) could help. After watching a practice, I realized she was right—the athletes weren't focused, but it was not because they were failing to pay attention. It was because their attentional system was overloaded. The practice

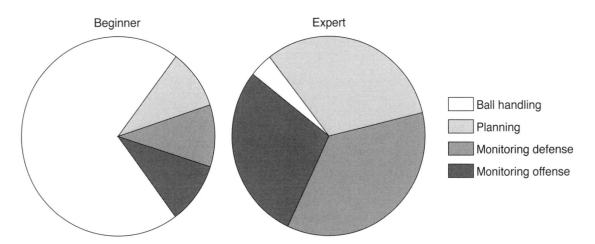

FIGURE 10.3 Differences in the attentional demands of novice and skilled athletes.

activities were too advanced for the athletes' skill level and beyond their attentional capacity. You can use the following strategies to prevent attentional overload in your athletes.

- *Simplify skills when athletes first learn them.* This can be done through developmental skill progressions or by dividing complex skills into meaningful components. For example, a youth hockey coach discovered that his players' attentional systems were overloaded when he tried to add stickhandling skills to the already attention-demanding task of learning to skate well. He decided to simplify the attentional requirements of stickhandling by using a larger puck, and his athletes were able to progress on skating and stickhandling at the same time.

- *Simplify strategy and decision-making requirements.* If a quarterback is running an option that requires him to decide whether to hand off, pitch, or keep the ball, his information processing ability may be exceeded if you don't limit the number of cues necessary to determine what option to choose. You might instruct him to base his decision on the actions of certain key defensive players rather than trying to read the whole field. Another way to reduce the amount of information athletes need to process is to increase their knowledge of the game and its strategies to make situations more predictable. Skilled tennis players know that a down the line shot will likely be followed with another down the line shot, so they put themselves in position to make a quick response.

- *Ensure that athletes overlearn and automate fundamental skills.* As your athletes overlearn skills, you can progressively increase the attentional demands placed on them. Overlearning skills helps free performers'

attention so they can focus on other task-relevant cues necessary for excellent performance. Rather than having to think about how to execute the skill, they can be more aware of what is going on around them and how the game is unfolding.

Selective Attention

A person can focus on only a limited number of stimuli at one time, and **selective attention** is the process by which we attend to some information and ignore or screen out the rest. Athletes must learn which information is critical to their performance success and then direct their attention to it. In many cases, athletes learn to focus on the right thing at the right time by means of trial and error and countless hours of practice. You can hasten and improve the learning process by teaching athletes what cues to focus on. For example, when a coach instructs a linebacker to drop into the short middle zone and watch for crossing receivers on drop-back passes, he is helping the player develop selective attention skills.

Focusing on Relevant Cues

To help your athletes develop selective attention, teach them to become aware of the cues they need to attend to in order to perform well and to block out distractors. You can do this by teaching athletes the following skills.

Develop a Mind-Set

Help athletes learn (and overlearn) what cues are critical to focus on and develop a mind-set to be

---

Anticipation Skills

Expert athletes often seem to have the uncanny ability to "read" what is happening and make the perfect move at the right time. One reason is that experts are skilled at using cues to anticipate what will happen and determine the appropriate response. In racket sports, skilled players predict where the ball will go by using cues—opponent's shoulder and trunk movements, racket position, ball toss—to anticipate the serve type and location before the ball is struck. In hockey, novice goaltenders tend to focus on the puck, whereas expert goalies focus on the shooter's stick to predict the location of a slap shot sooner and initiate the appropriate movements to make a save. Similarly, a baseball or softball fielder can get an idea of where a ball is likely to be hit by watching the batter's feet, and a basketball or football defender can anticipate the direction of a throw by watching the passer's eyes. The ability to anticipate or predict movements gives expert athletes a distinct advantage over their less experienced counterparts, and they do so by focusing on the right cues.

alert for those cues. In sports that require a broad focus of attention, such as basketball or soccer, you can teach athletes what cues they should focus on to read their opponents and to prepare for commonly used strategies. In situations where a narrow focus is needed, you should help athletes learn exactly where their focus should be directed. Tommy Moe, an Olympic gold medalist in men's skiing, describes his technique: "I just kept my thoughts real simple. I wanted to focus on making my turns with a strong edge on the outside ski, and keeping my hands forward. I knew if I concentrated on those two things, I would ski fast" (Murphy 1996, pp. 149–150).

Use Video Training

Show athletes a video depicting typical scenarios in their sport. Tell them what cues to watch for, then pause the tape at key moments so they can't see the result (e.g., show a pitcher in the midst of his delivery, a tennis player hitting a shot, or a soccer player attempting a goal). You might even block out certain cues (e.g., racket position) so the athlete has to use other cues to read the situation. Have your athletes try to determine what will happen next, then restart the video to show what actually took place. This training helps athletes learn to focus on task-relevant cues: Batters are better able to predict pitch locations, racket sport players better able to tell where serves will be targeted, and goalies better able to predict where a shot is directed (Abernathy, Wood, & Parks 1999; Starkes & Lindley 1994; Williams & Grant 1999).

Draw Attention to Important Cues

Make it a point to draw attention to important cues during practice. To help a shortstop who had a great arm but lacked accuracy because he simply threw toward first, a coach drew a target on the first baseman's mitt to provide a specific focal point. Similarly, to help a batter learn to focus on the seams of a baseball, which provide critical information about the type and speed of a pitch, a coach could brightly color the seams.

Use Performance-Related Cue Words

Many athletes find it useful to develop task-relevant, **performance-related cue words** to help them focus on the right information. In executing a forward three-and-a-half somersault dive, Olympic diver Greg Louganis used the cue words "relax, see the platform, spot the water, spot the water, spot the water, kick out, spot the water again" to help focus his attention (Wilson, Peper, & Schmid 2006). A hockey player might use the phrase "stick to ice" as a cue to focus on keeping his stick on the ice to maximize puck control. A punter in football might use the words "catch, drop, kick." The key is to find cue words that direct athletes' attention to critical task cues without causing them to think about the mechanics of performing the skill.

Use Focus Plans

Having a performance focus plan is like having a pilot's checklist. Athletes can simply run through the list without having to think about where to focus their attention. In sports that involve a race, the plan could specify where to focus attention during the event's different segments. In sports like soccer or basketball, a focus plan specifies where athletes should focus their attention in response to various scenarios in the course of a game. A well-developed focus plan that is overlearned prompts the right focus automatically.

Preparing for Distractors

Even if athletes have been trained to focus on the right cues, focusing on them can be incredibly difficult. A wide variety of external and internal distractors compete for an athlete's attention. Any intense or unexpected stimulus is especially likely to grab attention: a sudden loud noise, a flash of light, even a slight movement in the peripheral vision. The natural tendency to attend to this type of stimulus is called the **orienting response**. Golfers may have a hard time putting amidst crowd noise because they are used to a quiet gallery, whereas baseball players might be distracted in a quiet setting because they are used to performing in front of a noisy crowd.

Within and outside of sport, the orienting response sometimes serves a useful function, alerting us to potential danger or drawing attention to task-relevant cues. A skier may notice another competitor on the course in time to avoid a collision. A quarterback may notice a blitzing safety and throw to a receiver before being blindsided. A point guard may notice her coach's voice calling for a crucial time-out, for example.

But an orienting response to cues that are unrelated to safety and sport performance is just a distraction. A gymnast who orients to a cheering crowd, or a basketball player who attends to an opponent's antics, has lost focus. Athletes must block out irrelevant distractors and focus on the task at hand. Fortunately, they can learn to do just that. With repeated exposure to distractions, athletes become accustomed to the stimuli and no longer orient to them. The most effective way to prevent unwanted orienting responses is to make the unexpected expected, the abnormal normal, and the unusual usual.

Provide Simulations

Both NASA and the U.S. Air Force commonly use flight simulations to train astronauts and pilots to cope with flight and equipment problems that might cause them to lose focus. Successful coaches also use simulations to prepare athletes for potential distractors by creating gamelike situations in practice. They may simulate pressure situations, crowd noise, weather conditions, and the time of day or night of the actual event. For example, it is not uncommon in American football for teams to run their offense with a tape of loud crowd noise or the opposing team's fight song blaring from the public address system. A professional golfer who is distracted by the sounds of a camera click may have a person take pictures while he practices putting. An athlete who loses focus if an official makes an apparently bad call could have bad calls made against her during training sessions so she can practice her refocusing strategies. The point is to make anticipated distractions familiar.

Encourage Use of Imagery

It is, of course, impossible to simulate everything that may occur during competition, but you can teach athletes to avoid counterproductive orienting responses by having them imagine responding well to potential distractions (see chapter 5). As with practice simulations, this use of imagery can help athletes get used to certain stimuli and thus be less distracted by them during competition.

Sustaining Focus: Concentration

We have discussed ways to limit attentional overload and teach athletes to attend selectively to key task-relevant stimuli and block out all distractors. The final piece of the puzzle is learning to sustain focus, to concentrate on the task at hand. Although the terms *concentration* and *attention* are often used synonymously, they should not be. Concentration is the ability to sustain a focus of attention on selected stimuli over time. Helping athletes improve their concentration skills is a key ingredient of attention training. Concentrating on the task at hand can be quite challenging. External distractors such as a crowd noise can break athletes' concentration. Athletes can also be distracted by their own thoughts and feelings. And even if athletes block out all external and internal distractors, intense concentration is still difficult to sustain because it is energy demanding. When people concentrate for long stretches of time, they feel drained.

Trying to concentrate seldom yields positive results. The harder you try, the more elusive it becomes. Effective concentration actually requires "effortless effort," or allowing your mind to become absorbed in the here and now—in the task at hand—rather than trying to make yourself focus. For example, Tour de France winner Lance Armstrong is frequently asked what he thought about when riding for six or seven hours. "I get that question all the time, and it's not a very exciting answer. I thought about cycling. My mind didn't wander. I didn't daydream. I thought about the techniques at various stages" (Armstrong, 2000, p. 249). When athletes allow themselves to become completely involved in what they are doing, sustained concentration comes naturally and easily.

Concentration Is Energy Demanding

Athletes need to learn when and how to turn concentration off and on. Both in endurance sports and in events such as the decathlon and tournament sports—where athletes perform, then wait, then perform again—concentration must be managed prudently. If not, athletes are likely to experience mental fatigue: The correct stimuli are no longer selected efficiently, careless mistakes and poor decisions are made, and athletes are prone to being distracted.

Practice Concentrating

With practice, athletes will be able to concentrate for longer and longer periods of time. Some athletes are unaware of the need to practice this skill, and those who do practice it seldom do so for the full length of time their event takes in competition. Athletes should spend time in practice sustaining concentration in exactly the same way they must sustain it when competing. Coaches then can help athletes develop concentration skills by developing practice activities that require focused attention.

For example, the U.S. women's field hockey team used focused hitting drills in practice to develop concentration skills. Rather than just going through the motions while hitting, athletes were required to hit with awareness and hit the ball to exact locations (Ravizza 2006). A creative tennis coach fed athletes different colored balls during hitting drills. The athletes were told what type of return each color required. As they got better at concentrating, the coach made the colors lighter, and therefore harder to detect.

You can develop many practice activities that require performing with awareness and focused attention to develop your athletes' concentration skills. Timothy Gallwey (1997) encourages tennis students to focus on listening to the ball and discovering the distinct sound each shot makes. Attending to the sound of an opponent's serve puts a player's mind in a focused state of concentration. It also provides information that may help the player quickly anticipate the shot and choose the most appropriate response. Even simple activities such as stretching can be turned into a focused concentration exercise; for example, you can instruct athletes to focus closely on what each stretch feels like. If their minds wander, encourage them to redirect their attention back to stretching. With practice, they will get better at concentrating.

Roadblocks to Effective Concentration

Concentration requires quieting or "parking" the mind. When this was mentioned in a sport psychology class, a bright student asked, "And where should the athlete park it?" Good question. The answer is in the present, in the here and now. The athlete should focus on the current task and nothing else. This is, of course, easier said than done and can be hindered by internal factors, including excessive thinking, lack of trust, and fatigue.

Excessive Thinking

Some athletes have difficulty concentrating because they are holding onto things from the past, such as a poor call by an official, an opponent's style of play that has gotten under their skin, or a mistake they replay over and over. Athletes can also lose sight of the present because their minds are focused on the future—how great it would be to pull off the upset, or all the negative things that might occur if they have a bad performance. Their minds may be racing with all sorts of "what if" questions: "What if I miss

this shot?" "What if I blow this coverage?" "What if I mess up my routine?"

NBA coach Phil Jackson says, "Basketball is a complex dance that requires shifting from one objective to another at lightning speed. To excel, you need to act with a clear mind and be totally focused on what everyone else is doing. The secret is not thinking. That doesn't mean being stupid; it means quieting the endless jabbering of thoughts so that your body can do instinctively what's its been trained to do without the mind getting in the way" (Jackson & Delehanty 1995). In regard to tennis, Gallwey states, "Quieting the mind means less thinking, calculating, judging, worrying, fearing, hoping, trying, regretting, controlling, jittering, or distracting" (1997 p. 18). Figure 10.4 illustrates the difference between a cluttered mind and a calm, focused mind.

Lack of Trust

Trust is a skill that involves releasing conscious control over movements and allowing oneself to perform automatically. How would you react if we asked you to walk across a wide beam just above the ground? You would probably do so without a second thought. What if we asked you to walk across the beam again, but this time it was 100 feet (30 m) above the ground? Rather than trusting your walking ability, you would probably consciously try to keep your balance and focus on not falling, and this approach would make the task much more difficult. The same thing is true in sport. When competing, especially in major competitions, athletes desperately want to perform well and may start using controlled processing rather than trusting their training and skills. A pitcher may start "aiming," or consciously try to throw a strike rather than letting himself throw automatically. A mountain

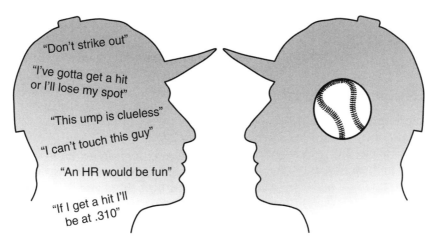

FIGURE 10.4 Effective concentration means quieting the mind and becoming absorbed in the activity.

Adapted from K. Ravizza and T. Hanson, 1995, *Heads up baseball: Playing the game one pitch at a time* (Indianapolis: IN: Masters Press), 34, by permission of The McGraw-Hill Companies.

Endurance Athletes: To Associate or Dissociate?

The demands of an endurance race go far beyond physical punishment. The athlete must also handle emotions related to the monotony, discomfort, fatigue, and pain that will almost always occur. How do these athletes sustain their concentration rather than succumbing to negative feelings? At any given moment, athletes can be either "tuned in" and focused on how they feel, or "tuned out," with their attention diverted from internal feeling states. These strategies are labeled **cognitive association** and **cognitive dissociation**. In cognitive association, athletes focus on bodily sensations, such as breathing patterns or stride mechanics. When dissociating, they shift attention away from feelings within their body to either an external focal point (e.g., scenery or surrounding events) or an internal diversion (e.g., daydreaming, singing to themselves, planning the rest of the day, or even solving math problems).

When should athletes associate, and when should they dissociate? Associating can help athletes manage their efforts—race with awareness, concentrate on maintaining stride length, monitor heart and breathing rates, and keep mindful of split times. Early in a race, associating could help a runner stick to a desired pace regardless of intense excitement. In later stages, association allows an athlete to quickly recognize potential problems and make the necessary adjustments to avoid pitfalls such as overexertion and excessive fatigue ("hitting the wall" in running or "bonking" in cycling). Dissociating can also be very beneficial. Intense concentration demands energy, and dissociation gives athletes a mental break. It can also help them work through fatigue by directing attention away from negative sensations, and it can reduce the monotony of long training runs. Athletes need to learn when each strategy is appropriate and develop the ability to switch from one to the other.

biker may try to consciously control the bike when going through a technical section rather than letting it go naturally through the obstacles.

Fatigue

Athletes with well-developed concentration skills seem to have an uncanny ability to block out feelings of fatigue. For those with less developed concentration skills, fatigue makes it difficult to sustain focus on the task at hand. Rather than becoming absorbed in their performance, they become completely preoccupied with their fatigue.

Overcoming Concentration Roadblocks

What can you do to improve your athletes ability to overcome concentration roadblocks? There is no single, foolproof strategy, but we can provide several tips on how to improve this important facet of attention.

Quieting Drills

Rather than *trying* to empty their mind of all thoughts, athletes should strive to quiet their mind by keeping it absorbed in the activity. The self-talk skills covered in chapter 7 can help athletes refocus whenever they

realize they are no longer focused in the present. As a coach, you can develop sport-specific strategies to help athletes quiet their minds and focus on the present. Tim Gallwey notes that, in racket sports, focusing on the ball can help maintain a quiet mind and a present focus. Players could be instructed to say the phrase "bounce-hit" either internally or aloud at the very moment the ball bounces on the court or makes contact with a player's racket. Saying "bounce-hit, bounce-hit," helps develop awareness of the rhythm and cadence of the rally and clears the mind of distractions, keeping the mind focused in the present and on the rally. If the athlete's mind wanders, the focus could be shifted to something more subtle and consequently more mind absorbing, such as the seams of the ball.

Triggers

Concentration can be improved through the use of **triggers**—words or actions that remind athletes to concentrate. Some use the word "focus" as a gentle reminder to direct their attention back to the task at hand after losing focus. In baseball and softball, fielders tend to lose concentration because of the inactive nature of much of the game. It is too much to expect them to maintain intense concentration for the entire time they are in the field. A useful concentration strategy before each pitch is to repeat in their minds where they will throw the ball given various situations, then use a trigger, such as touching the ground with their glove, to remind them to concentrate. Before the trigger, fielders can check out the crowd, adjust clothing, or move around, but after the trigger, they know they must concentrate only on the game.

Darrell Pace, Olympic gold medalist in archery, described the following technique to turn his concentration on and off: "I look in two places. I look either straight down at the ground in front of me or I'll see the center of the target. . . . From the time I cross the line, a switch goes on. They blow the whistle, I shoot, and then the switch turns off like a machine. It's like tunnel vision—nothing can interfere with it" (Vealey & Walter 1994). Did you notice how he used crossing the line to trigger his concentration?

Releases

Athletes can also learn to use **releases** to let go of negative thoughts and feelings that prevent them from concentrating on the present. Terry Orlick, a world-renowned sport psychology consultant, advocates using a "parking" routine to enable high-quality practices and help athletes focus. As athletes enter the training facility, they are instructed to place their hand on an object (e.g., the end of a bench) and imagine any personal problems or daily concerns flowing from their mind into that object. This frees their mind to focus during practice. After practice, the process is reversed and athletes can "unpark" those concerns and deal with them as needed. Athletes can also use releases to let go of mistakes or other distractions. An athlete can pick up an object, imagine the mistake or distraction moving into that object, then throw it away. A pitcher could use a foot to wipe the dirt from the pitching rubber, thus wiping away the mistake in order to focus on the next pitch with a clean mind (Ravizza & Hanson 1995).

Direct Attention Away From Distracting Thoughts and Feelings

Athletes can also use breathing control and rapid relaxation (see chapter 6) to divert concentration from distracting thoughts and feelings. Focusing attention on breathing helps athletes quiet the mind and focus on the present, and it facilitates concentration by reducing excessive arousal that interferes with optimal attention. Athletes can also use self-talk skills (see chapter 7) to regain composure and redirect their attention to the task at hand. Another strategy is to divert attention from conscious thinking by focusing on an object in the environment. A tennis player could focus on the strings of the racket, a diver on a spot on the wall, or a shotputter on a blade of grass to clear their mind. Learning to focus attention externally minimizes anxiety-producing thoughts. A runner might focus on the phrase "heel-toe" with each foot strike, or on a stop sign in the distance.

Being in Control: Having a Refocus Plan

All athletes have lost concentration at some point. It is inevitable. One factor that separates great athletes from other athletes is the ability to quickly regain their concentration after losing it. Rather than reacting to the situation that distracted them, mentally tough athletes have a recovery plan for regaining their focus, such as "recognize, relax, and refocus." The first step is to recognize that they have lost focus and need to regain concentration. Next, they use self-talk and diaphragmic breathing to relax. Then they refocus attention on the task at hand. Concentration is often lost when athletes react to situations rather than control how they respond. You'll learn more about refocusing plans in chapter 13, but for now recognize that they can be used to help athletes regain lost concentration.

Pitfalls of Being Too Focused

Although concentration skills are important, athletes can get stuck in one focus and fail to shift attention when needed, thus hurting their performance quality. Here, the final piece of the attention puzzle falls into place: Athletes need to be able to shift their focus depending on task demands. Shifting attention requires athletes to be aware of the type of attentional focus they need at various points during their performance, develop skills in selective attention so they can focus on task-relevant cues, and learn to manage stress so that it does not interfere with their ability to focus and shift attention when needed. Stress management is, in fact, one of the most important tools coaches can teach athletes to improve their attentional skills. In turn, if athletes have good attentional skills, they are less likely to experience stress because their minds will be absorbed in the game. Thus improvement in either area helps the other (more about this in the next chapter).

Implementing an Attentional Skills Program

Learning how to focus and block out all distractors goes beyond hoping that more practice, more experience, or more instruction to "concentrate" or "focus"

will bring improvement. The basic steps involved in developing mental skills such as attention are by now familiar to you: Education, acquisition, and implementation. The purpose of the education phase is multifold: to teach athletes how attentional systems work; to make them aware that they can improve their attentional skills through practice; to identify the specific attentional demands of the various skills and activities in their sport; to help athletes understand what factors cause attentional problems; and to teach them that they can learn to overcome such problems by using the strategies discussed in this chapter.

The next step is the acquisition phase, in which you create a training program to help each athlete learn to select which cues to attend to, sustain a focused state of concentration, and develop the flexibility to change focus as needed. The specific practice activities you structure should be sport specific, but the guidelines presented in this chapter provide a general foundation. For example, you could use video analysis or structured practice situations to help athletes learn which cues provide task-relevant information. You could take it one step further by devising practice activities that draw attention to important cues and using vivid performance-related trigger words. To enhance concentration, you can develop quieting drills and practice activities that help athletes perform with awareness. You can have your athletes practice regaining lost focus in the face of distractors by using releases, triggers, and developing a mind-set to focus on the present and on factors they can control. The possibilities are nearly endless.

In the implementation phase, you can begin to incorporate performance simulations that require athletes to deal with internal and external distractors, as well as shift their attention as the task requires. Imagery is also useful for creating competitive situations in order to identify cues to focus attention on and to practice sustaining focus as the situation changes. As attentional skills get stronger, introduce gamelike distractions so athletes have an opportunity to practice in an environment as close as possible to the real thing. Attentional skills should be developed to the point where athletes can focus on task-relevant cues, sustain that focus, and shift their attention without conscious thought.

As athletes put their attentional skills to work in competition, it is important to remember that the process of developing these skills continues to evolve as athletes grow. You should encourage your athletes to evaluate how well they focus on task-relevant cues and self-reflect to become aware of any problems that interfere with an optimal attentional focus. This awareness will serve as the foundation for continued development of athletes' attentional skills and of strategies for overcoming attentional obstacles.

SUMMARY

1. Attention is the mental process whereby athletes establish and maintain awareness of stimuli detected by their senses and use that information to make smart choices and decisions.

2. You should analyze the attentional demands for each specific skill in your sport. The attentional demands of any sport can be analyzed by considering the attentional dimensions of width (narrow or broad) and direction (internal or external) for each skill.

3. Well-developed attentional skills include the ability to focus on task-relevant cues, block out distractors, sustain concentration, and switch focuses as task demands change.

4. Key issues in understanding attention include attentional capacity, selective attention, and sustaining attention or concentration.

5. Well-developed attentional skills are required for achieving sport success, and expert athletes have better attentional skills than do novice athletes.

6. Given that athletes can only focus on a few things at a time, coaches need to prevent attentional overload when athletes are first learning a new skill.

7. Controlled processing is attention demanding, but automatic processing is not. With automatic processing athletes can perform basic skills without thinking about how to do them and can focus on other aspects of their sport performance and environment.

8. Athletes can develop a mind-set to be alert to certain cues in the environment or within themselves. Coaches can improve athletes' attention by teaching them which cues contain task-relevant information and how to focus on them.

9. We orient to unexpected stimuli, but by expecting and anticipating distractions we can learn to override unwanted orienting responses.

10. Concentration is the ability to sustain attention given to selected stimuli.

11. Concentration is improved not by forcing the mind to attend but by clearing the mind of distractors and becoming absorbed in the here and now. Concentration is hindered by excessive thinking, lack of trust, and fatigue.

12. It is difficult to shift attention away from powerful stimuli, such as fatigue, to focus on task-relevant stimuli. With the development of concentration skills, attention can be redirected from fatigue and other powerful stimuli to the right cues when performing the skill.

13. You should help your athletes recognize that concentration is energy demanding but can be improved through practice. When actually performing the skill, they should focus on the present.

14. Quieting drills, triggers, releases, distraction techniques, and refocus plans can be useful strategies for overcoming concentration roadblocks.

15. One of the most effective ways to develop concentration skills is to practice with focused attention and to redirect attention to the task at hand if distracted.

KEY TERMS

attention	cognitive dissociation	releases
attentional capacity	concentration	selective attention
attentional overload	orienting response	skill automaticity
cognitive association	performance-related cue words	triggers

REVIEW QUESTIONS

1. Explain why skilled athletes are able to perform multiple skills at once.

2. What is the distinction between external and internal distractors? Explain how they can interact to interfere with effective concentration.

3. Explain how endurance athletes can use cognitive dissociation and cognitive association to deal with fatigue.

4. Define the orienting response and give an example of it in your sport. What can coaches do to help athletes prevent counterproductive instances of the orienting response?

5. How does selective attention differ from concentration?

PRACTICAL ACTIVITIES

1. Describe a common situation for an athlete in your sport, then work through its attentional demands and indicate how each of the following demands is met: assessment, analysis and planning, rehearsal, and focusing and performing.

2. Imagine you are coaching a team that is physically talented but loses focus at critical times. What are some likely causes of your players' attentional problems, and what are some strategies you could use to improve their attentional skills?

3. You are coaching a group of athletes who are quite diverse in skill level. For those just learning the skill, how would you structure the learning environment to prevent attentional overload? For those who are more skilled, how would you structure the practice environment to ensure that they are not merely going through the motions?

4. Indicate what kind of focus is needed for each activity in the following table (internal versus external, and broad versus narrow). Answers are provided in the appendix.

Sport skill
A. Mentally rehearsing a golf swing
B. Developing a game plan for an important competition
C. Rebounding in basketball (ball has hit the rim)
D. Executing a gymnastics routine
E. Focusing on the next immediate hold while rock climbing
F. Planning a route for white water canoeing
G. Analyzing your skills and weaknesses as a coach
H. Watching how a football play develops

Stress Management

When you are finished reading this chapter, you should be able to

- understand common misconceptions about stress and its contemporary definition;
- describe Lazarus' stress model, including competitive demand, personal control, and coping strategies, and how they influence perceptions of stress;
- understand how athletes can use problem managment to manage stress by changing competitive demand or personal control and by using competitive engineering, personal engineering, problem solving, and mental plans;
- explain emotion management and arousal- and thought-triggered causes of stress;
- describe total emotion management packages, how they help athletes develop an integrated coping response, and total immersion versus gradual exposure practice strategies; and
- understand how to help athletes develop stress management skills using a three-phase program: education, acquisition, and implementation.

Most athletes, even longtime professionals, have failed to deal effectively with pressure at some point. A major league pitcher panics about facing the league MVP in the bottom of the ninth, a professional golfer gets the yips on an important putt, or an NFL quarterback chokes in the playoffs. If stress is a problem for these athletes, you can bet it's a concern for yours. Regardless of the sport, playing position, or competitive level, most athletes must deal with stress if they are to reach their performance potential and achieve their competitive goals.

Stress has a profound impact on athletes' sport experience. It can impair performance and deprive them of the satisfaction of demonstrating the skills they've mastered through countless hours of practice. Stress can destroy self-confidence by leading athletes to believe they are incompetent, and it can deprive performers of the joy of flow. Stress promotes interpersonal conflict, destroys teamwork, increases the likelihood of physical injury, and, when sustained, manifests itself as burnout that drives athletes to early retirement. Estimates suggest that one-third of all athletes suffer from chronic stress problems that reduce enjoyment, impair skill development, and stifle performance throughout their careers, and almost all performers experience occasional stress problems, which often strike at inopportune moments (Martens, Vealy, & Burton 1990). In either situation, if you are going to help your athletes, you must understand stress and know how to manage it effectively.

Understanding Stress

In chapter 9, you learned how arousal and anxiety affect performance, but we didn't discuss why athletes become anxious or how to manage arousal and anxiety effectively. To understand those issues, you need to grasp the stress process. This chapter will help you understand and manage your stress and help your athletes do the same. We start by identifying misconceptions about stress, then describe a model explaining how stress develops.

Common Misperceptions About Stress

Stress is blamed for many problems in sport, often due to two common misconceptions. First, it is commonly but incorrectly assumed that certain situations are inherently stressful because their excessive competitive demands result in extra pressure to perform well. Many athletes believe it is inherently stress

provoking to play for a state title, be an underdog against their crosstown rival, take a penalty kick with the game on the line, or bat with the game tied in the bottom of the ninth. But demanding competitive situations don't have to cause stress if athletes have the skills to deal with them effectively. In fact, you can probably think of times when an important competition didn't cause your athletes to experience stress. Thus it is clear that stress results from more than intense demands.

Another misconception is that stress consists of the physiological and psychological responses typically experienced in demanding competitive situations. Your players may experience a faster heartbeat, quicker and shallower breathing, sweaty palms, butterflies in their stomachs, and a frequent need to use the bathroom. Mentally, they may find it harder to focus—they think more (and more negatively), flash on images of disaster, and feel out of control. But not every athlete will find these responses detrimental to coping with competitive demands. These activation responses don't have to create negative emotions or impair performance. In fact, the same symptoms can be interpreted positively, prompting athletes to perform well. Stress, then, depends on how athletes interpret demanding competitive situations (the appraisal) based on their ability to meet those demands, and it can both help and hurt performance.

What Is Stress?

Most coaches and athletes have a basic idea of what stress is, but they may not fully understand its intricacies. **Stress** is a substantial imbalance between what we believe is demanded of us (competitive demand) and what we perceive our capabilities to be for meeting those demands (personal control), for situations in which success is important (McGrath 1970). Thus, perceptions—not competitive demands themselves—determine the amount and nature of stress we experience. As discussed in chapter 7, the premise of self-talk is that beliefs determine the impact of a competitive situation more than the situation itself does; our thoughts are more responsible for our actions than are the situations we practice and compete in. When appraisal is positive, we view a tough opponent as a challenge, which enhances performance, but negative appraisals prompt us to view difficult situations as threats, which hurts performance. One athlete may view a stadium full of people as "a great opportunity to show this crowd what I can do," while another may worry about "how embarrassed I'll be messing up in front of this crowd." It's the same stadium full of people, but different reactions can lead to either flow or choking.

Lazarus' Model of Stress

According to stress guru Richard Lazarus (1999), athletes weigh three types of information in appraising a potentially stressful situation: competitive demand, personal control, and coping strategies (see figure 11.1). If you want to help your athletes perform well under pressure, it is crucial to understand both the factors that cause stress and the strategies for managing it.

Competitive Demand

Competitive demand involves athletes' evaluation of how a demanding situation will affect their ability to attain important goals: the more important the goal, and the greater the **uncertainty** about reaching it, the greater the competitive demand. Playing a crosstown rival for the state title is a highly demanding competitive situation. In sport, stress occurs only if there is significant competitive demand—that is, if you are uncertain about attaining important goals.

Personal Control

Personal control refers to athletes' perceptions of how well they can manage competitive demands and achieve important goals. It hinges on two factors: whether they believe the sources of stress are surmountable, and whether they believe they have sufficient **performance capabilities** to do so. Performance capabilities include the knowledge, skills, tactics, and preparedness necessary to achieve valued goals—and the ability to harness them when it counts. Personal control is low if athletes perceive either that sources of stress cannot be eliminated or reduced, or that their performance capabilities are insufficient. High personal control results when athletes view stress sources as surmountable and believe their performance capabilities are sufficient to reach their competitive goals. Thus, the amount and type of stress experienced, and the quality of performance under pressure, depend on how performers appraise the balance between personal control and competitive demands.

Competitors who believe it is possible to achieve their goal (i.e., beating a tough opponent) and are confident that they have the capabilities to do so will view the situation positively, as a challenge, and select coping strategies designed to enhance their success. **Challenge appraisals** put a positive spin on competition and prompt athletes to focus on the opportunity to overcome obstacles and achieve success. This is a constructive way to deal with stress—when athletes appraise the situation as challenging, they develop optimistic emotions and choose constructive coping strategies that enhance performance. When athletes believe that competitive demands cannot be changed (e.g., they are hopelessly overmatched by an opponent) or that they lack the performance capabilities to meet demands (e.g., due to ineffective preparation), they think more about failure than success and appraise the situation as a threat. **Threat appraisals** highlight negatives and cause athletes to fear failure, feel pessimistic, and use ineffective problem-management strategies—thus impairing performance.

Coping Strategies

Coping strategies are the techniques that athletes use to deal with problems and to feel better emotionally in order to perform well in demanding competitive situations. Three major types are problem management, emotion management, and maladaptive coping. **Problem management** reduces or eliminates the sources of stress and includes a host of techniques for solving competitive problems (e.g., planning, increasing effort, and using preperformance routines). **Emotion management** entails decreasing emotional distress and enhancing positive well-being, even if the source of the problem remains unchanged (e.g., through social support, relaxation, positive thinking, and positive reinterpretation strategies). Maladaptive coping uses strategies that hurt rather than help (e.g., excessive venting of emotions, abusing drugs or alcohol, and withdrawing mentally or behaviorally). Coaches need to encourage athletes to use problem management and emotion management rather than maladaptive coping.

Athletes normally use a combination of problem management and emotion management, depending on the nature of the situation. When athletes appraise a situation as challenging, they tend to use problem-management strategies, adding emotion management as needed to maintain composure. But when athletes view a situation as a threat, they tend to make greater use of emotion-management strategies to enhance emotional well-being, whereas problem management receives limited attention because they believe that the problem can't be fixed or that they lack the capabilities to make things better.

Effects on Performance

Using effective problem-management strategies helps athletes perform better, whereas emotion management helps them develop a better mind-set but doesn't necessarily enhance performance. Effective coping helps athletes play at or beyond current performance

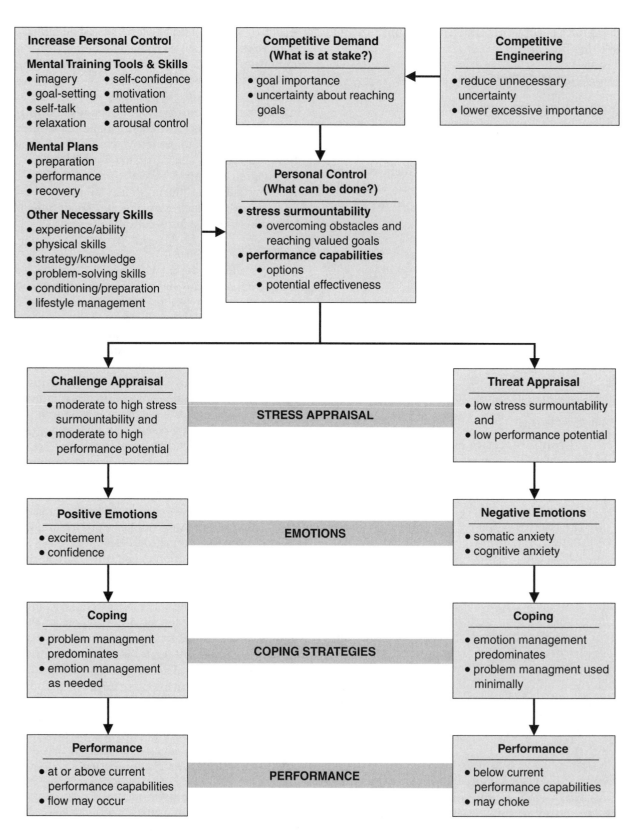

FIGURE 11.1 The Lazarus stress model.

Adapted from R. Lazarus, 1999, *Stress and emotion: A new synthesis* (New York, NY: Springer).

capabilities and on occasion experience flow, when things come together perfectly. Ineffective coping impairs top-level performance, prompting athletes to perform below their capabilities and even choke if negative emotions reach a critical point. As discussed in chapter 9, flow occurs when athletes become highly aroused, interpret arousal symptoms positively as challenge and readiness, and focus their thought patterns on the positive, the present, and the process of playing well. Performers choke when high arousal is interpreted negatively, as lack of readiness, and thought patterns are negative, failure oriented, and focused on uncontrollable factors such as outcome.

Personality and Situational Factors

Coaches need to be able to recognize athletes who are more vulnerable to stress as well as the types of situations that commonly increase stress responses. Athletes' stress levels, as well as their choices of coping strategies, are affected by trait anxiety and trait self-confidence (i.e., their personal tendencies toward high or low anxiety and self-confidence). Athletes who tend toward high anxiety and low self-confidence are more likely to appraise situations as threats and question their ability to succeed. Those who tend toward high self-confidence and low anxiety are more likely to appraise competition as a challenge and respond constructively.

Key situational factors—type of sport, importance of contest, uncertainty of outcome—can also affect how athletes view stress. Individual sports are typically more threatening than team sports because athletes have no one to share the blame with if they fail. Thus if you coach an individual sport, you should watch closely for stress-related problems in your athletes. And in all sports, the more important the competition is, or the more critical the situation, the greater the potential for stress. Finally, stress appraisal increases as athletes become more uncertain about how they will perform and whether they'll attain valued goals such as winning.

Stress Management

Coaching is a stressful profession. Coaches often demonstrate near maximal heart rates during competition while just sitting on the bench (Porter & Allsen 1978). Many critical situations require athletes and their coaches to successfully manage stress if they want to perform their best. The good news is that stress management is a skill you can master and teach

to your athletes, and the basic ideas discussed in this section can help both you and your team enhance your mental toughness.

Stress management is the process of reducing or eliminating the negative consequences of stress, particularly physical anxiety and mental anxiety, in order to feel better, experience positive emotions, and perform up to capabilities. Stress management strategies can target each component of the stress model: competitive demand, personal control, and coping strategies. You should help your athletes use problem management strategies whenever possible because they reduce or eliminate the sources of stress. If the stressor can't be changed, or athletes lack the capability to meet competitive demands, they can still modify how they view the situation in order to manage their emotions. Emotion management can help in these instances by reducing unwanted muscular tension, lowering excessive autonomic arousal, and countering negative thoughts.

Stress management strategies can be implemented both before and during practice and competition. Problem management is proactive and can be used before practice and competition to help coaches and athletes view stress as a surmountable challenge. Emotion management is more reactive and is used primarily *during* practice and competition to deal with stress as soon as it arises. Because there is little time for managing stress in the heat of practice and competition, emotion management is normally the first step. Once emotional control has stabilized, mental plans and problem solving can be used as time permits to overcome obstacles that hinder goal attainment.

Problem Management

Problem management is a proactive approach that reduces stress through competitive engineering, personal engineering, problem solving, and use of mental plans.

Competitive Engineering

Stress occurs when athletes are uncertain about being successful in important competitions, which means you can reduce stress by changing the situation. You do this through **competitive engineering**—eliminating unnecessary uncertainty and decreasing the inflated importance of the situation. To do so, you need to identify factors that raise your athletes' chances of experiencing stress and determine what can be done about them.

Reducing unnecessary uncertainty—The left-hand column of table 11.1 lists events that can increase uncertainty and over which athletes typically have minimal control. The right-hand column recommends ways to help athletes decrease unnecessary uncertainty. The list is merely illustrative, intended to stimulate your thinking about uncertainty in your sport: If you consider which aspects of your athletes' environment may cause excessive uncertainty and what you might do to alleviate it, then you will be effective in engineering a more constructive competitive environment. You may already use some strategies to reduce undesirable uncertainty, such as scouting reports and video study of opponents as you design game plans. Some uncertainty, of course, is inherent in sport, and uncertainty about outcome is part of what makes sport challenging and fun. You cannot and should not try to remove this uncertainty because your athletes need to develop

sufficient mental skills to cope with it. What should be eliminated is the *unnecessary* uncertainty that adversely affects you or your athletes.

Removing excessive importance—The other cause of elevated environmental demand is the excessive importance sometimes assigned to competitive outcomes (e.g., winning). Although intrinsic rewards are difficult to engineer, the extrinsic rewards available for winning (e.g., money, trophies, praise, playing time, and advancing to higher competitive levels) are more controllable. Table 11.2 provides an incomplete list of what makes events important and how you can decrease excessive importance for athletes experiencing competitive anxiety.

Athletes often feel that coaches and parents place too much pressure on them to perform well, and one important aspect of competitive engineering is to help those people provide better support. For

TABLE 11.1

Reducing Uncertainty for Athletes in Competitive Situations

Source of uncertainty	Action to reduce uncertainty
Waiting until only moments before the game to announce the starting lineup	Let athletes know well in advance of game time whether they will be playing and how much so they have the opportunity to mentally prepare.
Not letting athletes know where they stand on the team and particularly what their role will be	Clear role definition leads to greater team cohesion. Let athletes know what contributions they can make, what strengths they have, and what weaknesses they need to improve on. Make sure they understand what they have to do to expand their role.
Sending vague, nonverbal messages to athletes that they generally interpret negatively, leaving the cause of your disapproval unclear	Send clear, consistent, and specific messages, and provide corrective feedback on how to perform correctly. Use good confrontation skills if you feel an athlete's performance is not living up to your expectations.
Telling athletes one thing and then doing another, or telling them one thing today and another tomorrow	Be consistent in what you say and do. You can't behave the same way toward every athlete, but be consistent with your philosophy and how you treat each athlete across similar situations.
Creating uncertainty among the athletes about their physical well-being because of poor playing conditions or equipment	Improve the playing conditions and equipment. Discuss with your athletes the objective risks of injury in your sport and what can be done to minimize those risks, such as strength and conditioning training, safety precautions, equipment, skill improvement, following the rules, and matching players on size and ability.
Humiliating endurance athletes who drop out of a race, even though they are often uncertain about their ability to endure the pain of running a top time	Avoid using humiliation and help athletes develop their skills to manage arousal and reframe self-talk, thereby reducing their chances of dropping out.
Coaches, players, or spectators threatening an athlete's self-worth with negative evaluations or comments	Take any action within your power to prevent an athlete's self-worth from being threatened.

TABLE 11.2

Reducing Importance for Athletes in Competitive Situations

Source of importance	Action to reduce importance
Parents or coaches offer athletes money or other rewards for winning or achieving certain performance levels.	Ask parents not to do this, explaining that you believe this creates stress for the athletes. If you have a team policy of offering rewards for performance levels, discontinue it immediately.
The presence of important others such as parents, friends, and college or professional coaches or scouts at competitions can make the outcome more important.	Ask the spectators who are creating the stress not to attend until the player's skill level or confidence has improved. Don't tell players of the presence of coaches or scouts until after the competition.
Constructing a program to recognize outstanding play may cause some athletes to press too hard because they want the recognition.	Eliminate the recognition schemes or discuss with your athletes how to keep the recognition in proper perspective.
Certain athletes seek your approval because you help them get better and determine playing time.	Explain to your athletes that you value them as people, not just players who perform well, and act accordingly.
The league wants to recognize the most talented players by selecting an all-league team, thereby raising the stakes for playing well.	Encourage the league not to name an all-league team or to make the team as large as possible to recognize many athletes.
Parents or booster club members want to develop various types of awards (best offensive player, best defensive player, etc.), thereby increasing the importance of playing well.	Discourage parents and boosters from offering this type of award and explain the rationale behind your position.

example, you might establish a parent orientation program to educate parents about their child's participation and the level of importance they should assign to winning. It is also critical that athletes support each other, because they form the core of any team's social support system.

Personal Engineering

Your athletes can also use personal engineering to increase personal control in order to better cope with problems that arise during practice and competition.

Increasing personal control—In chapter 4, we suggested that keying goals to process and performance rather than outcome might be the most critical concept in mental training because it dramatically increases athletes' control over their own success. A winning outcome brings such attractive rewards that coaches and athletes are often enticed to set goals based on the level of play needed to win rather than a realistic level. The combination of excessive difficulty and minimal personal control associated with outcome goals often prompts threat appraisals and high anxiety in athletes. The best strategy for managing stress is to set realistic process and performance goals. Help your athletes

focus on highly controllable process and performance goals: staying in top physical condition; developing physical attributes such as strength, agility, endurance, and speed to their fullest; giving maximum effort; working to improve weaknesses; preparing mentally for practice and competition; and maintaining a flow mind-set. The more important the competition, and the more uncertain the outcome, the more critical it is to gear goals to process and performance. Such goals reduce threat and promote challenge, allowing athletes to play to their capabilities and have their best chance to win. Thus, in critical moments, top athletes experience great personal control by focusing on technical and tactical execution rather than on winning. No stress management strategy is more important in helping athletes view demanding situations as challenges, rather than threats, so they can play their best and rise to the occasion.

Enhancing performance capabilities—If you want your athletes to appraise demanding situations positively as a challenge, they must believe not only that problems are surmountable but also that they have the capabilities to attain their goals. For example, just standing at the top of a 90-meter ski jumping hill scares most people to death, and they think ski jumpers must be crazy. But ski jumpers don't consider their sport inordinately dangerous, because they have developed skills to meet the challenge. Jumpers' confidence comes from getting into the sport at a young age and starting on 5- and 10-meter jumps, where they could master the necessary skills to be successful before gradually working their way up to big hills. Thus, experience and skill development are important to acquiring effective performance capabilities.

You can help your athletes gain confidence in their capabilities by making sure they are physically and mentally prepared: The more performers develop physically (e.g., in terms of speed, strength, endurance, quickness, agility, and flexibility), the greater their coping skills will be. The more they automate key skills and strategies, the more confident they become about managing competitive demands. The more knowledge they accumulate, the more effective their problem-solving skills, and the better prepared they are to execute in specific competitions, the greater their overall performance capabilities will become. Lifestyle management also contributes to performance capabilities. Athletes will manage stress better if they sleep well, eat a nutritious diet, hydrate sufficiently, and manage their time effectively.

Developing Problem-Solving Skills

Enhancing personal control also requires systematically overcoming obstacles in demanding competitive situations. Good coaches teach their athletes to solve problems so that when situations change, game plans fail, opponents change tactics, or other problems arise, they can modify their strategies and techniques. For example, a basketball player adjusts how she comes off a screen depending on whether the defender slips under or fights over it. You also need to develop athletes' ability to solve technical problems so they can correct their own mechanics when needed. If a quarterback overthrows his first six passes, he should recognize the pattern and understand the technical adjustment necessary to correct his throwing mechanics.

In addition, you need to help your athletes develop their tactical problem-solving skills. Many coaches keep a list of demanding competitive situations (e.g., down a goal with one minute to go) and, several times a week, devote 10 to 15 minutes during practice to simulating one or two of them. Using problem-solving guidelines, athletes practice effectively dealing with each demanding situation, then critique themselves, identifying strengths and weaknesses in their execution, and generate alternate tactics to try next time. The more athletes practice this type of tactical problem solving, the better they perform in demanding competitive situations.

Mental Plans

Because competitions seldom follow a script, performances almost never go as planned, and problems inevitably arise, athletes must be able to cope effectively. As a result, personal control is greatly enhanced by having well-developed mental plans to deal with selected challenging situations. In fact, it is critical to sport success that athletes have a predetermined, structured plan describing how to cope with particular situations, as well as enough practice to execute the plan under adverse conditions. When athletes develop backup mental performance plans and a mental recovery plan, they feel greater personal control and thus less stress (see chapter 13 for more).

Emotion Management

While problem management is most effective *before* practice or competition (or, when time allows, during breaks in the action), emotion management is primarily carried out *during* practice or competition. Even when stress can't be reduced or eliminated, athletes can still exert control over their emotional responses and perform up to their capabilities.

To be effective, emotion management strategies must handle stress triggered by both thoughts and arousal. In fact, stress has been categorized based on which comes first—negative thoughts or excessive arousal (McKay, Davis, & Fanning 1981). Many athletes become conditioned to respond physically to specific competitive environments: As soon as a team steps into its archrival's gym, the players' hearts beat faster, butterflies form in their guts, and their palms get sweaty. These symptoms of increased arousal prompt negative thoughts, as players worry about a repeat of a game two years ago when they were upset and knocked out of the playoffs. Thus, the players' stress originates from increased arousal, prompted by a return to the scene of a negative experience, and which in turn triggers negative thoughts.

Stress can also be triggered in the opposite way, with negative thoughts prompting elevated arousal. Athletes may begin to have negative thoughts about their ability to win a big contest, then worry about the negative consequences of a loss. When they see their opponent during warm-ups, particularly if the other team looks more imposing than on video, performers' negative thoughts may ramp up (e.g., how humiliated they'll feel if they perform poorly in front of this large crowd). Suddenly, their hearts pound, butterflies flutter, palms get sweaty, neck and back muscles tighten, and lumps form in their throats. In this type of stress appraisal, negative thoughts prompt increased arousal.

Proactive Versus Reactive Emotion Management

Most stress management strategies can be used both proactively and reactively (see chapter 7). Proactive strategies help athletes develop greater emotional control, lower normal stress levels, and automate coping skills to deal with stressful competitive situations. We recommend taking time on a daily basis for total relaxation and for reading or playing a self-talk script to enhance general emotional control skills. Self-talk programming reminds athletes of their talent and skill, past successes, effective preparation, and adaptability, and it keeps performers focused on the present, on things they can control (task and effort factors), and on viewing problems as challenges. Reactive emotion management, on the other hand, is concerned with maintaining composure and emotional control in demanding competitive situations. Reactive strategies may include methods of reducing high physical and mental anxiety before taking a game-deciding free throw or penalty kick, controlling anger over being hit by a pitch or over an opponent's use of illegal tactics, and managing the frustration that accompanies playing poorly or making a key mistake.

Basics of Total Emotion Management Packages

No single strategy can deal effectively with stress from both arousal-induced and thought-induced anxiety (Schwartz, Davidson, & Goleman 1978). Thus, coaches will find it easiest to teach emotion management using **total emotion management packages** (TEMPs) that address both types of anxiety. TEMPs eliminate the need to diagnose what triggered the anxiety and allow you to teach one strategy rather than several different ones. TEMPs include a relaxation component to deal with the unwanted muscular tension and excessive arousal that promote physical anxiety as well as a self-talk component to counter the negative thoughts and irrational beliefs that trigger mental anxiety. This combined approach enables TEMPs to be effective against all types of stress problems.

Research assessing the effectiveness of TEMPs has been limited, but results have confirmed their effectiveness for managing stress (see Crocker, Kowalski, & Graham 2002 for a review). Performers should practice them regularly in order to become confident in their results, both in and out of sport: If you teach athletes TEMP skills to keep their composure so they can perform their best, they can apply the same skills to other situations and use them to help alleviate their fear of injury when learning how to execute a new Olympic lift (e.g., snatch) or dealing with anxiety about a test in the classroom. Because athletes can be confident that TEMPs will help them manage any kind of stress, they have good incentive to practice them regularly. TEMPs take a systematic approach to managing stress, but their success depends on automating component skills in order to create an integrated coping response.

Systematic approach to managing stress—TEMPs teach athletes to deal with stress systematically. First, stressful situations are chunked into parts, so specific thoughts can be used to handle each phase of the stress process. For example, athletes might have separate strategies for preparing to face a stressful situation, actually dealing with the problem, and managing extreme stress levels when they seem to be overwhelmed. Next, systematic, realistic process and performance goals are established to make success achievable and as personally controllable as possible. Athletes also create and maintain a flow mind-set, in which they are positive, confident, and composed; focused on task rather than self; and optimally aroused and motivated to push their limits. Finally, athletes practice their TEMPs to ensure they effectively manage emotions in most stressful competitive situations. Figure 11.2 illustrates the essential steps in developing a TEMP.

Automating component skills—Under stress, performers tend to revert to automatic responses. As a result, you must teach your players to automate physical relaxation and self-talk skills using the guidelines provided in chapters 5 and 7. This will enable them to execute TEMPs instinctively, without conscious thought; otherwise, TEMPs will seldom work effectively in demanding competitive situations.

Developing an integrated coping response—An **integrated coping response** (ICR) is a comprehensive strategy that quickly alleviates anxiety, whether it is caused by negative thoughts or excessive arousal (Smith 1980). Athletes initiate their ICR by inhaling deeply while repeating a counterargument (e.g., "I may not like this, but I can stand it and it will make me a better person"). As inhalation concludes, athletes repeat the transition word ("so") while they pause briefly. They then repeat their physical relaxation cue word (e.g., "relax") as they exhale deliberately. Effective ICRs must be practiced until they become highly automated—particularly the counterarguments, which must deal directly with negative, unproductive, or irrational thoughts.

Practice strategies—Total emotion management packages use two types of practice strategies: total immersion, in which athletes practice managing

Total Emotion Management Package

> ### Chunk Stressful Situations Into Phases

> ### Set Process and Performance Goals for Each Phase

> ### Develop and Maintain a Flow Mind-Set
>
> - Automate skills
> - Create ICR

> ### Practice Managing Emotions During Practice and Competition
>
> - Total immersion strategies
> - Gradual exposure strategies

FIGURE 11.2 A total emotion management package can help athletes deal with both arousal-induced and thought-induced anxiety.

maximal stress, and gradual exposure, in which athletes rehearse handling stress that increases in steps. Total immersion places athletes in extremely stressful competitive situations so they can get used to the high stress levels typical of demanding events (Smith 1980). Practice should be designed to help athletes use their ICR to handle a wide range of stressful situations. You can increase stress levels during practice by means of various strategies, including rewards and punishments. Once athletes are highly stressed, they use their ICR to turn off or manage the stress. Total immersion assumes that if athletes can handle high stress levels, they can adapt the same skills to manage lower stress levels. For a sample, see the Pressure Cooker drill (on page 179), a total immersion strategy for improving free-throw shooting.

Gradual exposure requires that athletes face a series of situations arranged in a hierarchy, with each one providing a slightly more stressful experience than its predecessor (Meichenbaum 1993). You first provide opportunities during sport practice for your players to handle low-stress situations, then move to moderate stress, and so on, until they have developed their ICR sufficiently to manage highly stressful situations in competition. In order to adapt the Pressure Cooker to a gradual exposure format, you might systematically increase the amount of preshot conditioning and raise the bar for success as players' ICR improves. You'll want to incorporate systematic practice using imagery, simulation, role playing, and homework assignments that allow your athletes to develop confidence in their ability to use emotion management skills.

Selection of a practice strategy—Both total immersion and gradual exposure are effective practice strategies (Meichenbaum 1993; Smith 1980). Your choice of which to use may be dictated by differences in sports,

Simulating Stress in Practice: Pressure Cooker Drill

When I (Damon Burton) was a high school basketball coach, my first team shot only 51% from the free throw line, costing us five or six ball games. For the next season, I developed a strategy to teach players how to shoot free throws under pressure. Two or three days a week, we concluded practice by simulating competitive pressure with a drill called Pressure Cooker. Each player was given a one-and-one free throw, and the team had to make 70% of all possible free throws to end the drill. Pressure was increased in three ways: players conditioned for 3 to 5 minutes before each turn, a missed first shot was scored as 0 for 2, and the drill was repeated until the team met the goal of 70%.

Players were taught to establish specific free throw routines; develop relaxation, imagery, and self-talk skills; focus on process cues; and manage their stress. The results of this emotion management program were dramatic. Over the course of the season, the players gradually became more consistent, as they automated their preshot routines to manage the stress of the Pressure Cooker drill. Not surprisingly, the team's free-throw percentage in games rose considerably (to 67%), and the team won at least three games with clutch free throw shooting in the final 2 minutes.

athletes, and your preferred way of organizing practice. If you're not getting desired results, don't be afraid to try an alternate approach; we have had good success with both formats, and our first choice was not always the one that worked. Having said all that, most coaches prefer to expose their athletes to stress gradually, allowing them to develop their ICR at a comfortable pace. But you must make sure that athletes don't get bored with the process and lose interest in practicing before they have the opportunity to deal with high stress levels. In order to maintain motivation, you may wish to use a total immersion strategy at least some of the time, exposing athletes to a level of stress they probably can't handle. This lack of success should motivate them to automate relaxation and self-talk skills and develop a more automated ICR.

Developing Athletes' Stress Management Skills

To develop stress management skills, athletes must use a combination of problem-management and emotion management strategies. Our program to automate these skills consists of the same three phases used to develop other mental training tools and skills: education, acquisition, and implementation.

Education Phase

The education phase of developing any mental skill consists of giving athletes general education on the skill and how it works, then moving to personal education, in which athletes develop self-awareness of their current stress-related patterns.

General Education

The material presented in the first part of this chapter should help you provide your athletes with a solid general education about stress management. You should teach them about common misconceptions regarding stress and help them understand the basics of the Lazarus stress model, highlighting the importance of competitive demand, personal control, and coping. Next, discuss specific problem-management strategies, such as personal engineering, competitive engineering, problem solving, and mental plans, and how they can be used to reduce unwanted stress. Finally, introduce emotion management strategies, especially TEMPs designed to simultaneously manage both types of anxiety.

Personal Education

Personal education involves helping your athletes understand their current stress and stress management patterns. Many coaches and athletes underestimate the stress they experience and overestimate how effectively they manage it. You may want to enhance players' awareness of their stress by assigning several types of homework. First, have them list common symptoms of stress such as those that appear in table 11.3.

You can also heighten athletes' awareness of their stress by using the Athlete Stress Management

TABLE 11.3

Common Stress Symptoms

Physiological	Psychological	Behavioral
Increased heart rate	Worry	Rapid talking
Elevated blood pressure	Feeling overwhelmed	Nail biting
Extensive sweating	Inability to think clearly	Foot or finger tapping
Elevated brain wave activity	Impaired decision making	Muscle twitching
Increased pupil dilation	Feeling confused	Pacing
Elevated respiration	Being easily distracted	Scowling
Decreased blood flow to skin	Inability to concentrate	Yawning
Greater muscular tension	Not feeling in control	Trembling
Increased oxygen uptake	Feeling strange or "different"	Frequent blinking
Elevated blood sugar	Narrowed attention	Poor eye contact
Dry mouth	Difficulty directing attention	Stammering
Frequent urination	Increased negativity	Rapid, high-pitched speech
Lump in the throat	Self-doubts and diffidence	
Increased adrenaline	Indecision	

Assessment Form (ASMAF). This inventory is particularly useful because it helps identify how stress affects practice and competitive performance (see figure 11.3). Have players complete the ASMAF for at least six practices and two competitions, so you can evaluate their stress levels before and during the event, along with their performance quality. Within 90 minutes before the start of practice or competition (as close to the start as possible), have athletes fill out row 1, using "prepractice" or "precompetition" as the situation and circling the responses that best describe their current feelings. Within an hour after the event, have them assess how well they maintained their optimal mind-set during the two most important stretches, briefly describing them in the first column of lines 2 and 3 and evaluating stress level during each. Finally, have athletes use the form to categorize their overall performance.

Help athletes examine their baseline information for both practice and competition in order to identify patterns of performance-related anxiety. Initially, have them concentrate on times when they performed well above or below normal and identify types of anxiety that seem to be most responsible for performance fluctuations—especially those that most hurt performance. For example, Samantha notices that her best competitive performances come when she is relatively free of negative thoughts, whereas muscular tension and unwanted arousal affect her performance less. In contrast, Steve recognizes that his poor performances are punctuated by excessive arousal and unnecessary muscular tension in the shoulders and upper back, whereas he performs well when arousal is optimal and tension minimal.

Information about midpractice or midcompetition patterns can also be helpful in developing performers' emotion management skills. Athletes should use specific strategies to target sources of stress that most impair their performance. For example, if players' confidence declines over the course of competition, they may want to employ their emotion management skills to reduce threat and enhance feelings of personal control. Keeping a log for a couple of weeks should help athletes get a good feel for the types, frequency, and intensity of stress problems they encounter.

Athlete Stress Management Assessment Form

Identify 3 situations that commonly stress you	How much do you notice unwanted muscular tension?	How much do you notice unwanted activation symptoms (e.g., pounding heart, butterflies, sweaty palms, & frequent urination)?	How much do you notice negative and distracting thoughts and personal put-downs?	How much do you notice negative images or nonspecific feelings of disaster?
	Low High	Low High	Low High	Low High
1.	1 2 3 4 5 6 7 8 9 Common symptoms _____	1 2 3 4 5 6 7 8 9 Common symptoms _____	1 2 3 4 5 6 7 8 9 Common symptoms _____	1 2 3 4 5 6 7 8 9 Common symptoms _____
2.	1 2 3 4 5 6 7 8 9 Common symptoms _____	1 2 3 4 5 6 7 8 9 Common symptoms _____	1 2 3 4 5 6 7 8 9 Common symptoms _____	1 2 3 4 5 6 7 8 9 Common symptoms _____
3.	1 2 3 4 5 6 7 8 9 Common symptoms _____	1 2 3 4 5 6 7 8 9 Common symptoms _____	1 2 3 4 5 6 7 8 9 Common symptoms _____	1 2 3 4 5 6 7 8 9 Common symptoms _____

Rate your overall practice or competitive performance

1   2   3   4   5   6   7   8   9
awful   average   great

From D. Burton and T. Raedeke, 2008, Sport Psychology for Coaches (Champaign, IL: Human Kinetics).

FIGURE 11.3 Athletes can use this form to evaluate their stress levels and how stress may be affecting their performance.

Case Study: Kerry, the Stressed-Out Basketball Player

Most veteran coaches have dealt with athletes whose stress problems hold them back. They tantalize coaches with exceptional skills that they never seem to harness effectively. During my (Damon Burton's) brief coaching career in high school basketball, I coached such a player, whom I'll call Kerry. A tall, well-built post player, Kerry was quick and rugged, had great hands, ran the floor well, featured a textbook jump shot and a soft touch, and had mastered an array of post moves that allowed him to score at will during practice. He was equally adept at almost every other phase of the game. From the first practice, Kerry played like a superstar and seemed to be a sure all-state pick. Kerry's team won almost every scrimmage, regardless of who was teamed with him. Regrettably, I soon found out that this was Kerry, the practice player.

Kerry was a totally different player in competition because of stress. In the locker room before our first game, Kerry was very nervous, and as soon as we tipped off he became a classic stress case. He was tentative about everything, fumbled almost every pass and rebound, and lost all the fluidity and touch on his shot. The longer the game went, the worse Kerry played, and his frustration quickly got him into foul trouble. This pattern worsened as the season went on, forcing me to play Kerry less and less. I tried various stress management strategies but nothing worked. By the end of the season, perhaps the most talented player in our classification was getting less than 10 minutes per game and contributing little to team success. Kerry was one of my biggest failures as a coach. We've since learned a great deal about stress management that can help you coach players like Kerry. We believe that the problem management and emotion management strategies described in this chapter could help your own "Kerry" manage stress, play better, and, over time, reach his competitive potential.

First, have Kerry set a series of process and performance goals that focus on controllable and realistic effort behaviors, such as playing good defense, running the floor, rebounding aggressively, and looking for open teammates when double-teamed. Work with Kerry's parents and teammates to provide support for keeping winning in perspective and focusing on process goals. Next, use competitive engineering to help him reduce unnecessary uncertainty and lower excessive perceived importance about competing. Use video and scouting reports of upcoming opponents. Enhance Kerry's conditioning, physical skills and strategies, and mental skills and problem-solving strategies, and automate them so they work even in pressure-packed situations. Additionally, teach him to develop mental plans to get in a flow mindset before practice and competition, maintain it during the event, and recover it if he loses focus. Use performance plans to target several situations that have stressed him in the past, such as double-teaming or physical play (see chapter 13 for more on mental plans).

When the uncertainty and importance of competition can't be changed, Kerry must learn how to manage his emotions and modify how he interprets the situation. First, he must automate the skills of goal setting, self-talk, and relaxation. Have Kerry focus on process goals, because these are realistic and controllable. Kerry can also use self-talk to build confidence, focus on controllable factors, change negative thoughts, reduce distorted thinking, and reframe irrational beliefs. You can teach Kerry to use rapid relaxation to lower unwanted tension and diaphragmic breathing to reduce excessive autonomic arousal. Encourage him to develop a self-talk script to help him create a favorable mind-set and counter problematic negative thoughts.

After automating component skills, help Kerry develop a total emotion management package for handling stressful competitive situations. Work with him to develop four or five affirmations and counterarguments to prepare for and confront problematic competitive situations. Put component skills together to develop an integrated coping response. For example, when worried about physical, double-teaming defense in the post, Kerry might counter, as he inhales, "What a compliment! If they double-team me, someone must be open. Stay composed and outsmart them by hitting the open man." He would then pause and repeat "so" as a transition phase before slowly and deliberately repeating his relaxation cue word (e.g., "chill") as he exhales.

Once Kerry masters his ICR, he needs to automate his TEMP. He can use imagery to re-create stressful competitive situations, then use his ICR to control his emotions in a gradual-exposure approach until he can perform successfully. During practice, you can simulate key situations anticipated with upcoming opponents to allow Kerry and his teammates the opportunity to automate ICRs to deal with stress. Finally, Kerry must utilize his ICR to manage stress in real competitive situations, enabling him to play in competition the way he performs in practice.

Acquisition Phase

The acquisition phase focuses on three objectives: help athletes develop basic emotion management strategies, have them combine those skills to construct an integrated coping response, and help them master problem-solving skills (see Case Study: Kerry, the Stressed-Out Basketball Player).

Develop Basic Stress Management Tools and Skills

In order to master an ICR, your athletes must develop and automate the key mental training tools of relaxation and self-talk (see chapters 5 and 7). Your athletes must practice these component skills enough to make them highly automated in order to be able to automate an integrated coping response.

Construct an Integrated Coping Response

An ICR combines emotion management strategies and typically occurs in three steps: addressing mental anxiety by thinking of compelling counterarguments as you inhale, saying the transition word "so" as you pause briefly, and alleviating physical tension and excessive autonomic arousal by repeating your relaxation cue word (e.g., "relax") as you exhale. Athletes can repeat this sequence as many times as necessary to manage stressful competitive situations.

Develop Problem-Solving Skills

Problem-solving skills and mental plans also need to be acquired and automated if athletes are to manage stress effectively. Coaches need to systematically assess team strengths and weaknesses and develop mental plans to deal with recurring problems (see chapter 13), while helping athletes sharpen problem-solving skills to deal with a variety of less common competitive challenges.

Implementation Phase

Athletes must practice their TEMP enough for it to become automated. Normally, practicing stress management skills involves going through imagery rehearsal, simulation during practice, and automation in lower-level competitions. Imagery is an effective initial practice approach that athletes can use in order to rehearse experiencing stress and using their personalized ICR to manage it. For gradual exposure, athletes need to develop a hierarchy of 10 or more situations, arranged in order from least to most stressful. Then they rehearse each situation in turn, moving on only when they have mastered the current one. For total immersion, players use imagery to immediately create a high level of stress related to their biggest competitive fear, then use their ICR to manage their stress by turning it off.

Once your athletes master their ICR during imagery, they can try it out in stressful simulations during practice to see if it transfers effectively to real-life situations. Practice simulations (e.g., Pressure Cooker) can be creative, as long as athletes have the opportunity to make use of their ICR. Finally, encourage your athletes to try their ICR in real competition, starting with minimally stressful competitions during the early or nonconference season, then working toward the more stressful competitions typical of the late season. Figure 11.4 summarizes what you can do to help athletes develop their stress management skills.

Stress Management Guidelines for Coaches

1. Help athletes set realistic process and performance goals that keep success challenging but realistic and personally controllable.

2. Assist athletes in minimizing unnecessary importance and uncertainty.

3. Develop athletes' basic problem-solving skills.

4. Use mental plans to deal with common problem situations and create a structured approach to unexpected problems.

5. Help athletes develop and automate a total emotion management package to effectively manage both types of anxiety.

6. Teach athletes to use integrated coping responses made up of counterarguments they think as they inhale, a transition phrase "so," and repetition of the relaxation cue word as they exhale to manage emotions.

7. Select problem management strategies when obstacles are surmountable, time is available, and performance capabilities meet competitive demands.

8. Choose emotion management strategies when time is limited, obstacles are insurmountable, and personal control fails to meet competitive demands.

9. Athletes should automate their TEMP by using imagery practice, sport practice simulation, and available competitive opportunities.

FIGURE 11.4 You can help athletes manage their stress by incorporating these steps into your mental training program.

SUMMARY

1. Two major misconceptions about stress are viewing it as equivalent to high competitive demand and viewing it as the physiological and psychological responses experienced in demanding competitive situations.

2. In fact, stress is a substantial imbalance between what we perceive is being demanded of us (i.e., competitive demand) and what we perceive our capabilities are for meeting those demands (i.e., personal control), for situations in which success is important.

3. The Lazarus model of stress suggests that it is determined by three factors: competitive demand, personal control, and coping strategies.

4. Competitive demand is what is being asked of performers and how those demands—particularly, the importance and uncertainty of competitive goals—affect physical and psychological well-being and sport success.

5. Personal control refers to the resources athletes have available to them, particularly control over surmounting sources of stress as well as the performance capabilities required to reach valued goals.

6. Stress appraisal (what athletes believe about the stress) determines whether uncertain competitive situations are viewed positively as a challenge or negatively as a threat.

7. Coping strategies are the techniques used to solve problems and feel better emotionally in order to achieve valued goals. Problem management (e.g., planning, increasing effort, and using preperformance routines) is designed to reduce or eliminate the source of stress. Emotion management involves using self-talk and relaxation techniques to reduce emotional distress. Maladaptive coping hurts efforts to manage stress.

8. Stress management is a process designed to reduce or eliminate the negative consequences of stress, particularly mental and physical anxiety, in order to help athletes feel better, experience positive emotions, and perform up to their capabilities. Stress management combines problem and emotion management strategies.

9. Problem management handles stress through competitive engineering, personal engineering, problem solving, and mental plans.

10. Emotion management helps performers feel better, even if the source of stress remains unchanged.

11. Total emotion management packages manage both anxiety types and involve a common rationale, a systematic approach to managing stress, automated component skills, and an integrated coping response.

12. TEMPs use the physical relaxation skills of deep breathing and rapid relaxation, combined with the reframing and reprogramming of self-talk skills, to develop an integrated coping response.

13. TEMPs can be developed using either total immersion or gradual-exposure practice strategies. Total immersion places athletes in the most stressful situation possible, whereas gradual exposure starts with low-stress situations and systematically increases stress as athletes demonstrate the ability to handle it.

14. Developing athletes' stress management skills follows the same three-phase process used with other mental training tools and skills: education, acquisition, and implementation.

15. In the education phase, coaches provide athletes with a good general education about stress and stress management, and athletes develop self-awareness about their current stress and stress management patterns.

16. During the acquisition phase, athletes develop basic stress management tools and skills, then combine them into an effective integrated coping response.

17. In the implementation phase, coaches use imagery rehearsal, practice simulation, and lower-level competitions to help athletes automate and fine-tune their stress management skills.

KEY TERMS

challenge appraisals
competitive demands
competitive engineering
coping strategies
emotion management

integrated coping response (ICR)
performance capabilities
personal control
problem management
stress

stress management
threat appraisals
total emotion management packages (TEMPs)
uncertainty

REVIEW QUESTIONS

1. What are the common misconceptions about stress, and what is its contemporary definition?

2. What are the three major components of Lazarus' stress model, and how do they influence perceptions of stress?

3. What is stress management? What is problem management, and how does it manage competitive stress?

4. What is emotion management, and what are the arousal- and thought-triggered causes of stress?

5. What are total emotion management packages (TEMPs)? How do they develop an integrated coping response? What is the difference between practice strategies that use total immersion and those that use gradual exposure?

6. How can you set up a program to help athletes develop their stress management skills?

PRACTICAL ACTIVITIES

1. Develop a list of situations that have caused you to become stressed and rank them from most to least stressful. For the least stressful situation, identify negative thoughts that contribute to your stress and generate one or two counterarguments for each. Use these counterarguments, combined with your relaxation cue word, to develop an integrated coping response, then rehearse your ICR until you feel comfortable with it. Finally, imagine your least stressful competitive situation and use your ICR to reduce or eliminate the stress.

2. Select the most stressful situation from your list, and identify the negative thoughts that prompted your stress. Generate one or two counterarguments for each negative thought, combine your counterarguments with your relaxation cue word to develop an ICR, and rehearse it until it becomes somewhat automated. Finally, imagine your most stressful situation fully, making sure you experience relatively high levels of stress, then use your ICR to turn off the stress so you can perform successfully.

Self-Confidence

© StockByte "Sport: The Will to Win" Royalty Free Images

After reading this chapter, you should be able to

- understand what self-confidence is and how it affects performance;
- explain the differences between three levels of confidence—optimal confidence, underconfidence (diffidence), and overconfidence;
- recognize why performance-based confidence improves performance quality and consistency more than outcome-based confidence does;
- describe how you can enhance self-confidence through performance accomplishments, vicarious experience, verbal persuasion, and control of emotional arousal;
- explain key factors in developing and maintaining confidence during competition;
- explain how the self-fulfilling prophecy can both boost and deflate self-confidence; and
- understand how to help athletes boost their self-confidence using a three-phase program.

We have never met a coach or athlete who does not believe that self-confidence is vital to individual and team success. Champion athletes invariably agree that the key to success is believing in themselves, and they back it up by exuding self-confidence in their play, even in pressure-packed situations. Michael Jordan believes that the ability to come through in the clutch comes from having confidence that you can do it: "Where does that confidence come from? From having done it in the past. Of course, you have to do it that first time, but after that, you've got a model you can always relate back to. It gives you comfort doing something you've done before" (Jordan & Telander 2001, p. 1).

Although you and your athletes probably realize that self-confidence is essential for success, you may be puzzled about how to develop consistent confidence, particularly in important competitions or when the game is on the line. It is a challenging task to raise the confidence of athletes who are insecure and full of self-doubt. They may recognize the trait in others and appreciate its importance, yet still have difficulty developing it in themselves. Most athletes and coaches recognize the reciprocal relationship between self-confidence and competitive success: Confidence is needed to succeed, but success is essential to developing self-confidence. One of the biggest dilemmas for coaches is how to help their athletes get off the downward spiral where failure leads to lower confidence and in turn to losing, which promotes repeated failure, and get on the upward spiral where success leads to increased confidence and in turn to winning, which breeds continued success.

This chapter shows you how to help your athletes develop and maintain a high level of confidence. We begin by defining self-confidence and describing three levels of confidence. We then illustrate the inverted-U relationship between confidence and performance. Next, we highlight how self-confidence affects performance, directly and indirectly, then identify strategies you can use to help athletes enhance their confidence before and during competition. We also describe how the self-fulfilling prophecy can both boost and deflate your athletes' confidence. Finally, we describe how you can build athletes' self-confidence through the three-phase process of education, acquisition, and implementation.

Understanding Self-Confidence

The first step toward helping your athletes become more self-confident is to understand what self-confidence is. It is also important to understand how self-confidence improves performance.

Self-Confidence Defined

Most coaches and athletes think self-confidence means believing they will win or outperform their opponent. One of the tenets of western sport is that athletes should always believe they will win; to think otherwise is akin to sacrilege. In fact, conventional wisdom dictates that if athletes don't believe they can defeat their opponent, then they are thinking like losers, which will cause them to become losers.

This mistaken belief often leads either to a lack of self-confidence or to overconfidence. True **self-confidence** is an athlete's realistic belief or expectation about achieving success. Self-confidence is an accumulation of one's unique achievements across many different tasks and situations, coupled with preparation for the upcoming event, which enables one to develop specific expectations of achieving future success (as in the opening quote from Michael Jordan). This performance history helps define how your athletes perceive themselves and their abilities, thus establishing their level of optimism. Self-confidence is a vital part of athletes' personalities, and others quickly recognize it in them. More important, having optimal self-confidence is probably the most critical aspect of developing a flow mind-set.

Yet there are many myths about self-confidence, and your athletes need to be able to separate fact from fantasy. Help them understand that self-confidence is not what they hope to do, but what they realistically expect to do. It's not necessarily what they tell others, but their innermost thoughts about their realistic capabilities. It's not just pride in what they have done, but their considered judgment of what they will be able to do, regardless of competitive pressure.

Does Self-Confidence Enhance Performance?

Most coaches put a lot of stock in developing self-confidence, but does it really improve performance? The short answer is yes. Both anecdotal and scientific evidence confirm that athletes who have a higher level of realistic self-confidence perform better than those who don't (Burton 1988; Moritz, Feltz, Mack, & Fahrbach 2000). This is a direct effect: The more confident athletes are, the better they perform. But self-confidence also indirectly improves performance because of its relationship with three other traits: anxiety, motivation, and concentration (see figure 12.1).

- When self-confidence is high, mental anxiety is low, and vice versa. Optimally confident athletes experience fewer self-doubts and worries

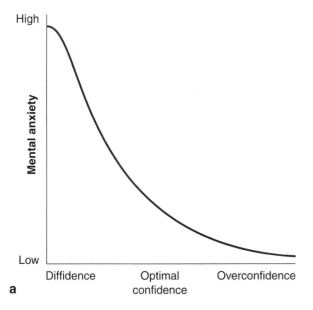

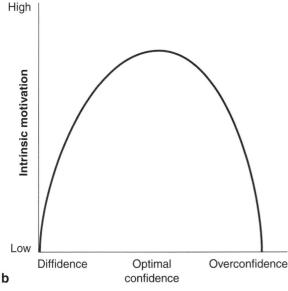

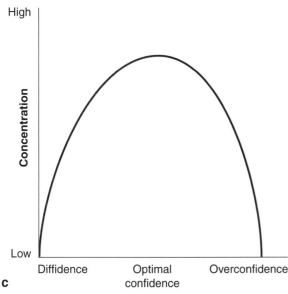

FIGURE 12.1 Relationship between self-confidence and three other mental skills.

than other athletes and are thus more likely to interpret high arousal positively, as readiness or excitement.

- Optimally confident athletes have strong intrinsic motivation to develop their game and continue to succeed. Diffident athletes do not feel competent enough to be optimally motivated, and overconfident athletes feel they are so talented that they do not need to work on their skills.

- Optimally confident athletes likely have optimal concentration—their confidence enables them to block out most distractions and helps them to focus on the attentional cues necessary to play their best. This allows them to execute skills more automatically, which can lead to flow.

Conceptualizing Self-Confidence

Coaches must work with athletes who have a wide range of self-confidence. You probably relish the opportunity to work with competitors who have an ideal level of self-confidence (**optimal confidence**). But most teams must also rely on performers who have too little confidence (underconfidence, or **diffidence**) or too much (**overconfidence**), either of which prevents them from performing their best. You can think of self-confidence as falling on a continuum, with diffidence at one end, overconfidence at the other, and optimal self-confidence in between. This continuum demonstrates the same inverted-U relationship with performance as does arousal (see figure 12.2). As self-confidence increases to an optimal level, performance improves, but when self-confidence exceeds this optimal level, performance deteriorates. Neither diffident nor overconfident athletes have the right amount of confidence to perform their best. Let's look at this model in more detail.

Optimal Confidence

Optimally confident athletes are competent and prepared. They have all the necessary physical and mental skills to achieve their realistic goals. They develop competence by being well-conditioned, mastering their sport's fundamentals, developing and executing effective strategies to maximize their strengths and minimize their weaknesses, and excelling at the mental skills necessary to create and maintain a flow mind-set. Optimally confident athletes play within themselves: They feel successful when they perform at the upper limits of their current capabilities but don't worry about achieving goals that are unrealistic for them.

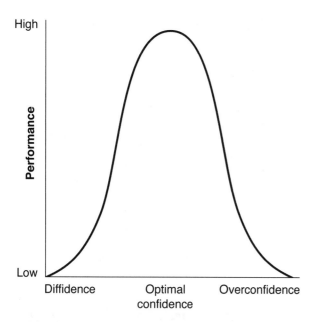

FIGURE 12.2 Relationship between self-confidence and performance.

Optimally confident athletes are also well prepared. The conditioning that athletes do to improve their flexibility, agility, speed, strength, power, endurance, and cardiovascular ability should improve their capabilities and prepare them to execute skills and strategies successfully in competition. Moreover, the harder they work in practice to develop and automate skills and accomplish performance objectives, the more prepared they should feel for important competitions. Athletes can't fool themselves. If they haven't done the preparation, their confidence will fluctuate and often plummet when they can least afford it. Confidence in the clutch requires that athletes pay the price in the off-season, in the weight room, and on the practice field or court, preparing sufficiently to create an optimal level of confidence.

Effort, and skill and strategy development are two types of preparation that are particularly important sources of confidence. Many athletes get a great confidence boost from knowing that no opponent can outwork them. At the 2000 Sidney Olympics, Rulon Gardner predicted his surprise victory over undefeated Greco-Roman wrestling legend Aleksandr Karelin due to superior conditioning, while swimmer Dara Torres attributed her four bronze medals at age 33 (in her fourth Olympics, after four years of retirement) to being in the best shape of her life. Most great performers continue to develop their skills, techniques, and strategies throughout their careers. Michael Jordan worked extensively on his game (especially his fundamental skills) during each off-season. This skill development enhanced

his confidence that, when the game was on the line, he could hit the shot, make the steal, or shut down his opponent. When athletes feel competent and prepared, they expect to do well, leading to optimal confidence, and in turn to top performance. You can see this success spiral in figure 12.3a.

Optimal confidence is usually necessary for great performance, but it does not guarantee top performance. Sometimes, despite being highly competent, preparing well, and feeling confident, athletes simply

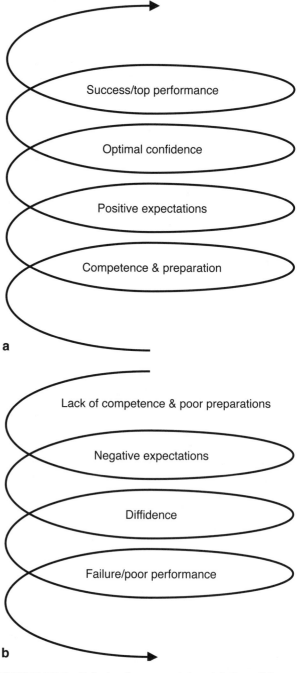

FIGURE 12.3 Spirals of success (a) and failure (b).

have off days and perform poorly. Optimally confident athletes recognize that self-confidence does not give them immunity against making errors. It does, however, give them a powerful tool in dealing with mistakes. When athletes' confidence is not in doubt, they feel free to correct errors in a constructive way and see mistakes as the stepping stones to future success. They are not afraid to try, because they know mistakes are the price that must be paid for getting better. Be sure not to chastise athletes for making errors, because you might deny them this powerful tool by tearing down their self-confidence.

Diffidence

Most coaches struggle in trying to help diffident (underconfident) athletes, particularly ones with the potential to be great performers. Some diffident athletes are being realistic in that they truly do not have the capabilities to perform well, but most merely underestimate their skills and preparation. These athletes may base their confidence too much on physical match-ups, which means trouble when they face physically superior opponents. They fail to recognize that they can overcome such opponents with well-developed mental skills and effective strategy. No matter how much they prepare for a particular competition, these performers don't really believe that they have the capabilities to compete successfully.

A mistake or loss does not shatter optimally confident athletes, who know that mistakes and losing are a normal part of sport, but diffident athletes fear failure so much that they are easily intimidated. They see themselves as losers and begin to behave accordingly. It's a vicious cycle, or self-fulfilling prophecy, that many performers find impossible to break: Because they lack or underestimate their preparation and competence, they expect to fail, leading them to feel underconfident, which, in turn, contributes to actual failure (see figure 12.3b). Poor performance then confirms their negative self-image, increasing their expectation of future failure. Alexandre Dumas (cited in Walker 1980) captured the diffident personality (which, of course, affects women as well the men Dumas posits): "A person who doubts himself is like a man who would enlist in the ranks of his enemies and bear arms against himself. He makes his failure certain by himself being the first person to be convinced of it" (p. 160).

Diffident athletes become tentative and blame themselves, even when responsibility should be placed elsewhere or simply chalked up to "one of those things." Their self-doubts cause them to experience high anxiety, and they lose concentration and resolve; they may even quit trying. Diffident athletes are underachievers whose lack of confidence limits both their development and their performance. For specific ideas about how to help them become optimally confident, see the Boosting Self-Confidence section on page 192.

Overconfidence

The term *overconfidence* is a misnomer. Athletes cannot be overconfident if their confidence is well-founded. When we say they are overconfident, we really mean they are unrealistically confident—their confidence is greater than their competencies and preparation warrant. By any name, however, overconfident athletes may be the most difficult group to coach, because they labor under two distinct misperceptions.

The first misconception we term **inflated confidence**, because some players honestly believe they are better than they really are, whether due to pampering from parents and coaches, playing against weak competition, or excessive media hype. These athletes are headed for disappointment. They are often very good—sometimes extraordinarily skilled—at their sport, but because they believe they have superior physical or mental skills, they often become complacent. Without adequate preparation, their once-superior skills are negated, leaving them wondering what happened and why they felt so lethargic, out of sync, and off their game. These athletes' confidence is easily shaken when they encounter obstacles, adversity, or failure. Moreover, because they overestimate their ability, they often respond to competitive adversity by trying to do too much rather than playing within themselves.

The second misconception, **false confidence**, is seen in athletes who believe that acting confident on the outside will overcome the diffidence and fear of failure they feel on the inside. Falsely confident athletes are often regarded as brash, cocky, and pretentious, but their arrogant facade is designed to mask their self-doubts. These athletes often fake it because they know how important self-confidence is to sport success. They avoid situations that threaten their self-confidence and try to avoid failure in order to protect their fragile egos. They fake injury or offer excuses when they perform poorly, and they are often difficult to coach because they will not take responsibility for their mistakes or accept constructive feedback about how to improve. Overconfident athletes misrepresent reality, confusing what *is* with how they wish things were. They may have fallen prey to the fallacy of simplistic "positive thinking," but simply thinking positively does not help athletes reach their goals. Confidence must be earned by working hard to develop skills and strategies, then preparing to use them effectively during competition.

Consistency of Self-Confidence

Both athletes and teams can develop higher and more consistent levels of confidence when it is based on performance rather than outcome. Recall from chapter 4 that process and performance goals are flexible and give athletes more control, allowing them to achieve success and take credit for it. Can you see how this approach would enhance self-confidence? Athletes with performance confidence believe they can execute key skills and strategies to perform well and reach their process and performance goals. Those with outcome confidence, in contrast, believe that a high-quality performance will allow them to compare well socially and win.

When athletes set process and performance goals, they are able to establish an optimal level of challenge and therefore experience more consistent success. Because these goals are more controllable, athletes internalize this success and feel more competent, which breeds strong and consistent self-confidence, unchanging from contest to contest. Most athletes find that their performance confidence is consistently higher than their outcome confidence (Bandura 1977, 1986).

Athletes who base their confidence on outcome criteria (the goal is winning) may be overconfident when facing a weak opponent, diffident when facing a superior rival, and optimally confident when matched up with an opponent of approximately equal ability. Thus outcome confidence fluctuates, sometimes wildly, as the quality of opponents varies. This pattern tends to inhibit long-term skill development and performance improvement. In contrast, performance confidence is much more stable from one competition to the next, allowing the slow, steady, systematic performance improvement that leads to better overall long-term development. To promote a high and consistent level of self-confidence in your athletes, help them base their goals, and thus their confidence, on process and performance, not outcome.

Boosting Self-Confidence

Self-confidence is a crucial mental skill; without a healthy foundation of realistic self-confidence, your athletes will not be able to reach their true potential. But how do you help your athletes develop and sustain confidence, especially those who are full of self-doubt and insecurity? You should start with four tried-and-true strategies (see figure 12.4): performance accomplishments, vicarious experience, verbal persuasion, and arousal control (Bandura, 1977, 1986; Feltz & Lirgg, 2001).

Performance Accomplishments

The best way to boost confidence is to build a history of **performance accomplishments**. As long as athletes take credit for their success as a reflection of their hard work and ability, each success should help them feel more confident. Generally, if athletes and teams have succeeded in the past, they expect to succeed in the future, whereas failure tends to promote negative expectations. Michael Jordan described his confidence this way: "My whole NBA career I always

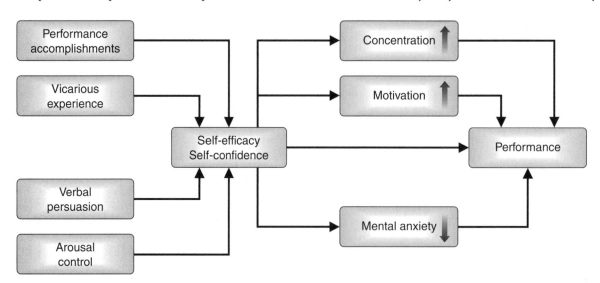

FIGURE 12.4   How self-confidence enhances performance: The strategies on the left enhance self-confidence, which boosts concentration and motivation and reduces mental anxiety. All of these factors work together to improve performance.

thought back to 1982 [i.e., his winning shot in the NCAA championship game]. I'm not saying you can't be confident in the clutch if you've never made the big play before—obviously, I was already confident before that shot. But that one moment initiated so much. Every shot after that, I felt I could make. I responded so well in those situations because I had such positive thoughts. I thrived on last-second shots. It became a trait for me." (Jordan & Telander 2001, p. 2)

Three aspects of performance accomplishment affect the development of confidence:

- *Consistency.* Confidence is buoyed by a pattern of success, even if improvements are small and opponents relatively weak. On the other hand, a stable failure history generally reduces confidence, even if a few big wins or performance gains are sprinkled into the mix.

- *Recency.* Athletes weigh recent experiences of success and failure more heavily than earlier ones.

- *Quality of success.* Confidence is enhanced more by success on difficult tasks and against tough opponents than by success on easy tasks and against mediocre opponents. Similarly, failure against weak opposition or on easy tasks is extremely damaging to self-confidence, whereas losing to a strong opponent or struggling on a difficult task is less harmful to confidence levels.

To highlight consistent, recent, and high-quality successes, you can use several practical strategies: goal setting, a personal Hall of Fame, and personal highlight videos.

Goal Setting

A systematic goal-setting program helps athletes develop a strong history of performance accomplishments. In a well-designed program, your athletes set daily and weekly goals that are evaluated regularly, boosting their confidence with each goal attained. Encourage your athletes to review goal logs often to remind themselves of the quality and quantity of their performance accomplishments. Have performers focus on both the magnitude and the consistency of their achievements, both in important competitions and in day-to-day practice sessions. Review the goal-setting program outlined in chapter 4 for specific strategies to maximize self-confidence. For skills that develop slowly, it is helpful to have athletes graph their progress to more readily see the gains they've made. Every few months, encourage athletes to systematically evaluate their long-term progress. They are usually amazed at the sheer magnitude of

what they've accomplished in just a few months. It's a great confidence builder.

Personal Hall of Fame and Highlight Videos

A personal Hall of Fame doesn't require a million-dollar building—just a few sheets of paper in a log where athletes list their accomplishments in sport and in life. I (Damon Burton) have used this strategy with athletes for years to help them recall the huge number of accomplishments in their lives (see figure 12.5 for a sample). It's not particularly important whether others would consider these accomplishments Hall-of-Fame–worthy, as long as they're meaningful to the athlete. Have athletes list everything they've done that was personally meaningful and gave them a sense of accomplishment, then add new successes as they occur. You and your athletes can also construct personal highlight videos showing outstanding swings, throws, jumps, plays, or other moments that remind them of their improvement and successes. Clips should be added to athletes' highlight sequences chronologically so they can easily see the progress they have made and the successes they've accumulated. Athletes should review their Hall of Fame and highlight video regularly to boost their confidence.

Vicarious Experience

Vicarious experience is the second-best strategy for developing confidence. It means helping athletes experience success indirectly, either through **modeling** (watching others demonstrate how to perform a skill or strategy) or through imagery (a type of self-modeling, in which athletes form a mental idea of how to perform a skill or mentally rehearse a well-learned skill). Imagined success is a powerful confidence builder.

Modeling

You are probably familiar with using modeling to help athletes learn or improve physical skills, and it can also be extremely valuable in enhancing confidence levels. It can be daunting to learn complex skills or face a difficult opponent, and watching a teammate (or opponent) meet the challenge can dramatically boost performers' confidence, particularly when they are similar to the model in experience and ability. A few years ago, I (Damon Burton) worked with two divers. Jill, the more skilled of the two, was reluctant to try new dives, and lead-up activities (e.g., trampoline work) did little to boost her confidence. Lisa, on the other hand, was less technically skilled but fearless, and she looked forward to the challenge of learning new dives. Because Jill knew she was a better

Excerpts From a Personal Hall of Fame

Tennis

- 1993: The legacy begins as I pick up a racket for the first time. I dream of becoming #1 in the world, the next Stefan Edberg.
- 1996: I play my first tournament and come in third at the age of nine.
- 2001–2005: I consistently help my high school team place high at the state tournament.
- 2001: I beat Mark from Lafayette. He's nationally ranked!
- 2002: What a great year. I felt "on" for almost every tournament and finally perfected my drop shot.
- 2004: Reach semifinals of State High School Doubles Tournament, place 3rd.
- 2005: Reach finals of State High School Doubles Tournament, place 2nd.

Academics

- 2000–2003: Honor roll student.
- 2003–2005: Honor roll student with 3.83 GPA.

Organizations

- 2003–2005: Member of high school Geography Club.
- 2005: Invited to speak at Kiwanis Club meeting. Given small scholarship.

Family

1987–present: My family is the center of my hall of fame; without them these pages would be blank. They are the ones who drove me to all the practices, brought me up, and supported me. Family has been the key to all my successes. They are my all-stars.

Other Life Accomplishments

- 2000–2003: Had a girlfriend. (It is an accomplishment.)
- 1987–present: Smoke- and drug-free.

FIGURE 12.5 Excerpts from a personal Hall of Fame.

diver than Lisa, it boosted her confidence to see Lisa master a new dive: "If Lisa can do it, so can I." Thus Jill used vicarious experience to get the confidence she needed to conquer her fear of new dives.

Modeling also works for developing confidence in tactics. Before the 1969 Super Bowl, New York Jets quarterback Joe Namath watched dozens of hours of film. He saw teams with skills similar to those of the Jets successfully exploiting the Baltimore Colts' weaknesses, in effect modeling a strategy the Jets could use to upset their heavily favored opponent. When asked by reporters how his team would fare,

Broadway Joe confidently guaranteed a Jets win. He then made history by using those borrowed strategies to lead the Jets to a shocking 16-7 victory, giving the upstart American Football League (now the NFL's American Football Conference) its first Super Bowl win and a major credibility boost.

It helps for the model to be similar to your athletes in experience or skill. Even though watching an elite performer may show your athletes how a skill should be performed, observing someone more on their level allows them to identify the performance cues necessary to take the next step in mastering the skill.

Imagery

Imagery is another important type of vicarious experience that can dramatically increase athletes' confidence. It was a key strategy in the development of Bill Russell, the centerpiece of the Boston Celtics dynasty. Imagining how to perform basketball skills or execute plays boosted Russell's confidence, because when he was on the court he felt as if he had already performed the move or play successfully. As Russell mastered the strategy, its confidence-boosting power grew, and he came to believe that if he could imagine it, he could perform it (Russell & Branch 1979). Follow these guidelines for incorporating imagery into your practices:

- Each day during imagery practice, have athletes imagine in great detail and with great frequency their successes, competitive triumphs, instances of good preparation, practice gains, and positive personal attributes.

- When watching video, help athletes dwell on success experiences, replaying them several times, but review mistakes or poor performance just enough to learn what they did wrong.

- Have athletes imagine their practice or game plan working well and see themselves confronting problems successfully. Make imagery a regular tool for confidence development.

Verbal Persuasion

Compliments, positive feedback, and even positive self-talk can be big confidence builders. Let's look at two forms of **verbal persuasion**: positive reinforcement from coaches, teachers, teammates, parents, and the media; and positive self-talk.

Feedback

Although it's always nice for competitors to hear good things about themselves, positive reinforcement or feedback helps most as a confidence builder when it comes from experts such as coaches or teachers. It boosts your athletes' confidence when you help them understand that they're performing a skill correctly, or at least improving their execution. So take a positive approach to skill development, using extensive encouragement, positive reinforcement, and corrective feedback delivered with respect. Use your knowledge and be sincere—the more respected, credible, trustworthy, authoritative, and sincere coaches are, the more their feedback helps athletes build confidence. And provide consistent reinforcement and feedback. It boosts athletes' confidence more than inconsistent feedback does. (See chapter 2 for specific ideas on using feedback to enhance confidence.)

Self-Talk

Self-talk is a form of personal verbal persuasion, and it can be a powerful tool for improving confidence (see chapter 7). Athletes can take themselves out of a game with negative self-talk, but they can also use self-talk to create a positive mind-set and boost their confidence. Help your athletes identify the negative or irrational thoughts that are most deflating to their confidence, develop and rehearse effective counterarguments, and use them whenever negative thoughts arise. Remember from chapter 7 that athletes can write scripts to systematize their self-talk, which could focus on statements of self-confidence or simply include a few quick reminders to maintain confidence. Self-talk scripts focused on self-confidence should remind athletes of personal strengths and assets; recall past successes, particularly in similar situations or in the face of obstacles, failure, or adversity; emphasize the amount and quality of their preparation; attribute successes and failures positively and optimistically; and appraise situations as challenges rather than threats (see sample in figure 12.6).

I (Damon Burton) recently worked with a talented distance runner named Margo, who ran well in smaller meets but performed poorly in major competitions. Margo's times confirmed that she had the talent to compete with the best runners in the Northwest, but she would often become intimidated and anxious and lose her concentration and confidence. I helped Margo develop a confidence script that she put on tape with her favorite music. The script emphasized her assets as a runner, her meticulous preparation, her previous successes, her ability to handle mistakes, and her extensive mental skills. Margo played the tape four or five times daily and before she competed. It helped her build confidence to race well regardless of the competition and helped her finish second at our conference championships and qualify for nationals.

Arousal Control

Arousal is simply a state of physiological readiness, and symptoms such as pounding heart, sweaty palms, and butterflies can be interpreted negatively as anxiety or positively as excitement. If physiological arousal symptoms become overwhelming, athletes interpret them negatively as anxiety, experience problems with focus or concentration, or feel ill prepared, all of which can lower their confidence. Thus athletes feel more confident when they have stronger **arousal control**. You can help athletes control their arousal levels using techniques learned in chapters 6 and 9,

Sample Self-Confidence Script

I don't want to imitate anyone, I want to be the best I can be!

My Strengths and Assets

- I'm a talented person with skills and abilities that allow me to be successful in life.
- I have the ability to make myself a better performer and help my team in many ways.
- On any given day I have the ability to play with anyone; it's a matter of my commitment to succeed.

Final Thought: I've got the goods!

Goals and How I Will Achieve Them

- My goal is to become the best I am capable of being.
- Dreams become reality through hard work and sacrifice.
- Give the game the best you have and the best will come back to you.

Final Thought: Stay focused and in the present.

My Past Performances and Learning From Them

- I've overcome similar obstacles before and I can do it again.
- Failure helps me by making me see where I can improve.
- I know it's only a matter of time before my hard work pays off.
- Remember all your success in the past and become the player you know you are capable of being.

Final Thought: Take the good and bad and use it to become better.

The Quantity and Quality of My Preparation

- I will work as hard or harder than anyone else; when crunch-time comes, they will fold and I will stand tall.
- I take pride in my work and practice; this will give me the confidence to overcome adversity.
- I have prepared myself well to maximize strengths and minimize weaknesses.

Final Thought: I am prepared and ready.

Situations Are Challenges, Not Threats

- Everyone encounters failure and adversity; champions rise above adversity and see problems as opportunities for excellence.
- I will approach each problem as a challenge—an opportunity to get better as a person and an athlete.
- Mistakes will happen and when they do, I will make the best of them and learn from them.

Final Thought: Challenges separate champions from wannabes.

(continued)

FIGURE 12.6 A sample self-confidence script.

No Negative Thoughts, Only Positive Ones

- "Labeling is disabling"—don't label yourself or others.
- I can't control my opponent or other variables; all I can control is my effort.
- Don't feel sorry for yourself. Life could be worse. No complaints!

Final Thought: Resilience is my middle name.

Success Comes From Hard Work

- I know hard work and consistent practice have paid off and allowed me to achieve success.
- I will not let failure defeat me, I will overcome it.
- Champions are made, not born!

Final Thought: I'm committed to personal excellence.

The thing that will make me a player is my love for the game.

FIGURE 12.6 *(continued)*

which will in turn help them interpret their arousal positively, thus enhancing their confidence (Jones, Hanton, & Swain 1994; Jones & Swain 1995).

In summary, you can help athletes develop self-confidence by helping them remember their accomplishments, watch others achieve success or imagine their own success, receive feedback and use positive self-talk, and learn to control their arousal. Now let's look at developing and maintaining *team* confidence.

Developing Team Confidence

In team sports, **collective confidence** is probably more important than the confidence of individual athletes. Personal and team confidence are decidedly different. Athletes may feel confident in their own ability to perform well, yet have little confidence in their team's ability to succeed. Others may feel confident that their team will perform well, even as they doubt their own capabilities. Teams have the ability to come together and achieve synergy, in which the team plays better than the performers' individual capabilities would seem to allow. This happens most when a team has a strong success history and outstanding leadership (Feltz & Lirgg 2001). Collective confidence plays a big role in synergy, as it does in all areas of team performance. Several factors are key in developing team confidence (in addition to the factors that promote personal confidence): understanding individual roles that must be performed to maximize the team's effectiveness;

developing the skills to perform these roles successfully; constructing a positive environment that supports teamwork and cohesion and fosters high productivity; and developing collective problem-solving strategies.

Teams are more confident when each team member understands his or her role and feels prepared to fulfill it. If roles are left unfilled, then team performance, and therefore team confidence, suffers. Most players would prefer to play the glamour roles that gain recognition and media attention, but when performers unselfishly accept lower-profile roles, team effectiveness soars. You must define the role that each athlete needs to play and help him or her see its importance. Athletes feel more confident when they know exactly what their role is. Help them set goals based on those expectations, so they are not left to base their confidence only on outcome goals. When many individual athletes achieve their role-based performance goals, team synergy should develop, leading the team to experience the success spiral.

Collective confidence also benefits from a positive team environment that fosters cohesion and high productivity. For a team to succeed, players have to trust their teammates to do their jobs, just as they are trusted in turn. The more positive and supportive the team environment is, the more teammates can trust each other, strive to get better, and build their confidence.

Finally, team confidence is affected by how issues are resolved. The more systematic and efficient a team's problem-solving process, the higher the quality of decisions made, and the greater the consensus about how to implement solutions, the greater a team's collective confidence should be. For example, attacking an opponent's pressure defense in basketball requires an effective team strategy as well as individual recognition and skills to implement the strategy. Team strategies must focus on creating passing outlets to alleviate the pressure and adjusting movement patterns to attack the defense's weak spots. Individual players must recognize what the defense is trying to exploit and calibrate individual technique to mesh with the team's strategy by adjusting roles, using different patterns to move the ball, modifying screening techniques, and using backcuts to attack the basket.

Developing and Maintaining Self-Confidence During Competition

As important as it is to develop confidence in practice, you are probably most interested in how to maintain high levels of confidence during competition, particularly during major momentum shifts. How athletes appraise the situation and cope with stress has a big influence on self-confidence during the ebb and flow of competition.

Remember from chapter 11 that stress is a substantial imbalance between what people believe is demanded by the situation and what they believe they are capable of doing. When athletes view this imbalance as a threat, confidence is reduced, but when they appraise it as a challenge, they maintain or even increase their confidence. Your athletes tend to label stressful situations as challenges or threats based on their answers to two key questions: Can the source of stress be reduced or eliminated through effective coping? Do I (or does my team) have the necessary skills and preparation to cope effectively? If the answers to both questions are yes, the situation is normally viewed as a challenge and confidence is maintained or increased, whereas a negative answer to either question may prompt a threat appraisal that reduces confidence.

Consider the following ideas for reducing confidence fluctuations during competition:

- Help your athletes prepare and develop the physical and mental skills to be confident when facing any opponent. This will enable them to appraise situations positively, helping them stay confident even when they are behind.

- Be sure your team is prepared to cope with expected problems, obstacles, and adversity. In the heat of competition, the ability to adjust strategy, tactics, and skills to meet changing demands is directly linked to confidence

level. Develop plans to overcome anticipated obstacles and rehearse them until they can be executed automatically.

- Of course, you will still face unforeseen events and circumstances. You can help your athletes maintain their confidence by developing accurate scouting reports, waiting for the right moment to act, putting skilled problem solvers in leadership roles, and working through problems in a systematic fashion. These approaches help athletes stay calm, poised, and emotionally centered.

- Even in the heat of competition, keep your athletes focused on process and performance (not outcome) goals to reduce feelings of threat and retain a positive outlook. Above all, be a confident role model.

Now that you understand how to develop and maintain confidence during competition, let's look at the role that expectations play in confidence development, as we examine the special case of the self-fulfilling prophecy.

Self-Fulfilling Prophecy: Confidence Booster or Deflator?

Coaches can affect their athletes' confidence in a variety of ways, but one factor often overlooked is how coaches' expectations influence athletes' performance. Can you remember a coach who believed in you so much that he or she inspired you to be better than you thought you could be? Have you had a coach who expected the worst of you and prompted you to perform down to his or her expectations? Although expectations influence confidence indirectly, the powerful nature of what is commonly called the **self-fulfilling prophecy** makes it critical for you to understand this process.

Self-fulfilling prophecies occur when coaches' expectations prompt athletes to behave or perform in ways that conform to those expectations. In a classic study, Rosenthal and Jacobson (1968) matched two groups of students on academic ability and then investigated how teachers' expectations for each group influenced their academic progress. Teachers were told that testing had demonstrated that selected students in their classes were academic late bloomers who could be expected to make large educational gains over the next year. Amazingly, by the end of the school year, the supposed late bloomers had made greater achievement gains than the control group for whom teachers had normal expectations.

How does the self-fulfilling process work? It is quite subtle, and the "expectation–performance process" in sport can be described as a series of four key steps (Horn, Lox, & Labrador 2006):

1. Coaches develop expectations for how athletes should perform.

2. Coaches' expectations influence their treatment of individual performers (i.e., the frequency, duration, and quality of interactions).

3. Coaches' behaviors affect athletes' rate of learning and level of performance.

4. The cycle is completed when athletes' behavior or performance conforms to coaches' expectations (see figure 12.7).

In addition to affecting performance, others' expectations can also influence athletes' self-confidence. Athletes are quite aware of the treatment they receive from coaches, and over time their development and performance are affected by subtle variations in how they are coached. As a result of this differential treatment, high-expectation athletes develop physical skills faster and to higher levels, are more confident and motivated, experience less anxiety, perform better and more consistently, and come closer to reaching their performance potential than do their low-expectation counterparts. When athletes' performance conforms to coaches' expectations, the process has come full circle. Conformity of performance with expectations further reinforces the perceived accuracy of coaches' original judgments, making it more likely that the self-fulfilling prophecy will perpetuate itself, particularly for athletes more

susceptible to its effects because they are younger, less experienced, lower in self-esteem, more coachable, or more likely to value success.

You may think that you have not fallen into this type of self-fulfilling prophecy. Consider these questions:

- Do you believe some of your athletes have great potential and others only average potential?

- Do you spend more time with some athletes than with others? Are you more warm and caring with some athletes than with others?

- Do you expect some athletes to learn more skills, and persist in teaching these athletes difficult skills when they have problems learning them immediately?

- Do you give some athletes more, and more specific, feedback about how to correct or improve their performance than you give to others?

- Do you credit some athletes' success to hard work and others' to luck or an easy opponent?

- Do you credit some athletes' failures to things that can be improved and others' to low ability?

If you answered yes to any of these questions—as many coaches would—then self-fulfilling prophecy may be alive and well on your team. How can you change this? First, keep your expectations fluid. One of my favorite players was Bob, a walk-on offensive lineman who went on to earn a scholarship and enjoy a lengthy professional career. At 6 feet 2 inches (1.9 m) and 260 pounds (118 kg), Bob was considered too small to play offensive line collegiately,

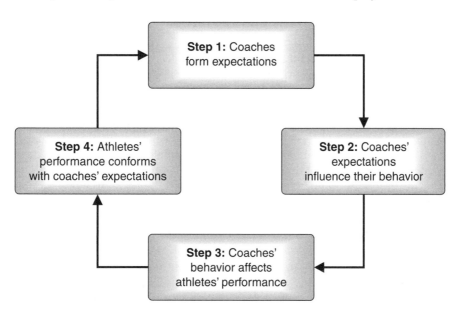

FIGURE 12.7 The cycle of self-fulfilling prophecy.

but his athleticism soon caught the coach's eye, and he became a starter midway through his redshirt freshman year because of his ability to make plays in practice and competition. Although Bob didn't meet the size stereotype his coaches had for offensive linemen, their expectations remained flexible, and when Bob demonstrated the athleticism to be an outstanding player, they changed their assessment. Remember that the self-fulfilling prophecy can be a confidence booster as well. It is a two-edged sword; to use it to your advantage, you must communicate positive expectations to all of your athletes.

Developing Athletes' Self-Confidence

As with the other mental training tools and skills described in this book, developing self-confidence is easiest when you implement a systematic program involving education, acquisition, and implementation phases.

Education Phase

This phase of developing athletes' self-confidence has two objectives: to provide a solid general education about confidence and to encourage athletes to assess their confidence patterns. First, use a team meeting to educate your athletes about self-confidence and how it benefits performance in practice and competition. Describe the three major types of self-confidence and the roles that competence and preparation play in developing optimal confidence. Emphasize the importance of performance-based confidence, and lay out the four major strategies for enhancing confidence. Sell the importance of boosting confidence by discussing times when your athletes could have benefited from greater confidence (you can also use examples of teams or athletes who know how to maximize it). We recommend concluding this initial session by helping your athletes identify one major strategy they can try out to enhance their confidence.

In terms of personal education, your athletes should develop a good understanding of their own self-confidence and the role that competence and preparation play in optimizing their confidence and performing their best. They should become aware of the factors that boost their confidence and those that deflate it. We recommend that athletes heighten their self-awareness by systematically logging key information about their confidence level and subsequent performance (as described in chapter 14). Athletes who understand what helps them develop their own

optimal confidence will be able to create a confident mind-set that helps them play their best.

Acquisition Phase

Confidence doesn't develop overnight, and building athletes' confidence can be challenging for coaches who have many other things to worry about. However, because you know how important self-confidence is to optimal performance, you probably are willing to spend time on confidence development. If initial efforts are successful, your athletes will become more enthusiastic about future mental training efforts, particularly for building confidence. Such efforts are most effective when athletes follow these five steps:

1. Prioritize the four confidence development strategies (i.e., performance accomplishments, vicarious experience, verbal persuasion, and arousal control) based on their effectiveness for each athlete.
2. Develop a plan for using the highest-priority strategy to boost confidence.
3. Try the strategy for a week in practice and competition.
4. Assess how well this confidence-building strategy works and fine-tune it in order to maximize its effectiveness.
5. Use this strategy systematically until confidence is optimal for each athlete.

Confidence development is an ongoing process. Various problems and obstacles arise to test athletes' confidence, often requiring the development of new strategies to boost confidence as situations change.

Implementation Phase

During this phase, you help your athletes automate their confidence development and maintenance skills. Acquiring confidence skills is of little value if athletes don't practice them enough to automate them. If confidence is not highly automated, most competitors suffer the same fate as Kerry, the basketball player whose confidence was easily shaken in competition. Such performers' confidence crumbles in important, pressure-packed competitions—the ones in which it is needed most. Automating confidence is tedious and time-consuming, but it is necessary for developing optimal confidence that won't crack at crunch time. In pressure-packed situations, performers must have the optimal confidence that allows them to react instinctively, relying on the execution of automatic responses with minimal conscious thought.

Confidence is more likely to remain optimal when practice simulates the conditions athletes will face in competition. When athletes practice developing and maintaining confidence in a distracting, pressure-packed environment, they are more likely to be able to automate optimal confidence and transfer it to competition. We recommend using three types of simulation. First, have athletes use imagery to simulate competition and practice becoming and remaining confident in order to play their best. A swimmer might rehearse the 500-meter freestyle race at the conference championships so many times in the month before the event that when he steps on the blocks he's totally confident in his ability to swim his best race. Second, devise practice situations to simulate competition as realistically as possible, so that each athlete can practice creating and maintaining her optimal confidence under any conditions, no matter how stressful. Finally, treat early-season or less important competitions as opportunities to simulate more important ones that athletes will encounter later in the season, when confidence is more critical.

Final Thoughts: Developing Ultimate Confidence

The most important self-confidence athletes can possess is not the conviction that they will always win or never err, but the belief that they can correct errors and improve consistently by working to become the best they can be. Athletes need to believe in their ability to improve by developing their physical and mental skills and preparing to the fullest extent possible.

Armed with confidence in their ability to become competent and prepared, athletes will not be intimidated by opponents' successes or disturbed by their own temporary failures. Wins and losses will be given appropriate weight in view of athletes' long-term objectives. Competitors will more likely view a particular contest and its outcome as a test to measure their progress as they pursue their objectives. Winning the game is no longer the most important objective; becoming better is.

SUMMARY

1. True self-confidence is an athlete's realistic belief or expectation about achieving success.

2. Self-confidence is not what you hope to do but what you realistically expect to do. It's not what you tell others, but your innermost thoughts about your realistic capabilities. It's not just pride in what you've done, but your considered judgment about what you will be able to do, regardless of the circumstances.

3. Self-confidence can be conceptualized as a continuum, with diffidence (underconfidence) at one end, overconfidence at the other, and optimal or ideal confidence in the middle. Self-confidence demonstrates an inverted-U relationship with performance.

4. Optimal confidence is based on competence and preparation. Athletes must have the knowledge, skills, and strategies to perform at a high level, and they must be fully prepared to use that knowledge and execute those techniques and tactics in the upcoming competition.

5. Diffidence is underconfidence that comes primarily from the inability to develop adequate knowledge, techniques, and tactics for success. Diffident athletes are full of self-doubts and play not to fail rather than striving to succeed.

6. Overconfidence comes in two forms. Inflated confidence occurs when performers honestly believe they are better than they are. False confidence is seen in diffident athletes who attempt to hide their insecurities by acting cocky.

7. Self-confidence is seldom stagnant. It is normally in either a positive, upward spiral or a negative, downward one. Athletes must work to get on a success spiral and avoid the pitfalls of failure spirals.

8. Self-confidence not only enhances performance directly; it also indirectly promotes improved productivity through relationships with three other mental skills—motivation, attention, and stress management.

9. The four major ways to boost self-confidence are performance accomplishments (goal setting, personal Hall of Fame, and personal highlight videos), vicarious experience (modeling and imagery), verbal persuasion (feedback and self-talk), and arousal control.

10. Team confidence is influenced by team members understanding and performing their roles, establishing a positive team climate, and developing effective collective problem-solving skills.

11. Self-confidence during competition hinges on appraisal and coping skills. The more athletes feel in control and believe they have effective coping skills, the more likely they are to view uncertainty as a challenge rather than a threat, thus maintaining confidence.

12. A self-fulfilling prophecy occurs when coaches' expectations prompt athletes to behave in ways that conform to those expectations. Coaches can use positive aspects of the self-fulfilling prophecy to bring out the best in athletes and avoid undesired effects that impair their development.

KEY TERMS

arousal control

collective confidence

diffidence

false confidence

inflated confidence

modeling

optimal confidence

overconfidence

performance accomplishments

self-confidence

self-fulfilling prophecy

verbal persuasion

vicarious experience

REVIEW QUESTIONS

1. What is self-confidence?

2. How does self-confidence affect performance, and what are the differences between optimal confidence, diffidence (underconfidence), and overconfidence?

3. What are the key components of optimal confidence?

4. What are the differences between performance confidence and outcome confidence? Which type of confidence will develop higher and more consistent overall confidence?

5. How can you enhance your athletes' self-confidence?

6. What are the key factors in developing and maintaining confidence during competition?

7. What is a self-fulfilling prophecy, and how does it boost or deflate self-confidence?

PRACTICAL ACTIVITIES

1. Construct a self-talk script to boost self-confidence.

2. Develop a systematic program for building your athletes' self-confidence using the four major types of confidence development strategies.

PART IV

Integrating Mental Training Tools and Skills

The final section contains two chapters that demonstrate how to combine mental training tools and skills into mental plans and build those into mental training programs. The thirteenth chapter, Mental Plans, emphasizes how to package multiple mental training tools and skills into three types of mental plans designed to attain, maintain, and regain a flow mind-set. Chapter 14, Mental Skills Training Programs, provides a master plan and systematic strategies to help you construct and implement your MST program successfully.

13

Mental Plans

When you have finished reading this chapter you should be able to

- explain mental toughness and how it helps athletes play their best under any circumstances;
- describe mental plans and their role in mental training;
- explain how mental plans help athletes create, maintain, and regain a flow mind-set to promote better performance and greater enjoyment of sport;
- lay out the benefits of mental plans;
- describe the three primary types of mental plans—mental preparation, mental performance, and mental recovery;
- help your athletes use triggers, releases, and cue words to initiate mental plans;
- explain how each type of plan is developed; and
- describe how to help athletes learn mental toughness skills through a systematic, three-phase process: education, acquisition, and implementation.

Early in my (Damon Burton's) career, I learned an important lesson about implementing mental training from Brenda, an outstanding player on our women's basketball team. Brenda's insightful discussion and outstanding performance in my applied sport psychology class confirmed that she understood and valued mental training. However, when I watched Brenda play, I was surprised at her lack of mental toughness. When things went poorly, Brenda got anxious, lowering both her concentration and confidence, and her game fell apart. I bumped into her several days later, and Brenda confirmed that she was having a hard time being mentally tough. My next question was obvious: "You know a lot about mental training. Why don't you use that knowledge to improve your mental toughness?" Her response was typical but eye-opening. "I know I'm not mentally tough, especially when things go wrong. I understand mental training and I've developed basic relaxation, self-talk, and goal-setting skills, but I'm having trouble figuring out how to use them in basketball."

This story points out a common problem with mental training. Knowing about mental training tools and skills is one thing, but integrating mental training techniques into sport and developing mentally tough athletes is a completely different challenge. Developing mental toughness in your athletes cannot be left to chance, and finding ways to implement mental skills training programs is critical to helping athletes deal with problems and adversity in competition. **Mental toughness** is the ability to play one's best in any situation, particularly when encountering problems, obstacles, adversity, or failure. It brings out the best in performers when they have the most at stake. However, mental toughness is not a single skill but a constellation of the skills discussed in earlier chapters. These skills must be integrated to promote optimal performance in challenging competitive situations. Mental toughness revolves around creating and maintaining an ideal mental performance state, a **flow mind-set**. How can you help your athletes integrate all of these skills and become mentally tough? Mental plans are the answer.

Understanding Mental Plans

Your athletes probably play well when things are going well, but can they perform at a high level when problems arise? It depends on how well they have prepared mentally. Many coaches and athletes leave mental toughness to chance, resulting in inconsistent or subpar performance and preventing athletes from

developing as much as their talent warrants. The champion athletes we've worked with leave nothing to chance. They are mentally tough because they use systematic mental and physical preparation to consistently create and maintain a flow mind-set in practice and competition. Elite performers' systematic approach to mental preparation and their execution of mental plans help them develop more fully than their counterparts who train less systematically. They also employ mental toughness more consistently when confronting adversity and enjoy their sport experience more fully. We believe athletes can develop mental toughness most effectively through systematic planning.

What Are Mental Plans?

Pioneered in applied sport psychology by Terry Orlick (1986), **mental plans** involve a series of systematic, individualized strategies designed to build mental skills into an athlete's game. Mental plans help athletes develop, maintain, or regain their flow mind-set so that they can remain mentally tough during the ebb and flow of competition and play their best. Mental plans are a means of implementing mental training tools and skills so that your athletes become more systematic in their mental, as well as physical, approaches to practice and competition.

Mental plans designed to *prepare* athletes for practice and competition (mental preparation plans) consist of steps to help them reach the mental state needed to perform their best. Athletes move deliberately through the steps—which might include goal setting, self-talk, imagery, energization, or any other mental training tool or skill—in an order that helps them personally create a flow mind-set. Mental plans for use *during* practice and competition include steps designed to maintain a flow mind-set and reach critical goals. Athletes also need to develop mental plans to help them get *back* on track when things go wrong in practice or competition.

Mental plans should become routines that your athletes follow to combine mental and physical skills in order to enhance performance. They differ from the inflexible and impractical superstitious rituals that many performers blindly follow. Such rituals control the athlete and prompt repeated robotic behavior that cannot enhance performance (e.g., put left sock on before right, or jersey before shorts; never step on lines when walking to or from the mound; always warm up with the same partner), whereas athletes are in control of mental plans and can use them to realistically promote better performance. Mental plans are based on sound research and theory and are designed to help performers promote, sustain, and regain a flow mind-set. They enhance automaticity and mental toughness, thus helping athletes perform optimally in pressure-packed competitive situations. Mental plans are athletes' blueprints for excellence.

Benefits of Mental Plans

Mental plans benefit your athletes in many ways. Here are four of the best: creating and maintaining a flow mind-set, enhancing performance quality, increasing performance consistency, and dealing more effectively with failure and adversity. Let's look at each.

Creating a Flow Mind-Set

We believe the ultimate goal of mental training is to help athletes maximize flow experiences. The flow mind-set stimulates optimal performance, and athletes who can achieve, maintain, and regain it are mentally tough. Mental plans help them do just that. Though experiencing flow in every practice and competition is unrealistic, we want athletes to strive to attain the flow mind-set, where they are confident, optimistic, and in control when they practice or compete.

Mental plans help athletes focus on needed improvements in order to enable a flow mind-set. Targeted mental skills vary by the athlete, even on the same team. The point guard may have rock-solid self-confidence, with little trouble controlling her arousal, yet feel her concentration and motivation weaken when she performs poorly. Meanwhile, the power forward may have an easy time with concentration and motivation but need help controlling arousal, boosting confidence, and managing stress. Each player would create her own mental plan to address weak areas and to attain, maintain, or regain the flow mind-set, thus enabling personal excellence.

Enhancing Performance Quality

Mentally tough athletes seem to maintain an optimal mind-set throughout competition, whereas their mentally weaker opponents become distracted or lose confidence at critical times and thus perform poorly. The great basketball coach John Wooden always wanted his team to remain emotionally stable, eliminating the peaks and valleys that interfere with top performance. Mental plans provide athletes with the needed tool for practicing and playing with composure. When athletes experience flow, they have a better chance of achieving their goals, can concentrate intently on performance-relevant cues, are physically and mentally relaxed yet energized, experience optimal arousal, and feel positive and worry free, so they can focus on executing automatically. These are the ingredients of optimal performance.

Increasing Consistency

Consistency in physical training leads to good physical conditioning, and athletes who follow a systematic mental training schedule experience more and better mental gains than teammates who train haphazardly. Champion athletes use a consistent mental preparation routine regardless of opponent, circumstances, or what's at stake—from practice to an easy nonconference opener to a championship game. Less successful athletes often have no plan or vary their competitive approach widely, sometimes replacing effective mental preparation strategies with less effective ones during their most important competitions. For example, a 5000-meter runner with whom I (Damon Burton) worked on stress management experienced so much stress 45 minutes before a championship race that she completely changed her mental preparation routine and performed a total relaxation session. She felt less nervous but was so lethargic that she had one of her poorest races of the season. Champion athletes perform consistently because they prepare and execute consistently, using systematic mental plans to automate the mind-set needed for top performance.

Dealing With Adversity

Even the most gifted athletes face failure and adversity, but mentally tough performers such as Anika Sorenstam, Peyton Manning, Roger Federer, and Tiger Woods consistently perform well and rise to big occasions because they plan for and deal with foreseeable problems. Handling adversity is difficult for anyone, but what seems to separate champions from the rest is their willingness to admit that competition seldom follows a script and develop plans to handle problems. Mentally tough competitors can win without their A-game. If Roger Clemens doesn't have his fastball working, he focuses on winning with his breaking stuff. When Tiger Woods isn't driving well, he uses his three wood. We'd bet you already use some mental strategies to help your athletes perform better, but perhaps like many coaches you have not been as systematic as you could be. Mental plans will help you and your athletes become systematic about mental training. Rifle shooter Launi Meili used systematic mental plans to overcome problems she encountered in Seoul and win the Olympic gold medal in Barcelona (see Launi Meili Automates Her Mental Plan and Strikes Gold on page 208).

Launi Meili Automates Her Mental Plan and Strikes Gold

Launi Meili went into the 1988 Seoul Olympics as U.S. national champion and world-record holder in three-position smallbore rifle shooting, in part because of her development and **automation** of two mental plans: a precompetition mental preparation plan and a mental performance plan based on an effective preshot routine. During the preliminary round of Olympic competition, Launi set an Olympic record and shot her way into first place. Unfortunately, a new final-round format had just been adopted in international competition that required the top eight shooters to fire 10 additional shots, each individually timed and scored to enhance the drama for the television audience. Launi had competed in this format in only two international competitions, struggling each time to adapt her deliberate preshot routine to the requirement of shooting at a faster pace. During the Olympic final, she felt rushed and shot poorly, slipping from first to sixth place and out of the medals.

Launi's frustration spurred her to commit to four more years of training so she could try again for the gold in Barcelona. This time, she refined her preshot routine to better meet the challenging demands in the Olympic finals. The routine helped her change the timing of her shift from broad to narrow focus while waiting for the command to take the next shot, thus better adjusting to the restrictive time limit in the finals. Happily, Launi's hard work in developing and automating the new routine through thousands of hours of practice—and a number of competitive trials—paid off. As before, she entered the Olympics as the reigning national champion and team world champion and set a new Olympic record in the preliminary round. But this time her highly automated preshot routine for the finals allowed her to perform well when the pressure was on, and she took home the gold.

Types of Mental Plans

As shown in Figure 13.1, the role of mental plans is to develop, maintain, and regain a flow mind-set. Mental *preparation* plans help performers create a flow mind-set before practice and competition. Mental *performance* plans help athletes maintain their flow mind-set while practicing and competing. And mental *recovery* plans help competitors regain their emotional composure and get back into a flow mind-set when they've been taken out of their game.

Mental Preparation Plans

Mental preparation plans help your athletes warm up mentally by using a structured routine to promote a flow mind-set that will enable them to practice and play at their best. Most athletes find it helpful to integrate their mental warm-up into their physical one, thus readying their mind and body together. Preparation plans include a basic plan for ideal conditions and a backup plan for use when the warm-up is constrained by time or circumstance. Your athletes' mental preparation plans should be designed like a pilot's preflight

checklist—to be worked step by step. Preparation plans for practice and competition should be quite similar, with changes made only in those steps that must differ based on the situation. This continuity helps athletes seamlessly transfer skills from practice to competition.

Mental Performance Plans

Mental performance plans are used during practice and competition to help athletes perform their best by maintaining and using their flow mind-set. They typically include a **standard mental performance plan** for use when things go well and **backup mental performance plans** to cover several common contingencies when problems occur or when the standard plan proves ineffective.

Standard mental performance plans focus on athletes' goals for practice or competition and on action plans for attaining them. These plans are usually tailored to one of three main categories of competition: races or routines, **self-paced tasks**, and **interactive sports**. For races and routines, standard mental performance plans focus on developing specific strategies to maintain a flow mind-set during each major segment of the event. Self-paced

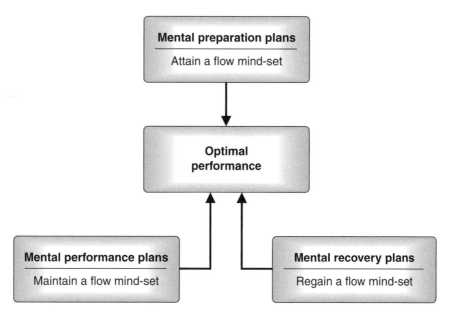

FIGURE 13.1 Mental plan model.

tasks (e.g., golf, field events, archery, basketball free throws, and tennis and volleyball serves) are repetitive, and athletes should construct and automate **preperformance** and **between-performance routines** that will maximize the quality and consistency of their performance. Finally, for interactive sports, where it is hard to predict what will happen, standard mental performance plans should focus on strategies for anticipated critical points during the contest (e.g., last 3 minutes of the game, or first play after a time-out) or for reacting to specific good or bad performance trends (e.g., after a turnover, or a run of points by the opponent). Between-play (or between-point) plans can be devised for interactive sports with breaks in the action, such as tennis and American football.

Backup mental performance plans emphasize overcoming specific problems that regularly arise, or adjusting goals to get the most out of practice or competition in the face of trouble. Problems in practice might include sluggishness due to lack of sleep, a lack of focus, or a coach's bad mood. Problems in competition might include a large early deficit, an unruly crowd, or fallout from a key mistake. Backup mental performance plans help athletes forge ahead even when conditions are not optimal.

Mental Recovery Plans

Backup mental performance plans address recurring or predictable problems; **mental recovery plans** help you recover from unexpected or uncommon setbacks where you become emotionally flustered and get taken out of your game. Mental recovery plans don't necessarily allow performers to completely return to form, but they do help them make the best of difficult situations and perform as well as circumstances allow. A mental recovery plan is a simple routine designed for the wide range of unexpected practice and competitive situations that occasionally catch competitors off guard and cause them to lose composure (e.g., distracting nonsport problems, controversial officiating decisions, trash talking by opponents, or stupid mistakes of their own). Mental recovery plans are general in design to provide a standard coping routine that can be used regardless of the problem that caused the loss of composure.

Role of Triggers, Releases, and Cue Words

An important component of any mental plan is the behavior or word designed to initiate the routine. For mental plans to be effective, they must be practiced until they are automatic, and shorthand methods are needed to focus attention and initiate action without prompting excessive analysis. This need is filled by triggers, releases, and cue words; in addition, triggers and releases provide a tangible way for coaches to see if athletes are following their routines.

Triggers

Athletes use a variety of triggers to initiate mental plans: A runner laces up her shoes to trigger her mental preparation plan, a golfer pulls a club from his bag to trigger his preshot routine, and a basketball player slaps both palms on the floor to trigger a mental recovery plan. Volleyball players form a quick huddle and look each other in the eye to trigger their between-point routine, and a tennis player focuses on his racket strings between points to trigger greater concentration. You can help your athletes identify triggers to initiate their own mental plans.

Releases

Releases are specific behaviors used to shed the effects of bad plays, stupid mistakes, missed assignments, poor decisions, and bad calls that create negative thoughts, frustration, and anxiety. A basketball player can walk away and count to 10 after a bad call. An infielder can pick up a handful of dirt and throw it down after making an error. A volleyball team can huddle after a bad point and chant "out of here" to exorcise their competitive demons. Our favorite release comes from colleague Ken Ravizza, who takes a plastic toilet into the dugout and has players flush their bad plays, poor at-bats, errors, and negative thoughts away to put these problems behind them. Coaches must help their athletes develop effective releases in order for mental plans to work.

Cue Words

Cue words remind athletes of process concerns that enhance performance while helping eliminate the distracting, confidence-deflating effects of negative thoughts. However, personal experience has shown that using cue words sometimes causes athletes to overanalyze, which can interfere with their ability to get into flow. Thus, we recommend using cue words that emphasize feel and trust to promote automatic skill execution. For example, during practice, a golfer may want to use cue words to remind herself to maintain a structured preshot routine (e.g., "one step at a time") or a swing cue (e.g., "smooth") when she hits a long iron shot. Cue words can be automated through extensive practice, so that during competition athletes can use them minimally and execute automatically based on trust and feel. Diver Greg Louganis used cue words such as "see the water, see the water, see the water, push out" to spot his dives, whereas NBA great Larry Bird focused on the cue words "nothing but net" when shooting free throws. See table 13.1 for cue words that can be used in a race plan.

TABLE 13.1

Cue Words for a 100-Meter Dash

Stage of race	Cue words
Prestart	Ready, alert, energized
Start	Explode, drive, react, go
First 10 strides	Low, power, accelerate, boom
Middle	Pump, kick, cruise, smooth
Finish	Lunge, push hard, go for it

Developing Mental Plans

How do you help your athletes develop mental plans? It's not as hard as it might seem. Although we strongly recommend that your athletes develop mental preparation, performance, and recovery plans, they don't have to be done all at once. Although starting with a preparation plan helps athletes develop a flow mind-set, we often start with a plan that makes a more immediate impact, such as a between-performance plan in team sports or a **race plan** or preperformance routine in individual sports. However, the decision is yours, because you must consider your athletes' current capabilities and needs. Regardless of which plan you teach first, we believe the investment in developing mental plans will pay huge dividends. You'll develop mentally tough athletes who will rise to the occasion in competitions and develop their capabilities fully. Let's look at specific steps for developing each type of plan.

Mental Preparation Plans

Mental preparation plans provide a blueprint for athletes' mental warm-up to maximize their chances of creating a flow mind-set and practicing and competing at their best. Athletes need to develop a mental warm-up routine that can be performed each day in practice and, with minor adjustments, before competition. Mental preparation plans must be highly individualized to meet each athlete's specific needs, but most include two basic steps: using mental training tools to develop mental preparation skills and strategies, and combining physical and mental warm-ups.

Using Mental Training Tools to Develop Mental Preparation Plans

The goal of mental preparation plans is to help athletes create a flow mind-set that solidifies their confidence; eliminates distractions and negative thoughts; concentrates on realistic process goals; controls arousal so they feel relaxed, energized, and in control; enhances motivation to push their limits; and helps them remain positive, poised, and optimistic in the face of failure and adversity. Athletes can use each mental training tool as needed to develop the mental skills that enable a flow mind-set.

Goal setting—Goal setting is an important component of any mental preparation plan. In the sample plan shown in figure 13.2, 400-meter runner Kim focuses on her goals and race plan during five steps in her mental preparation plan. During her jog and static stretching, she focuses on her goals and goes over her race plan. Later, during race simulation, she focuses on her overall goal and the subgoals to make it happen. Finally, during the last 20 minutes before the race, Kim focuses on her goal time, race plan, and splits to enhance her focus and readiness and to help her remain process oriented. Goal setting should be used in mental preparation plans to maintain task focus rather than self-focus and to motivate athletes to strive for excellence.

Imagery—Using imagery helps athletes boost confidence, program goals, and create a feeling that will help them perform optimally. Kim uses imagery early, during the jog and static stretching portions of her warm-up, to get the feeling of running with perfect form and enhance readiness by focusing on quick clips of key portions of her race. She also uses imagery during race simulation to imagine competitors beside her, and again during isolation to review her overall race plan and focus on key parts of the race. Imagery is a versatile tool that athletes use at various points in mental preparation plans to play out possible competitive scenarios, re-create positive performance feelings, practice strategy recognition, imagine achieving goals by following specific action plans, boost confidence, and try out possible strategies.

Relaxation and energization—Most athletes use relaxation and energization in a variety of ways in constructing and implementing their mental preparation plans. Kim uses relaxation in 7 of her 11 steps. She relaxes to control anxiety during initial race check-in. During static stretching she uses relaxation to enhance her flexibility and continue to control anxiety, and while running drills and strides she works to maintain relaxation, particularly in her jaw and arms. Next, during her bathroom break and race check-in, Kim uses relaxation to deal with prerace jitters, then, as she isolates herself from other

competitors, she uses relaxation as needed to calm her nerves. Finally, she focuses on staying relaxed as she drives out of the blocks during race-start practice. Athletes should use relaxation in their mental preparation plans as often as necessary to get and stay relaxed and control anxiety.

Normally, athletes have more need to relax than energize before competition because of the natural arousing effects of performing. Kim focuses on energization during five steps of her mental preparation routine. First, during dynamic stretching, she aims to feel strong and powerful, then, during strides, she increases arousal to enhance her motivation. During race simulation she tries to feel the energy of the crowd, whereas during isolation she feels electricity running through her body to signal readiness. Finally, as she conducts start preparation, Kim wants to feel explosive as she drives out of the blocks. Thus, she uses energization skills during those steps of her plan where she needs to feel strong and vigorous.

Self-talk—Self-talk is a critical part of mental preparation plans; it helps athletes become and remain positive, focused, confident, motivated, and poised. Kim uses self-talk in five steps of her mental preparation plan, starting with her jog and static stretching, where she listens to her self-talk script and repeats positive affirmations. During strides, she focuses again on maintaining a positive mental attitude, and during race check-in and isolation she focuses on staying positive and uses cue words such as "quick feet," "fast turnover," and "maintain form when I'm hurting." Self-talk also helps athletes manage stress and get motivated to push their limits.

Putting it all together—Your athletes can use the questions in figure 13.3 on page 214 to begin designing their mental preparation plans. These questions help athletes identify the mental training tools that will be most beneficial for them and decide how to use those tools in their mental preparation plans. They can then figure out how to combine their mental and physical warm-ups.

Combine Mental and Physical Warm-Up

In developing mental preparation plans, the length and sequencing of steps is critical. The plan must fit into the time available for warm-up, and the sequencing must feel comfortable and mesh with the athlete's physical warm-up routine. For most athletes, the physical warm-up is more systematic than the mental one. To combine the two, have athletes first write out their physical warm-up routine in

Mental Preparation Plan for a 400-Meter Runner

Step 1. Initial Race Check-In (80 minutes before competition, for 5 minutes)

Pick up number, check spike length, and get lane assignment.

Find heat number and check competitors in the race.

Control anxiety level using deep breathing and cue word.

Find a shady spot to put stuff and stretch.

Step 2. Jog (75 minutes before competition, for 8 minutes)

Nice and easy to start the blood pumping.

Go over race plan from assigned lane, imagining competitors in their lanes.

Image running with perfect form; particularly focus on the feelings.

Go over backup plans and how you want to use them.

Listen to self-talk script to focus only on positive thoughts.

Step 3. Static Stretching (67 minutes before competition, for 15 minutes)

Breathe into each stretch, focusing on getting muscles really loose.

Control anxiety and focus on race plan.

Be confident and use positive self-talk as I do quick imagery clips of key portions of my race.

Step 4. Dynamic Stretching (52 minutes before competition, for 7 minutes)

Create feeling of strength and power in muscles.

Stay tall, drive legs, and use good form with "pawing" action.

Step 5. Drills (45 minutes before competition, for 10 minutes)

Feel light and powerful with a strong push-off.

Look stylish with proper technique.

Toe up, heel up, knee drive, hips up, and stay tall.

Shoulders down, relaxed arm swing, relaxed jaw.

Step 6. Strides (35 minutes before competition, for 10 minutes)

Accelerate and drive off the ground with a quick first step.

Push, push, push while staying low.

Transition into driving taller while remaining relaxed.

Feel fast, confident, and totally positive.

Keep PMA (positive mental attitude) high, increase arousal while developing strong motivation—get psyched.

Step 7. Race Simulation (25 minutes before competition, for 5 minutes)

120 meters simulating the first part of the race and the corner.

Imagine competitors beside me as I feed off the energy from the crowd and my competitors.

Focus on my personal goal and the subgoals that will make it happen.

(continued)

FIGURE 13.2 Encourage your athletes to design personal mental preparation plans that will help them get into a flow mind-set.

Step 8. Bathroom Break (20 minutes before competition, for 3 minutes)

  Better safe than sorry.

  Use rapid relaxation to deal with race jitters.

Step 9. Check-In (17 minutes before competition, for 2 minutes)

  Place my number on my hip.

  Stay positive and confident.

  Don't let other competitors sidetrack me—stay focused on my race plan.

Step 10. Isolation (15 minutes before competition, for 10 minutes)

  Lie down in the shade away from others.

  I'm now physically ready to race and in a good flow mind-set.

  If needed, do rapid relaxation to stay relaxed.

  Feel the electricity running through my body as a sign of readiness.

  Go over my overall race plan and key parts again in my mind.

  Vividly see running my goal time by hitting each split on the button.

  Think of positive cue words: "quick feet," "fast turnover," "maintain form when I'm hurting."

  Be in the zone to run my own race—I'm totally prepared and ready.

  Now compete.

Step 11. Start Preparation (5 minutes before competition, for 5 minutes)

  Set up the blocks and do three starts.

  Feel explosive and drive off the blocks.

  Get out of warm-ups.

  Stay relaxed but drive the ground.

  "Be hungry" and "feel fast."

  Think only of the gun and react.

FIGURE 13.2 *(continued)*

the proper sequence, noting how long each part takes (see figure 13.4) and how long before practice or competition they normally start their physical warm-up. Next, they should write out their mental warm-up, first listing the mental training tools they will use to create a flow mind-set, then sequencing them in a routine that will be stable and easy to follow. Athletes must also estimate how long each step will take in order to determine when to start their preparation routine for practice or competition. Athletes who become highly aroused while doing precompetition imagery, for example, may schedule it for several hours before the actual competition and use short imagery bouts as needed later in their preparation plan so that they benefit from the imagery but also maintain their desired level of composure.

Finally, athletes should integrate their mental and physical warm-ups into a combined routine by finding ways to perform mental warm-up activities while conducting physical warm-up drills. For example, a sprinter might combine sprints with energization and motivation work, or relax her muscles and do final imagery as she stretches. Even then, combined preparation plans take considerably longer than physical warm-up routines, so athletes must design their routines to fit into the available time. (Depending on the time constraints of the sport, combined preparation routines take anywhere from 20 minutes to several hours.) And you must make sure your team arrives at the competitive venue in time for an adequate warm-up. It's also a good idea to develop a streamlined backup preparation plan for use when travel problems or other issues prevent athletes from

Strategies for Developing Mental Preparation Plans

1. How will you get focused for practice or competition?

    a. What are your goals for this practice or competition? What do you want to accomplish or focus on?

    b. Do you have a focus cue word or phrase for this event?

    c. What type of imagery would help you focus better?

2. How will you develop a positive mental attitude for practice or competition?

    a. How will you keep your goals challenging but realistic?

    b. Does playing your self-talk script create a strong positive mental attitude (PMA)?

    c. Do you have a PMA cue word or phrase?

    d. What type of imagery might create a more PMA?

3. How will you develop an optimal level of self-confidence for practice or competition?

    a. How will you use your goals to develop optimal self-confidence?

    b. Does playing your self-talk script create optimal confidence?

    c. Do you have a self-confidence cue word or phrase?

    d. What type of imagery helps you create an optimal level of confidence?

4. How will you develop optimal arousal for practice or competition?

    a. How will you use your relaxation and energization skills to create optimal arousal?

    b. How will you use your goals to enhance your optimal energy level?

    c. How helpful is your self-talk script in creating optimal arousal?

    d. Do you have an optimal energy cue word or phrase?

    e. What type of imagery helps you achieve optimal arousal?

5. How will you develop motivation to push your limits for practice or competition?

    a. How will you use your goals to enhance your motivation?

    b. How helpful is your self-talk script in enhancing your motivation?

    c. Do you have a motivation cue word or phrase?

    d. What type of imagery helps you achieve optimal motivation?

6. How will you combine this mental warm-up with your physical warm-up?

FIGURE 13.3 Athletes should ask themselves these six questions as they design their mental preparation plans.

Physical and Mental Preparation Plan Development Form

Identify the sequence of your physical and mental warm-ups, looking for ways to combine physical and mental warm-up activities. Write out each step, noting steps that include both physical and mental warm-up activities. Make sure that your routine allows you to warm up completely, both mentally and physically. Make sure your mental warm-up helps develop high levels of focus and concentration, self-confidence, positive mental attitude, and motivation and gets your arousal to the optimal energy zone.

Crucial Steps in Physical Warm-up Routine	Time Required	Concerns	Crucial Steps in Mental Warm-up Routine	Time Required	Concerns	Combined Physical & Mental Warm-up
1.						
2.						
3.						
4.						
5.						
6.						
7.						
8.						

From D. Burton and T. Raedeke, 2008, *Sport Psychology for Coaches* (Champaign, IL: Human Kinetics).

FIGURE 13.4 Athletes can use the Physical and Mental Preparation Plan Development Form to ensure that their preperformance warm-up routine addresses all aspects of performance readiness and helps create a flow mind-set.

Hank Aaron's Mental Preparation and Performance Plans

Baseball great Hank Aaron believes that the secret to his success as a hitter was a disciplined mental routine that gave him an edge over other major league hitters (Hanson 1992). Aaron used a combination of mental preparation and performance plans. He would arrive at the ball park early each day so he could spend several hours preparing mentally for the game, primarily visualizing himself facing the pitchers he might hit against that day in a variety of situations. Aaron's internal imagery helped him feel in tune with how the ball was likely to come at him, enhancing his pitch recognition skills and the automaticity of his swing. During the game, he continued his visualization and studied the pitcher, even watching the pitcher's release point through an eyelet of his cap if he was struggling to see the ball. At bat, after anticipating what the next pitch was likely to be, he simply watched the ball and tried to use a relaxed swing to put the ball in play. Aaron credits his mental routines for helping him become a career .305 hitter, baseball's longtime career home run leader (755), and an amazingly consistent performer in the field, on the base paths, and at the plate.

implementing their normal plan. Note that the 400-meter runner's integrated preparation plan begins 80 minutes before competition and ends when she sets up in her blocks and clears her mind so she can react to the gun. Mental preparation plans are very effective for team sports as well (as illustrated above in Hank Aaron's Mental Preparation and Performance Plans).

Mental Performance Plans

These plans provide a blueprint for remaining in a flow mind-set throughout practice and competition. Standard mental performance plans proactively enhance performance when things go according to plan, whereas backup mental performance plans cover common contingencies that can reduce performance quality. Standard mental performance plans form the foundation of athletes' mental approach to practicing and competing. They focus on athletes' goals for practices or competitions that go as expected and provide specific action plans for maintaining a flow mind-set. They also include periodic checks (at specific times during a race or during scheduled breaks in team sports) on athletes' mind-set so that mental skills can be adjusted if needed to maintain a flow feeling. If problems consistently arise, review the related mental skills with your athletes to identify whether an adjustment is needed. Athletes should know which mental skills are most beneficial personally and be sure to use them.

As helpful as standard mental performance plans can be, backup plans are often the key to success, because they prepare athletes to handle problems that arise frequently. Due to time constraints, most athletes and teams will be able to create only two or three backup plans. But because they deal with spe-

cific anticipatable problems and are rehearsed extensively, they greatly enhance the chance of success. An example: Julie was the only dependable scorer on our basketball team, and opponents knew that if they shut her down they would probably win. One favorite tactic was to rough her up physically, which sparked her temper and took her out of her game. I helped Julie develop a backup plan to handle the problem. We changed her mind-set to view these tactics as a form of flattery and emphasized that if our team was to win, she had to score in spite of them. We focused on using her speed to outmaneuver opponents, run them through numerous screens, and create good shots for her. These points were the focus of her imagery, her self-talk script, and her goals. The strategy worked, and Julie's scoring average went up three points per game during the conference season.

In this section, we look briefly at the basics for developing each of the three types of mental performance plans: races and routines, self-paced tasks, and interactive sports.

Races and Routines

Races involve a competitive task of somewhat fixed difficulty—the task doesn't change a lot from race to race. Uncontrollable factors such as weather conditions and quality of the race field may affect performance, but athletes can develop a systematic race plan to employ with minimal modification each time they race. Step one is to chunk the race into three to seven meaningful parts (e.g., start, first 400 meters, middle 700, and last 400), then develop goals and action plans for each segment. During the first 400 meters, a runner's main goal may be to "relax and hang back at a 64-second pace." Athletes should choose cue words that trigger the correct feeling and focus for each race segment. Possible cue words for the start include "explode and push" to get out fast, or "control and pace" to stay within oneself. For the finish, possible cue words include "relax and maintain form" to avoid tightening up, or "reel them in" to catch the runner ahead. Performance plans for gymnastics and figure skating routines can be set up in similar fashion.

Backup plans deal with adverse weather conditions, strategy problems (e.g., going out too fast or slow), and race performance concerns (e.g., feeling lethargic, worried about a rival competitor, or concerned about performance). For each problem situation, have athletes identify what cues they will use to implement their backup plan, how they will resegment the race if their original plan becomes ineffective, and how they can reestablish the desired feeling for the remainder of the race. Use figure 13.5 on page 218 to help athletes develop their race plans.

Self-Paced Tasks

Self-paced tasks are sports, or isolated tasks within sports, in which athletes perform at their own pace. They usually require repetitions of the same or similar movement patterns. Self-paced tasks are common in accuracy sports (e.g., bowling, billiards, golf, archery, and shooting) and in accuracy tasks in interactive sports (e.g., shooting free throws, kicking field goals, or serving in tennis or volleyball). Other examples include diving, ski jumping, and most throwing and jumping events in track and field. The two major ingredients of any mental performance plan for self-paced sports or tasks are a preperformance routine and a systematic between-performance routine. Preperformance routines create and maintain a flow mind-set that helps athletes trust their bodies and execute with greater automaticity. (See Tom Amberry's Preshot Routine for Free Throws below for information on the preshot routine that helped him make 2,750 straight free throws.)

Tom Amberry's Preshot Routine for Free Throws

Tom Amberry is a retired podiatrist who started going to the gym for exercise. By pure chance, he became interested in free throw shooting and started shooting 500 per day. Within several months, he had become proficient enough to attempt to set the world record for consecutive free throws made, and, at age 73, he did just that, hitting an astounding 2,750 in a row. In truth, he never even missed. He had started at 9 a.m. and was still shooting after 10 p.m. but had to quit because the gym owner wanted to lock up. Amberry says his secret to success is his seven-step preshot routine, and it is a good model for athletes who want to develop their own preperformance routines (Amberry & Reed 1996).

Step 1: Feet square to the line.

Before stepping to the line, do several deep knee bends, clinch your fists for 3 to 5 seconds, and shake them out to relax your hands and arms.

Step 2: Bounce the ball three times with the inflation hole up.

The inflation hole is your focus or concentration cue, so stare at it as you bounce the ball deliberately.

Step 3: Put your thumb in the channel, with your third finger pointing at the inflation hole.

Take a deep breath to relax and get rid of the butterflies.
Mental imagery should focus on how perfect your shot looks and feels.

Step 4: Elbow in the shot pocket.

Step 5: Bend your knees.

Step 6: Eyes on the target.

Repeat cue words "nothing but net."

Step 7: Shoot and follow through completely, with your "hand in the cookie jar."

Race Plan Development Form

Race Segment	RACE SEGMENT GOALS		Cue Words
	Physical	**Mental**	
Example: Race start	React quickly, stay low and drive hard; be with the leaders out of the blocks	Focus only on the gun; keep it positive; be confident in your start	"Be explosive," "drive low and hard," "I always get great starts"
1.			
2.			
3.			
4.			
5.			
6.			
7.			

From D. Burton and T. Raedeke, 2008, *Sport Psychology for Coaches* (Champaign, IL: Human Kinetics).

FIGURE 13.5 Plotting physical and mental goals and cues for each segment of the race and creating backup plans for overcoming potential difficulties helps athletes automate their execution and achieve a flow mind-set.

Preperformance Routine Development Form

Identify the steps in your current preperformance routine and any concerns about those steps. Next look at the required steps for preperformance routines. Make any additions of required steps to your current routine. Finally, write out your final preperformance routine that includes all personal and required steps. Write out each step in your Final Routine in as much detail as possible. Make sure that your new Preperformance Routine works for you and is short enough to fit within the time constraints of your sport.

Steps in Current Preperformance Routine	Concerns	Required Steps for Preperformance Routines	Additions of Required Steps to Routine	Final Routine: Combined Current and Ideal Steps
1.		**Step 1**: Relax and remove unwanted tension from performing muscles.		
2.		**Step 2**: Use goals and self-talk to promote focus and concentration.		
3.		**Step 3**: Adjust arousal to ensure you're in your optimal energy zone.		
4.		**Step 4**: Use imagery and positive self-talk to become optimally confident in performing your best.		
5.		**Step 5**: Develop a positive mental attitude that is stress-free but challenged.		
6.		**Step 6**: How will you maximize a highly automated, feeling-oriented performance?		
7.		**Step 7**: Streamline your routine to make it quick, effective and consistent to execute.		
8.				

From D. Burton and T. Raedeke, 2008, *Sport Psychology for Coaches* (Champaign, IL: Human Kinetics).

FIGURE 13.6 Athletes can use the Preperformance Routine Development Form to analyze and refine their existing routine.

Use the Preperformance Routine Development Form (figure 13.6 on page 219) to guide your athletes in developing their own routine (which should not be dramatically longer than their current one). Have them try the routine on their own a few times to make sure that they like its flow and that it creates the feeling state and automaticity they're looking for. Remember that feel and automaticity come with practice, so it takes time to finalize preperformance routines.

As with mental preparation plans, athletes in self-paced tasks or sports will want to create backup mental performance plans. If competition is delayed, weather interferes, or the athlete loses focus, what will he or she do? Athletes should identify what cue they'll use to start their backup plan, how they will develop new goals and action plans based on the situation, and how they will regain a flow mind-set or positive outlook for the rest of the competition.

Athletes performing self-paced tasks or sports often need to develop a between-performance routine, as well. What should golfers or shot-putters do with the time between shots or throws? How can place-kickers or pitchers best use the time between kicks or pitches? We recommend structuring this time with a consistent between-performance routine to maintain a flow mind-set that ensures athletes are relaxed, focused, and confident. Moreover, maintaining intense concentration throughout a three-hour baseball game or four-hour round of golf is virtually impossible. Performers need to learn to turn concentration on and off (e.g., a pitcher turns his concentration on when he toes the rubber, and stepping off is his cue to relax). Between-performance routines feature three main components:

1. *React.* Using relaxation and self-talk skills, develop a composed **reaction** to the previous performance—good or bad—in order to stay on an even keel.

2. *Reflect.* Quickly reflect on and learn from the previous performance, but do not dwell on poor performance. Use a cue to end reflection and move on to **readying** (e.g., putting a golf club back in the bag, or turning to face the net in tennis or volleyball).

3. *Refocus and ready.* The cue to end reflection triggers athletes to repeat their preperformance routine to help them refocus on the task at hand and get ready to perform automatically.

Interactive Sports

Interactive sports vary in difficulty, even during one event, because the nature of the task changes according to the caliber of the opponent and the type and effectiveness of offensive and defensive strategies that each athlete or team employs. Most team sports are interactive, as are such individual sports as tennis, wrestling, boxing, and martial arts. Because interactive sports are fast-paced and only somewhat predictable, mental performance plans for them focus on responding systematically to anticipatable critical situations or events (during practice or competition) and reacting to specific good or bad performance trends.

The first step is to have your athletes identify four to eight important situations that occur during practice or competition. They can start by using a plan development form (figure 13.7) to select two to four critical times during practice (e.g., scrimmage situations, one-on-one drills, or two-minute offense) and competition (e.g., beginning or end of a quarter, half, or period; or first action after a timeout). They should also select two to four good or bad performance events, both during practice (e.g., poor early performance, losing a one-on-one drill, or making critical mistakes) and competition (e.g., a run of points by the opposing team, being confronted by a press, or a turnover). Next, develop goals and action plans for each situation. In the first two minutes of a half, a team might emphasize defense to take advantage of high arousal levels. During one-on-one drills, a player might focus on using good technique and exploiting the opponent's weaknesses. Teach athletes to check and adjust their flow mind-set as needed. If they normally experience high stress in the first minute, they should focus on relaxing and having fun. They can use cue words to trigger automated responses. (See figure 13.8 on page 222 for a sample plan for basketball.)

Numerous situations in interactive sports require backup plans: bad calls, rowdy fans, turnovers and other mistakes, an angry coach, a run of points by the opponent. Have your athletes develop backup plans for two to four major problems that have been the hardest for them to handle. Athletes in interactive sports (e.g., volleyball, tennis, and American football) that have breaks in the action will also benefit from between-play routines. The basic "react" principles remain similar for interactive sports, but "reflect" is constrained by time limits, and "refocus" cues become more concrete, such as stepping into the football huddle or facing the volleyball or tennis net. "Readying" still triggers pre-serve routines in tennis and volleyball and presnap routines in football. (See Ready, Respond, Refocus on page 223 for a sample between-play routine in a team sport.)

Interactive Sport Performance Plan Development Form

Predetermined Critical Situations	SITUATION GOALS		Cue Words
	Physical	Mental	
Example: First 3 minutes of the game	Emphasize defense and rebounding to take advantage of high arousal level.	Focus on being relaxed but aggressive; try to intimidate opponent physically; keep things simple until in flow of the game.	"Be quick but don't hurry," "be aggressive but in control," "let the game come to you," "be unselfish and put the team first."
1.			
2.			
3.			
4.			

Reactions to Good and Bad Performance Trends	SITUATION GOALS		Cue Words
	Physical	Mental	
Example: Opponent reels off 10 straight points	Play under control to reduce turnovers; be more patient to get better shots; increase defensive intensity; put more pressure on opponent's guards.	Focus on increasing energization and motivation; restore confidence and PMA; focus on more physical defense and more patience on offense.	"Poise and composure under pressure," "make the extra pass to get a good shot," "pressure them into hurrying," "ball pressure and shoot down the passing lanes."
1.			
2.			
3.			
4.			

From D. Burton and T. Raedeke, 2008, *Sport Psychology for Coaches* (Champaign, Il: Human Kinetics).

FIGURE 13.7 Athletes can use the Interactive Sport Performance Plan Development Form to set specific goals and cue words for critical situations.

Sample Interactive Sport Performance Plan for Basketball

Predetermined Critical Situations	SITUATION GOALS		Cue Words
	Physical	Mental	
Critical Situation 1: first 3 minutes of the half or game	Emphasize defense and rebounding to take advantage of high arousal level.	Focus on being relaxed but aggressive; try to intimidate opponent physically; keep things simple until in flow of the game.	"Be quick but don't hurry," "be aggressive but in control," "let the game come to you," "be unselfish and put the team first."
Critical Situation 2: last 3 minutes of the half or game	Emphasize getting a spurt before half; turn up the aggressiveness on defense; look for every fast break opportunity; emphasize high percentage shots in half court; good time for pressure.	Approach this period confidently and aggressively; maintain a high PMA; focus on pushing the pace without becoming careless; raise arousal level and motivation to push limits	"Turn up the pressure," "look for every opportunity to run," "only want high percentage shots," "jump on them before half," "act confident and aggressive."
Critical Situation 3: after a time-out we call	Emphasize getting a stop or score on the next possession; turn up the intensity; adjust either offense or defense to create a positive mismatch; increase aggressiveness	Regain confidence; enhance PMA; focus on one possession at a time and how to exploit our strengths or minimize our weaknesses; raise arousal and motivation to create a burst.	"Critical time for a stop or score," "turn it up," "be positive and find the mismatch," "play to our strengths," "jump on them."

Reactions to Good and Bad Performance Trends	SITUATION GOALS		Cue Words
	Physical	Mental	
Performance Reaction 1: opponent reels off 10 straight points	Play under control to reduce turnovers; be more patient to get better shots on offense; increase defensive intensity and put more pressure on guards to keep them from getting into their offense.	Focus on increasing energization and motivation; restore confidence and PMA; focus on more physical defense and more patient offense.	"Poise and composure under pressure," "make the extra pass to get a good shot," "pressure them into hurrying," "ball pressure and shut down the passing lanes."
Performance Reaction 2: make lots of turnovers against the press	Understand where defense is vulnerable; play under control and understand multiple options on where to pass; once break pressure, look to score.	Focus on relaxation and positive self talk to regain confidence and combat negative thoughts; stay under control; be aggressive when pressure broken.	"Poise and composure under pressure," "be quick but don't hurry," "always an outlet pass," "once press broken, look to score."
Performance Reaction 3: officials' calls consistently going against us	Recognize that the aggressive player/team usually gets the calls; be more aggressive; concentrate on moving feet rather than reaching; penetrate and pass rather than try to score.	Focus on energizing and raising motivation; regain confidence & PMA; counter negative thoughts, emphasize that we can't control officials' decisions; play our game and don't worry about officials.	"Champions keep their composure in the face of adversity," "don't worry about things we can't control," "aggressive teams make their own breaks and calls," "just do your best."

From D. Burton and T. Raedeke, 2008, *Sport Psychology for Coaches* (Champaign, IL: Human Kinetics).

FIGURE 13.8   A basketball player's completed form might look like this.

Ready, Respond, Refocus: Nebraska Football's Between-Play Routine

In the early nineties, Nebraska football coach Tom Osborne and sport psychology consultant Ken Ravizza developed a between-play routine to help players take one play at a time by remaining relaxed, focused, and confident in order to maximize execution (Ravizza & Osborne 1991). Nebraska's mental training program was built on two basic concepts: taking personal responsibility and maintaining self-control. Because a missed assignment by just one player can lead to a blown play, the program was designed to develop consistency in mental and physical preparation.

Nebraska's between-performance routine centered on the three Rs—ready, respond, and refocus—to maximize concentration on one play at a time. In step one, "ready" is the verbal cue given by the signal caller (quarterback or linebacker) to focus attention totally on his directions and on the next play. Players must put the last play behind them and focus on what they have to do next. As the play is called, offensive players have two responsibilities: reviewing their assignment and repeating the snap count to themselves. As players break the huddle, they must recognize what their opponent is doing tactically by reading their cues and communicating adjustments to their teammates. As soon as players finish checks or audible calls, they shift to automatic pilot and focus on "just reacting."

Step 2 (respond) is the athletes' execution at the snap of the ball. They must respond automatically as they've learned through thousands of hours of practice. Trust is encouraged during portions of practice when players are given little feedback from coaches in order to teach them to react instinctively. The importance of performing on automatic pilot is reinforced in meetings, on the field, and during film sessions.

Step 3 (refocus) is where players review the completed play, then put it behind them and refocus their attention on the next play as soon as possible. The time between the end of the play and the next team huddle gives athletes time to reflect, identify anything learned, and decide on any adjustments to make for upcoming plays. This is also the time for the players to put the previous play behind them, particularly if a mistake was made, so they can focus on the next play. Players should acknowledge their feelings (e.g., celebrate a good play or allow momentary anger over a bad one), then move on.

Mental Recovery Plans

Coaches and athletes can't anticipate all problems, and mental recovery plans provide a general coping strategy to help athletes recover from unanticipated problems, particularly when their goals become unattainable or they lose their composure. A mental recovery plan is a single, all-purpose solution with a set procedure for getting back on track after disaster and salvaging as much benefit from the practice or competition as possible (see Mental Recovery in Basketball on page 224). Although recovery plans occasionally allow competitors to completely return to form, they usually just provide a means of damage control and help athletes take something positive away from a negative event. How complete a recovery an athlete makes depends on how quickly he or she identifies the need to use the mental recovery plan and how effectively it is then implemented. We recommend incorporating the following five steps:

1. Develop a physical trigger to start the recovery plan.

2. Relax and adjust arousal level.

3. Revise goals so they are realistic for the current situation.

4. Use affirmations and counterarguments to reduce stress, increase positive mental attitude, and boost confidence.

5. Imagine regaining a positive mind-set and attaining the revised goals.

A recovery plan can work only if athletes know when to implement it. Ken Ravizza uses a mental trigger in which athletes imagine a stoplight. A green light indicates that athletes have attained a flow

Case Study: Mental Recovery in Basketball

The opposing team has just exploded for 12 straight points, 8 of them by the player Rob is guarding. Rob looks panicked and reports that he can't stop his man. His confidence is gone, and he's focusing on what a rotten defender he is. Rob had used his size advantage to score 10 points earlier in the game, but now he's too flustered to take advantage of the mismatch. Rob and his teammates have lost their composure and been taken completely out of their game. You call a time-out and remind them to use their mental recovery plans. Rob has automated a good plan using these five steps:

1. Rob cues his mental recovery plan by slapping the floor with both hands.

2. He uses rapid relaxation (combining deep breaths with his cue phrase "chill out") to lower his arousal to a better level.

3. Rob then revises his goals so they are realistic given the current situation. His offensive goal is to take advantage of the size mismatch down on the block. On defense, he wants to beat his opponent to his favorite shooting spots and overplay him to force him left, while being more physical in fighting through screens off the ball.

4. Rob counters his negative thoughts by reminding himself, "I am a good player who just isn't play-ing well at the moment." He emphasizes that if he plays harder and smarter, as he did in the first half, he can hold his opponent in check and start scoring again. He reminds himself that no matter how the game comes out, he wants to play well and try to get back into it.

5. Rob uses quick imagery of how he wants to play and of regaining the flow mind-set that will allow him to reach his revised goals. He flashes quickly on images of himself posting up his opponent, holding him in check, and helping teammates who get beat. He imagines getting that smooth, fluid feeling on his jump shot and hitting three or four in a row.

Rob and his teammates do recover. After the time-out, they start playing better and outscore their opponents the rest of the way. They do not make up the 14-point deficit, but they play well during the last 7 minutes of the game and lose by only 8 points. Despite their disappointment about losing com-posure, Rob and his teammates are excited that their recovery plans worked and are ready to continue developing them.

mind-set, a yellow light indicates potential problems, and a red light indicates the need to use a recovery plan. You and your athletes can adopt that approach or create your own.

Developing Athletes' Mental Toughness Skills

Mental toughness means performing one's best under any circumstances, and developing mental toughness skills is critical to your athletes' com-petitive success. The key is to help your athletes create, automate, and implement a structured series of mental plans aimed at attaining, maintaining, and regaining a flow mind-set. As with any other mental training tools or skills, developing mental toughness through the use of mental plans involves the three phases: education, acquisition, and implementation.

Education Phase

This phase has two objectives: provide a general education about mental toughness and mental plans, and encourage personal education so that your athletes become aware of their own strengths and weaknesses in using mental plans. You can usually do this in one or two team meetings. First, educate them about mental plans and their benefits in practice and competitive performance. Describe the three major types (preparation, performance, and recovery), along with strategies for using each. Sell the importance of mental plans by citing times when your athletes could have benefited from using them, and give examples of athletes who have used them well. We recommend concluding this initial session by helping your athletes start the process of developing their first mental plan. We suggest that a between-performance routine is a good starting place for team sports because it benefits performance and is a collective routine that should boost team cohesion. For individual sports, we recommend starting with a race plan or preperformance routine.

Your athletes should develop a good understanding of what helps them achieve their own flow mind-set and how they already use routines to enhance performance. We recommend that athletes heighten their self-awareness by systematically logging key information about their flow mind-set and subsequent performance as described in chapter 14. Athletes with this kind of self-understanding will be better able to create effective, individualized mental plans.

Acquisition Phase

Mental plans can be time-intensive to develop and implement, and they can seem overwhelming for coaches who have only limited time for mental training. If you feel you do not have time to develop all three types of plans, start by developing one, perhaps a pre- or between-performance plan. If your athletes find that this plan works, it will be easier to add other plans in the future. Thus it is often best to implement mental plans using a phased approach grounded in four basic strategies:

1. Identify the mental plan that would be most valuable for athletes to develop first.

2. Develop that plan using the guidelines discussed in this chapter.

3. Assess how well the plan works and revise it until it works optimally.

4. Practice systematically until the plan is highly automated.

Implementing mental plans is a trial-and-error process. Have your athletes try out plans and evaluate their effectiveness, modifying them as necessary

until they have one they like. First, they should test their plans using imagery, attending to each plan's rhythm and flow, its length, and the degree to which they feel it will do what it is designed to do. If any aspect of a mental plan feels uncomfortable, revise it freely. Second, have athletes try their mental plans in practice and continue to record data in their mental training log. They should note whether their plan helps them prepare mentally and whether their performance meets the plan's goal, then modify the plan in any problem areas. The more comfortable athletes become with their plans, the better the plans will work, creating the physical feeling and positive mind-set that maximize performance.

Implementation Phase

In this phase, you help your athletes automate their mental skills, and they'll get best initial results from simulation. Unless mental skills are highly automated, most competitors suffer Launi Meili's fate at the Seoul Olympics: Their mental skills break down in important, pressure-packed competitions when they are needed most. Automating mental plans is the tedious part of learning, because it requires hundreds, even thousands, of repetitions of already-learned skills and strategies. Automation is laborious, but it is necessary to develop the mental blueprint of the skills to the point where athletes can execute them without thinking. In pressure-packed situations, performers experience so much stress that they cannot rely on thinking their way through their performance. Instead, they must react instinctively, relying on the execution of automatic responses with minimal conscious thought.

As with other mental training tools and skills, automating mental plans is most effective when practice simulates the conditions athletes will face in competition. When athletes practice using their mental training tools, skills, and plans in a distracting, pressure-packed environment, they are better able to fully automate those skills and transfer them to competition. We recommend using three types of simulation. First, have athletes practice using their mental plans during imagery (e.g., imagine using a race plan in an upcoming home meet). Second, use practice situations such as scrimmages to simulate competition as realistically as possible so athletes can use their mental plans in live action. Finally, treat early-season or less important competitions as opportunities to simulate major competitions where execution of mental plans is most critical.

SUMMARY

1. Mental toughness is the ability to play one's best in any situation, particularly in the face of problems, adversity, or failure. It is not a single mental skill but a constellation of mental training tools and skills promoting a flow mind-set. Mental plans seem to be the best strategy for incorporating and automating these skills in order to promote mental toughness.

2. Mental plans are systematic, individualized strategies designed to help athletes develop, maintain, and regain a flow mind-set so that they can remain mentally tough and play their best.

3. Mental plans have four major benefits: creating a flow mind-set, enhancing overall performance quality, increasing performance consistency, and dealing with adversity.

4. Athletes should develop three types of mental plans: mental preparation plans, mental performance plans, and mental recovery plans.

5. Mental preparation plans provide a blueprint for athletes' mental warm-up to help them create a flow mind-set. Athletes can develop standard and backup mental preparation plans.

6. Mental performance plans provide a road map for remaining in a flow mind-set throughout practice and competition in order to accomplish key goals. Standard and backup mental performance plans can be developed for races and routines, interactive sports, and self-paced tasks. Self-paced mental preparation plans also include preperformance and between-performance routines.

7. Mental recovery plans provide a generic solution for coping with unforeseen problems that cause athletes to lose their emotional composure. These are single, all-purpose plans that help athletes recover from severe problems, regain composure, and make the best of bad situations.

8. Developing athletes' mental toughness skills through mental plans helps them develop, automate, and implement a structured series of steps aimed at enhancing practice and competitive performance. As with other mental tools and skills, you can develop athletes' mental toughness in three phases: education, acquisition, and implementation.

9. During the education phase, coaches provide athletes with general knowledge about designing and implementing mental plans, and athletes develop an awareness of their strengths and weaknesses in developing a flow mind-set.

10. In the acquisition phase, you and your athletes decide which mental plan to create first, develop the plan, assess its effectiveness and revise as needed, and practice systematically until the plan is highly automated.

11. In the implementation phase, athletes automate their mental plans through overlearning and simulation.

KEY TERMS

automation

backup mental performance plans

between-performance routines

flow mind-set

interactive sports

mental performance plans

mental plans

mental preparation plans

mental recovery plans

mental toughness

preperformance routines

race plan

reaction

readying

self-paced tasks

standard mental performance plan

REVIEW QUESTIONS

1. What is mental toughness, and how does it help athletes?
2. What are mental plans, and what is their role in mental training?
3. What are the benefits of mental plans?
4. What are the three major types of mental plans, and what is each designed to do?
5. How do triggers, releases, and cue words help athletes initiate mental plans?
6. How are mental plans developed?

PRACTICAL ACTIVITIES

1. Identify which type of standard mental performance plan is most appropriate for your primary sport (i.e., races and routines, self-paced tasks, or interactive sports) and determine the order in which you would develop plans for mental preparation, performance, and recovery.
2. Develop a first draft of your highest-priority plan.

Mental Skills Training Programs

After reading this chapter, you should be able to

- understand the need to implement a mental skills training (MST) program with your team;
- understand how to develop and implement a basic MST program that fits your coaching philosophy and competitive constraints;
- describe the components of effective MST programs: using a systematic implementation process, identifying strengths and weaknesses, personalizing programs to meet individual needs, monitoring progress, and making adjustments as needed;
- explain the importance of the educational phase and how it combines a general MST education with a personal education to assess athletes' strengths and weaknesses;
- understand how the acquisition phase can help develop mental training tools, skills, and plans; and
- describe the implementation phase, in which athletes automate mental training techniques, build them into their games, and enhance execution in stressful situations.

If you've stuck with us this far, you've developed a basic understanding of applied sport psychology. Now is the time to put that knowledge to work by implementing a mental skills training (MST) program with your team. You may have dozens of reasons you don't feel ready to do it—at least not now. You're busy! It's too hard to sell to your team! You're confused about how to start! You're overloaded just dealing with the physical side of your sport! You're afraid of messing it up! Maybe you're still not sure it's worth it. But can you really afford to wait? We can understand that you may not feel completely comfortable yet with the material presented here; it's only natural to be a bit overwhelmed with so much new information. However, if you're convinced that mental training will benefit your athletes, then you have to make a commitment to start somewhere and take the first steps toward implementing an MST program. So how do you get started?

Getting Started

We believe that you must start with your coaching philosophy. Throughout this book, we've espoused a number of key concepts that are the foundation to our approach to coaching and mental training. These concepts include the following:

- Sport is a test of athletes' physical and mental skills, and learning to master both the physical and mental game is the best way to maximize competitors' chances of success.
- The mental skills needed for success in sport and life can be learned through systematic practice.
- Self-awareness is the first step toward learning to master the mental game.
- Coaches need to help athletes take personal responsibility for their actions.
- Athletes can't always control what happens to them, but they can control how they respond to difficult or untimely events.
- Mental skills training is a systematic process for developing important mental training tools, skills, and plans.

For MST to be effective, you must buy into the tenets of this coaching philosophy. If not, please reread chapter 1, on coaching philosophy, and chapter 3, which introduced mental skills training. If you're still not convinced, then this program is probably not for you. However, we believe that the logic supporting MST programs is compelling and that the potential benefits are too great not to at least give one a test drive. Mental skills, like their physical counterparts, don't develop overnight, so be patient and give your program a full season in order to realistically evaluate its effectiveness.

Components of Effective MST Programs

Before we get down to the nitty-gritty of designing and implementing MST programs, it's important to address four components that underlie effective self-change programs such as MST:

1. Implementation must use a systematic process.
2. A needs assessment should be used to identify strengths and weaknesses and guide development.
3. Strategies must be personalized to meet individual needs and situational demands.
4. Regular self-monitoring should be used to assess progress and identify areas to modify.

Use a Systematic Implementation Process

As discussed throughout the book, MST programs involve three phases: education, acquisition, and implementation. The educational phase gives athletes a general education about mental training tools, skills, and plans, including their key benefits and how to develop them (you can use the information presented in chapters 4 through 13). This phase also includes an extensive personal education, in which performers learn about their own mental patterns through a systematic needs assessment that identifies personal strengths and weaknesses. The acquisition phase then helps athletes acquire the mental training tools, skills, and plans needed to make MST programs work. And the implementation phase teaches athletes to automate these components, systematically build them into their game, and execute them under pressure. The type of mental skills training program you develop depends on several factors: the sport you coach; your understanding of MST concepts and your ability to teach them; your athletes' knowledge, talent, and experience; and the time and resource constraints you must work around.

Develop Self-Awareness: Initial Needs Assessment

Making MST programs work requires helping athletes understand their mental strengths and weaknesses and the situations that enable and undercut their mental toughness. Athletes can enhance their self-awareness and participate in their own **needs assessment** by using performance profiling and mental skill assessment. Both of these techniques provide athletes with valuable information, but if you feel you do not have the time or expertise to use both, select the one that best meets your needs. Helping your athletes identify their mental strengths and weaknesses allows you to determine which skills to include in your mental training program—usually either weaknesses that must be remediated or critical skills that need to be developed more fully.

Performance Profiling

Performance profiling is a relatively simple way to help athletes and teams identify their physical and mental strengths and weaknesses. For both individual and team profiling, use the Performance Profile Form (figure 14.1 on page 232) to list 10 to 20 mental and physical characteristics that you and your athletes believe are essential to success. Have players use whatever terminology they prefer, but the final team list should reflect as much of a group consensus as possible. (See table 14.1 for performance profile lists from three sports.) Each physical or mental skill can then be rated on two dimensions: athletes' current skill level as a percentage of their perceived ultimate potential, and the importance of the skill to overall success in their sport. Not all needed physical and mental attributes are equally important. For an offensive lineman, strength may be twice as important as speed, but for a cornerback, speed may be two or three times more important than strength. Communication may be very important in team sports but less so in individual sports, whereas self-motivation may be more valued by individual sport performers.

TABLE 14.1

Skills and Attributes Identified as Essential to Success

Tennis player	Volleyball player	Javelin thrower
1. Confidence	1. Aggressiveness	1. Focusing skills
2. Toughness	2. Willingness to do whatever it takes	2. Visualization skills
3. Enjoying your sport	3. Willingness to give 110%	3. High mental toughness
4. Believing in yourself	4. Competitiveness	4. Blocking out pain
5. Imagery skills	5. Being a good team player	5. Resisting boredom
6. Desire to succeed	6. Building up others	6. Independence
7. Being happy with yourself	7. Unselfishness	7. Speed
8. Knowing you're the best	8. Taking responsibility for mistakes	8. Flexibility
9. Learning from others	9. Not dwelling on uncontrollable factors	9. Strength
10. Upper-body strength	10. Physical fitness and strength	10. Power
11. Fast low movements	11. Fast, high jump	11. Good technique
12. Perfect timing on shots	12. Being flexible and adjustable	12. Strong legs, back, and shoulders
13. Aerobic fitness	13. Quick body and mind	13. Small biceps and triceps like a gymnast
14. Excellent agility	14. Playing smart and under control	
15. Overall power on shot	15. Athleticism	

Performance Profile Form

Physical and Mental Skill or Attribute	Percent of Current Skill Level Compared to Performance Potential	Importance of Skill or Attribute
1.	10 20 30 40 50 60 70 80 90 100	1 2 3 4 5 6 7 8 9 10
2.	10 20 30 40 50 60 70 80 90 100	1 2 3 4 5 6 7 8 9 10
3.	10 20 30 40 50 60 70 80 90 100	1 2 3 4 5 6 7 8 9 10
4.	10 20 30 40 50 60 70 80 90 100	1 2 3 4 5 6 7 8 9 10
5.	10 20 30 40 50 60 70 80 90 100	1 2 3 4 5 6 7 8 9 10
6.	10 20 30 40 50 60 70 80 90 100	1 2 3 4 5 6 7 8 9 10
7.	10 20 30 40 50 60 70 80 90 100	1 2 3 4 5 6 7 8 9 10
8.	10 20 30 40 50 60 70 80 90 100	1 2 3 4 5 6 7 8 9 10
9.	10 20 30 40 50 60 70 80 90 100	1 2 3 4 5 6 7 8 9 10
10.	10 20 30 40 50 60 70 80 90 100	1 2 3 4 5 6 7 8 9 10
11.	10 20 30 40 50 60 70 80 90 100	1 2 3 4 5 6 7 8 9 10
12.	10 20 30 40 50 60 70 80 90 100	1 2 3 4 5 6 7 8 9 10
13.	10 20 30 40 50 60 70 80 90 100	1 2 3 4 5 6 7 8 9 10
14.	10 20 30 40 50 60 70 80 90 100	1 2 3 4 5 6 7 8 9 10
15.	10 20 30 40 50 60 70 80 90 100	1 2 3 4 5 6 7 8 9 10
16.	10 20 30 40 50 60 70 80 90 100	1 2 3 4 5 6 7 8 9 10
17.	10 20 30 40 50 60 70 80 90 100	1 2 3 4 5 6 7 8 9 10
18.	10 20 30 40 50 60 70 80 90 100	1 2 3 4 5 6 7 8 9 10
19.	10 20 30 40 50 60 70 80 90 100	1 2 3 4 5 6 7 8 9 10
20.	10 20 30 40 50 60 70 80 90 100	1 2 3 4 5 6 7 8 9 10

From D. Burton and T. Raedeke, 2008, *Sport Psychology for Coaches* (Champaign, IL: Human Kinetics).

FIGURE 14.1 Use this form to help your athletes or team identify skills and attributes they believe are most important to their success.

Once each individual (or the team) has rated all skills, athletes should transfer this information to circular performance profile graphs (see example in figure 14.2). First, divide the graph into as many pie-shaped wedges as you have skills or attributes, with the thickness of each wedge reflecting the item's importance (thus the wedge for a skill rated 8 should be twice as thick as that for a skill rated 4). Next, for each skill or attribute, shade part of the graph to reflect current skill level, starting at the center, with each circle

PREFORMANCE PROFILE: ATHLETE VERSION

8 Most Important Characteristics

1.	5.
2.	6.
3.	7.
4.	8.

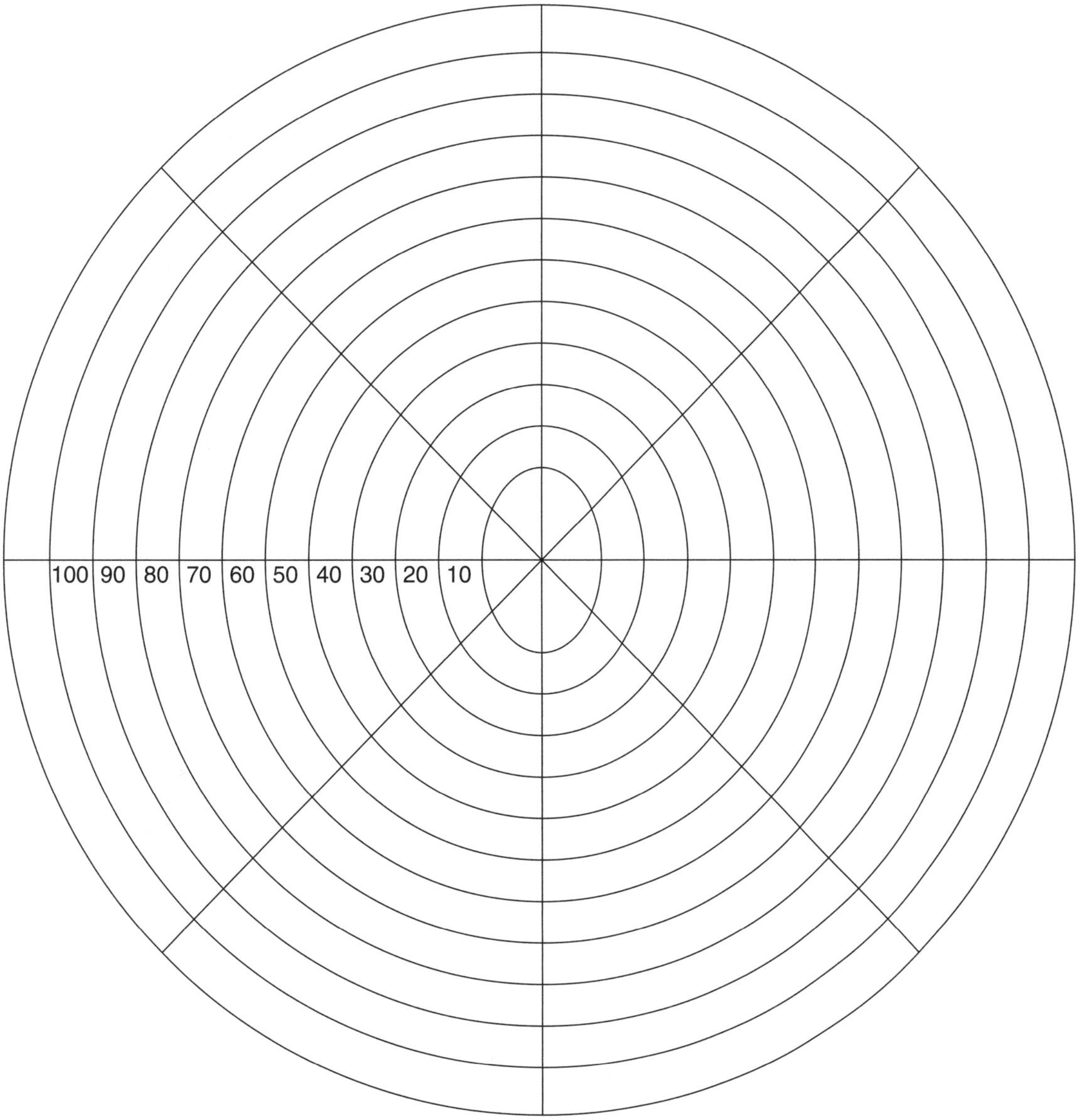

From D. Burton and T. Raedeke, 2008, *Sport Psychology for Coaches* (Champaign, IL: Human Kinetics).

FIGURE 14.2   Circular performance profile graph.

representing a 10% increment. Thus a completed performance profile graph (see example in figure 14.3) clearly shows the skills needed for success, the relative importance of each skill, and current skill level for each athlete. Team profiles can be generated independently or composited from the individual profiles.

Mental Skills Assessment

We also recommend that you have your athletes complete one of the inventories that assess mental skills in sport, such as the **Test of Performance Strategies** (TOPS; Thomas, Murphy, & Hardy 1999) or the **Athletic Coping Skills Inventory–28** (ACSI-28; Smith,

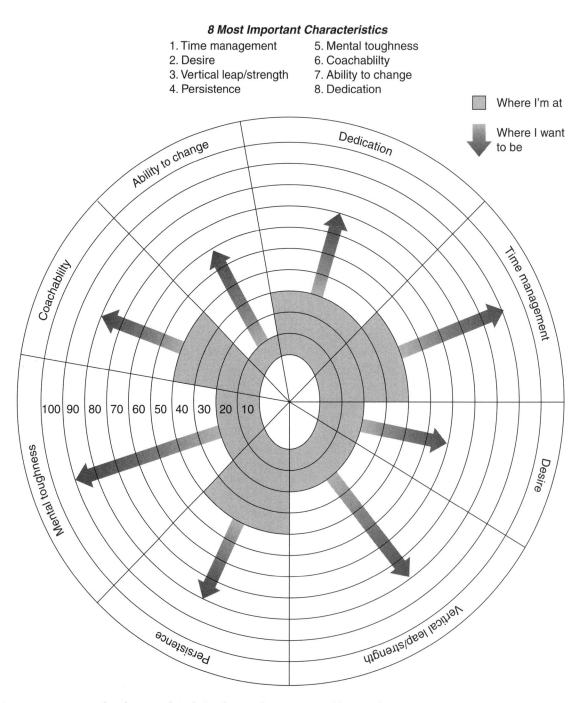

PREFORMANCE PROFILE: ATHLETE VERSION

8 Most Important Characteristics

1. Time management
2. Desire
3. Vertical leap/strength
4. Persistence
5. Mental toughness
6. Coachablilty
7. Ability to change
8. Dedication

Where I'm at

Where I want to be

FIGURE 14.3   Example of a completed circular performance profile graph.

Schutz, Smoll, & Ptacek 1995). These well-designed instruments are easy to administer and they provide a systematic way to assess athletes' proficiency in a number of mental training tools and skills. The 64-item TOPS, presented in Appendix C on page 263, consists of eight subscales for competition (goal setting, self-talk, imagery, emotional control, relaxation, automaticity, positive thinking, and activation) and eight for practice (with attention control replacing positive thinking). The 28-item ACSI-28 is comprised of seven 4-item subscales that measure proficiency in coping with adversity, peaking under pressure, goal setting and mental preparation, freedom from worry, confidence and achievement motivation, concentration, and coachability. Show athletes how to score themselves, then go over their scores with them and help them identify areas of personal strength and weakness.

Personalize MST Programs

MST programs are most effective when personalized to meet athletes' needs and competitive constraints. **Personalization** strategies that provide information to enhance the fit between program demands and athletes' needs include mental training logs and observation and interview strategies.

Mental Training Logs

Keeping a **mental training log** helps athletes develop self-awareness and personalize their MST program. Have athletes collect baseline data for several weeks using the Practice Flow Mind-Set Assessment Form (PFMAF), which tracks performers' pre- and mid-practice levels on five mental skills and overall performance (figure 14.4). Athletes should rate themselves within 20 minutes of the start of practice; then, within an hour after practice, they should rate their mental skill levels for the most important portion of practice, as well as their overall practice performance quality.

After several weeks, go over each athlete's data with him or her in order to identify patterns in the relationship between mental skills and performance. (Graphing often makes patterns more evident.) Most athletes will find consistent relationships between some, but not all, of these mental training skills and their performance, thus suggesting ways to personalize their MST programs. Identify the mental skills most closely related to an athlete's performance extremes (practices in which he or she performed particularly well or poorly). For example, you may notice that when an outside hitter practices well, her confidence and focus are higher than normal,

whereas on subpar days she feels less confident and less focused.

Although you want athletes to prepare and perform as similarly as possible for practice and competition, some differences must be planned for. The competitive log-keeping process is similar to that for practice. It is initiated by collecting baseline data to develop awareness of how mental factors affect athletes' competitive performance, especially factors that differ from practice or are unique to competition. Have your athletes complete the Competitive Flow Mind-Set Assessment Form (CFMAF) for several competitions to evaluate how well they were able to create and maintain an optimal mind-set. Have them monitor the same five mental skills before and during competition, along with overall performance (figure 14.5). The CFMAF should be completed as close to the start of competition as possible (within 90 minutes) and again within an hour after competition, in order to see how well performers maintained their flow mind-set during the most important part of competition. Concentrate on performance extremes where patterns are most obvious. Help your athletes identify patterns that most affect their competitive performance, then use this information to personalize their program.

Encourage athletes to create personalized log forms by placing copies of generic forms on a Web site and allowing athletes to modify them in any way that's helpful. Athletes need to record enough information to assess patterns that help or hurt mental training and accurately evaluate progress. Logs also need to make **self-monitoring** as quick and easy as possible, because most athletes won't diligently keep a log if the process is too time-consuming. Some athletes prefer to use rating scales, others would rather describe their experiences in a diary or journal format, and still others like a combination of the two. However, evaluation is of little value unless it is based on honest, accurate data, particularly where thoughts and feelings are concerned. Journal-size logs seem to be used more regularly and filled in more fully than bulkier logs, because they are easier for athletes to carry wherever they go.

You may also want to include some of the log sheets introduced in the chapters on mental training tools. For example, we put self-talk sheets in the back of most logs for athletes to complete on days when positive mental attitude (PMA) is low. Many athletes also like room to describe their mental training experiences in detail, so we provide both journal- and objective-style log sheets for each day. In compiling logs, we copy enough pages to get athletes through the season, color code different forms, add plastic

Practice Flow Mind-Set Assessment Form

	M	T	W	Th	F	Game	Perf. avg.	
Positive mental attitude (PMA)								**If PMA < 7** 1. self-talk script or tape 2. identify negative thoughts & use counterargument 3. imagery
Prepractice PMA (1-10 rating)								
Midpractice PMA (1-10 rating)								
Self-confidence (SC)								**If SC < 7** 1. goal setting 2. self-talk 3. imagery
Prepractice self-confidence (1-10 rating)								
Midpractice self-confidence (1-10 rating)								
Focus/Concentration (FOC)								**If FOC < 7** 1. review plans 2. focus on goals 3. adjust OAL
Prepractice concentration (1-10 rating)								
Midpractice concentration (1-10 rating)								
Commitment to push limits (COM)								**If COM < 7** 1. review goals 2. self-talk 3. imagery
Prepractice commitment (1-10 rating)								
Midpractice commitment (1-10 rating)								
Optimal arousal level (OAL)								**If OAL > or < 5** 1. < 5 use rapid energization 2. > 5 use rapid relaxation
Prepractice OAL (1-9 rating, 5=optimal)								
Midpractice OAL (1-9 rating; 5= optimal)								
Overall performance (PERF) (1-10 rating)								

From D. Burton and T. Raedeke, 2008, *Sport Psychology for Coaches* (Champaign, IL: Human Kinetics).

FIGURE 14.4 Athletes can use this form to track pre- and midpractice levels of mental skills.

Competitive Flow Mind-Set Assessment Form

	M	T	W	Th	F	Game	Perf. avg.	
Positive mental attitude (PMA)								**If PMA < 7** 1. self-talk script or tape 2. identify negative thoughts & use counterarguments 3. imagery
Precompetition PMA (1-10 rating)								
Midcompetition PMA (1-10 rating)								
Self-confidence (SC)								**If SC < 7** 1. goal setting 2. self-talk 3. imagery
Precompetition self-confidence (1-10 rating)								
Midcompetition self-confidence (1-10 rating)								
Focus/Concentration (FOC)								**If FOC < 7** 1. review plans 2. focus on goals 3. adjust OAL
Precompetition concentration (1-10 rating)								
Midcompetition concentration (1-10 rating)								
Commitment to push limits (COM)								**If COM < 7** 1. review goals 2. self-talk 3. imagery
Precompetition commitment (1-10 rating)								
Midcompetition commitment (1-10 rating)								
Optimal arousal level (OAL)								**If OPL > or < 5** 1. < 5 use rapid energization 2. > 5 use rapid relaxation
Precompetition OAL (1-9 rating, 5=optimal)								
Midcompetition OAL (1-9 rating; 5= optimal)								
Overall performance (PERF) (1-10 rating)								

From D. Burton and T. Raedeke, 2008, *Sport Psychology for Coaches* (Champaign, IL: Human Kinetics).

FIGURE 14.5 Have athletes use this form to track their competitive levels of mental skills.

cover pages (embossed with the school or university logo) to enhance durability, and put them in a spiral binder. Construct your logs in whatever way is most effective for you and your athletes.

Observation and Interviews

Objective data help you understand your athletes and team, but even more revealing is subjective assessment through normal coaching observations and individual meetings. As a coach, you gather much information by observing your athletes' performances, both live and on video. If you are an empathic and careful observer, you can learn a lot about your athletes' mental strengths and weaknesses in practice and competition. It's easy for athletes to act confident, motivated, and focused in the locker room, on the bus, even in practice. But can they *play* that way, particularly in stressful competitions? Athletes may present a composed, relaxed exterior for fans and opponents, but can they compete with confidence and poise? Careful observation helps you answer these questions, as do individual meetings with your players. Getting useful information from such meetings depends on your ability to develop a good relationship with your athletes, so that they feel comfortable honestly discussing their mental strengths and weaknesses. Part of that task is to convince players that the information you collect will be used only to help them improve.

If you want to maximize self-awareness and personalize MST programs, it is critical that you guide athletes' interpretation of any data collected. Emphasize that self-monitoring strategies will be used for self-evaluation, not comparison with teammates. Questionnaires and logs are not designed to evaluate athletes, decide who makes teams, or determine playing time. They provide a way to assess personal strengths and weaknesses; gauge progress in developing mental training tools, skills, and mental plans; and personalize implementation strategies. Use them to help athletes identify where they've improved, as well as areas for development.

Monitor Progress

You will want to objectively monitor the progress of your athletes or team to assess whether programs are meeting objectives or need to be modified or extended. Use logs to monitor the development of mental training tools, skills, and plans as well as to evaluate short-term progress. Use assessment to evaluate more long-term development. Failure to monitor progress makes it difficult to develop and automate mental training tools, skills, and plans.

To be effective, assessment must be used not for evaluating athletes but for helping them develop. Most assessment techniques use straightforward questions that make it easy for athletes to distort their responses, or simply lie, in order to look better to coaches. Athletes are much more likely to do this if they believe assessment is about comparing them with teammates and competitors for selection purposes or to determine playing time. Assessment is much more effective if athletes know it is designed to enhance personal development. Distorted responses will only reduce the quality of planning and ultimately limit the effectiveness of MST programs. Don't conduct assessment if you are not committed to using it for the right reasons. Sell your athletes on assessment as a personal development strategy and convince them you will use this information exclusively to enhance their long-term development.

As athletes learn more about mental tools and skills, their subjective rating criteria tend to change. Initially a volleyball player might naively rate herself as good (as a 4 on a 5-point scale) at goal setting because she has set goals for much of her career and seen some positive results. After several months of systematically setting goals, she may rate herself as fair (as a 3 on a 5-point scale). This player has not become a less effective goal setter, nor has she lost confidence. Instead, her goal-setting program has enhanced her awareness of her true goal-setting skill and how much room there is for improvement, which enables her to take the needed steps to get better. Help your athletes recognize that scales often change as players develop more self-awareness and skill, especially during the first 3 to 6 months of any MST program. And keep this phenomenon in your mind when evaluating initial progress on any mental training tool or skill.

Implementing a Basic MST Program

Basic MST programs are designed for coaches who want to get started with mental training while making sure to keep program demands manageable. They offer a good way to introduce mental training to your athletes, because they are not overly time-consuming, and you can learn to teach them as you go along, assuming you follow mental training principles and implementation guidelines. In basic MST programs, you set up team sessions and homework to help athletes learn to systematically develop several chosen tools and skills throughout the season. You also integrate mental training into practice sessions.

Programs are designed to help athletes' learn the mental side of sport and develop key mental training tools, skills, and plans. Implementation is partially left up to athletes.

To develop and implement a basic MST program, follow the basic format used throughout this text. First, educate athletes about MST programs. Once they understand what to do and are aware of their typical mental patterns, shift to the acquisition phase, in which they identify the mental training tools, skills, and plans that they want to systematically acquire. Once athletes have acquired the basic techniques, the implementation phase helps them automate tools, skills, and plans through extensive overlearning; builds those strategies into their game; and teaches them how to use them consistently and effectively, even in pressure-packed competitive situations.

Education Phase

The foundation of any basic MST program is effective education, and the education phase has two general objectives. First, you should provide athletes with a good general education about the mental training tools, skills, and plans that you have chosen to incorporate into your program, drawing from the content in chapters 4 through 13 of this text. Second, you should help athletes develop awareness of their personal strengths and weaknesses related to the mental aspects of sport, so that acquisition and implementation strategies are based on accurate information.

General Education: MST Orientation

Whether you develop a small-scale program that is highly focused (e.g., on goal setting) or a broader, more comprehensive MST program, you should start by gaining athletes' commitment to what you want to accomplish. Athletes must be educated about the mental training tools, skills, and plans in your program, and they must be shown how to develop, automate, and integrate each one into their game. Whether you use lecture and discussion, workbooks, videos, homework assignments, or some combination thereof, athletes must learn MST basics, commit to developing and using them, and understand how to build them into their games and perform them effectively. You also need to find interactive ways to engage athletes in the learning process and help them gain a practical understanding of how beneficial MST programs can be to their long-term development and their performance in critical situations.

You can best launch your MST program in an orientation meeting during the off-season or the very early preseason. The meeting should be long enough to introduce the basic concepts of mental skills training discussed in chapter 3. Some teams hold a one- or two-day retreat to start formal practice for the season and initiate an MST program, scheduling three or four MST sessions around sport practices. Your presentation should be relevant and practical. Use examples of local and elite athletes who use mental training to excel in your sport, as well as performers whose lack of mental skills held them back. The main objective for this session is to convince your athletes that psychological attributes affect competitive success and that mental skills can be learned and developed through systematic practice. The session should be an informal discussion in which you engage your athletes as much as possible and encourage them to ask questions and provide examples from their own experience. Conclude the session by handing out any questionnaires that you've decided to use as part of your initial mental skills assessment and give instructions about how to complete and score each instrument.

Ongoing Education About Mental Training

MST programs should include weekly or semiweekly team sessions in which a topic (e.g., goal setting) is presented and discussed in terms of benefits to individual or team performance. Although you have to keep demands realistic in light of athletes' busy schedules, you should usually assign homework between sessions to enhance understanding and promote basic skill development. Individual sessions are not usually included in basic MST programs, but if deemed necessary, they should involve minimal time (e.g., 10–20 minutes every other week).

Personal Education: Initial Needs Assessment

Start by giving your athletes the TOPS, ACSI-28, or another instrument you have chosen to use in evaluating their mental training needs. Show athletes how to develop a performance profile and have them come up with their list of 10 to 20 mental and physical characteristics as homework. During the second full session, have your athletes complete individual and team performance profiles. Also have them log data on the five key mental skills (self-confidence, positive mental attitude, focus and concentration, commitment to push their limits, and arousal level), as well as performance for several weeks in order to identify which skills most affect how they perform. Finally, observe your athletes carefully and schedule time to talk to them about mental training issues in order to get a complete picture of strengths and challenges.

Acquisition Phase

The acquisition phase of MST programs helps athletes develop mental training tools, skills, and plans. The premise behind basic MST programs is that increasing athletes' knowledge of sport psychology can change their perceptions of competition, of their performance, and of their skills, and motivate them to acquire needed mental training tools and skills.

Initial Acquisition of Mental Training Tools, Skills, and Plans

Development of the four basic mental training tools (chapters 4–7) greatly enhances acquisition of mental skills (chapters 8–12) and construction of mental plans (chapter 13). You must ensure that players put sufficient time into developing tools (e.g., goal setting, self-talk, imagery, relaxation, and energization), and you should also devote time to developing these tools yourself. Performers must also develop competence in key mental skills, typically concentrating on those most closely linked to their own performance. For example, if Mary, a soccer midfielder, finds her performance affected more by arousal and stress than by self-confidence, motivation, or attentional issues, then she can focus her acquisition strategies on developing arousal control and stress management skills. Finally, mental plans are a great way to combine mental training tools and skills into a systematic routine to enhance performance directly. However, because mental plans are time-consuming to develop and difficult to master, we recommend limiting your initial efforts to one plan that will provide the greatest performance benefits for your team.

It is particularly important in basic MST programs to make the skill acquisition and development process as systematic as possible. In fact, you don't need to develop all of the tools and skills in one season. We recommend a staggered approach, in which athletes work for two weeks on each attribute before a new tool, skill, or plan is introduced. Thus it takes 14 weeks to introduce four mental training tools, two mental skills, and one mental plan. For shorter seasons, simply target fewer elements. Although you can shorten the introduction period or introduce several attributes at once, development is more effective when athletes have an opportunity to concentrate on the tool or targeted skill, do enough focused practice to acquire and begin to automate it, and learn through practical experience how it can benefit their performance—and only then move on to the next technique.

Goal setting is a great starting point because it helps your athletes identify what they want to accomplish and prompts them to develop a systematic action plan for meeting their long-term objectives. We recommend that you sequence tools in the program according to athletes' perception of their importance. Thus, perhaps introduce self-talk second, imagery third, and relaxation and energization fourth, if you believe this reflects their importance to your team.

Once athletes have developed all four mental training tools, focus on targeted mental skills. Most athletes have already developed a few mental skills to the point where additional work is not a high priority. But most also struggle with one or two mental skills that consistently hinder their practice or competitive performance. Ideally, log data will pinpoint one or two mental skills that need to be targeted for individual or team development. If not, confidence and concentration (focus), are always good choices.

Although time is limited in basic MST programs, we also like to help athletes develop one basic mental plan so they can better appreciate how these integrated strategies can enhance performance, particularly pre- or between-performance routines. Both types are relatively quick and easy to develop and automate, yet they make a solid, positive difference in performance. Make sure that the initial plan you choose is easy to teach and learn.

Team Acquisition Sessions

Most basic MST programs are focused on team sessions designed to develop mental training tools, skills, and plans. Team sessions are typically held once or twice a week, with content focused more on education and acquisition than on practicing. We recommend using most of your first team acquisition session to develop individual and team goals for that season, as well as action plans for systematically accomplishing those goals. Based on your needs assessment, develop a schedule to discuss each of the four mental training tools, or follow the generally recommended format. Devote part or all of the initial team session for each tool to the education phase, teaching athletes about the tool and how it works, and giving them a chance to assess their skills in that area. Most of the remaining time should be focused on acquiring and automating these tools and using them effectively to enhance performance.

You need to come up with three or four basic exercises or drills that can be used to acquire each mental training tool. You can find ideas for exercises in the chapters (4–7) that discuss acquiring and practicing individual tools. Remember that you need to develop a solid progression for the acquisition of each mental training tool, so exercises or drills should be sequenced to start simple and gradually become more complex. Repeat this process for the selected mental skills and the basic mental plan. Once mental training tools, skills, and plans have been introduced, any remaining sessions you have time for can be devoted to automating these attributes. Make team sessions fun and hands-on, and try to involve each athlete in a meaningful way.

Individual Acquisition Sessions

Generally, basic MST programs minimize individual sessions, primarily due to time constraints. However, if possible, try to have occasional individual meetings with your athletes to discuss their needs, how to personalize their MST program, and how to deal with any problems. Use this time to get to know your athletes better, identify their mental strengths and weaknesses, set goals, practice skills to enhance acquisition, and troubleshoot any problems that may be impairing MST effectiveness.

Implementation Phase

This phase is crucial to the success of any basic MST program because mental training tools, skills, and plans must be automated, built into athletes' games, and performed successfully under stressful competitive situations.

Automating Mental Training Tools, Skills, and Plans

The key here is extensive overlearning. Many athletes believe they need only to practice enough to acquire the tool, skill, or plan. But being able to perform a skill does not ensure that an athlete can execute it automatically, especially in critical competitive situations. Under stress, performers lose their ability to think their way through things and must react instinctively based on highly automated responses. If your athletes haven't automated their key mental training tools, skills, and plans, their execution will break down under pressure. In contrast, performers with highly automated mental and physical skills will execute successfully in decisive competitive situations. Thus you need to help your athletes automate their mental and physical skills through practice strategies that emphasize overlearning.

Basic MST programs assign the athlete much responsibility for practicing mental training tools, skills, and plans, but well-designed programs give them multiple strategies to work with: team MST practice, individual MST practice, and simulation training. Try to make team automation drills consistent with physical practice, so that athletes practice key mental and physical skills at the same time and in a way that simulates competitive demands. Don't be afraid to take these sessions to the field, court, or track to make

them more relevant and realistic. For example, a basketball rebounding drill might emphasize physically blocking out the opponent and aggressively going after the ball at its highest point. At the same time, you might want to teach players to relax their hands on contact, making them soft to secure the rebounds they touch. Thus, this blockout drill helps automate advanced relaxation skills.

Help athletes develop an individual MST practice schedule that focuses at least half of their time on automating mental training tools, skills, and plans; the rest of the time should be devoted to building skills into their games and performing them effectively under stressful circumstances. Identify games and drills that allow athletes to automate skills while fitting them into team offensive and defensive objectives. For example, athletes should automate self-talk skills until counterarguments become second nature, so that when they make a key mistake that previously would have lowered their confidence, they counter effectively, almost without thinking.

Building Basic MST Programs Into Practices and Competitions

Having well-developed mental training tools, skills, and plans is of little value if athletes can't build them into their game. How will golfers use relaxation skills to lower their handicap? When and how will soccer players use imagery to play better? How can setting goals systematically help a shot-putter reach long-term objectives? What mental plans will help a young hockey player maximize long-term development? A critical part of facilitating a basic MST program for your players is to show them how to build mental training tools, skills, and plans into their game so they maximize long-term development, perform optimally in stressful competitions, and enjoy their competitive experience. Simulation training puts the finishing touches on the practice and performance phase by helping your athletes learn how to automate responses for particular situations. For example, if you simulate coming back from being a goal down in the last two minutes, it helps your athletes automate mental training tools and skills necessary to relax, stay positive and focused, and make effective adjustments that will give you a chance to win.

Encourage athletes to set daily goals for practice and competitions and evaluate goal attainment. Plan practices to encourage flow and allow time for flow practice. Regularly simulate competitive pressure during practice and help athletes learn how to use their mental training tools and skills to cope with elevated demands. Basic MST programs help performers manage stress, maintain mental toughness, and execute under pressure. Your role is twofold: You must help athletes understand the demands of the situation and develop the mental training tools, skills, and plans to deal with stress. And you must simulate stressful situations in practice so athletes have the opportunity to automate their stress management and mental toughness skills. Be creative in designing stress simulations, and be patient in helping athletes learn to use mental techniques to handle these situations.

Typically, you should simulate competition in three ways. First, have athletes practice mental training tools and skills on their own while imagining competitive pressures. Next, have them tackle simulated competitive situations in practice that are as realistic as possible. Finally, allow athletes to try their mental abilities in easier or less important competitions in order to simulate conditions that will be encountered in bigger contests later in the season. Each of these simulation strategies helps athletes learn how to make mental training tools, skills, and plans an integral part of their game and learn to perform their best when their best is needed.

Evaluating Progress

We recommend that at the end of your season you audit the MST program to monitor your athletes' or team's progress. You can use mental training logs, follow-up assessment, observation, and interviews. Have performers use the data from their logs to graph their performance along with key mental skills in order to evaluate whether they progressed during the season. We also recommend that you conduct follow-up assessment using the same psychological instruments used during the initial needs assessment. For example, have each athlete complete his or her performance profile again, identifying areas of improvement and lack of progress. You probably also want to have your athletes complete the TOPS, ACSI-28, or another measure of targeted mental skills again in order to assess progress. Finally, use your observations of each athlete in practice and competition, along with an exit interview, to learn more about how they are reacting to the MST program. Equipped with this program audit information, you can plan how to adjust MST programs to help your athletes further develop and automate their physical and mental skills.

SUMMARY

1. If you're convinced that mental training can help your athletes, then it's time to make a commitment to develop and implement some type of MST program for your team.

2. MST programs must be compatible with your coaching philosophy and competitive constraints.

3. Well-designed MST programs use a systematic implementation process to develop awareness of personal strengths and weaknesses, personalize strategies to meet individual needs, monitor progress, and make needed adjustments.

4. A basic MST program allows you to implement mental training while keeping program demands manageable. It follows the three-phase development model: education, acquisition, and implementation.

5. Self-awareness is enhanced through performance profiling and mental skills assessment.

6. MST programs can be personalized based on information from logs, observations, and interviews.

7. Monitoring progress through log keeping helps you document development and make program modifications.

8. An MST program's education phase helps athletes learn generally about mental training tools, skills, and plans, and develop awareness of personal strengths and weaknesses.

9. The acquisition phase allows athletes to acquire basic mental training tools, skills, and plans.

10. In the implementation phase, athletes automate mental training tools, skills, and plans; build them into their games; and learn to execute them in stressful competitive situations.

11. It is essential to evaluate ongoing progress and conduct a yearly MST audit. Use performance profiling, mental skills assessment, MST logs, observation, and interviews to assess progress and inform program refinements.

KEY TERMS

Athletic Coping Skills
Inventory–28 (ACSI–28)
basic MST programs
mental training logs

needs assessment
performance profiling
personalization

self-monitoring
Test of Performance Strategies
(TOPS)

REVIEW QUESTIONS

1. Why is it important to develop and implement an MST program?
2. What are the components of effective MST programs?
3. What role does the education phase play in implementing MST programs?
4. How does the acquisition phase help athletes acquire mental training tools, skills, and plans?
5. What role does the implementation phase play in ensuring the success of MST programs?

PRACTICAL ACTIVITIES

1. Identify at least five ways that a mental skills training program could benefit your individual athletes or your team as a whole.
2. Based on the implementation strategies presented in this chapter, outline a 12-week MST program that addresses your athletes' biggest mental training need. Your program should include a needs assessment, a systematic program involving at least two mental skills, assessment procedures, and a mechanism for making necessary program adjustments.

APPENDIX A

Answers to Review Questions

Chapter 1: Coaching Philosophy

1. A coaching philosophy is a set of beliefs guiding how you coach and what kind of relationships you develop with your athletes. Your philosophy reflects the values you hold in life.

2. A sound coaching philosophy helps identify what you believe in and how you want to conduct yourself as a coach. These values guide how you interpret situations and provide direction for how you think, act, and relate to others. A coaching philosophy becomes a blueprint for how you coach in practice and competition and provides a set of principles that helps you handle difficult situations. By identifying your values ahead of time, you are more likely to handle difficult situations in a way that is consistent with those values.

3. A coaching philosophy is always a work in progress, and you must constantly evaluate information and experiences to cultivate a clear awareness of what you value so that you can prioritize your competitive objectives based on those values. Developing a sound coaching philosophy first requires developing awareness of who you are and what you believe in. You will find feedback from others helpful in this process. Next, prioritize your competitive objectives for winning versus development and construct clear strategies about how to achieve them.

4. You can enhance athletes' development by using competition as a powerful motivator, a valuable strategy for improving athletes' skills, a way to develop positive character traits, and a means of developing cooperation as well as competition skills. Competition motivates most effectively when challenge is moderate (approximately equal to athletes' capabilities). Competition maximizes quality control when striving for excellence is seen as the ultimate goal and when you put time and effort into helping athletes perfect their skills. If competition is to develop positive character traits, coaching objectives have to emphasize character development. Finally, cooperation is integral to competition, and athletes must be taught cooperative as well as competitive skills.

5. This is a trick question. Competition is neither good nor bad. It is simply a neutral process. Whether the consequences of competition turn out to be positive or negative depends on how competition is organized and conducted. Because adults typically determine how competition is implemented, it should be a high priority to teach coaches, as well as administrators and parents, how to develop and run competitive programs that actively maximize benefits and minimize negative consequences.

Chapter 2: Communication

1. Coaches should reinforce successful approximations, effort and improvement, use of social and emotional skills, and good behavior.

2. A coach should respond to a good performance with descriptive feedback about what the athlete did well.

3. A coach should respond to a performance mistake with encouragement and instructional feedback, which should be specific and should highlight what an athlete needs to do to improve, rather than merely pointing out what the athlete did wrong.

4. Half of the communication process involves listening and receiving messages from others. Listening skills are important in understanding and establishing good relationships with your athletes. Coaches should develop a mind-set to listen, encourage athletes to share their views, summarize the core message and feelings athletes are communicating, ask athletes to elaborate on or clarify what they are saying, check to make sure they are understanding correctly, and convey through nonverbal behaviors that they are listening.

5. The sandwich approach to providing feedback involves placing the instructional feedback (the meat of the sandwich) between positive comments. Start by letting athletes know what they did well, provide instructional feedback, then end on a note of encouragement.

6. The five conflict styles that Johnson (2003) describes are turtle (withdrawing), shark (attacking), teddy bear (smoothing things over), fox (compromising), and owl (collaborating).

7. The steps for effective conflict resolution are to think before you act, understand the views of the other person, describe your views and feelings, and seek action.

Chapter 3: Introduction to Mental Skills Training

1. Athletes can't control whether they get into flow, but they can set the stage to make it more likely to happen through MST.

2. MST can enhance athletes' sport enjoyment and satisfaction. It can also be used as a tool to help develop life skills and facilitate athletes' development.

3. At the foundation of mental toughness are well-developed mental skills, which are much like physical skills in that they can be learned and refined. It is true that some athletes are more mentally tough than others due to their personality. Others have learned to be mentally tough through experience. However, all can improve their mental toughness through mental skills training. Mental toughness is a skill that can be developed through systematic practice.

4. Mental skills are the attributes or qualities we want athletes to develop in order to be mentally tough. Mental training tools are the techniques coaches use to develop those qualities.

5. No. Mental skills take time and practice to learn. In fact, introducing mental skills right before an important competition may hurt athletes' performance by disrupting routines or causing them to think too much. Athletes may even believe that abruptly introducing mental skills is a sign that their coaches have doubts about their readiness to compete.

6. If athletes are struggling with issues that affect everyday life functioning, they should be referred to professional counselors or psychologists. Coaches can help athletes learn mental training tools and skills that can improve their sport performance.

Chapter 4: Goal Setting

1. Goals are aims that give athletes purpose and direction and provide a standard for measuring progress.

2. Goals enhance focus and concentration and boost self-confidence. Keeping goals realistic is an important strategy for managing stress, creating a positive mental attitude, and remaining optimistic in the face of failure and adversity. Goals are also instrumental in fostering a positive and cohesive team climate. Most important, goals are a great tool for enhancing playing skills, techniques, and strategies. For experienced and skilled goal setters, the process can ultimately become more important than the product. Goals are the destination, but the joy is the journey.

3. Process and performance goals are more flexible and controllable than outcome goals. This flexibility allows goals to be readily adjusted to establish optimal goal difficulty, thus enhancing motivation. Controllability allows athletes to exercise greater influence over their own success, so that when they succeed, they can take credit for it and strengthen their self-confidence.

4. In addition to setting process, performance, and outcome goals, good goal setters make their standards specific and measurable, positively focused, and moderately difficult. Athletes also need to use a combination of individual and team goals, short- and long-term goals, and practice and competitive goals to maximize goal effectiveness.

5. Goal implementation is most effective when it follows a five-step process. In step 1, you set goals systematically by creating a vision, developing a mission statement, conducting a needs assessment, and prioritizing and coordinating goals. Step 2 involves developing goal commitment by involving athletes and selling them on the value of goals. In step 3, you construct a systematic action plan for achieving goals and overcoming potential obstacles. Step 4 focuses on obtaining feedback to allow for accurate evaluation of goals. And in step 5, you reinforce goal attainment to help develop intrinsic motivation that will fuel future goal-setting efforts.

6. In order to set up effective goal-setting programs, coaches should emphasize the education, acquisition, and implementation phases recommended for developing any mental training tool or skill. The educational phase helps athletes understand the basics of goal setting and builds their awareness of personal goal-setting skills and patterns. The acquisition phase helps athletes develop basic skills such as choosing goals and using the goal implementation process to pursue them. Finally, the implementation phase focuses on automating goal-setting skills, making them part of athletes' game, and using goals to perform their best.

Chapter 5: Imagery

1. Visualization involves the visual sense—seeing yourself perform in your mind's eye. Imagery involves more than vision; it can, in fact, involve all the senses.

2. Internal imagery is viewing your performance through your own eyes. External imagery is like seeing yourself on-screen. Thus internal imagery uses a first-person perspective, and external imagery uses a third-person perspective. Neither is better than the other. It just depends on the athlete and how vividly he or she can create internal and external images. It also depends on what the athlete is trying to accomplish; internal perspective is better for creating kinesthetic feel, and external is better for analyzing form and seeing the big picture.

3. Imagery is most effective when it supplements physical practice, but it can be used when physical practice is impossible due to bad weather, illness or injury, or excessive fatigue that prevents high-quality practice.

4. Compared with novices, experienced athletes can create more vivid, lifelike, and controlled images due to their greater familiarity with the sport. Also, experienced athletes tend to use imagery for different reasons than novice athletes. Although novice athletes use imagery to help learn and improve physical skills, experienced athletes also use imagery to develop their mental skills.

5. Stress often occurs when something unexpected happens and the competition does not go as planned. Under these circumstances, athletes may feel pressure and lose composure. Through imagery, they can anticipate stressors and imagine themselves coping effectively, thus establishing a plan for dealing with adversity and remaining confident.

Chapter 6: Relaxation and Energization

1. Relaxation is the ability to decrease unwanted muscular tension, reduce excessive activation of the sympathetic nervous system (SNS), and calm the mind by keeping it productively occupied. Total relaxation is when athletes take as long as needed to relax as deeply and completely as possible, whereas rapid relaxation is when performers quickly relax as much as needed to perform optimally on the spot.

2. Total relaxation benefits athletes by alleviating chronic stress to help them enjoy life more fully, promoting recovery from workouts and injuries, enhancing sleep quality, and developing rapid relaxation skills. Rapid relaxation enhances performance by reducing athletes' tension, promoting better arousal control, breaking the stress spiral, promoting an unconscious trusting attitude toward performance, conserving energy, and increasing enjoyment.

3. One's choice of a total relaxation strategy is typically based on subjective criteria: comfort level, personal effectiveness, ease of use, and personal enjoyment. Total relaxation uses a selected strategy and as much time as needed to get deeply relaxed. A conditioning process is then initiated to pair this deeply relaxed state with a relaxation cue word. In daily life, rapid relaxation involves repeating the cue word twice when exhaling a deep diaphragmic breath in order to relax as much as needed to perform optimally.

4. Energization, the opposite of relaxation, involves activating the body to prepare for optimal performance. It requires that athletes learn how to speed up heart rate and respiration, stimulate greater blood flow to muscles, and enhance brain activity. Total energization involves taking as long as needed to get as highly energized as possible, whereas rapid energization helps performers quickly energize as much as needed to perform optimally.

5. The benefits of energization include controlling arousal, enhancing concentration, and boosting confidence.

6. One's choice of a total energization strategy is normally based on such subjective criteria as comfort level, personal effectiveness, ease of use, and personal enjoyment. Total energization uses a selected strategy and as much time as needed to get highly energized. A conditioning process is then initiated to pair this highly energized state with an energization cue word. In daily life, rapid energization involves repeating the cue word twice when exhaling after each third "psych-up" breath in order to energize as much as needed to perform optimally.

7. In order to set up effective relaxation and energization programs, coaches follow the same format (education, acquisition, and implementation) recommended for developing all mental training tools and skills. The education phase helps athletes gain a basic understanding of relaxation and energization, while enhancing their awareness of their own relaxation and energization skills and patterns. The acquisition phase helps athletes develop basic relaxation and energization skills and teaches them how to use

those skills to perform their best. And the implementation phase focuses on automating relaxation and energization skills, making them part of the athlete's game, and using them to enhance performance.

Chapter 7: Self-Talk

1. Self-talk is the steady stream of thoughts and internal dialogue that goes on in the mind almost constantly. It consists of the ongoing thoughts that determine moods and emotions and affect performance.

2. In the ABCs of self-talk, A represents an activating event (e.g., needing to make a critical adjustment in strategy), B represents the athlete's beliefs about the situation, and C represents consequences (emotional and behavioral). Self-talk theory suggests that stress is based more on our perceptions of or beliefs about a situation (B) than on the situation itself (A). Thus, to change negative emotions and behaviors, coaches and athletes need to change negative or irrational beliefs to more positive and productive thought patterns.

3. Be an optimist, not a pessimist; make the choice to view each situation in a positive way. Remain realistic and objective and keep self-talk grounded in reality rather than wishful thinking. Focus on the present and play your best, rather than dwelling on the past or future, which cannot be changed or controlled. Appraise problems as challenges rather than as threats, in order to maintain an optimistic perspective about competition. View successes as replicable and failures as surmountable, in order to create confidence and positive expectations. Concentrate on process, not product, because personal excellence is the foundation of competitive success. Focus on what you can control, because stress often results from trying to change things over which you have minimal control. Separate your performance from your self-worth; self-worth is innate, not earned.

4. The critic is the inner voice that attacks and judges you. It is the negative side that constantly reminds you us of failures and shortcomings. The critic is impossible to satisfy and always ready to criticize. It is always trying to tear down your self-esteem. It thrives on distorted thoughts, which are self-talk problems that occur due to faulty thinking, incorrect inferences, and failure to separate fantasy from reality. *Catastrophizing* involves expecting the worst and exaggerating negative consequences. *Overgeneralization* involves forming faulty conclusions based on insufficient information. *Blaming* involves holding others responsible for negative events. *Mustification* involves believing that life should be lived according to rigid rules, everyone should follow them without exception, and everything in life should be the way you want it. *Polarized thinking* involves viewing things in all-or-nothing terms, either all good or all bad.

5. Irrational beliefs are more specific types of negative thoughts that commonly create negative emotions and impair performance. The following five irrational beliefs, all common in sport, are typically based on partial fact, unsound evidence, and questionable logic. *Perfectionism* is the belief that you should be thoroughly competent in everything you do and never be inconsistent or make mistakes. Instead, athletes should view mistakes as stepping stones to future success. *Fear of failure* involves feeling that it is terrible when your game is not where it should be, but this fear itself can prompt failure. In reality, everyone plays poorly sometimes, but it doesn't ruin your life. What's the worst that can happen? Even though it may not be pleasant, you've probably survived something similar before and can do so again if you have to. *Social approval* problems involve excessive worry about impressing others with your performance. The approval of others is an uncontrollable factor, and it makes sense to focus instead on controllable goals, such as pleasing yourself and having fun. *Equity* problems involve the belief that life should always be fair and you should always be rewarded for hard work. Regrettably,

life is often unfair, particularly in the short run. Forget about things you can't control; focus instead on performing your best, because persistence is eventually rewarded. *Social comparison* places too much importance on largely uncontrollable outcomes, such as winning and outperforming others, rather than concentrating on controllable factors, such as playing your best. Winning is ability-limited, so you can play your best but still not win against talented opponents. However, opponents have no direct control over your performance. Get the most out of the ability you have and play your game.

6. In order to program self-talk, you must first heighten awareness of current self-talk patterns by using imagery of good and bad performances, negative thought counts, and postpractice and competition logbooks. Next, develop self-talk scripts that can be read or played frequently to automate positive, productive thoughts. Scripts should serve several selected purposes, with two to four thoughts for each purpose. Scripts can be put on a CD to make them easier to use, but effectiveness comes from repetition (four or five times a day) to automate positive thoughts.

7. The three-Ds process is useful for reframing negative thoughts. First, detect negative thoughts that are causing problems. Second, disrupt them by using thought stopping or thought changing to halt them as quickly as possible. Finally, use counterarguments to dispute negative thoughts, thus reducing or eliminating their negative influence.

Chapter 8: Motivation

1. The four needs underlying intrinsic motivation are as follows:
   - The need for fun and stimulation. Coaches can include variety in practice and create games and competitions that target certain skills.
   - The need for acceptance and belonging. Coaches can include team-building activities in practice and make sure each athlete realizes he or she plays an important role on the team.
   - The need for control and autonomy. Coaches can help athletes develop ownership by involving them in decision making and giving them responsibilities.
   - The need to feel successful and competent. Coaches can design practice activities that challenge athletes at a level on which they can succeed. Creating a mastery-oriented team climate is also an effective way to meet this need.

2. If extrinsic motivators are contingent on performance quality and make the person feel competent, they raise intrinsic motivation. If they make the person feel less competent or are structured in a way that lowers autonomy, they lower intrinsic motivation.

3. Playing for a democratic coach gives athletes some ownership and thus can increase autonomy and raise intrinsic motivation. Playing for a micromanager or an autocrat who makes all the decisions lowers autonomy and intrinsic motivation.

4. Success-seeking athletes will have high motivation if they feel they can do well compared with others.

5. Mastery-oriented athletes believe the keys to success are hard work and skill development. Success seekers see the keys as talent and being naturally gifted.

6. They both feel successful. Sydney feels successful because she showed improvement by running a personal best. Andi feels successful, even though her personal performance was not great, because she compared well with other athletes,

Chapter 9: Energy Management

1. Arousal is the energy that fuels athletes' performance. It is the general physiological and psychological activation (on a continuum from deep sleep to intense excitement) that prepares the body for action. Arousal results from activation of the sympathetic component of the autonomic nervous system, which makes wholesale changes in the

body's physical and mental readiness to prepare it to fight or run when confronted with real or imagined danger.

2. The inverted-U relationship predicts that performance will peak when arousal is moderate. When arousal is too low, athletes lack sufficient physical and mental energy to perform their best. When arousal is too high, players may suffer from a variety of problems related to tension, attention, motor control, and interpretation that prevent them from performing optimally.

3. Underarousal hurts performance because the physiological changes associated with activation of the body either don't occur or fail to reach the level necessary to promote top performance. Overarousal hurts performance in three major ways: First, it can cause excessive muscular tension and coordination problems, because antagonistic muscles become too tense, reducing range of motion and disrupting the rhythm, touch, timing, and feel needed to perform skillfully. Second, attentional problems arise. As arousal increases, attention narrows, helping athletes focus on crucial aspects of competition. But overarousal narrows attention too far, blocking awareness of important cues needed for top performance. It also robs athletes of their ability to shift attention, causing them to get stuck in one attentional style rather than adjusting to situational demands. Third, excessive arousal causes performers to lose their ability to switch smoothly between controlled and automatic processing. Flow requires athletes to use primarily automatic processing, but high arousal often prompts them to overcontrol performance rather than trust their bodies to perform as they have been trained to do through long hours of practice.

4. Personality factors affect athletes' arousal–performance relationships and optimal energy zones. Each athlete's inverted-U curve will differ from all others based on personality, attitudes, values, learning experiences, and motivation. The arousal–performance relationship is also affected by three task dimensions: fine versus gross motor control, short- versus long-duration, and simple versus complex. Fine motor tasks requiring accuracy have narrower and lower optimal energy zones than do gross motor tasks. Short-duration tasks require more precise and more highly focused arousal levels than do long-duration tasks, where athletes have plenty of time to adjust arousal and still perform well. Complex tasks (e.g., shooting a basketball) require narrower and lower optimal energy zones than do simple tasks (e.g., playing physical defense).

5. Arousal is not just physical—it also includes athletes' interpretations of physical symptoms. The physical component of arousal is neutral; it simply reflects the activation of the body. It is how this activation is interpreted that determines whether arousal is facilitative or debilitative. The mental interpretation of arousal includes a combination of thoughts, images, types of focus, and perceptions of control. Facilitative arousal is viewed as excitement or challenge, whereas debilitative arousal is typically labeled as anxiety.

6. Athletes perceive arousal as facilitative when mental anxiety is low, self-confidence is high, and focus is on process and performance. Debilitative arousal occurs when mental anxiety is high, self-confidence is low, and focus is on outcome. Neutral arousal falls between these extremes—anxiety and self-confidence are moderate, and some combination of performance and outcome orientation is established. Under neutral conditions, arousal and performance should demonstrate a classic inverted-U relationship. Under facilitative conditions, athletes should conform to a reversal model and perform best when arousal is high, whereas debilitative conditions should prompt a catastrophic drop in performance (as predicted by the catastrophe model).

Chapter 10: Attention

1. Skilled athletes are able to perform multiple skills at once because they have overlearned skills so that they can perform them automatically, without conscious thought. Performing a skill without conscious thought is not attention demanding; thus it allows athletes to focus on more than one thing at a time.

2. An external distractor is something in the environment that distracts athletes (e.g., crowd noise, fan behavior, or a stimulus that is out of the ordinary that draws an athlete's attention). Internal distractors involve thoughts and feelings that hinder athletes from focusing on the task at hand. External distractors can trigger negative thoughts and feelings, thus causing athletes to lose focus as they become preoccupied.

3. It is hard to block out feelings of fatigue, especially as they intensify. With cognitive association, athletes focus on bodily sensations such as heart rate, breathing patterns, and stride length to make sure they are following their plan for the race or routine. This strategy can help athletes avoid overexerting due to excitement, and, if they stay focused on task-relevant cues, they may notice fatigue less. Cognitive dissociation, however, is probably more effective as fatigue becomes more pronounced. When dissociating, athletes divert their attention away from feelings within their body, tuning out fatigue in favor of an external focus (e.g., scenery) or an internal diversion (e.g., a daydream or a math problem).

4. The orienting response occurs when an athlete is distracted by an out-of-the-ordinary stimulus—something very intense (loud noise), unusual or unexpected, or involving movement. With repeated exposure, athletes become accustomed to these stimuli and no longer get distracted by them. To prevent unwanted orienting responses, athletes should practice with distractions.

5. Selective attention involves learning to focus on the right things, on task-relevant cues. Concentration involves being able to sustain that focus.

The following table contains answers to Practical Activities question 4:

Sport skill	Answer
A. Mentally rehearsing a golf swing	Narrow-internal
B. Developing a game plan for an important competition	Broad-internal
C. Rebounding in basketball (ball has hit the rim)	Narrow-external
D. Executing a gymnastics routine	Narrow-external
E. Focusing on the next immediate hold while rock climbing	Narrow-external
F. Planning a route for white water canoeing	Broad-external
G. Analyzing your skills and weaknesses as a coach	Broad-internal
H. Watching how a football play develops	Broad-external

Chapter 11: Stress Management

1. Two common misconceptions about stress are that it results from high situational demand, and that it is the debilitating response sometimes experienced in demanding competitive situations. The first misconception suggests that some situations are inherently stressful, but demanding competitive situations don't have to provoke stress if athletes have the skills to deal with them. Neither does high arousal have to interfere with coping effectively in demanding situations. It can, in fact, enhance performance when appraised positively. Contemporary definitions characterize stress as a substantial imbalance between what is being asked of us (i.e., competitive demand) and what we believe our capabilities are for meeting those demands (i.e., personal control), for situations in which success is important.

2. According to Lazarus, performers weigh three types of information in determining the amount and quality of stress they experience: competitive demand, personal control, and coping strategies. Competitive demand involves athletes' evaluation of the impact of demanding situations on their ability to attain important goals that they are uncertain about reaching. Personal control refers to athletes' sense of whether they can meet competitive demands and achieve important goals, based on two factors: Can they change the source of stress, and, if competitive demands are surmountable, do they have the performance capabilities to meet those demands and reach their goals. Finally, coping strategies are the cognitive and behavioral techniques that athletes employ to deal with problems and feel better emotionally. When personal control and coping strategies exceed competitive demand, stress is viewed as a challenge, prompting a positive attitude and effective coping. But when competitive demand is greater than control and coping resources, stress is perceived as a threat, generating negative emotions and less effective coping.

3. Stress management is the process of reducing or eliminating the negative effects of stress, particularly physical and mental anxiety, in order for athletes to feel better, experience positive emotions, and perform effectively. Problem-management strategies reduce or eliminate the sources of stress. Problem management is a proactive stress management approach that reduces stress through competitive engineering, personal engineering, problem solving, and use of mental plans to remove the reasons for concern about the situation.

4. Even if the sources of stress can't be changed, emotional distress can be managed by lowering unwanted muscular tension, reducing excessive autonomic arousal, and countering negative thoughts in order to promote reappraisal of the situation, so that performers can perform as well as circumstances allow. Stress has been categorized in two ways depending on which occurs first—negative thoughts or excessive arousal. Arousal-triggered stress occurs when athletes get physically aroused in response to environmental stimuli, then experience negative thoughts. Thought-triggered stress works in the opposite way, with negative thoughts stimulating increases in arousal.

5. TEMPs are a comprehensive stress management approach to address arousal- and thought-triggered stress simultaneously. TEMPs eliminate the need to diagnose the anxiety experienced because they work in any type of anxiety-provoking situation. They are easy to use, effective, and generalizable to most athletes and situations, because they address both excessive arousal and negative thoughts. TEMPs develop integrated coping responses by combining relaxation and self-talk skills in a systematic format. As athletes inhale deeply, they repeat an adaptive counterargument. As inhalation ends, they say the transition phrase "so" as they pause briefly, then they repeat their relaxation cue word as they exhale slowly. If practiced until automatic, an integrated coping response can help with all types of stress responses. TEMPs can be used in practice with total immersion or gradual exposure. Total immersion places athletes in the most stressful situation possible, so they can learn to handle high levels of stress typical of demanding events. Gradual exposure slowly increases the amount of stress athletes are asked to handle as they develop the skills to meet demands. Both are effective; the choice is typically based on athletes' preferences and success in learning the technique.

6. In order to set up effective stress management programs, coaches should follow the three-phase approach recommended for developing any mental training tool or skill: education, acquisition, and implementation. The education phase helps athletes understand the basics of stress management and enhances their awareness of their personal patterns of stress and stress management. The acquisition phase helps athletes develop basic skills needed to construct a TEMP, including a consistent integrated coping response and a practice strategy for automating the skills. Finally, the implementation phase automates stress management skills, particularly the ICR, so that the skills become part of sport performance and athletes can readily use their TEMP to manage stress and enable top performance.

Chapter 12: Self-Confidence

1. Self-confidence is an athlete's realistic belief or expectation about achieving success.

2. Self-confidence has an inverted-U relationship with performance. Performance is highest when self-confidence is optimal but declines when athletes become diffident (underconfident) or overconfident. Optimally confident athletes are both competent and prepared, whereas diffident athletes lack competence or underestimate their ability. Overconfident athletes fall into two categories. Inflated confidence occurs when athletes honestly believe they are better than they are (often due to being pampered by parents and coaches, playing against weak competition, or buying into excessive media hype). Falsely confident athletes act confident on the outside but are actually diffident and worried about failing.

3. Optimal confidence rests on a foundation of competence combined with preparation. Athletes must have high competence, including all the necessary physical and mental skills to achieve their realistic goals, yet play within themselves. Competent athletes also need to be well prepared. The harder performers work in practice to develop and automate skills and accomplish performance objectives, the more prepared they should feel in approaching important competitions. Two types of preparation that are important sources of confidence are effort and development of skills and strategies.

4. Performance confidence is based on consistent success at attaining process and performance goals, whereas outcome performance is contingent on consistently winning and comparing well socially. Because performance confidence is based on attaining more flexible and controllable goals, it should develop a higher and more sustainable level of confidence than outcome confidence.

5. The four major strategies for developing self-confidence are performance accomplishment, vicarious experience, verbal persuasion, and arousal control. The best way to boost confidence is to build a history of successful performance accomplishments. The consistency, recency, and quality of accomplishments influence how they affect confidence. Goal setting, a personal Hall of Fame, and highlight videos are great ways to identify accomplishments and reinforce their importance. Athletes can also benefit from vicarious experiences of success by either observing others doing a task (modeling) or imagining themselves performing it successfully (imagery). Confidence can also be enhanced through verbal persuasion, particularly feedback or reinforcement from others, as well as positive self-talk. Both strategies remind performers of their skills, knowledge, and positive personal qualities that can feed healthy confidence. Finally, arousal control involves keeping arousal in the optimal range and interpreting arousal positively as challenge or excitement.

6. The secret to developing and maintaining confidence during competition is to appraise competitive uncertainty positively, as a challenge, rather than negatively, as a threat. Challenge appraisals that boost confidence view uncertainty as surmountable and hold that the athlete has the knowledge and skills to meet the challenge. Coaches and athletes must also have the coping skills to solve problems that arise during competition. Confidence can also be boosted during competition by using backup mental performance plans (to handle common, predictable problems) and all-purpose recovery plans (to deal with unexpected adversity).

7. A self-fulfilling prophecy (SFP) occurs when coaches' expectations prompt athletes to behave or perform in ways that conform to those expectations. An SFP develops in four stages: Coaches develop expectations for how athletes should perform, then these expectations influence their treatment of individual performers. Next, coaches' behavior affects athletes' rates of learning and levels of performance. And, finally, athletes' behavior conforms to coaches' expectations. When coaches expect the best from athletes, the SFP can boost confidence, but if coaches' expectations for athletes are negative, the SFP can reduce performers' confidence and performance quality.

Chapter 13: Mental Plans

1. Mental toughness is the ability to play one's best in any situation, particularly when encountering problems, adversity, or failure. Mental toughness is a constellation of mental skills combined in a way that brings out the best in performers when they have the most at stake.

2. Mental plans are a series of systematic, individualized strategies that build mental skills into an athlete's game. They are a means of implementing mental training tools and skills so that athletes become more systematic in their mental and physical approach to practice and competition. They help athletes develop, maintain, and regain their flow mind-set so that they can remain mentally tough and play their best in challenging situations.

3. Mental plans have four primary benefits: creating and maintaining a flow mind-set, enhancing performance quality, increasing performance consistency, and handling failure and adversity.

4. Mental plans fall into three categories: preparation, performance, and recovery. Mental preparation plans create a flow mind-set before practice and competition. Mental performance plans help performers maintain their flow mind-set while practicing and competing in races or routines, self-paced tasks, or interactive sports. Mental recovery plans help competitors regain their emotional composure when they've been taken out of their game.

5. For mental plans to be effective, athletes must develop shorthand methods to focus attention and initiate action automatically, without excessive analysis. Triggers are behaviors designed to initiate a routine. Releases are behaviors used to get rid of negative thoughts, images, or feelings that develop after mistakes or bad plays. Cue words are abbreviated reminders designed to focus attention on goals and promote automated responses.

6. As with any mental training tool or skill, mental plans follow the three-stage learning process, including education, acquisition, and implementation. In the education phase, one or more team meetings will be held to explain mental plans and how they are developed and to help athletes build awareness of their mental toughness patterns. The acquisition phase uses three basic strategies to begin implementing one mental plan: identify the mental plan that would be most valuable, develop the plan by following guidelines in the chapter, and assess plan effectiveness and revise it until it works well. Finally, in the implementation phase, athletes should practice the plan until it is highly automated and use imagery, practice, and competitive situations in which the plan must be implemented effectively in order to enable optimal performance.

Chapter 14: Mental Skills Training Programs

1. If you've developed a good coaching philosophy, you understand how important the mental side of competition is and want to do everything you can to help your athletes develop their mental as well as their physical skills. Moreover, we believe the logic presented in this book in support of mental training is compelling, and the potential benefits are too enticing not to at least implement a basic MST program on a trial basis.

2. Four key components underlie the development of effective MST programs: a systematic implementation process, a needs assessment that pinpoints strengths and weaknesses to guide development, personalized implementation strategies to meet individual needs and address important situational factors, and regular self-monitoring to assess program progress and identify areas for modification.

3. Effective education is the foundation of any MST program. It has two objectives. First, it should provide athletes with a good general education about the mental training tools,

skills, and plans being incorporated into your program. Second, it should enhance athletes' personal education by helping them develop awareness of the mental side of sport and of their personal strengths and weaknesses, so that acquisition and implementation strategies are based on accurate information.

4. The acquisition phase of MST programs helps athletes actually develop mental training tools, skills, and plans. Athletes must first learn how the desired tools, skills, and plans work and what strategies are most effective to promote their development. The key component of the acquisition phase is designing and implementing a program to learn how to perform the tool, skill, or plan reasonably well.

5. The implementation phase is where mental training tools, skills, and plans get automated, built into an athlete's game, and performed successfully under demanding competitive conditions.

APPENDIX B

Relaxation and Energization Scripts

Sample Progressive Muscle Relaxation Script

Progressive muscle relaxation helps you to first tense each of four muscle groups, part by part, in order to tire it out and then relax it deeply. When you tense a muscle group, gradually build up the tension. Like a car gradually accelerating, work up to 100 mph by starting at 10, then increasing to 20, then 30, 40, 50, 60, 70, 80, 90 and finally 100% maximum tension. Then you're going to hold that all-out tension for 5-7 seconds before letting it all go at once. When you do, relax those muscles as deeply and completely as possible for 20-30 seconds. (Standard protocol is to relax each muscle group twice before moving on, but this should be adjusted up or down to meet individual needs.) To begin, get into a comfortable position, seated or lying down.

To tense the muscles of **muscle group 1,** the **shoulders, arms, and hands**, make a tight fist with both arms and push the elbows down and into your sides. Ready—go! 10, 20, 30, 40, 50, 60, 70, 80, 90, 100. Hold the tension, feel it pull, tighter, tighter, RELAX. Just let it all go now. Let all the tension go from the muscles of your shoulders, arms, and hands, allowing those muscle fibers to loosen up, to smooth out, to unwind, and to relax. Let the tension flow down your arms and out the tips of your fingers. Use your breathing to fuel your relaxation, allowing those muscles to go deeper and deeper into relaxation. With each breath, feel the relaxation deepening and spreading. Concentrate on learning to recognize what relaxation feels like so you can compare and contrast it to the tension you experienced before. Use your deep diaphragmic breathing to allow those muscles to relax as deeply and completely as possible. Feel your muscles getting very loose, limp, heavy, and relaxed. (Repeat cycle for group 1 as needed.)

Keeping the muscles of the shoulders, arms, and hands as relaxed as possible, move to **muscle group 2,** the muscles of the **face and neck**. Tense these muscles by lifting the eyebrows high, wrinkling up your nose, biting down hard, and pulling the corners of your mouth back while doing an isometric contraction with your neck (i.e., use the muscles of the front part of the neck to try to touch your chin to your chest as you use the muscles of the back part of the neck to try to prevent that from happening). Ready—go! 10, 20, 30, 40, 50, 60, 70, 80, 90, 100. Hold the tension, feel it pull, tighter, hold it, hold it, RELAX. Just let all of the tension go and feel it slowly draining out of your face and neck. Feel those muscle fibers loosening up, smoothing out, unwinding, and gradually relaxing. Use your breathing to help that relaxation to deepen and spread. Consciously focus on the feelings of relaxation. Learn what those feelings of relaxation are like and how they differ from the feelings of tension that you sometimes have. Allow your breathing to continue to promote greater relaxation of the face and neck as more and more muscle fibers unwind and relax with each breath. Allow those muscles to get very loose, limp, heavy, and relaxed. Concentrate on letting go the final residual tension from your face and neck, along with your shoulders, arms, and hands. Relax these muscles deeply and completely. (Repeat cycle for group 2 as needed.)

While maintaining the relaxation in your shoulders, arms, and hands and your face and neck, move to the **third muscle group**—the **chest, back, and stomach**. Tense these muscles by taking a deep breath and holding it while pulling your shoulders back and together and making your stomach hard. Ready—go! 10, 20, 30, 40, 50, 60, 70, 80, 90, 100. Hold the tension, feel it pull, tighter, hold it, tighter, hold it, RELAX. Just let all the tension flow out of your chest, back and stomach. Allow those muscles to loosen up, smooth out, unwind, and relax. Use your breathing to promote deeper and more complete relaxation, helping the relaxation deepen and spread with each breath. Be aware of how your relaxation feels and distinguish it from the tension you were experiencing before. Concentrate on the differences as well as the similarities so that you'll be able to diagnose even small levels of tension in your chest, back, or stomach when they occur. Use your breathing to help promote deeper levels of relaxation. Remember that the longer you relax, the more muscle fibers will let go and get loose, limp, heavy, and relaxed. (Repeat cycle for group 3 as needed.)

Keeping the muscles in the upper body relaxed, move to the **fourth and final muscle group**—the **hips, thighs, calves, and feet**. Tense this muscle group by making your upper legs—both quads and hamstrings—hard using an isometric contraction, pulling your toes back toward you or pointing them away from you—whichever gets the best tension in your calves—and turning your feet slightly inward and curling your toes slightly. Ready—go! 10, 20, 30, 40, 50, 60, 70, 80, 90, 100. Hold the tension, feel it pull, hold it, tighter, hold that tension, tighter, RELAX. Just let it all go now. Feel all of that tension draining down your legs and out your toes. Feel those muscle fibers slowly letting go as they loosen up, smooth out, unwind, and relax. Let your breathing fuel your relaxation, with each slow, deep, regular diaphragmic breath helping your muscle fibers to go deeper and deeper and deeper into relaxation. Feel relaxation slowly consuming these muscles, and feel it deepen and spread. Concentrate on those feelings of deep relaxation and distinguish them from the tension you experienced before. Learn to diagnose even minute levels of tension in your muscles and relax it away. Use your breathing to continue to relax more and more muscle fibers. Feel your relaxation deepening and spreading. Feel those muscles becoming very loose, limp, heavy, and relaxed. Let it all go and allow yourself to experience deep, enjoyable levels of relaxation. (Repeat cycle for muscle group 4 as needed.)

To ensure that you are completely relaxed, go back and scan each muscle group in turn for any remaining tension. If you are already relaxed in a muscle group, continue relaxing. If you have residual tension, do another tension-relaxation cycle to help you relax again as deeply and completely as possible.

Having scanned your body for any residual tension in the four muscle groups and eliminated it, you should feel pretty relaxed throughout your entire body. Shift your attention from specific muscles groups to the relaxation throughout your entire body and how that relates to your deep, regular diaphragmic breathing. Continue breathing deeply and regularly and focusing totally on the feelings of relaxation in every part of your body.

Follow with a conditioned relaxation process. Each time you exhale say your relaxation cue word to yourself while focusing on your breathing and what it feels like to be deeply relaxed. Pairing those feelings of deep relaxation with your cue word each time you exhale strengthens the association between the two, so that you can use your cue word to trigger rapid relaxation in your daily life. If you happen to have any stray thoughts, worries, or concerns, just let them go and allow them to float out of your mind as you continue to focus on your breathing and the feelings of deep relaxation throughout your body. Focus on those feelings of relaxation, and contrast them to the tension you felt before so that you can diagnose and release even minute levels of tension as needed. Continue to take slow, deep, and regular breaths, and each time you exhale say that cue word to yourself.

Once you've counted 15-20 breaths during conditioned relaxation, end the session by counting backward from four to one. At 4, begin to move your legs and feet to get the circulation going again. At 3, move your arms and hands. At 2, roll your head and neck. At 1, open your eyes when it feels comfortable. Your body should feel very relaxed, as if you've just awoken from a refreshing nap. Your mind should be calm and relaxed but alert and focused on the goals you must accomplish today.

Adapted from D.A. Bernstein, T.D. Borkovec and H. Hazlett-Stevens, 2000, *New directions in progressive relaxation training: A guidebook for helping professionals* (New York, NY: Praeger).

Sample Self-Directed Relaxation Script

With Self-Directed Relaxation (SDR) you use the power of your mind and positive suggestion to command each of four muscle groups, in turn and as a unit, to attain deep relaxation. You will focus on four major areas of the body: the shoulders, arms and hands; the head and neck; the chest, back, and stomach; and the hips, thighs, calves, and feet.

To begin the session, get into a comfortable position and close your eyes. Begin by doing 6 to 8 deep, diaphragmic breaths, breathing in deeply through your nose, feeling your diaphragm and then your chest expand completely, holding the breath briefly, and then exhaling slowly through your mouth. Keep your breathing slow, deep and regular, and take approximately the same amount of time to inhale as you do to exhale. Each breath allows you to exhale tension and anxiety and to take in soothing, refreshing oxygen. Concentrate on this simple process now. Allow yourself to totally let go of all tension and sink down deeper into your chair or bed as you become more deeply and completely relaxed.

Focus your attention on the muscles of your **head and neck**. Command these muscles to relax and feel them begin to respond. Feel the tension draining out as each individual muscle fiber loosens up, smoothes out, unwinds, and relaxes deeply and completely. Each breath takes you deeper and deeper into relaxation, as your facial and neck muscles let go and unwind. Concentrate on using your breathing to fuel relaxation, as you exhale tension and anxiety and breath in soothing, invigorating oxygen. Focus on your breathing, and allow it to help the muscles of your face and neck to go down, down, down, deeper and deeper into relaxation. Be aware of how the relaxation feels and contrast it to the tension you experienced in these muscles before. Use imagery to further enhance the effectiveness of the technique. You might imagine your tension falling gradually, like dried leaves, off your muscles. You may envision little men with brooms sweeping the tension away, or imagine tension as a yellow or red liquid that drains slowly from the muscles. Feel the muscles of your face and neck gradually let go and get very loose, limp, heavy, and relaxed.

Allow the relaxation you have achieved in your head and neck to begin to spread down your body to your **shoulders**, then your **arms**, and finally to your **hands**. See the tension slowly draining out of these muscles and feel relaxation steadily radiate into your shoulders and down your arms. Imagine these muscles relaxing and feel them respond, allowing more muscle fibers to loosen up, smooth out, unwind, and relax as the tension slowly drains away. Concentrate on your breathing, with each inhalation bringing in relaxing and soothing oxygen while each exhalation slowly expels tension and anxiety from your body. Focus on letting go all remaining tension from your shoulders, arms, and hands. Identify these feelings of relaxation and contrast them to the tension you experienced before. Little by little, slowly and deliberately, more and more muscle fibers relax, bringing you to a deep level of relaxation in which all the muscles of your shoulders, arms, and hands feel very loose, limp, heavy, and relaxed.

Continue to breathe deeply and regularly, allowing your breathing to deepen your relaxation. Use your breathing to help extend your relaxation down your body to your **chest, back, and stomach**. Let go of the tension in these muscle groups, imagining the muscles relaxing and feeling them respond. Feel your breathing help each muscle fiber loosen up, smooth out, unwind, and relax. See the tension slowly draining out of these muscles and feel relaxation steadily spreading into your chest, back, and stomach. Concentrate on your breathing, allowing yourself to inhale soothing, refreshing oxygen and exhale tension and anxiety. Focus on letting go all remaining tension from your chest, back and stomach. Recognize these feelings of relaxation and compare them to the tension you experienced before. Little by little, slowly and deliberately, more and more muscle fibers relax and unwind, bringing you to a deep level of relaxation where the muscles of your chest, back, and stomach feel loose, limp, heavy, and relaxed. Your entire upper body is now deeply relaxed.

Maintain your slow, deep and regular breathing, use it to help spread relaxation from your upper body to your **hips, thighs, calves, and feet**. Let go of the tension in these muscle groups, imagining the muscles relaxing and feeling them respond. Use your breathing to help each muscle fiber loosen up, smooth out, unwind, and relax. See the tension slowly draining out of your lower body. Feel the relaxation move steadily into your hips, thighs, calves, and feet. Concentrate on your breathing, inhaling refreshing oxygen to promote relaxation and exhaling tension and anxiety. Focus on letting go all remaining tension from your lower body. Notice these feelings of relaxation and contrast them to the tension you felt in these muscles before. Little by little, slowly and deliberately, more and more muscle fibers relax and unwind, bringing you to a deep level of relaxation where the muscles of your lower body feel loose, limp, heavy, and relaxed.

Now that you have relaxed each major muscle group, your entire body is comfortably relaxed. Quickly go back and **scan each group** in turn for any residual tension, letting it go so the muscles relax more deeply and completely. Start with the muscles of the head and neck. If you find any residual tension there, just let it go and let those muscles relax. Use your breathing to fuel relaxation and help it to deepen and spread. Now focus on the muscles of the shoulders, arms, and hands, letting go of any remaining tension. Each breath exhales tension and anxiety and brings in refreshing oxygen to promote relaxation, allowing muscles to relax deeply and completely. Next scan your chest, back, and stomach and let go of any remaining tension. Allow yourself to go deeper and deeper into relaxation with each breath so your entire upper body is now comfortably relaxed. Finally, scan your hips, thighs, calves, and feet, eliminating any tension that remains. Concentrate on your feelings of relaxation and enhance them with controlled breathing and conscious effort to relax deeply and completely. Again focus on the feelings of deep relaxation throughout your entire body, feeling physically very loose, limp, heavy, and relaxed physically and very calm, peaceful, tranquil, and comfortable mentally. Sink down deeply in your chair or bed, and enjoy the feelings of being totally relaxed.

Follow with a conditioned relaxation process. Each time you exhale say your relaxation cue word to yourself while focusing on your breathing and what it feels like to be deeply relaxed. Pairing those feelings of deep relaxation with your cue word each time you exhale strengthens the association between the two, so that you can use your cue word to trigger rapid relaxation in your daily life. If you happen to have any stray thoughts, worries, or concerns, just let them go and allow them float out of your mind as you continue to focus on your breathing and the feelings of deep relaxation throughout your body. Focus on those feelings of relaxation, and contrast them to the tension you felt before so that you can diagnose and release even minute levels of tension as needed. Continue to take slow, deep, and regular breaths, and each time you exhale say that cue word to yourself.

Once you've counted 15-20 breaths during conditioned relaxation, end the session by counting backward from four to one. At 4, begin to move your legs and feet to get the circulation going again. At 3, move your arms and hands. At 2, roll your head and neck. At 1, open your eyes when it feels comfortable. Your body should feel very relaxed, as if you've just awoken from a refreshing nap. Your mind should be calm and relaxed but alert and focused on the goals you must accomplish today.

Adapted from D.A. Bernstein, T.D. Borkovec and H. Hazlett-Stevens, 2000, *New directions in progressive relaxation training: A guidebook for helping professionals* (New York, NY: Praeger).

Sample Energy Machine Script

Close your eyes and take several deep, diaphragmic breaths: breathe in through your nose, feeling your diaphragm expand, then your chest; hold the breath briefly, and then exhale through your mouth. Each breath helps you to relax more and more deeply and more and more completely.

Picture yourself in a large house at the bottom of a long staircase. You can select any type of house and any type of staircase you like. Slowly begin to climb the stairs, smoothly and effortlessly. With each step you become more energized, more invigorated, more revitalized, and more rejuvenated. As you ascend you continue to build strength, power, stamina and energy.

At the top of the staircase you find a room with a strange looking machine in the center. When you approach the machine and step onto a raised platform, a large, glass cylinder is lowered around you. The energy source inside the cylinder engages, transfusing you with power and energy from the top down. The energy core surrounds your head and neck, and energy pulsates through your facial and neck muscles, infusing your mind with a keen, sharp aptitude and a confident attitude. This positive energy field spreads downward to rejuvenate and invigorate your upper body, pulsing strength and power through your chest, shoulders, back, and arms. The energy penetrates your physical and mental core, rejuvenating tired and sore muscles, reviving and rehabilitating all tissues and structures. Feel the growing strength and power radiating through each muscle fiber of the shoulders, arms, and torso, rendering them quick, agile, forceful, flexible, and energized. Each breath adds to the reservoir of energy and power within you, making you feel stronger and stronger.

The energy core descends around the muscles of your hips, thighs, calves, and feet. Waves of pulsating energy from the core infuse your lower body with strength and power, rejuvenating tired and injured muscles and increasing their stamina and endurance. Your muscles tingle with strength, vitality, power, and energy. Your heart powerfully pumps revitalizing oxygen to every muscle.

To maximize the power and energy flowing within you, channel your personal energy field to flow down the sides of your body and pulsate up through your body from your feet to the top of your head in rejuvenating waves. Feel your power, stamina, and energy growing stronger and stronger with each breath and each pulsating wave. Every muscle fiber in your body is now poised for peak performance, waiting for the next challenge to confront or goal to accomplish. You're totally positive, energized and ready to meet all challenges and to accomplish all goals.

Follow with conditioned energization. Count 15-20 breaths, repeating your energization cue word after each set of three psych-up breaths. Focus your mind on the feelings of energization throughout your body and on your energy-promoting breathing.

Count backward from 4 to 1, becoming more in touch with what's going on around you with each number, but feeling very confident, focused, and energized.

Sample Healing White Light Script

Concentrate on an area in the middle of your forehead. Notice a tingling sensation that is growing as you bring all of your attention and concentration to this area. By directing your consciousness, you can use the full power of your mind and body to enhance your focus, your energy, and your health. Now project this pinpoint of consciousness to a point about a foot over your head and let it grow into a large, glowing sphere of radiant white light and energy. Feel the heat as the ball of energy radiates above you. As the bottom opens, the sphere begins to pour out fiery, radiant energy down through your body, from the top of your head, down through your torso, and out your feet and into the floor or ground. As the fiery, radiant energy flows through your body, it incinerates and consumes all mental and physical defects, impurities, or problems. The energy downpour destroys anything that impedes its flow through your body, including illness, injury, fatigue, negative thoughts, distractions, and self-doubts.

The sphere rotates in a clockwise direction, surrounding each major part of your body in turn, starting with your head and then moving down your torso and arms and finishing with your legs and feet. The radiant energy sphere acts like a vacuum cleaner to suck all the waste, impurities, and debris from every part of you so that you're cleansed of all the mental and physical problems and impediments that reduce your focus, energy, or health.

The radiant energy sphere then rotates in the opposite direction, surrounding your feet and slowly ascending up your body, infusing each area with strength, power, stamina, energy, and vitality. Waves of revitalizing energy surge through your body as the sphere slowly works its way to your head. Each muscle fiber feels stronger and more powerful, imbued with great suppleness and flexibility, and stocked with vitality and energy.

Fatigue is erased as your body develops a level of stamina and endurance beyond anything you've ever experienced. Your mind is energized and rejuvenated. You feel keen, sharp, focused, and confident that you can accomplish any goal and overcome all obstacles. Pulsating waves of radiant energy revitalize every particle of your being. You are a strong, powerful, vibrant, energized, dynamic individual just waiting to unleash the unlimited power and energy within you.

Having reached the top of your head, the sphere stops revolving and shrinks back to a tiny pinpoint of consciousness in your forehead region. You are now energized, but that pinpoint of consciousness remains poised to help you psych up and energize whenever you need a revitalizing energy burst.

Follow with conditioned energization. Count 15-20 breaths, repeating your energization cue word after each set of three psych-up breaths. Focus your mind on the feelings of energization throughout your body and on your energy-promoting breathing.

Count backward from 4 to 1, becoming more in touch with what's going on around you with each number, but feeling very confident, focused, and energized.

APPENDIX C

Test of Performance Strategies

This questionnaire measures performance strategies used by athletes in various sport situations. Because individual athletes are very different in their approach to their sport, we expect the responses to be different. We want to stress, therefore, that there are no right or wrong answers. All that is required is for you to be open and honest in your responses.

Each of the following items describes a specific situation that you may encounter in your training and competition. Please circle how frequently these situations apply to you on the following 1-5 scale:

		Never	Rarely	Sometimes	Often	Always
1	I set realistic but challenging goals for myself.	1	2	3	4	5
2	I say things to myself to help my practice performances.	1	2	3	4	5
3	During practice I visualize successful past performances.	1	2	3	4	5
4	My attention wanders while I am training.	1	2	3	4	5
5	I practice using relaxation techniques at workouts.	1	2	3	4	5
6	I practice a way to relax.	1	2	3	4	5
7	During competition I set specific goals for myself.	1	2	3	4	5
8	When the pressure is on at competitions, I know how to relax.	1	2	3	4	5
9	My self-talk during competition is negative.	1	2	3	4	5
10	During practice, I don't think about performing much—I just let it happen.	1	2	3	4	5
11	I perform at competitions without consciously thinking about it.	1	2	3	4	5
12	I rehearse my performance in my mind before practice.	1	2	3	4	5
13	I can raise my energy level at competitions when necessary.	1	2	3	4	5
14	During competition I have thoughts of failure.	1	2	3	4	5
15	I use practice time to work on my relaxation techniques.	1	2	3	4	5
16	I manage my self-talk effectively during practice.	1	2	3	4	5
17	I am able to relax if I get too nervous at a competition.	1	2	3	4	5
18	I visualize my competition going exactly the way I want it to go.	1	2	3	4	5

(continued)

		Never	Rarely	Sometimes	Often	Always
19	I am able to control distracting thoughts while I am training.	1	2	3	4	5
20	I get frustrated and emotionally upset when practice does not go well.	1	2	3	4	5
21	I have specific cue words or phrases that I say to myself to help my performance during competition.	1	2	3	4	5
22	I evaluate whether I achieve my competition goals.	1	2	3	4	5
23	During practice, my movements and skills just seem to flow naturally from one to another.	1	2	3	4	5
24	When I make a mistake in competition, I have trouble getting my concentration back.	1	2	3	4	5
25	When I need to, I can relax myself at competition to get ready to perform.	1	2	3	4	5
26	I set very specific goals for competition.	1	2	3	4	5
27	I relax myself at practice to get ready.	1	2	3	4	5
28	I psych myself up at competitions to get ready to perform.	1	2	3	4	5
29	At practice, I can allow the whole skill or movement to happen naturally without concentrating on each part of the skill.	1	2	3	4	5
30	During competition I perform on "automatic pilot."	1	2	3	4	5
31	When something upsets me during a competition, my performance suffers.	1	2	3	4	5
32	I keep my thoughts positive during competition.	1	2	3	4	5
33	I say things to myself to help my competitive performances.	1	2	3	4	5
34	At competitions, I rehearse the feel of my performance in my imagination.	1	2	3	4	5
35	I practice a way to energize myself.	1	2	3	4	5
36	I manage my self-talk effectively during competition.	1	2	3	4	5
37	I set goals to help me use practice time effectively.	1	2	3	4	5
38	I have trouble energizing myself if I feel sluggish during practice.	1	2	3	4	5
39	When things are going poorly in practice, I stay in control of myself emotionally.	1	2	3	4	5
40	I do what needs to be done to get psyched up for practice.	1	2	3	4	5
41	During competition, I don't think about performing much —I just let it happen.	1	2	3	4	5
42	At practice, when I visualize my performance, I imagine what it will feel like.	1	2	3	4	5

(continued)

		Never	Rarely	Sometimes	Often	Always
43	I find it difficult to relax when I feel too tense at competition.	1	2	3	4	5
44	I have difficulty increasing my energy level.	1	2	3	4	5
45	During practice I focus my attention effectively.	1	2	3	4	5
46	I set personal performance goals for competition.	1	2	3	4	5
47	I motivate myself to train through positive self-talk.	1	2	3	4	5
48	During practice sessions I just seem to be in a flow.	1	2	3	4	5
49	I practice energizing myself during the training sessions.	1	2	3	4	5
50	I have trouble maintaining my concentration during long practices.	1	2	3	4	5
51	I talk positively to myself to get the most out of practice.	1	2	3	4	5
52	I can increase my energy level to just the right level for performance.	1	2	3	4	5
53	I have very specific goals for practice.	1	2	3	4	5
54	During competition I play/perform with little conscious effort.	1	2	3	4	5
55	I imagine my competitive routine before I do it at a competition.	1	2	3	4	5
56	I imagine screwing up during competition.	1	2	3	4	5
57	I talk positively to myself to get the most out of competitions.	1	2	3	4	5
58	I don't set goals for practices; I just go out and do it.	1	2	3	4	5
59	I rehearse my performance in my mind at competitions.	1	2	3	4	5
60	I have trouble controlling my emotions when things are not going well at practice.	1	2	3	4	5
64	When I perform poorly in practice I lose focus.	1	2	3	4	5
62	My emotions keep me from performing my best at competitions.	1	2	3	4	5
63	My emotions get out of control under pressure of competition.	1	2	3	4	5
64	At practice, when I visualize my performance, I imagine watching myself as if on a video replay.	1	2	3	4	5

(continued)

Scoring

TOPS is a 64-item inventory that is scored as 16 separate subscales, 8 measuring practice usage and 8 measuring competitive usage of mental training tools and skills. All scales are scored by summing the 4 items, but 1-2 items on 4 subscales are reversed scored. Reverse scoring means that the score that is summed to get the subscale total is reversed from the item actually circled. Thus, on the five-point scale, a 1 is scored as a 5, a 2 is scored as a 4, 3 stays the same, a 4 is scored as a 2 and a 5 is scored as a 1 (i.e., 1 = 5, 2 = 4, 3 = 3, 4 = 2, and 5 = 1). (R) means the item is reverse scored.

PRACTICE SUBSCALES

Goal Setting = Item 1 + Item 37 + Item 53 + Item 58 (R)

Emotional Control = Item 20 + Item 39 + Item 60 + Item 61

Automaticity = Item 10 + Item 23 + Item 29 + Item 48

Relaxation = Item 5 + Item 6 + Item 15 + Item 27

Self-Talk = Item 2 + Item 16 + Item 47 + Item 51

Imagery = Item 3 + Item 12 + Item 42 + Item 64

Attentional Control = Item 4 (R) + Item 19 + Item 45 + Item 50 (R)

Activation = Item 35 + Item 38 + Item 44 + Item 49

COMPETITIVE SUBSCALES

Goal Setting = item 7 + item 22 + item 26 (R) + item 46

Emotional Control = item 24 + item 31 + item 62 + item 63

Automaticity = item 11 + item 30 + item 41 + item 54

Relaxation = item 8 + item 17 + item 25 + item 43

Self-Talk = item 21 + item 33 + item 36 + item 57

Imagery = item 18 + item 34 + item 55 + item 59

Positive Thinking = item 9 (R) + item 14 (R) + item 32 + item 56 (R)

Activation = item 13 + item 28 + item 40 + item 52

Adapted, by permission, from P.R. Thomas, S.M. Murphy and L. Hardy, 1999, "Test of performance strategies: Development and preliminary validation of a comprehensive measure of athletes' psychological skills," *Journal of Sport Sciences* 17(9): 697-711.

GLOSSARY

Acquisition phase—Stage of mental skill training that helps athletes learn and actually develop various mental training tools and skills.

Action-oriented feedback—Feedback that focuses on what athletes should accomplish rather than what they should avoid.

Action plan—Detailed plan that identifies the specific steps and strategies to be used in attempting to overcome obstacles and achieve a goal.

Activating event—Event experienced during practice or competition that stimulates an emotional or behavioral response.

Active listening—Process of participating firsthand in the communication process as a listener, rather than just passively hearing what is said.

Anxiety—Negative state characterized by feelings of nervousness, worry, and apprehension; has mental and physical components.

Appraisal—Cognitive evaluation of competitive demand and perceived control that determines whether a situation is interpreted positively as a challenge or negatively as a threat.

Arousal—Physiological activation of the body and the interpretation of that activation that collectively prepare performers for competitive situations.

Arousal control—Self-confidence development strategy that emphasizes remaining poised and composed; involves monitoring one's level of arousal, interpreting it positively, and adjusting as needed.

Association—Combination of competition and cooperation necessary for most social institutions, and for sport in particular, to function effectively.

Athletic Coping Skills Inventory–28 (ACSI–28)—28-item self-report inventory designed to measure seven coping skills critical for sport success, including coping with adversity, peaking under pressure, goal setting/mental preparation, freedom from worry, confidence/achievement, motivation, concentration, and coachability.

Attention—Process that directs our awareness to information available through our senses and uses that information to make decisions and choose responses; involves focusing on task-relevant cues and blocking out internal and external distractors.

Attentional anticipation—Ability to "read" what is happening and make the perfect move at just the right time by using advance cues to predict what will happen next and determine the appropriate response.

Attentional capacity—Amount of information a person can attend to and process at one time.

Attentional dimension—Aspect of attention that describes the width or scope of focus; an athlete's attention will fall somewhere between the extremes (internal to external; broad to narrow) of each dimension depending on the task and the situation.

Attentional narrowing—Process by which an athlete hones in on stimuli related to his performance.

Attentional overload—State experienced when attentional demands exceed an athlete's ability to handle the information.

Attentional shifting—Act of changing attentional focus according to task demands.

Attentional style—Manner in which an athlete executes four critical behavioral components of performance: analyzing and planning, assessing the situation, mentally rehearsing key skills and strategies, focusing and performing.

Attribution—Explanation for success or failure.

Automatic processing—Fluid performance of a sport skill without conscious awareness of the component steps involved.

Automation—Overlearning a mental or physical skill to the extent that it can be executed with minimal, if any, conscious thought.

Autonomic nervous system (ANS)—Portion of the nervous system that controls most of the automated systems within the body (e.g., organs and glands) and is responsible for physically preparing performers for action.

Autonomy—A sense of having control over one's behavior (whereas low autonomy reflects a sense of being pressured or obligated to act, think, or feel a certain way).

Backup mental performance plan—Systematic set of strategies designed to effectively deal with a limited number of foreseeable problems.

Basic MST program—Initial program that introduces mental skills training to athletes while keeping demands manageable. Such programs use team sessions and homework to develop a small number of mental training tools or skills while integrating them into practice.

Belief—Highly automated thought pattern that represents an athlete's interpretation of specific situations.

Between-performance routine—Structured routine for maintaining a flow mind-set and maximizing performance and consistency by planning how to react, reflect, refocus, and get ready to return to the task at hand.

Blaming—Type of distorted thinking that holds others responsible for negative events or outcomes.

Catastrophe theory—Theory that predicts that the inverted-U relationship between arousal and performance will demonstrate a catastrophic drop in performance on the right-hand side of the curve when mental anxiety is high.

Catastrophizing—Type of distorted thinking that focuses on the worst in any situation and exaggerates the consequences of real or imagined events.

Challenge appraisal—Constructive way to deal with stress in which athletes put a positive spin on competition and focus on the opportunity to overcome obstacles and achieve success.

Coaching philosophy—Set of value-based beliefs that dictate how you coach, particularly how you interact with athletes, parents, officials, administrators, and fans.

Cognitive association—"Tuning in" to physiological feedback and focusing on bodily sensations, such as heart rate, breathing patterns, and stride length.

Cognitive dissociation—"Tuning out" and disconnecting from feelings within one's body by directing attention elsewhere.

Collective confidence—Joint confidence that players on a team have in the team's ability to reach its goals.

Communication—Act of expressing or transmitting ideas, information, knowledge, thoughts, and feelings, as well as understanding what is expressed by others.

Competition—Process in which performance is compared to a standard in the presence of another person who knows the standard and can evaluate its attainment. The comparison is influenced by the competitor's personality, attitudes, and values; prompts a variety of physiological, psychological, and behavioral responses; and results in positive or negative consequences that impact the athlete's emotions, competence, and future behavior.

Competitive demand—Athletes' evaluation of the capability required to attain important goals in challenging situtions.

Competitive engineering—Changing the situation in order to reduce competition stress by lowering unnecessary uncertainty and decreasing excessive importance.

Concentration—Ability to sustain a nondistractable focus of attention on selected stimuli for a period of time.

Confidence—Athlete's realistic expectation of achieving success.

Confrontation—Technique used to resolve conflicts by expressing one's views and feelings about the conflict and inviting the others involved to express their views and feelings as well in order to negotiate a mutually beneficial solution.

Constructive criticism—Well-intentioned feedback following a mistake or performance error that may come across in a negative fashion.

Contingent reward—Reward based on attaining a standard of excellence or accomplishing a goal; can raise perceived competence and intrinsic motivation.

Controlled processing—Step-by-step performance of a sport skill with conscious awareness of the mechanics involved.

Cooperation—Process in which two or more competitors work together to accomplish goals and enhance team chemistry.

Coping strategy—Cognitive and/or behavioral technique athletes employ to deal with problems or to feel better emotionally so that they can perform effectively in demanding situations.

Corrective feedback—Communication that describes what the athlete needs to accomplish next time to perform well.

Counterargument—Self-talk strategy used to debate or dispute negative thinking by first identifying the faulty logic behind the thought and then identifying a more logical, productive thought to concentrate on instead.

(the) Critic—Negative internal voice of self-doubt that attacks, judges, and blames the performer and worries about performing poorly.

Cued energization—Strategy for conditioning feelings of strong energization to a "cue word" so that with repetition, the cue word will trigger rapid energization in a few seconds.

Cued relaxation—Strategy for conditioning feelings of deep relaxation to a "cue word" so that with repetition, the cue word will trigger rapid relaxation in a few seconds.

Cue words—Quick self-talk reminders used to focus attention in order to enhance performance and attain goals.

Current performance capability—Standard that reflects an athlete's average current performance level.

Debilitative arousal conditions—Conditions that detract from an athlete's performance; mental anxiety is high, self-confidence is low, and focus is on the outcome.

Descriptive feedback—Communication that, rather than simply saying "good job" or making a general statement, describes the performance and what the athlete did well.

Diaphragmic breathing—Type of breathing in which athletes fill their lungs fully by expanding the diaphragm; also a yoga-based relaxation strategy.

Diffidence—Underconfidence that arises from a lack of competence and/or preparation.

Distorted thinking—Type of self-talk that includes faulty thought processes, incorrect inferences based on inadequate or erroneous information, and failure to separate fantasy from reality.

Dream goal—Highly challenging goal that is achievable only if athletes perform their best and experience flow.

Education phase—Stage of mental training in which athletes learn the importance of a mental training tool or skill as well as how to develop it, then build greater awareness of their strengths and weaknesses in that area.

Emotion management—Collection of strategies that decrease emotional distress and enhance positive feelings of well-being. These include social support, relaxation, positive thinking, and positive reinterpretation.

Empathetic listening—Process of hearing what others say with the intent of deeply and completely understanding their perspective.

Energization—Process of getting into an optimal energy zone, the psychological state that helps athletes perform their best.

Energy machine—Imagery strategy in which athletes imagine receiving an energy transfusion from a powerful outside source.

Energy management—Ability to get into an optimal energy zone (the psychological state that helps athletes perform their best).

Equity—Concept that life should always be fair, regardless of situation or circumstance.

External imagery—Imagery done from a third-person perspective in which athletes experience a performance from outside their body, seeing and hearing the image as they would on a screen.

Extrinsic motivation—Desire to participate in sport as a means to an end, such as to obtain a particular benefit.

Facilitative arousal conditions—Conditions that improve an athlete's performance; mental anxiety is low, self-confidence is high, and focus is on the process or performance.

Failure avoiders—Outcome-oriented athletes who doubt themselves and focus on avoiding failure rather than striving for success because they doubt they can compare well with others.

False confidence—Form of overconfidence in which performers act self-assured but feel diffident.

Fear of failure—Irrational belief that places excessive weight on failure and its negative consequences.

Fight or flight syndrome—Physical response to real or imagined physical danger; the activation of the autonomic processing system triggers a readiness to fight or flee.

Flow—An optimal psychological state involving total absorption in an activity that can occur when athletes are both mentally and physically prepared; enables best performance.

Flow mind-set—Frame of mind that stimulates flow by helping performers to solidify confidence, eliminate negative thoughts, focus on process goals, optimize arousal levels, enhance motivation, and manages stress.

Goal commitment—The level of motivation athletes possess to reach a goal.

Goal evaluation—Process of checking goal attainment by comparing performance to the original goal.

Goal importance—Value placed on the attainment of a goal.

Goal setting—Process of establishing a standard of accomplishment.

Healing white light—Imagery technique in which athletes imagine a personal power source that both heals and energizes their body.

Idealized standard—Commonly recognized level of superior performance that athletes try to attain; examples include a 4-minute mile in running, a hat trick in hockey, and breaking par in golf.

Imagery—Using all the senses to create or re-create an experience in one's mind; similar to physically performing the skill but experienced in the absence of external stimuli.

Imagery control—Degree to which an athlete can create images that do what they want them to do.

Imagery energization—Energy technique that involves imagining a previous experience in which the performer was highly activated and energized.

Imagery relaxation—Relaxation technique that involves imagining a visit to a place that promotes feelings of comfort, safety, and relaxation.

Imagery vividness—Degree to which imagined images are lifelike and have a clear focus and sharp details.

Implementation phase—Stage of training in which athletes practice a mental training tool or skill until it is overlearned in order to be able to use it automatically in competitive situations without having to think about it consciously.

Individual zone of optimal functioning (IZOF)—Bandwith of arousal within which performance is at or near optimal.

Inflated confidence—Type of overconfidence in which athletes honestly believe they are better than they really are.

Instructional feedback—Corrective or desciptive feedback.

Integrated coping response (ICR)—Comprehensive strategy that combines counterarguments with rapid relaxation in a systematic routine for coping quickly with mental and physical anxiety.

Interactive sports—Sports that require direct competition against an opponent and in which the difficulty of the task fluctuates based on the opponent's level of skill and the effectiveness of the strategies employed.

Internal imagery—Imagery done from a first-person perspective in which athletes see the image through their own eyes and feel kinesthetic movements as if actually performing the skill.

Intrinsic motivation—Desire to participate in sport for the sheer pleasure and inner satisfaction that athletes obtain from the experience, such as playing for love of the game.

Inverted-U hypothesis—Relationship between arousal and performance that forms an upside-down "U" when graphed. As arousal increases from low to moderate, performance improves to its highest level. Further increases in arousal prompt steady declines in performance.

Irrational beliefs—Highly specialized negative thoughts that occur frequently; they are easily believed because they are based on partial fact, enticing but unsound evidence, and somewhat questionable logic.

Kinesthetic feel—Sensation of body position, presence, or movement that arises from stimulation of sensory nerve endings in muscles, tendons, and joints.

Long-term objective—More a quest for improvement than a standard, long-term objectives help athletes progress systematically along a performance continuum toward a desired accomplishment.

Mastery orientation—Inclination to define success based on personal standards such as effort, improvement, personal development, and task mastery.

Mastery-oriented team atmosphere—Climate in which the emphasis is on learning, participation, skill mastery, and effort.

Mental anxiety—Cognitive component of anxiety that focuses on negative expectations of success or negative consequences of failure, both of which impair performance.

Mental performance plans—Systematic plans used by athletes during practice or competition to perform optimally by maintaining and making use of a flow mind-set.

Mental plans—Series of systematic, individualized strategies designed to build mental skills into athletes' games by helping them develop, maintain, and regain a flow mind-set so that they can become mentally tough and play their best.

Mental preparation plans—Systematic plans designed to help athletes warm up mentally using a structured routine to promote a flow mind-set that will ensure that they practice and play their best.

Mental recovery plans—Preplanned strategies that help athletes recover from unexpected situations in which they have become flustered, choked, or been taken out of their game.

Mental skills—Psychological attributes, typical of mentally tough athletes, that coaches want their athletes to have, including motivation, energy management, attention, stress management, and confidence.

Mental skills training—Systematic practice and use of mental training tools to develop mental skills in order to improve performance, increase enjoyment, and develop life skills.

Mental toughness—Athletes' ability to play their best in any situation, particularly in the face of problems, obstacles, failure, or adversity.

Mental training logs—Forms for monitoring and recording critical mental training tools and skills to develop self-awareness and identify personal patterns; results can be used to refine mental plans and MST programs.

Mental training tools—Mental training strategies that are the cornerstones for developing mental skills; include goal setting, imagery, relaxation and energization, and self-talk.

Mindfulness—Process in which athletes direct attention toward cues where greater awareness is desired by becoming more attuned to their sensory experience while performing a skill.

Mind-to-muscle techniques—Strategies such as imagery relaxation designed to calm the mind in order to relax the body.

Modeling—Process of learning how to perform a skill or strategy by watching others demonstrate it.

Moderately difficult goals—Goals that are slightly (5-15%) beyond athletes' current performance capabilities.

Motivation—Desire to pursue a goal, reflected in three behaviors by athletes: the choices they make, their effort level, and their task persistence. This construct is reflected in athletes who work hard, persist even in the face of adversity, and view challenging tasks as an opportunity.

Muscle to mind techniques—Relaxation strategies such as diaphragmic breathing designed to relax the body in order to calm the mind.

Mustification—Must thinking; type of distorted thinking based on the belief that life must be lived according to a rigid set of rules or must correspond to one's own idealized view.

Needs assessment—Self-awareness technique that systematically identifies strengths and weaknesses in order to better target critical skills for inclusion in MST programs.

Negative thought count—Identification of all the negative, irrational, or unproductive thoughts that occur within a particular time interval.

Neutral arousal conditions—Conditions that have neither a debilitative or a facilitative effect on performance; mental anxiety and self-confidence are moderate and focus is on a combination of the process or performance and the product or outcome.

Nonreinforcement—Failure of coaches to acknowledge athletes' effort, skill execution, and performance improvements.

Nonverbal communication—Kinds of communication other than words, such as actions, facial expressions, body positioning, and gestures.

Objective performance measure—Type of performance standard that is quantifiable and easily counted; often takes the form of a sport statistic such as a batting average in baseball, distance in shot putting, or time in running.

Optimal confidence—Self-assurance that comes from a high level of competence and preparation.

Optimal energy zone—Range in the middle of the inverted U-curve in which arousal is moderate and performance is best.

Orienting response—Human tendency to direct attention to any intense or unexpected stimulus; can be helpful or distracting to athletes.

Outcome goals—Goals that emphasize outperforming other competitors and attaining valued outcomes such as winning or placing high.

Outcome orientation—Perspective in which athletes define success and failure based on how they compare with others, feeling successful if they do better than others but feeling like a failure if their performance does not measure up.

Outcome-oriented team atmosphere—Climate in which the emphasis is on interpersonal competition, public evaluation, and normative feedback.

Overconfidence—Unrealistic confidence that is greater than performers' competence and preparation warrant.

Overgeneralization—Type of distorted thinking in which athletes erroneously form conclusions based on an isolated incident or insufficient information while ignoring conflicting facts.

Paraphrasing—Actively listening to the message communicated by another person, then describing the essence of the message in your own words.

Peaking—Hitting an optimal level of readiness and performance ability; athletes try to peak during, rather than before or after, their most important competitions.

Perceived competence—Extent to which athletes have positive perceptions of their skills and abilities and feel capable of succeeding in sport.

Perfectionism—Irrational belief that suggests performers should always perform perfectly and never make mistakes, experience inconsistency, or exhibit flaws.

Performance accomplishments—Self-confidence development strategy in which athletes view their history of success as a reflection of their hard work and ability.

Performance capabilities—Knowledge, skills, tactics, and preparedness necessary to successfully execute a task.

Performance goals—Goals that focus on improving overall performance, such as running a faster time, throwing farther, or shooting a lower score.

Performance profiling—Type of needs assessement in which athletes or teams identify the chararcteristics necessary for success and then evaluate the degree to which they have developed each in relation to their ultimate performance potential.

Performance-related cue words—Phrases or words that direct athletes' attention to critical tasks, without causing them to think about the mechanics of performing the skill.

Personal control—Ability to manage competitive demands; based on the degree to which sources of stress are surmountable and on the sufficiency of performance capabilities.

Personal excellence—Goal of striving to learn and improve in order to become the best that you are capable of becoming.

Personalization—Process of individualizing strategies to meet each athlete's needs and competitive demands.

Physical anxiety—Physiological component of anxiety that includes muscular tension, butterflies, increased heart rate, and sweaty palms and is interpreted as detrimental to performance.

Physical cue—Overt physical movement such as turning to face the net or slapping the floor that can be used to initiate mental recovery plans.

Polarized thinking—Type of distorted thinking in which things are viewed as being at either of two extreme ends of a continuum: all or nothing, black or white, good or bad, etc.

Positive affirmations—Self-talk reminders of skills, abilities, and desirable personal qualities.

Positive mental attitude—Subjective evaluation about the degree to which self-talk remains positive and productive; an expectation of effectiveness.

Preperformance routines—Strategies used for self-paced tasks designed to help athletes create and maintain a flow mind-set in order to trust their bodies and perform with greater automaticity.

Problem management—Strategies used to reduce or eliminate the source of stress; encompasses a host of techniques for addressing competition difficulties (planning, increasing effort, preperformance routines, etc.).

Process goals—Goals that enhance form, technique, and strategy.

Programming—Focusing on positive thoughts and repeating them frequently in order to increase confidence, improve concentration and focus, enhance motivation, control stress, and perform optimally.

Progressive muscle relaxation (PMR)—Relaxation strategy used to diagnose and relieve excess tension by first tensing and then relaxing specific muscle groups.

Psych-out zone—Right-hand portion of the inverted-U curve in which arousal is too high to allow for ideal performance.

Psych-up breathing—Energization strategy that helps increase symptoms of autonomic arousal through a quick, shallow breathing process that is associated with sport and with the Lamaze childbirth technique.

Psych-up zone—Left-hand portion of the inverted-U curve in which arousal is too low to allow for ideal performance.

Punishment—Consequence that decreases the likelihood that an athlete will repeat a certain behavior or action in the future.

Race plan—Systematic strategy that chunks a race into parts, develops goals and techniques for maintaining a flow mind-set during each phase, and uses cue words to preserve mental toughness and stimulate automated performance during each phase.

Rapid energization—Abbreviated energization strategy designed to allow athletes to energize optimally in a few seconds.

Rapid relaxation—Abbreviated relaxation strategy designed to allow athletes to relax optimally in a few seconds.

Reaction—Composed, strategic, between-play response to specific good or bad performance trends (e.g., after a turnover, or a run of points by the opponent).

Readying—Between-play strategy in which athletes use a cue word to end reflection on the previous play and initiate a repeat of their preperformance routine in order to refocus on the task at hand and prepare to perform automatically.

Realistic goal—Moderately difficult goal that can be attained with a good, not great, performance.

Reframing—Changing self-talk in order to view a situation in a new, more positive way.

Reinforcement—Consequence that increases the likelihood that an athlete will try to repeat a given behavior in the future.

Relaxation—Process of decreasing unwanted muscular tension, reducing excessive activation of the sympathetic nervous system, and calming the mind by keeping it productively occupied.

Releases—Techniques for letting go of negative thoughts and feelings that prevent athletes from concentrating on the present.

Reprogramming—Process of helping performers think more constructively by developing and repeating smart-talk scripts designed to encourage positive emotions and productive behavior.

Response characteristics—How athletes respond to a situation being imagined, including actions, physiological feelings, and emotions.

Reversal theory—Theory that predicts that the inverted-U relationship between arousal and performance is prompted by a shift from a process or performance orientation to product or outcome orientation and that high arousal combined with a process orientation stimulates optimal performance.

Selective attention—Process by which we attend to some pieces of information and ignore or screen out others.

Self-awareness—An understanding of the self, especially of personal strengths and weaknesses.

Self-confidence—An athlete's realistic belief about achieving success; based on performance history and preparation.

Self-directed relaxation (SDR)—Relaxation strategy that is an abbreviated version of progressive muscle relaxation; involves focusing on specific muscle groups and systematically releasing tension.

Self-evaluation—Process of measuring success based on comparison of an athlete's own performance over time; focused on learning and self-improvement.

Self-fulfilling prophecy—Phenomenon in which performance conforms to the expectations of the coach.

Self-monitoring—Comparison of performance or log data to individual and team goals in order to assess improvement; used to enhance both motivation and self-confidence.

Self-paced tasks—Activities in which athletes perform repetitious or similar movement patterns and in which they have significant flexibility as to the pace of their performance (e.g., bowling, golf, shooting free throws).

Self-talk—Steady stream of thoughts and internal dialogue that has a significant impact on mood, emotions, and performance.

Self-talk script—Smart-talk tool designed for a variety of specific purposes that facilitates positive, productive belief patterns.

Sensory awareness—Process of becoming more aware of one's internal and external sensory experiences while performing, such as body position, footwork, timing, flow of movement, change of direction, and preparatory movements before striking or hitting an object.

Shaping—Reinforcing successive or close approximations of a desired behavior.

Short-term goal—Specific target behavior to be achieved within a period of six weeks.

Simulations—Training technique in which coaches incorporate common distractions into imagery or practice sessions to help athletes habituate to stimuli that create unwanted orienting responses.

Situational characteristics—Aspects of a situation that athletes respond to, such as the content of an imagined scenario (e.g., various circumstances one might face in an upcoming competition).

Skill automaticity—Performance of sport skills automatically, without conscious thought or attention.

Smart-talk—Positive thought patterns that help create a flow mind-set.

Social approval—Irrational belief that places excessive importance on pleasing others and maintaining a positive image.

Social comparison—Irrational belief that the behavior and performance of other competitors is important and has the power to negatively affect one's own.

Social evaluation—Method of measuring success that focuses on winning or achieving a particular rank.

Social loafing—Performance problem that plagues teams in which individuals working together on a task tend to exert less individual effort and perform at a lower level than when they perform the task alone.

Standard mental performance plan—Plan designed to facilitate athletes' attainment of practice and performance goals for races or routines, self-paced tasks, and interactive sports by helping them maintain a flow mind-set and remain mentally tough.

Stress—Imbalance between (competitive) demands and perceived abilities to meet those demands for situations in which success is important.

Stress management—Process of reducing or eliminating the negative consequences of stress, particularly mental and physical anxiety, in order to help athletes feel better, experience positive emotions, and perform effectively.

Subjective performance measure—Standard for assessing performance of tasks or skills in which performance is not easily quantified; requires educated observational assessment such as rating a player's footwork using a 10-point scale.

Success seekers—Outcome-oriented athletes who are confident in their ability to win.

Test of Performance Strategies (TOPS)—64-item, self-report inventory used to assess eight critical mental training tools and skills (goal setting, self-talk, imagery, emotional control, relaxation, automaticity, activation, and attention control [practice] or positive thinking [competition]) for practice and competition.

Threat appraisal—Assessment of a situation that highlights the negative aspects and prompts athletes to feel pessimistic and think more about failure than success; fueled by a product- or outcome-based orientation and athletes' perception of excessive difficulty and minimal personal control.

Threshold level—Upper limit of tension at which relaxation strategies can be used effectively to manage stress symptoms.

Total emotion management package (TEMP)—Comprehensive stress management strategy that combines problem management and emotional management techniques into a system that enables athletes to perform effectively regardless of the situation or type of stress involved.

Total energization—Full-length strategy designed to help athletes energize as completely as possible.

Total relaxation—Full-length strategy designed to help athletes relax as completely as possible.

Triggers—Words or actions that remind athletes to concentrate.

True competitor—Athlete who places personal excellence ahead of winning and focuses on the journey rather than the destination.

Uncertainty—Indecision or ambiguity about attaining a goal.

Verbal persuasion—Strategy in which performers use feedback or reinforcement from others, or their own positive self-talk, to develop or enhance self-confidence.

Vicarious experience—Strategy in which performers experience success indirectly by observing the successful performances of others or imagining their own successful performances as a means of developing or enhancing self-confidence.

REFERENCES AND RESOURCES

Abernathy, B. (2001). Attention. In R.N. Singer, H.A. Hausenblas, & C.M. Janelle (Eds.), *Handbook of sport psychology* (2nd ed., pp. 53–85). New York: Wiley.

Abernathy, B., Wann, J., & Parks, S. (1998). Training perceptual-motor skills for sport. In B. Elliot (Ed.), *Training in sport: Applying sport science*. West Sussex, England: Wiley.

Abernathy, B., Wood, J.M., & Parks, S. (1999). Can the anticipatory skills of experts be learned by novices? *Research Quarterly for Exercise and Sport*, 70, 313–318.

Allen, J.B., & Howe, B. (1998). Player ability, coach feedback, and female adolescent athletes' perceived competence and satisfaction. *Journal of Sport and Exercise Psychology*, 20, 280–299.

Amberry, T., & Reed, P. (1996). *Free throw: 7 steps to success at the free throw line*. New York: Harper Collins.

Ames, C., & Archer, J. (1988). Achievement goals in the classroom: Students' learning strategies and motivation processes. *Journal of Educational Psychology*, 80, 260–267.

Apter, M.J. (1982). *The experience of motivation: The theory of psychological reversals*. London: Academic Press.

Armstrong, L. (2000). *It's not about the bike*. New York: Putnam.

Bandura, A. (1977). Self-efficacy: Toward a unifying theory of behavioral change. *Psychological Review*, 84, 191–215.

Bandura, A. (1986). *Social foundations of thought and action*. Englewood Cliffs, NJ: Prentice Hall.

Beck, A.T. (1976). *Cognitive therapy and emotional disorders*. Madison, CT: International Universities Press.

Beilock, S.L., Afremow, J.A., Rabe, A.L., & Carr, T.H. (2001). "Don't miss!" The debilitating effects of suppressive imagery on golf putting performance. *Journal of Sport and Exercise Psychology*, 23, 200–221.

Beller, J.M., & Stoll, S.K. (1995). Moral development of high school athletes. *Journal of Pediatric Science*, 7(4), 352–363.

Benson, H. (1975). *The relaxation response*. New York: Avon.

Bernstein, D.A., Borkovec, T.D., & Hazlett-Stevens, H. (2000). *New directions in progressive relaxation training: A guidebook for helping professionals*. New York: Praeger.

Brown, B.E. (2001). *1001 motivational messages and quotes*. Monterey, CA: Coaches Choice.

Burton, D. (1988). Do anxious swimmers swim slower? Re-examining the elusive anxiety–performance relationship. *Journal of Sport Psychology*, 10, 45–61.

Burton, D. (1989). Winning isn't everything: Examining the impact of performance goals on collegiate swimmers' cognitions and performance. *The Sport Psychologist*, 3, 105–132.

Burton, D. & Naylor, S. (1997). Is anxiety really facilitative? Reaction to the myth that cognitive anxiety always impairs sport performance. *Journal of Applied Sport Psychology*, 9, 295–302.

Burton, D., & Naylor, S. (2002). The Jekyll/Hyde nature of goals: Revisiting and updating goal setting in sport. In T.S. Horn (Ed.), *Advances in sport psychology* (2nd ed., pp. 459–499). Champaign, IL: Human Kinetics.

Burton, D., Naylor, S., & Holliday, B. (2001). Goal setting in sport: Investigating the goal effectiveness paradox. In R.N. Singer, H.A. Hausenblas, & C.M. Janelle (Eds.), *Handbook of sport psychology* (2nd ed., pp. 497–528). New York: Wiley.

Burton, D., Pickering, M.A., Weinberg, R.S., Yukelson, D., & Weigand, D. (2007). The competitive goal effectiveness paradox revisited: Examining the goal practices of Olympic athletes. Submitted to *The Sport Psychologist*.

Burton, D., Weinberg, R.S., Yukelson, D., & Weigand, D. (1998). The goal effectiveness paradox in sport: Examining the goal practices of collegiate athletes. *The Sport Psychologist*, 12, 404–418.

Burton, D., & Weiss, C. (2008). The Jekyll/Hyde nature of goals: Fine-tuning a performance-based goal-setting model for promoting sport success. In T.S. Horn (Ed.) *Advances in sport psychology* (3rd ed.) Champaign, IL: Human Kinetics.

Chambers, H.E. (2001). *Effective communication skills for scientific and technical professionals*. Cambridge, MA: Perseus.

Coakley, J. (1980). Play, games and sport: Developmental implications for young people. *Journal of Sport Behavior*, 3, 99–118.

Coakley, J. (2001). *Sport in society: Issues and controversies* (7th ed.). New York: McGraw-Hill.

Crocker, P.R.E., Kowalski, K.C., & Graham, T.C. (2002). Emotional control and intervention. In J.M. Silva & D.E. Stevens (Eds.), *Psychological foundations of sport* (pp. 155–176). Needham Heights, MA: Allyn & Bacon.

Csikszentmihalyi, M. (1990). *Flow: The psychology of optimal experience*. New York: Harper & Row.

Csikszentmihalyi, M. (1997). *Finding flow*. New York: Harper Collins.

Cumming, J., & Hall, C. (2002). Deliberate imagery practice: The development of imagery skills in competitive athletes. *Journal of Sport Sciences*, 20, 137–145.

Dagrou, E., Gauvin, L., & Halliwell, W. (1992). Effects of positive, negative and neutral language on motor performance. *Canadian Journal of Sport Sciences*, 17, 145–147.

Deci, E.L., & Flaste, R. (1996). *Why we do what we do: Understanding self-motivation*. New York: Penguin.

Duval, D. (1998) www.asapsports.com/show_interview.php?id=9847. August 29.

Dweck, C.S. (1999). *Self-theories: Their role in motivation, personality, and development*. Philadelphia: Taylor and Francis.

Dweck, C.S. (2006). *Mindset: The new psychology of success*. New York: Random House.

Egan, G. (1990). *The skilled helper: A problem management approach to helping* (5th ed.). Pacific Grove, CA: Brooks/Cole.

Ellis, A. (1996). *Better, deeper, and more enduring brief therapy: The rational emotive behavior therapy approach*. New York: Brunner/Mazel.

Epstein, J. (1988). Effective schools or effective students? Dealing with diversity. In R. Haskins & B. MacRae (Eds.), *Policies for America's public schools* (pp. 89–126). Norwood, NJ: Ablex.

Epstein, J. (1989). Family structures and student motivation: A developmental perspective. In C. Ames & R. Ames (Eds.), *Research on motivation in education* (Vol. 3, pp. 259–295). New York: Academic Press.

Ericsson, K.A., & Charness, N. (1994). Expert performance: Its structure and acquisition. *American Psychologist*, 49, 725–747.

Ewing, M.E., & Seefeldt, V. (1990). *Participation and attrition patterns in American agency-sponsored and interscholastic sports: An executive summary* (pp. 20–84). East Lansing, MI: Youth Sports Institute, Michigan State University.

Feltz, D. (1988). Self-confidence and sport performance. In K.B. Pandolf (Ed.), *Exercise and sport science reviews* (pp. 423–457). New York: Macmillan.

Feltz, D.L., & Landers, D.M. (1983). The effects of mental practice on motor skill learning and performance: A meta-analysis. *Journal of Sport Psychology*, 5, 25–57.

Feltz, D.L., & Lirgg, C.D. (2001). Self-efficacy: Beliefs of athletes, teams and coaches. In R.N. Singer, H.A. Hausenblas, & C.M. Janelle (Eds.), *Handbook of sport psychology* (2nd ed., pp. 340–361). New York: Wiley.

Gallimore, R. & Tharp, R. (2004). What a coach can teach a teacher, 1975–2004; Reflections and reanalysis of John Wooden's teaching practices. *The Sport Psychologist*, 18, 119–137.

Gallwey, W.T. (1997). *The inner game of tennis* (Rev. ed.). New York: Random House.

Goleman, D. (narrator). (1976). *Flow and mindfulness: An instructional cassette*. New York: Psychology Today.

Goleman, D. (1998). *Working with emotional intelligence*. New York: Bantam Books.

Gould, D., Eklund, R.C., & Jackson, S.A. (1993). Coping strategies used by U.S. Olympic wrestlers. *Research Quarterly for Exercise and Sport*, 64, 83–93.

Gould, D., Finch, L.M., & Jackson, S.A. (1993). Coping strategies used by national champion figure skaters. *Research Quarterly for Exercise and Sport*, 64, 453–468.

Gould, D., Greenleaf, C., Lauer, L., & Chung, Y. (1999). Lessons from Nagano. *Olympic Coach*, 9, 2–5.

Gould, D., Tammen, V., Murphy, S.M., & May, J. (1989). An examination of U.S. Olympic sport psychology consultants and the services they provide. *The Sport Psychologist*, 3, 300–312.

Greenfield, E. (1997). *For the love of the game: Michael Jordan and me*. New York: Harper Collins.

Greenspan, M., & Feltz, D. (1989). Psychological intervention with athletes in competitive situations. *The Sport Psychologist*, 3, 219–236.

Hale, B.D. (1994). Imagery perspectives and learning in sports performance. In A.A. Sheikh & E.R. Korn (Eds.), *Imagery in sports and physical performance* (pp. 75–96). Amityville, NY: Baywood.

Hall, C.R. (1997). Lew Hardy's third myth: A matter of perspective. *Journal of Applied Sport Psychology, 9,* 310–313.

Hall, C.R. (2001). Imagery in sport and exercise. In R.N. Singer, H.A. Hausenblas, & C.M. Janelle (Eds.), *Handbook of sport psychology* (pp. 529–549). New York: Wiley.

Hall, C.R., & Rodgers, W.M. (1989). Enhancing coaching effectiveness in figure skating through a mental skills training program. *The Sport Psychologist, 2,* 142–154.

Hall, C.R., Schmidt, D., Durand, M., & Buckolz, E. (1994). Imagery and motor skills acquisition. In A.A. Sheikh & E.R. Korn (Eds.), *Imagery in sports and physical performance* (pp. 121–134). Amityville, NY: Baywood.

Hanin, Y.L. (1986). State-trait anxiety research on sports in the USSR. In C.D. Spielberger & R. Diaz (Eds.), *Cross-cultural anxiety* (Vol. 3, pp. 45–64). Washington, DC: Hemisphere.

Hanin, Y.L. (2000). Individual zones of optimal functioning (IZOF) model: Emotion–performance relationships in sport. In Y.L. Hanin (Ed.), *Emotions in sport* (pp. 65–89). Champaign, IL: Human Kinetics.

Hanson, T. (1992). The mental aspects of hitting a baseball: A case study of Hank Aaron. *Contemporary Thought on Performance Enhancement, 1,* 49–70.

Hardy, C.J., & Latane, B. (1988). Social loafing in cheerleaders: Effects of team membership and competition. *Journal of Sport and Exercise Psychology, 10,* 109–114.

Hardy, L. (1990). A catastrophe model of anxiety and performance. In J.G. Jones & L. Hardy (Eds.), *Stress and performance in sport* (pp. 81–106). Chichester, UK: Wiley.

Hardy, L. (1997). Three myths about applied consultancy work. *Journal of Applied Sport Psychology, 9,* 277–294.

Hardy, L., & Callow, N. (1999). Efficacy of external and internal visual imagery perspective for the enhancement of performance on tasks in which form is important. *Journal of Sport and Exercise Psychology, 21,* 95–112.

Hardy, L., Jones, G., & Gould, D. (1996). *Understanding psychological preparation for sport: Theory and practice of elite performers.* Chichester, UK: Wiley.

Hird, J.S., Landers, S.M., Thomas, J.R., & Horan, J.J. (1991). Physical practice is superior to mental practice in enhancing cognitive and motor task performance. *Journal of Sport and Exercise Psychology, 8,* 281–293.

Holmes, P.S., & Collins, D.J. (2001). The PETTLEP approach to motor imagery: A functional equivalence model for sport psychologists. *Journal of Applied Sport Psychology, 13,* 60–83.

Horn, T.S. (1985). Coaches' feedback and changes in children's perceptions of their physical competence. *Journal of Educational Psychology, 77,* 174–186.

Horn, T.S., Lox, C.L., & Labrador, F. (2006). The self-fulfilling prophecy theory: When coaches' expectations become reality. In J.M. Williams (Ed.), *Applied sport psychology: Personal growth to peak performance* (5th ed., pp. 52–108). Mountain View, CA: Mayfield.

Isaac, A.R. (1992). Mental practice—does it work in the field? *The Sport Psychologist, 6,* 192–198.

Jackson, P., & Delehanty, H. (1995). *Sacred hoops: Spiritual lessons of a hardwood warrior.* New York: Hyperion.

Jackson, S. (1995). Factors influencing the occurrence of flow in elite athletes. *Journal of Applied Sport Psychology, 7,* 135–163.

Jackson, S.A. (1992). Athletes in flow: A qualitative investigation of flow states in elite figure skaters. *Journal of Applied Sport Psychology, 4,* 161–180.

Jackson, S.A., & Csikszentmihalyi, M. (1999). *Flow in sports: The keys to optimal experiences and performance.* Champaign, IL: Human Kinetics.

Jacobson, E. (1938). *Progressive relaxation.* Chicago: University of Chicago Press.

Janssen, J. (1999). *Championship team building.* Tucson, AZ: Winning the Mental Game.

Janssen, J., & Dale, G. (2002). *The seven secrets of successful coaches.* Cary, NC: Winning the Mental Game.

Johnson, D.W. (1981). *Reaching out: Interpersonal effectiveness and self-actualization* (2nd ed.). Engelwood Cliffs, NJ: Prentice Hall.

Johnson, D.W. (2003). *Reaching out: Interpersonal effectiveness and self-actualization* (8th ed.). Needham Heights, MA: Allyn & Bacon.

Johnson, M. (1996). *Slaying the dragon.* New York: Regan Books.

Jones, G. (1993). The role of performance profiling in cognitive behavioural interventions in sport. *The Sport Psychologist, 7,* 160–172.

Jones, G., Hanton, S., & Swain, A.B.J. (1994). Intensity and interpretation of anxiety symptoms in elite and non-elite sports performers. *Personal Individual Differences, 17,* 657–663.

Jones, G., & Hardy, L. (1990). *Stress and performance in sport.* Chichester, UK: Wiley.

Jones, G., & Swain, A.B.J. (1995). Predisposition to experience debilitative and facilitative anxiety in elite and nonelite performers. *The Sport Psychologist, 9,* 201–211.

Jones, L., & Stuth, G. (1997). The uses of mental imagery in athletics: An overview. *Applied and Preventive Psychology, 6,* 101–115.

Jordan, M., & Telander, R. (2001). May 15. My first time. ESPN MAG.com., pp. 1–4.

Kennedy, S. (1998). *Winning at life.* (p. 25) Bloomington, MN: Garborg's Inc.

Kerr, J.H. (1989). Anxiety, arousal and sport performance: An application of reversal theory. In D. Hackfort & C.D. Spielberger (Eds.), *Anxiety in sports: An international perspective* (pp. 137–152). New York: Hemisphere.

Kerr, J.H. (1993). An eclectic approach to psychological interventions in sport: Reversal theory. *The Sport Psychologist*, 7, 400–418.

Kingston, K.M., & Hardy, L. (1994). Factors affecting the salience of outcome, performance and process goals in golf. In A. Cochran & M. Farrally (Eds.), *Science and golf* (Vol. 2, pp. 144–149). London: Chapman-Hill.

Kingston, K.M., & Hardy, L. (1997). Effects of different types of goals on processes that support performance. *The Sport Psychologist*, 11, 277–293.

Kohn, A. (1999). *Punished by rewards: The trouble with gold stars, incentive plans, A's, praise, and other bribes.* Boston: Houghton Mifflin.

Krane, V., & Williams, J.M. (2006). Psychological characteristics of peak performance. In J.M. Williams (Ed.), *Applied sport psychology: Personal growth to peak performance* (5th ed., pp. 207–227). New York: McGraw-Hill.

Kyllo, L.B., & Landers, D.M. (1995). Goal-setting in sport and exercise: A research synthesis to resolve the controversy. *Journal of Sport and Exercise Psychology*, 17, 117–137.

Landers, D.M., & Arent, S.M. (2001). Arousal–performance relationships. In J.M. Williams (Ed.), *Applied sport psychology: Personal growth to peak performance* (4th ed., pp. 206–228). Mountain View, CA: Mayfield.

Lang, P.J. (1979). A bio-informational theory of emotional imagery. *Psychophysiology*, 16, 495–512.

Lazarus, R. (1991). *Emotion and adaptation.* New York: Oxford University Press.

Lazarus, R. (1999). *Stress and emotion: A new synthesis.* New York: Springer.

Locke, E.A. (1996). Motivation through conscious goal setting. *Applied and Preventative Psychology*, 5, 117–124.

Locke, E.A., & Latham, G.P. (1990). *A theory of goal setting and task performance.* Englewood Cliffs, NJ: Prentice Hall.

Locke, E.A., Shaw, K.N., Saari, L.M., & Latham, G.P. (1981). Goal setting and task performance, 1969–1980. *Psychological Bulletin*, 90, 125–152.

Luschen, G. (1970). Cooperation, association and contest. *Journal of Conflict Resolution*, 14, 21–23.

Marks, D. (1977). Imagery and consciousness: A theoretical review from an individual difference perspective. *Journal of Mental Imagery*, 2, 285–347.

Martens, R. (1975). *Social psychology and physical activity.* New York: Harper & Row.

Martens, R. (1987). *Coaches guide to sport psychology.* Champaign, IL: Human Kinetics.

Martens, R., Vealey, R.S., & Burton, D. (1990). *Competitive anxiety in sport.* Champaign, IL: Human Kinetics.

Martin, K.A., Moritz, S.E., & Hall, C.R. (1999). Imagery use in sport: A literature review and applied model. *The Sport Psychologist*, 13, 245–268.

Masters, K.S., & Ogles, B.M. (1998). Associative and dissociative cognitive strategies in exercise and running: 20 years later, what do we know. *The Sport Psychologist*, 12, 253–270.

McGrath, J.E. (1970). *Social and psychological factors in stress.* Ft. Worth, TX: Holt, Rinehart & Winston.

McKay, M., Davis, M., & Fanning, P. (1981). *Thoughts and feelings: The art of cognitive stress intervention.* Richmond, CA: New Harbinger.

McKay, M., & Fanning, P. (1992). *Self-esteem* (2nd ed.), New York: MJF Books.

Meichenbaum, D. (1993). Stress inoculation training: A 20-year update. In P.M. Lehrer & R.L. Woolfolk (Eds.), *Principles and practices of stress management* (2nd ed., pp. 373–406). New York: Guilford Press.

Meyers, A.W., Whelan, J.P., & Murphy, S.M. (1996). Cognitive behavioral strategies in athletic performance enhancement. In M. Hersen, R.M. Miller, & A.S. Belack (Eds.), *Handbook of behavior modification* (Vol. 30, pp. 137–164). Pacific Grove, CA: Brooks/Cole.

Mills, B. (1990). An open letter to U.S. distance runners. *American Athletics*, Fall/Winter, pp. 34–36.

Ming, S., & Martin, G.L. (1996). Single-subject evaluation of a self-talk package for improving figure skating performance. *The Sport Psychologist*, 10, 227–238.

Moran, A.P. (1996). *The psychology of concentration in human performers: A cognitive analysis.* East Sussex, UK: Psychology Press.

Moritz, S.E., Feltz, D.L., Mack, D.E., & Fahrbach, K.R. (2000). The relation of self-efficacy measures to sport performance: A meta-analytic review. *Research Quarterly for Exercise and Sport*, 71, 280–294.

Moritz, S.E., Hall, C.R., Martin, K., & Vadocz, E. (1996). What are confident athletes imaging? An examination of image content. *The Sport Psychologist*, 10, 171–179.

Munroe, K.J., Giacobbi, P.R., Hall, C., & Weinberg, R. (2000). The four w's of imagery use: Where, when, why, and what. *The Sport Psychologist*, 14, 119–137.

Murphy, S. (1996). *The achievement zone: Eight skills for winning all the time from the playing field to the boardroom.* New York: Putnam.

Murphy, S.M., & Jowdy, D.P. (1992). Imagery and mental practice. In T.S. Horn (Ed.), *Advances in sport psychology* (pp. 221–250). Champaign, IL: Human Kinetics.

Murphy, S.M., Jowdy, D., & Durtschi, S. (1990). *Report on the U.S. Olympic Committee survey on imagery use in sport.* Colorado Springs: U.S. Olympic Training Center.

Murphy, S.M., & Martin, K.A. (2002). The use of imagery in sport. In T. Horn (Ed.). *Advances in sport psychology* (2nd ed., pp. 405–439). Champaign, IL: Human Kinetics.

Murphy, S.M., & Woolfolk, R.L. (1987). The effects of cognitive interventions on competitive anxiety and performance on a fine motor skill accuracy task. *International Journal of Sport Psychology, 18,* 152–166.

Nicklaus, J. (1974). *Golf my way.* New York: Simon & Schuster.

Nicklaus, J. (1976). *Playing better golf.* New York: King Features Syndicate.

Nideffer, R.M. (1976). *The inner athlete: Mind plus muscle for winning.* New York: Crowell.

Nideffer, R.M., & Sagal, M.S. (2001). Concentration and attention control training. In J.M. Williams (Ed.), *Applied sport psychology: Personal growth to peak performance* (4th ed., pp. 312–329). Mountain View, CA: Mayfield.

Orlick, T. (1986). *Psyching for sport: Mental training for athletes.* Champaign, IL: Human Kinetics.

Orlick, T., & Partington, J. (1988). Mental links to excellence. *The Sport Psychologist, 2,* 105–130.

Pierce, B.E., & Burton, D. (1998). Scoring the perfect 10: Investigating the impact of goal-setting styles on a goal-setting program for female gymnasts. *The Sport Psychologist, 12,* 156–168.

Porter, D., & Allsen, P. (1978). Heart rates of basketball coaches. *The Physician and Sports Medicine, 6,* 85–90.

Ravizza, K. (2006). Increasing awareness for sport performance. In J.M. Williams (Ed.), *Applied sport psychology: Personal growth to peak performance* (5th ed., pp. 228–239). Mountain View, CA: Mayfield.

Ravizza, K., & Hanson, T. (1995). *Heads up baseball: Playing the game one pitch at a time.* Indianapolis: Masters Press.

Ravizza, K., & Osborne, T. (1991). Nebraska's 3 R's: One-play-at-a-time preperformance routine for collegiate football. *The Sport Psychologist, 5,* 256–265.

Riley, P. (1996). *The winner within: A life plan for team players.* New York: Berkley.

Rosenthal, R., & Jacobson, L. (1968). *Pygmalion in the classroom: Teacher expectations and pupils' intellectual development.* New York: Holt, Rinehart & Winston.

Rotella, R., & Cullen, R. (1995). *Golf is not a game of perfect.* New York: Simon & Schuster.

Rotella, R.J. (1997). *The golf of your dreams.* New York: Simon & Schuster.

Russell, B., & Branch, T. (1979). *Second wind: The memoirs of an opinionated man.* New York: Random House.

Schwartz, G.E., Davidson, R.J., & Goleman, D.J. (1978). Patterning of cognitive and somatic processes in the self-regulation of anxiety: Effects of meditation versus exercise. *Psychosomatic Medicine, 40,* 321–329.

Seefeldt, V.D., & Ewing, M.E. (1997). Youth sports in America. *President's Council on Physical Fitness and Sport Research Digest, 2,* 1–11.

Seefeldt, V., Ewing, M., & Walk, S. (1992). *Overview of youth sports programs in the United States.* Washington, DC: Carnegie Council on Adolescent Development.

Sharples, P. (1992). The impact of goal-setting styles on the effectiveness of a goal-setting training program for women's collegiate cross-country runners. Master's thesis, University of Idaho, Moscow.

Sheikh, A.A., & Korn, E.R. (1994). *Imagery in sports and physical performance.* Amityville, NY: Baywood.

Shill, T., Monroe, S., Evans, R., & Ramanaiah, N. (1978). The effects of self-verbalizations on performance: A test of the rational-emotive position. *Psychotherapy Theory, Research and Practice, 15,* 2–7.

Shoop, R.J., & Scott, S.M. (1999). *Leadership lessons from Bill Snyder.* Manhattan, KS: AG Press.

Short, S.E, Bruggeman, J.M., Engel, S.G., Marback, T.L., Wang, L.J., Willadsen, A., & Short, M.W. (2002). The effect of imagery function and imagery direction on self-efficacy and performance on a golf-putting task. *The Sport Psychologist, 16,* 48–67.

Singer, R.N. (2000). Performance and human factors: Considerations about cognition and attention for self-paced and externally-paced events. *Ergonomics, 43,* 1661–1680.

Singer, R.N. (2002). Preperformance state, routines, and automaticity: What does it take to realize expertise in self-paced events? *Journal of Sport and Exercise Psychology, 24,* 359–375.

Smith, R.E. (1980). A cognitive-affective approach to stress management training for athletes. In C. Nadeau, W. Halliwell, K. Newell, & G. Roberts (Eds.), *Psychology of motor behavior and sport—1979* (pp. 54–73). Champaign, IL: Human Kinetics.

Smith, R.E. (2006). Positive reinforcement, performance feedback, and performance enhancement. In J.M. Williams (Ed.), *Applied sport psychology: Personal growth to peak performance* (5th ed., pp. 40–56). Mountain View, CA: Mayfield.

Smith, R.E., Schutz, R.W., Smoll, F.L., & Ptacek, J.T. (1995). Development and validation of a multidimensional measure of sport-specific psychological skills: The Athletic Skills Coping Inventory–28. *Journal of Sport and Exercise Psychology, 17,* 379–398.

Smith, R.E., & Smoll, F.L. (1996). *Way to go, coach! A scientifically-proven approach to coaching effectiveness.* Portola Valley, CA: Warde.

Smoll, F.L., & Smith, R.E. (2006). Development and implementation of coach-training programs: Cognitive behavioral principles and techniques. In J.M. Williams (Ed.), *Applied sport psychology: Personal growth to peak performance,* (5th ed., pp. 458–480). New York: McGraw-Hill.

Starkes, J.L., Helsen, W., & Jack, R. (2001). Expert performance in sport and dance. In R.N. Singer, H.A. Hausenblas, & C.M. Janelle (Eds.), *Handbook of sport psychology* (2nd ed., pp. 53–85). New York: Wiley.

Starkes, J.L., & Lindley, S. (1994). Can we hasten expertise by video simulations? *Quest, 46,* 211–222.

Suinn, R.M. (1980). Psychology and sport performance: Principles and applications. In R.M. Suinn (Ed.), *Psychology in sports: Methods and applications* (pp. 26–36). Edina, MN: Burgess International.

Suinn, R.M. (1997). Mental practice in sport psychology: Where have we been, where do we go? *Clinical Psychology: Science and Practice*, 4, 189–207.

Thomas, P.R., Murphy, S.M., & Hardy, L. (1999). Test of Performance Strategies: Development and preliminary validation of a comprehensive measure of athletes' psychological skills. *Journal of Sport Sciences*, 17, 697–711.

Van Dyken, Amy. (1995). Visualize. *Swimming World and Junior Swimmer*. November, p. 27.

Van Raalte, J.L., Brewer, B.W., Rivera, P.M., & Petitpas, A.J. (1994). The relationship between observable self-talk and competitive junior tennis players' performance. *Journal of Sport and Exercise Psychology*, 16, 400–415.

Vealey, R.S. (1988). Future directions in psychological skills training. *The Sport Psychologist*, 2, 318–336.

Vealey, R.S. (1994). Current status and prominent issues in sport psychology interventions. *Medicine and Science in Sports and Exercise*, 26, 495-502.

Vealey, R.S., Hayashi, S.W., Garner-Holman, G., & Giacobbi, P. (1998). Sources of sport-confidence: Conceptualization and instrument development. *Journal of Sport and Exercise Psychology*, 20, 54–80.

Vealey, R.S., & Walter, S.M. (1994). On target with mental skills: An interview with Darrell Pace. *The Sport Psychologist*, 8, 427–441.

Walker, S.H. (1980). *Winning: The psychology of competition.* New York: Norton.

Weinberg, R.S. (1984). The relationship between extrinsic rewards and intrinsic motivation in sports. In J.M. Silva & R.S. Weinberg (Eds.), *Psychological foundations of sport* (pp. 177–187). Champaign, IL: Human Kinetics.

Weinberg, R.S., Burton, D., Yukelson, D., & Weigand, D. (1993). Goal setting in competitive sport: An exploratory investigation of practices of collegiate athletes. *The Sport Psychologist*, 7, 275–289.

Weinberg, R.S., Burton, D., Yukelson, D., & Weigand, D. (2000). Perceived goal setting practices in Olympic athletes: An exploratory investigation. *The Sport Psychologist*, 14, 279–295.

Weinberg, R.S., & Comar, W. (1994). The effectiveness of psychological interventions in competitive sport. *Sports Medicine*, 18, 406–418.

Weinberg, R.S., Gould, D., & Jackson, A. (1980). Cognition and motor performance: Effect of psyching-up strategies on three motor tasks. *Cognitive Therapy and Research*, 4, 239–245.

Whelan, J.P., Elkins, C.C., & Meyers, A.W. (1990). Arousal intervention for athletic performance: Influence of mental preparation and competitive experience. *Anxiety Research*, 2, 293–307.

Williams, A.M., & Grant, A. (1999). Training perceptual skills in sport. *International Journal of Sport Psychology*, 30, 194–220.

Wilson, V.E., Peper, E., & Schmid, A. (2006). Strategies for training concentration. In J.M. Williams (Ed.), *Applied sport psychology: Personal growth to peak performance* (5th ed., pp. 404–422). New York: McGraw-Hill.

Wooden, J.R. (1988). *Practical modern basketball.* (3rd ed.) New York: Macmillan.

Wooden, J.R. (2004). Personal communcation to Damon Burton, June 6, 2004.

Wooden, J.R. (with Jamison, S.) (1997). *Wooden: A lifetime of observations and reflections on and off the court.* Chicago, IL: Contemporary Books.

Yukelson, D.P. (2001). Communicating effectively. In J.M. Williams (Ed.), *Applied sport psychology: Personal growth to peak performance* (4th ed., pp. 135–144). Mountain View, CA: Mayfield.

Zaichkowsky, L.D., & Baltzell, A. (2001). Arousal and performance. In R.N. Singer, H.A. Hausenblas, & C.M. Janelle (Eds.), *Handbook of sport psychology* (2nd ed., pp. 319–339). New York: Wiley.

Ziegler, S.G., Klinzing, J., & Williamson, K. (1982). The effects of two stress management training programs on cardiorespiratory efficiency. *Journal of Sport Psychology*, 4, 280–289.

INDEX

Note: The italicized *f* and *t* following page numbers refer to figures and tables, respectively.

ABOUT THE AUTHORS

Damon Burton is a professor of sport psychology at the University of Idaho and has taught undergraduate and graduate applied sport psychology courses since 1983. At Idaho, Burton created master's and doctoral programs to develop sport psychology consultants with strong backgrounds in both counseling and performance enhancement. A fellow and former president of the Association for Applied Sport Psychology (AASP), he is an AASP-certified consultant and past chair of the certification committee. A former athlete and coach who has worked extensively in coaching education for almost 30 years, educating over 4,500 coaches, Burton has consulted with coaches and athletes from youth sport to Olympic and professional levels on the development of mental skills in both individual and team settings. He coauthored *Competitive Anxiety in Sport*, authored or coauthored numerous research studies evaluating the effectiveness of mental skills training programs, and supervised or mentored many master's and doctoral students in their work helping coaches and athletes develop mental skills. Burton is past chair of the American Alliance for Health, Physical Education, Recreation and Dance (AAHPERD) Sport Psychology Academy and a longtime member of the North American Society for the Psychology of Sport and Physical Activity (NASPSPA). He earned a master's degree in sport psychology from the University of Wisconsin at Madison and a PhD in sport psychology from the University of Illinois, specializing in applied sport psychology and coaching education.

Photo courtesy of Joe Pallen, University of Idaho Photographic Services

Thomas D. Raedeke is associate professor of sport and exercise psychology at East Carolina University. Since 1993, Raedeke has taught graduate and undergraduate applied sport psychology courses focusing on coaching education and mental skills training at the University of Oregon, University of Colorado, and East Carolina University, earning the University of North Carolina's Board of Governor Distinguished Professor for Teaching Award in 2007. A research expert on motivation, stress, and burnout, Raedeke has worked with athletes and coaches from a variety of sport types and skill levels. He is a certified consultant through the Association of Applied Sport Psychology (AASP), where he is chair of the Health and Exercise Psychology Committee. He is also a member of the North American Society for the Psychology of Sport and Physical Activity (NASPSPA) and the American Alliance for Health, Physical Education, Recreation and Dance (AAHPERD). Raedeke is past chair of the National Association for Sport and Physical Education (NASPE) Sport and Exercise Psychology Academy. A former collegiate wrestler, Dr. Raedeke earned his master's degree from the University of Idaho and a PhD from the University of Oregon, with a focus on sport and exercise psychology. He has also served as a research assistant in sport psychology at the United States Olympic Training Center in Colorado Springs and as an instructor for American Sport Education Program (ASEP) coaching courses.

Photo courtesy of the author

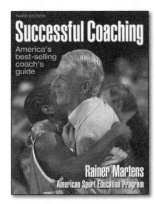
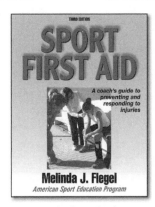

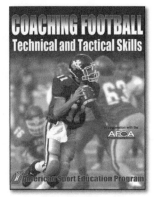